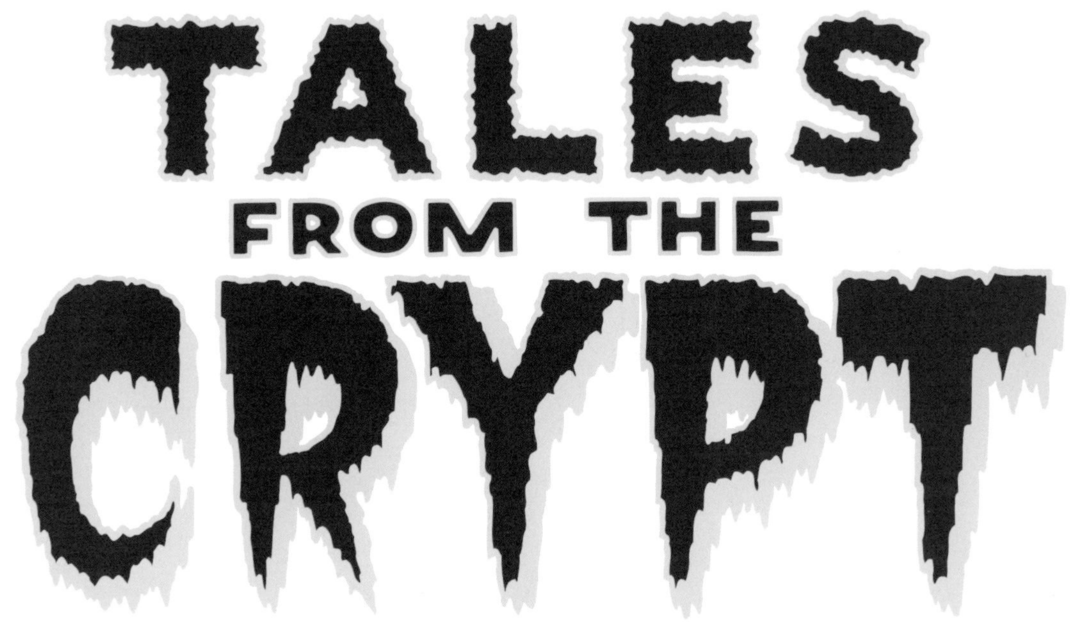

by Digby Diehl

Designed by David Kaestle and Rick DeMonico

St. Martin's Press New York

Diehl, Digby.
Tales from the Crypt:the official archives/by Digby Diehl.
p. cm.
ISBN 0-312-14486-5
1. Tales from the crypt (Comic strip) — Micellanea. 2. Tales from the crypt (Television program) — Micellanea. I. Title.
PN6728.T25D54 1996
741.5'973 — dc20 96-3078
CIP

First Edition: October 1996
10 9 8 7 6 5 4 3 2 1

Acknowledgments

The most enduring legacy of Bill Gaines is laughter, as I have discovered in my research for this book. He had the King Comus touch: his friends, his colleagues, and his family—apparently, everyone whose life he touched—partake of the infectious good humor. The same spirit, obviously passed on through the EC comics, runs through the creative crew connected with Tales from the Crypt Productions in Hollywood. I haven't stopped laughing since I began this project—and I can assure you that this is not always the case in researching and writing books.

Any large picture book is a collaborative undertaking, and this one has been more so than most. I am greatly indebted to many people who are listed below, but there are four whose contributions have been at least equal to my own:

Kay Beyer Diehl, my wife, my partner in life and in literary crime; she has researched, written, edited, typed, proofread, and struggled through every phase of this book, shoulder-to-shoulder with me with extraordinary good spirits and a sharp eye; she gave her all even when my energies were flagging, and lifted the enterprise to new heights; she is the living definition of true love.

David Kaestle and Rick DeMonico, the most intelligent and sensitive designers with whom I have ever worked; in their hands, a picture really is worth a thousand words; they read the text and know how to utilize images to express ideas (many times, they developed and extended my ideas in ways I had not imagined); right from the start, they loved this *Tales* material as much as I did and their love and tireless effort shows on every page.

Rich Barber, who was my dear friend long before he was my agent; his skill and patience as a negotiator and his knowledge as an editor kept all of the many parts of this enterprise together when the wheels threatened to fly off; in addition to being a great ringmaster, he also provided many key creative suggestions.

Where do I begin to list the rest of my collaborators? In my mind, I go back to a superb dinner in Madison, Wisconsin, where Wendy Gaines Bucci, with her warm and vivid stories, brought her father alive for me as though he were sitting with us at the table. From the "vault" (one of many in this saga) in her basement, she extracted loads of EC and family materials that were the cornerstones of my research. I am also grateful to Wendy's mother, Nancy Gaines, her sister, Cathy Mifsud, and her brother, Mike Gaines, for their memories and contributions to this book.

In a converted railroad station in West Plains, Missouri, I had an excellent porterhouse steak with Russ Cochran and his family at the end of several days of immersion in Russ' EC publishing empire (which is discussed in the pages to follow). Russ told me about his early fascination with comics and about his adventures with Bill Gaines while we played with his chimps—Sammy, Sally, and Buck. I also had the good fortune to meet with his son-in-law, Bruce Hershenson, one of the partners in the EC Convention of 1972 and purveyor of the finest movie posters in the world.

In Livingston, Montana, I reveled in the hospitality of Al Feldstein and his wife, Michelle, on their beautiful ranch. Al, of course, was there at The Creation, and his remarkable memory took me back to enjoy all of the zany scenes at 225 Lafayette Street. Al's generous participation in every aspect of this book and Michelle's Montana-style cooking have made them special friends.

We all laughed so long and so loudly when I had dinner with Annie Gaines and Don Ashton at Nimrod in New York City that the owner threatened (jokingly, I think) to throw us out. In addition to wonderful stories, Annie dug into her "vault" for pictures and memorabilia and was endlessly patient in assisting me with contacts.

The first time Grant Geissman and I had lunch at Hamburger Hamlet in Sherman Oaks, California, I didn't even know the questions to ask. As David acknowledges below, Grant has been generous with his encyclopedic knowledge of EC lore and equally generous with access to his renowned collection. This book could not exist without his unfailing assistance.

Jerry Weist gave me an exhilarating sense of his passion for comics when I visited him at his home in Brooklyn. Over the course of other meetings during this project he has shared with me his lifetime of EC wisdom, from *Squa Tront* to Sotheby's. (When he showed me his extensive collection of vintage jazz LPs, I also began to develop a theory about the relationship between EC and jazz—but that's another story.)

More than thirty years ago, Ray Bradbury adopted me as an "honorary son," and he has treated me lovingly and generously as family ever since. He and his bibliographer, Donn Albright, gave me lots of useful research regarding his pieces of the EC puzzle.

My friend Lyle Stuart, the publisher of Barricade Books, gave me important insights into EC during a long, noisy lunch at Patria. He was one of Bill Gaines' closest friends and was kind enough to read my manuscript at an early stage and offer corrections.

During an elegant lunch at Aquavit in Manhattan and then, over Indian food at Akbar (when we were joined by Jack Albert), Dorothy Crouch (and Jack) provided good suggestions and anecdotes for this book. Thanks also to Dorothy's associate, Edna, for her help in a crucial phase of our preparations.

Of course, there would be no book without the artistic geniuses of EC, and I want to thank them for their creativity and for sharing their memories with me: Joe Orlando (who regaled me with great stories over lunch at the Illustrators' Club), Jack Davis, Johnny Craig, Will Elder, George Evans, Jack Kamen, Marie Severin, Al Williamson, and—again—Al Feldstein.

I want to acknowledge several others whose help in researching the EC years was vital: Betty Ballantine and Bernie Shir-Cliff, who clarified the history of Ian Ballantine's EC reprints; Harlan Ellison, a great friend, writer, and EC collector who sent me off in all the right directions, as usual; Maggie Thompson, who generously shared the resources of the Comic Buyer's Guide; Tom Spurgeon, who provided indispensable EC background from *The Comics Journal*; Sam Kingston, who publishes *Horror from the Crypt of Fear*, one of the best EC horror fanzines; Sigurd Case, whose new *Post Crypt* magazine is adding to EC scholarship with every issue; and Ella Wells, a wonder of efficiency who guided me through the complexities of DC Comics' rights and permissions department.

Meanwhile, back in Hollywood...

Behind the scenes, making it all happen—as usual—was Joel Silver. Not only did Joel make time in his insanely busy schedule to talk with me, but he generously has lent the support of his organization, most especially the beautiful, calm, and efficient Michela. If you ever want to reach anyone in the movie business, just say, "I'm calling at the suggestion of Joel Silver...."

Each of Joel's partners in Tales took time out from their projects to talk with me: Richard Donner, the calm in the eye of the storm; Robert Zemeckis, truly brilliant and modest; Walter Hill, a secret intellectual; and David Giler, the phantom. Special thanks to Alex Collett, who patiently gave me a road map to understanding the television *Tales*.

Jack Wohl, president of Tales from the Crypt Productions, Inc., is the godfather of this book. He originally conceived of the idea and has contributed tirelessly to every phase of its development. I cannot thank him, and his assistant, Scott Brisbane, enough. I also want to thank Garrick Dion, who brought his own considerable knowledge of *Tales* to the job of organizing the filmography.

Former Tales producer Bill Teitler offered the most articulate and insightful analysis of those crucial early seasons, and Russell Mulcahy was funny and helpful in giving me the director's point of view. Kevin Yagher gave me a dazzling tour of his amazing illusion shop and explained the inner workings of the Crypt Keeper. Alan Katz inspired me with his hints on pun-filled C.K. commentary. In some part of his mind, John Kassir IS the Crypt Keeper, as he proved in an hilarious interview. Warden Neil and Todd Masters are artists of costume and illusion who shared their secrets with me. Mike Vosberg offered me a few especially useful thoughts about the preproduction activities on Tales. Max Rosenberg, producer of the 1970s *Tales* films, is a charming and perceptive man who was the first to bring EC to the big screen; he was generous in assisting my research in that area. Freddie Francis, who lives in England, provided long-distance anecdotes and patiently answered my questions about his work as a director. Elaine Lindeloff, at her offices not far from my home in Pasadena, gave me a tour of the *Tales* website and shared resources from her archives.

Behind almost every nonfiction book, one of the unsung heroes—in this case, heroine—is the transcriber who accurately captures hundreds of hours of interviews on computer disk. Sandy Taylor, who has worked with me on many other projects, typed away night after night, often under tight deadline conditions, to provide the material for my text. And I am sincerely grateful.

Thanks, too, to ace photographer Christie Vance and her assistants Lars Larsen and Sara Diehl for making me look at least as good as the Crypt Keeper.

Finally, I sincerely wish to thank the impressive team of professionals at St. Martin's Press, beginning with the president, Sally Richardson, a special friend who fought hard to bring this project to her house and won. Our editor, Jim Fitzgerald, was a constant source of guidance and support. I will never forget one day when we were long past our deadlines, and he called with what I expected, realistically, to be a tough tongue-lashing. Instead, he invited the entire book team to a marvelous dinner at America and told us he loved what we were doing. Over coffee, he quietly suggested that it might improve our life expectancies if we delivered the missing chapters by the end of the week. Special thanks also to John Cunningham, John Murphy, Amelie Littell, and Jim's assistant, Regan Good.

Design Credits

Produced by **David Kaestle, Inc.**, New York

Art directed and designed by **David Kaestle** and **Rick DeMonico**

Acknowledgments

The Art

This book showcases some of the best comic art ever created, and derives a good measure of its visual impact from that art. The cadre of artists who worked at EC in the early fifties is legendary. I owe a very special thanks to these guys and a gal...they make us, the designers of *this* EC book, look good.

The Photography

I would also like to thank the talented photographers who worked behind the scenes documenting the television and film productions.

For the HBO series (principally): **Michael Paris**, **Cliff Lipson**, **Sam Emerson**, **Randy Tepper**, **Doug Hyun**, and **Martin Black.**

For Universal Studios: **Peter Sorel** and **Robert Isenberg** (*Demon Knight*) and **Joe Lederer** (*Bordello of Blood).*

Studio still life photography produced for this book was shot by **Lee Varis** (Los Angeles) and **Christie Sherman** (New York City).

Cover photograph by **Aaron Rapaport.**

Picture research by **Rick DeMonico, Penelope Orfino,** and **Louisa Grassi.**

Special Thanks

The *most* special thanks goes to **Grant Geissman.** Probably the premier EC collector on the planet, Grant's knowledge is as vast and astounding as his collection. He was our trusted expert and prime resource for almost all of the comic material and collectibles depicted herein. Thanks to Grant, this *is* the definitive look at the EC horror comics phenomenon.

Grant is also one of the premier jazz guitarists on the planet (his "day job," you might say). His is a talent of rare skill and imagination, and in the course of this project I fell in love with his music...a rich reward for which I am also thankful.

And as Bill Gaines said, "First comes the word." And the words, of course, came from **Digby Diehl**. Without Digby's brilliant take on this subject, the design would have no reason for being. No author in my considerable experience has ever been more understanding of the design process. This book is a word and picture collaboration of the highest order. And I leave this venture with a new friend.

This book would have been a pale version of what it is were it not for the talents of **Rick DeMonico.** Rick is the senior designer at David Kaestle, Inc., and this project is yet more evidence that he is one of the best young designers working anywhere. I greatly admire his skills, and I benefit every working day from his knowledge, his loyalty, and his company.

Our thanks to the many individuals and institutions who provided images for this book, most notably: the Gaines family (thank you in particular **Wendy Gaines Bucci** and **Annie Gaines**), publisher **Russ Cochran**, the ultimate keeper of the EC flame, Crypt Keeper creator **Kevin Yagher**, special fx makeup wizard **Todd Masters,** costume designer **Warden Neil**, **Tales from the Crypt Productions** (thank you **Jack Wohl**), EC comics collector **Bill Spicer**, **DC Comics**, and **Boss Film Studios.**

Stock Photography provided by: The Bettmann Archive, Wide World Photos, FPG, Superstock, and Archive Photos.

Thanks too to **Jim Fitzgerald**, our editor at St. Martin's Press, and to **Twisne Fan**, our production honcho, for their support throughout, to **Mark Hecker** for his layout assistance, to **Jacqueline Norris** of the HBO photo library, and to **Peter Maresca**, my friend and comic strip collector.

And finally, thanks to my precious six-year-old son, **David Joseph Kaestle**, who—during this project's tenure—developed a craving for the *Goosebumps* books. It provided a wonderful reminder of the fundamental fascination so many of us have for a good scary tale.

—David Kaestle

"A lot of people have the idea we're a bunch of monsters who sit around drooling and dreaming up horror and filth. That's not true. We try to entertain and educate. That's all there is to it."

— Bill Gaines

CONTENTS

THE CRYPT OF TERROR
NO. 17
10¢

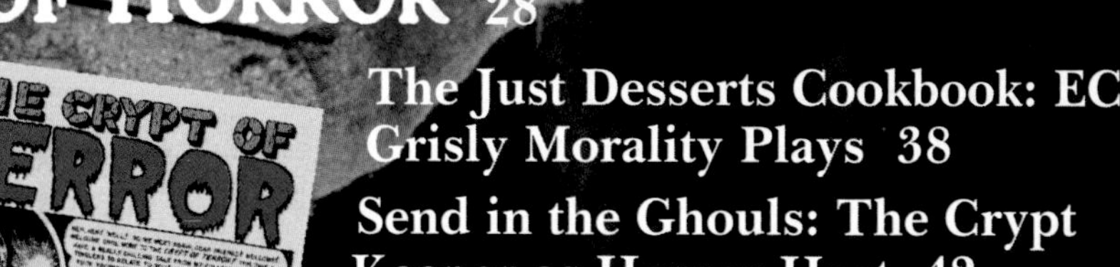

TALES FROM THE CRYPT
TERROR

MAD MEMBER
EC
FAN-ADDICT CLUB

WESTWOOD VILLAGE
TALES FROM THE CRYPT DEMON KNIGHT
TALES FROM THE CRYPT

Archie
Prayers
Gene Autry
Roy Rogers
Mysterious
Traveler
Johnny
Mack Brown

We in the United States have come to only a late-blooming appreciation of comic books as a mirror of our culture. In Europe and Japan, comic books and graphic novels have been revered as art forms for decades. Here, however, for most of their existence, comics were looked down upon as unworthy and insignificant reading matter. Comic books were considered mindless, often scurrilous trash, consumed by children and young adults with too much time and too little intellectual capacity. Lost upon the adults who disparaged them was an enduring truth that was obvious to every kid who ever bought one—comic books are great fun.

The comic book as we have come to know and love it is a hybrid—a cross between the newspaper comic strip and the "pulp" magazine.

In 1896, Richard F. Outcault's *The Yellow Kid* hit the streets, first in Joseph Pulitzer's *New York World*, then in *The New York Journal*, a paper published by newspaper magnate William Randolph Hearst. Part of what was appealing about the Yellow Kid was that he really *was* yellow—he was often clad in a bright yellow nightshirt (upon which his dialogue was written). This was a new wrinkle in the newspaper business. Up until that time, the presses had been able to crank out a sickly jaundiced yellow, but an honest-to-goodness egg yolk or daffodil hue had been unattainable. Now that they could do so, many newspapers went overboard on the use of bright yellow; often they were dailies that featured reportage on the more sensational crimes and juicy scandals of the day. Hence the term "yellow journalism" was born (and frequently applied to newspapers in the Hearst chain.) With his bad grammar, his *dis dat dem dose* spelling, and his irreverence, the Yellow Kid was a child of the streets (most precisely of Hogan's Alley). A true populist, his spunky attitude matched the elbows-out brashness of New York itself.

The Yellow Kid was christened "Mickey Dugan" in August of '96, but it was two months later that he cemented his place in comic history. On October 25, 1896, he appeared not just in a single frame diorama with the other motley denizens of Hogan's Alley (who share much in common with Spanky & Our Gang), but in a series of five drawings that also featured a parrot and a phonograph—in other words, a comic strip. Within just a few weeks, Outcault ruled in fine lines to separate the drawings, which became numbered panels.

Throughout the teens and Roaring Twenties, the comic strip continued to grow in popularity. For the most part during these decades, however, the strips were quite literally comic, generally focusing on the trials and tribulations of daily domestic life, not unlike early TV sitcoms. In that regard there is much that links Jiggs and Maggie of *Bringing Up Father* with Lucy and Desi or Ralph and Alice Cramden. (Although it

One of Outcault's innovations was the introduction of balloon dialogue that was essential to understanding the comic strip.

Munsey's magazine became a success, the more so after his top writer, Edgar Rice Burroughs, began a series of stories starring a white man who went native in Africa. In 1912, Tarzan of the Apes became the first hero of pulp fiction, and spawned a whole industry of spinoffs and imitations.

Before it was a movie title, "pulp fiction" was a type of popular literature.

came later, Chic Young's *Blondie* (1930) was yet another link in the same chain.)

Before it was a Quentin Tarantino movie, "pulp fiction" really was a type of popular literature. The name of the genre is rooted in its means of publication. Just before the turn of the century, the cheapest grade of paper was called "wood pulp" or simply "pulp." In 1896, the same year that *The Yellow Kid* debuted, a publisher named Frank Munsey began putting out an inexpensive magazine named *The All-Story Magazine*, later renamed *Argosy*. *Argosy* specialized in short tales of action and adventure, and was printed on pulp-grade paper.

From dime store novels to bodice rippers to true crime to supermarket tabloids, pulps are the ancestors of a wide range of "trashy" literature—the kind of reading matter every parent feared was hidden in the bookshelf behind the Charles Dickens, *Anne of Green Gables*, or Rudyard Kipling. (Never mind that it was also the kind of reading matter that mother and father picked up surreptitiously themselves.) A heady mix of adventure, fantasy, and violence, early pulps also featured a whiff of sexual innuendo, with well-muscled heroes, damsels in distress, and Snidely Whiplash villains out to "get the girl."

RILEY DILLON in a Thrilling Novelette
DETECTIVE FICTION WEEKLY
APR. 20
10¢
Formerly Flynn's
"Death to a Tenor" by Fred MacIsaac
IBS
10¢
DIME MYSTERY MAGAZINE
MARCH
COMING OF THE FACELESS KILLERS
THRILL-PACKED MYSTERY NOVEL by FRANCIS JAMES
SATAN'S PIGMY HORDE by JOHN HAWKINS
Weird Tales
OCT.
25¢
KISS
story
DREAMER'S WORLDS—Brilliant Novelette by EDMOND HAMILTON
15¢
15¢
HORROR STORIES
APRIL MAY
FOOD FOR THE FLAMES!
by GEORGE EDSON
THE BLACK MASK
AMAZING STORIES
UNCANNY, SPOOKY, CREEPY TALES
Ghost STORIES
July
25¢
The GHOST of a BURNING SHIP
PARK AVENUE VAMPIRE
LON CHANEY'S Favorite Ghost Story
AMAZING STORIES
Stories by H.G.WELLS
A. HYATT VERRILL
JULIAN HUXLEY

Two of the most important pulps were *Black Mask* (1920), which showcased hardboiled detective fiction by Dashiell Hammett and Raymond Chandler, and *Weird Tales*, a horror pulp that carried stories by H. P. Lovecraft and later Ray Bradbury.

Another was *Amazing Stories* (1926), the first science fiction pulp, where futuristic trailblazer Buck Rogers first appeared in 1928. He became a comic strip one year later.

In 1929, the comic strip and pulp fiction merged.

On January 7 of that year, both Tarzan and Buck Rogers made the transition from prose to picture, becoming comic strip characters. The stage was now set for the introduction of drama (both melo- and otherwise) in the comics, and more sophisticated characters and stories with sustained plot and action began to appear.

It was one of the many moments when trends in the comics reflected events in society. The freewheeling, fun-loving twenties slammed into the beginning of the hard-luck thirties with the stock market plunge on October 25, 1929. Harsh times called for sterner heroes. Chester Gould's *Dick Tracy* was the right man for the early 1930s, when organized crime was gaining a foothold, and newspapers reported regularly on gangland murders. (Not surprisingly, he debuted in Chicago, where mob strife was particularly bloody.) America still loved to laugh at humorous characters in *Gasoline Alley*, but the adventures of poor *Little Orphan Annie* and her wealthy guardian, arms manufacturer and war profiteer Daddy Warbucks, became increasingly poignant in a country where the disparity between legions of unemployed men and women and the privileged few took on distinctly Dickensian overtones. In these grim days a salesman at Eastern Color Printing Company in New York noted the successs of the newspaper comic strips and had an idea about how to capitalize on them.

Dick Tracy decided to become a cop after gangsters brutally shot his fiancée's father. His murder was the first contemporary urban homicide in the comics.

The Birth of the Comic Book

Max Gaines is rightly credited as the Father of the Comic Book. Max had struggled through the twenties and early thirties and failed to make a living at a variety of schemes. He'd been an elementary school principal, munitions factory worker, and haberdasher before finding work as a salesman for Eastern Color Printing. Because finances were tight, he and his family (consisting of his wife, Jessie, and his two children, Elaine and Bill) were living with Max's mother in the Bronx when Max found inspiration in a stack of old Sunday funnies in her attic. In 1933, the heart of the Depression, Max caught himself laughing at the old strips over again. Other people might laugh at them too, he reasoned; the trick was to figure out how to make it pay off.

Eastern's main asset was a state-of-the-art color printing press, and it was here that the Sunday funnies were printed for many of the major newspapers along the East Coast. Eastern's presses, which were set up for a standard newspaper page, were the determining factor in establishing the size of the contemporary comic book. Max and Eastern sales manager Harry Wildenberg realized that the standard page, folded twice (folded once it became tabloid size), made a handy size for a book or booklet (about the size of a piece of business stationery). One page of newsprint yielded eight pages; two made a sixteen-page pamphlet; four produced a respectable-size booklet of thirty-two pages.

In one of the earliest financially remunerative examples of recycling, Max Gaines literally created a market that did not exist before.

Calling them **Funnies on Parade**, he published the thirty-two-page reprinted comics as giveaway premiums to boost the sales of comsumer products such as Canada Dry ginger ale and Wheatena breakfast cereal. Manufacturers were pleased as customers by the hundreds of thousands clipped coupons and sent away for the comics. Within Eastern Color Printing, Max became the man to see about premium comic books.

After Eastern paid a syndicate $10 per page to reprint newspaper comic strips, Max Gaines convinced Procter & Gamble to order a million copies of the first Funnies on Parade. However, the soap company made no long-term publication commitment.

Eastern continued to put out **Famous Funnies** for twenty-two years, concluding with issue #218 in 1955. First published in 1936, Dell's **Popular Comics** ran through 1948.

At this point, comic books were merely an inducement to buy something else. In effect they were no different from the prize in the Cracker Jacks box. However, they were so successful that Max came to believe comics had a value in their own right.

The time had come to float a trial balloon. Ever the salesman, Max convinced George Delacorte of Dell Publishing to finance a print run of 35,000 copies. He priced his half-tabloid-size sixty-four-page comic books at 10 cents a copy, called them **Famous Funnies**, and test-marketed a batch at local mom and pop groceries near his home. Much to Max's delight, they sold out over a weekend. Delacorte remained unconvinced that the phenomenon could be repeated and abandoned support of **Famous Funnies**. Gaines then talked Eastern into publishing directly, and ordered up a larger print run of 250,000.

The circulation of Max Gaines' Famous Funnies increased with each issue until sales approached a million copies a month.

Following the success of **Famous Funnies**, Eastern expressed its gratitude by firing Max. Gaines hired on with McClure Syndicate, which had a brace of two-color presses acquired from a failed newspaper. Max hitched them together to get four-color capability and picked up where he left off. He rekindled his relationship with Dell and founded **Popular Comics**, which premiered the comic book appearances of **Dick Tracy**, **Little Orphan Annie**, **Terry & the Pirates**, and **Gasoline Alley**.

The comic book was born.

The Beginning of the Golden Age

In an effort to keep the McClure presses fully engaged, Max was also printing *Detective Comics* for his friend, pulp publisher Harry Donenfeld. In 1937, Gaines was approached by two young cartoonists, Jerry Siegel and Joe Shuster, with a strip they'd been trying to peddle for four years without success. Thinking that it might interest Harry, Gaines showed him a strip featuring a square-jawed man with one curly forelock. Clad in garish underwear (bright blue union suit, red trunks) and red cape, he was endowed with extraordinary physical powers.

Even though Donenfeld had his doubts about the appeal (and credibility) of the character, he published the new strip as one of his *Action Comics*. Issue #1 hit the streets in June of 1938, starring Siegel and Shuster's hero, *Superman*. It was an immediate runaway hit, and *Superman* became comics' first superstar. He is also the most durable. Having spawned radio and television shows, four major motion pictures, cartoons, a Broadway musical, and a pantheon of imitations,

A rejection letter received by Siegel and Shuster said, "We feel that the public have had their fill of superhuman subjects." A very fine *Action Comics* #1 (left), the first appearance of *Superman*, sold for $30,000 in 1991. A mint copy recently sold for $137,500.

Superman remains the single most important character in comic book history.

Donenfeld kept *Superman* within the DC fold, but joined in partnership with Gaines to produce the affiliated *All-American* line of comics, whose heroes included *The Flash*, *Hawkman*, and *Green Lantern*. In what was to become a tradition among superheroes, within a couple of issues they banded together to form *The Justice Society of America*.

The appearance of *Superman* was the dawn of what has become known as the Golden Age of comic books. During that era, victory of the superheroes over the forces of evil was never in doubt. Increasingly in the late thirties and early forties, the specific identity of those forces of evil was implied, if not stated. Even before war against Germany was declared, the superheroes had gone on the offensive against sinister but unnamed enemies. After Pearl Harbor, the sinister cads flaunted their swastikas, and the Nazis provided Superman and the other heroes with a never ending skein of villains to vanquish. (Social historians have made much of the fact that Siegel and Shuster borrowed the Nietzschean concept of the *Ubermensch*, or superman, and turned it against the Germans who claimed to be the inheritors of Friedrich Nietzsche's legacy. Indeed, it is said that an irate Joseph Goebbels, Hitler's Minister of Propaganda, once brought a meeting at the Reichstag to a screeching halt over the matter. Gesticulating with an *Action Comic*, he supposedly then vehemently reviled *Superman* as a Jew.)

Because *Superman* always made a point of defending the underdog, Hitler and Stalin, with their goals of world domination, were tailor made as villains.

Wonder Woman was added to the *All-American* lineup in 1942. A strong, self-sufficient female character, she was the creation of Harvard psychologist William Moulton Marston. Max had brought him in to develop a hero that appealed to female readership and who would be a positive role model for children. (Marston was also the inventor of the systolic blood pressure deception test, aka the lie detector.) Everyone was astonished when Moulton's hero turned out to be a heroine, but *Wonder Woman* is another manifestation that currents in society are reflected in the comics.

This Fall 1942 cover shows Princess Diana, aka Diana Prince or *Wonder Woman*, sending Mars, the Roman god of war, head over heels. William Moulton Marston, *Wonder Woman*'s creator, personally selected Mars as her adversary.

This superwoman who could hold her own with the superguys came along at the same time that Rosie the Riveter took her place on the assembly line as the men went to war.

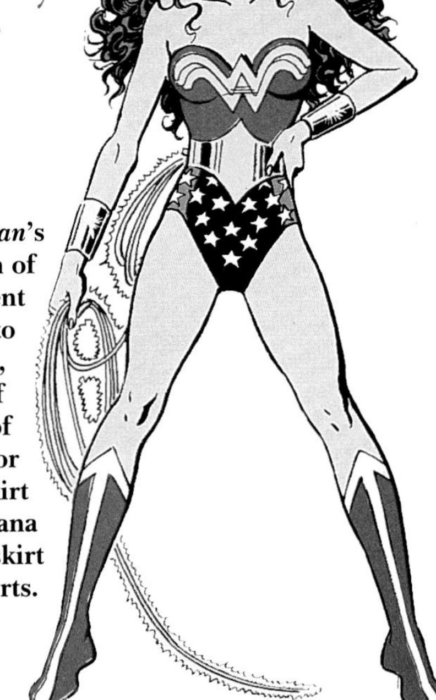

***Wonder Woman*'s mother, the Queen of the Amazons, sent her daughter off to fight for "America, the last citadel of democracy, and of equal rights for women," in a skirt (left), but Diana jettisoned the skirt for a pair of shorts.**

Despite paper shortages, the war was good for Gaines and Donenfeld. By 1943, they were publishing twenty titles that accounted for one-third of the 25 million comics being sold in America every month.

The once-cozy relationship between Max and Harry soured when Harry unilaterally gave half of his half of the business to his accountant, Jack Liebowitz. Max was not consulted, perhaps because Liebowitz and Gaines had rubbed each other the wrong way for years. Max disdained Liebowitz as a bean counter and believed he was determined to wring the last penny from the bottom line in the comic book ventures. Gaines was particularly aggravated by Liebowitz's insistence on increasing the number of advertisements in the comic books. Screaming matches among the partners became increasingly frequent until early in 1945, when Max asked for and got $500,000 from Jack and Harry for his interest in *Action Comics*. Part of what made Jack and Harry meet Gaines' asking price was that Max held the paper contracts—and since newsprint was still a controlled substance due to wartime shortages, Jack and Harry were very much tied to Max until he released them. (Shortly thereafter, of course, the war ended and the paper shortage ended—from that perspective, at least, Max had maximized his opportunity.) In accepting the buyout, Gaines surrendered his rights to *The Flash*, *Wonder Woman*, *The Green Lantern*, and the other All-American action heroes and announced his retirement. "Retirement" lasted two weeks, after which Max founded *Educational Comics*, publishing the more sedate titles that Donenfeld and Liebowitz had ceded to him.

Above, The original partners in *Action Comics* (left to right): Jack Liebowitz, Harry Donenfeld, an unidentified associate, and Max Gaines.

At right, Max Gaines poses at the helm of his *Educational Comics* empire, with a selection of titles behind him.

The Grisly Creativity of William Gaines

The Enfant Terrible

Born in 1922, Bill Gaines hated comics when he was growing up. He was a klutzy, rebellious kid who couldn't seem to do anything right, and his father Max didn't miss many opportunities to tell him so. The elder Gaines was convinced his kid had been dredged from the bottom of the family gene pool, and was doomed to be a failure. For his part, Bill did his best to live down to his father's expectations.

Max was a strong, old-fashioned father in the Prussian tradition, who felt that his job was to mold his children and instill discipline, not to show affection. He was also a screamer at home, and more often than not the target of his high-decibel ire was his son. Perhaps as a defense mechanism, young Bill developed a proclivity for practical jokes and a puckish literal-mindedness that drove his father bananas (as it was no doubt calculated to do). If Max sternly summoned him to "drop whatever you're doing," to give him a hand, Bill complied to the letter with his father's directive—and let the pile of books or cup of coffee slip from his fingers before presenting himself on the double before the family commander-in-chief. "I was always a bumbling idiot around my father," Gaines confessed to Frank Jacobs in *The MAD World of William M. Gaines*, "I don't know whether it was because I knew it would drive him out of his mind, which it did, or because he *scared* me into being a bumbling idiot."

After high school he enrolled in Brooklyn Poly but was expelled in his junior year because of his poor grades and his relentless tomfoolery (dueling with slide rules, chalk and eraser battles). To hide his disgrace from Max, he continued to leave the house each morning as if going to school. Finally, despite his asthma and poor eyesight, he was drafted. At this stage in his life, the younger Gaines was a withdrawn, rather nerdy young man. He dated little if at all throughout high school. Because he lacked much in the way of savoir faire with the ladies, in 1944 his mother Jessie all but arranged his marriage to his first halfway serious romance, his second cousin, Hazel Grieb.

As Max prospered, he moved the family to a comfortable house in Brooklyn. Eventually he bought a more elegant home in White Plains and a summer house on Lake Placid. Bill, shown above with his father Max and below with his mother Jessie and his sister Elaine, spent his childhood summers on the lake.

After an uneventful stint as a photographer in the Army Air Corps, Bill decided that he wanted to teach high school chemistry. He certainly had no desire to join the family business and work under his father's thumb on a daily basis. After his discharge from the army, Bill enrolled in NYU and was within a few months of earning his teaching credential in 1947 when his marriage unraveled. To comfort his distraught wife, Max took her and some family friends, Sam and Helen Irwin and their son Billy, to their vacation home on Lake Placid. Sam and Billy Irwin were with Max in the Gaines family boat when the front of the boat was rammed by another speeding vessel. Max and Sam were killed instantly; ten-year-old Billy survived. Billy Irwin's account of the accident suggests that Max Gaines died a hero. As the other boat bore down on them and the crash became inevitable, at the last possible moment Max picked up Billy and threw him from the front of the boat to the rear, saving his life.

The Court Jester Becomes King

At Jessie's behest, young Bill, just twenty-five and newly divorced, reluctantly took over EC Comics, his father's publishing business. At first, he went into the office about once a week, primarily to sign checks and to humor his widowed mother. He believed his presence at the company was temporary, and among some of Max's veteran staff there was the ill-disguised hope that this would indeed be the case. (As a teen, Bill had made a few forays into his father's office during school vacations, and had displayed an uncanny penchant for getting in the way, or worse, into mischief.) In the first few months following his father's passing, it was not unusual to find him sitting at his father's desk, playing gin rummy with his cousin for hours on end.

Bill inherited a mess of titles competing with each other to lose the most money.

Bill may have had no prior experience running a company, but it didn't take a CPA to see that the business was failing. When Max Gaines was bought out by Harry Donenfeld and Jack Liebowitz, all rights to the superheroes remained with *Action Comics*. Perhaps it was a holdover from Max's days as an elementary school principal, but he never gave up on the potential for comic books as a teaching tool. (His use of the psychologist William Moulton Marston to create *Wonder Woman* was perhaps an earlier effort in the same vein.) When he came back from his two-week "retirement," he set about trying to demonstrate this theory on the newsstands of America.

It wasn't working. His EC or Educational Comics were far more popular with parents than with children. Max Gaines had deliberately stayed away from the most popular comic trends of the postwar era—and the market was punishing him for it. At a time when kids were plunking down their dimes in record numbers for westerns, romances, and crime comics, EC put out innocuous publications like *Picture Stories from the Bible*, *Picture Stories from American History*, *Tiny Tot Comics*, and *Animal Fables*. There was nothing inherently wrong with *Animal Fables*; funny animal comics (led by Dell's *Looney Tunes* and *Merrie Melodies*, with Bugs Bunny, Elmer Fudd, Daffy Duck and Porky Pig, as well as Disney's Donald Duck and Mickey Mouse) held strong appeal throughout the late forties and early fifties as the vanguard of the Baby Boom learned to read. However, with sterile and even downright inane offerings like *Bouncy Bunny in the Friendly Forest*, it was

In 1945, Max Gaines distributed over $5,000 worth of proceeds from sales of *Picture Stories from the Bible* to various religious organizations. One of the recipients was Dr. Norman Vincent Peale, then pastor of the Marble Collegiate Church of New York.

not surprising that EC Comics was hemorrhaging red ink. When Max Gaines died, in August 1947, it was $100,000 in the hole.

Bill Gaines probably would have been an excellent chemistry teacher (the kind who would blow things up just to see what would happen, or make hydrogen sulfide just before an inspection visit by the school board), but he never lit a Bunsen burner again. With the shadow of his overbearing father suddenly absent, Bill fell head over heels in love with Max's medium, if not his message. "First thing I knew, I had to read comics. Next thing I knew, I was in love with them," he said simply.

By his own description, Bill inherited "a mess of titles competing with each other to lose the most money." As he slowly grew more familiar with the business, he wanted to make changes, both to improve the fiscal health of the company and to move the comics closer in line with his own interests. At first, he took the lead from other publishers, putting out imitations of other successful comics.

Bill Gaines never thought he could fill his father's shoes. When his mother insisted he take his father's place at the office, he complained, "If he was losing money, what do you expect *me* to do?"

Sol Cohen had been Max Gaines' circulation manager and, with business manager Frank Lee, he was keeping a eye on EC while Bill got up to speed with the business. Cohen got word to a young cartoonist working at Fox Features Syndicate that Bill was interested in putting out a teen comic, something in the vein of the popular *Archie* series.

The artist came in with his portfolio. Gaines was particularly attracted to the artist's ability to render voluptuous young ladies, and put him under contract to do a teenage comic book called *Going Steady with Peggy*. The artist's name was Al Feldstein—and the rest, as they say, is history.

In March of '48, Feldstein went right to work on *Peggy*. He got as far as writing the first stories and penciling in the drawings when Gaines called him into his office. With furrowed brow he told Feldstein that he wasn't going to publish *Going Steady with Peggy*. In 1948, publishing practices in the comic book industry resembled nothing so much as a game of "follow the leader"—played by a colony of suicidal lemmings. With the lifting of wartime rationing on paper, there was an explosion of comic book titles, all vying for the attention of schoolchildren, teens, and young adults.

Hello, creeps! Here's a putrid peek at what's ahead after you're done being gored stiff with pre-Crypt tedium, heh, heh, heh.

The market was glutted, as comics fought for space in drugstores and newsstands. The first comic to break new ground was almost immediately followed by a tidal wave of comic clones, but the original usually held an edge it never relinquished. In the wake of an innovation, new knockoff titles came and went with dizzying speed, sometimes lasting just a couple of issues—or less. Before *Going Steady with Peggy* ever left Feldstein's drawing board, the entire teenage comic market collapsed from supersaturation. Almost everything except *Archie* was dying on the shelves.

Feldstein was then just twenty-two, but was not entirely surprised when Gaines told him *Peggy* was dead. Even when he was still at Fox, he'd seen the teen trend begin to wane. Still it was not good news. "I had a child and was living in a three-room apartment in Brooklyn. I had to make a living and I was desperate," he remembers. He had nothing to lose by taking his best shot with EC. "Okay, tear up the contract," he told a relieved Gaines. "I'll come to work for you and help you develop some more marketable titles." Keeping Al Feldstein was Bill Gaines' first major independent business decision as the head of EC Comics. Together they began a metamorphosis of the EC line, taking a hard look at what other publishers were offering and jettisoning the bland, wholesome comic books championed by Bill's father.

For obvious reasons, comics featuring well-endowed young women were known within the industry as "headlight" comics.

Al Feldstein's penchant for bad puns, which found full expression in the Crypt Keeper, can be seen in the title of the only surviving pencil renderings in the EC archives, "Lashes to Lashes."

Teenage Comics: A Boom Goes Bust

It all started with **Archie**, who was spawned in December 1941 (about the same time as Pearl Harbor). Created by Bob Montana, he got his own magazine in February of 1943, and his antics with pals Betty, Veronica, and Jughead provided relief to war-weary GIs scarcely out of high school themselves.

Archie had the teen market to himself for most of the Second World War. DC came out with its **Archie** wannabe, **Buzzy**, in 1944. Targeting the teenage girl market, Marvel debuted **Tessie the Typist** in the same year. In 1945 they came out with **Millie the Model** and **Nellie the Nurse** (all three bosomy alliterative females were created by Stan **Spider-Man** Lee), as well as **Patsy Walker**. **Archie**'s publishers countered with **Katy Keene**. None of them ever rivaled the success of the original; **Archie** got his own radio program in 1945. His success ultimately prompted his publishing house, MLJ Magazines, to change its name in his honor.

In 1948, Al Feldstein was freelancing at Fox Features Syndicate, drawing and writing some teen comics called **Sunny—America's Sweetheart**, **Junior**, and doing a comic book adaptation of a popular radio show called **Meet Corliss Archer**. Sol Cohen reached Feldstein through the letterer who was working on Al's panels and told him that EC was considering coming out with a teenage comic. Unhappy at Fox, he made an appointment to meet with Bill Gaines.

The youthful Bill Gaines and dapper Al Feldstein relax at an early EC office party in the days when they were about to become the hottest creative team in horror comics.

The Bill & Al Show

The new approach was heralded by a subtle but important name change—within a year, Bill made the "E" in EC comics stand for "Entertaining," rather than "Educational." After the war, crime comics, all of them the illegitimate offspring of Lev Gleason's *Crime Does Not Pay* (1942), were the most popular, but westerns and romances were also selling well. Trying to grab a piece of the current trend, Bill changed the name of *International Comics* to *International Crime Patrol*, rebaptized the hapless *Happy Houlihans* as *Saddle Justice*, and put Al to work illustrating crime and western stories. So that Feldstein's talent for drawing buxom beauties didn't go to waste, they also started a romance comic called *Modern Love*. Al found himself working side-by-side with another artist whom Gaines had hired early in his tenure as head of EC, Graham Ingels.

Feldstein began illustrating scripts that Gaines had commissioned, but soon complained about their quality. "Look," he groused to Bill, "I can do better than this." Feldstein had been writing and editing for Fox's teenage series before coming to EC, so Gaines greenlighted him to write his own crime and western stories.

With the new comic books, EC had become more competitive, but it was a long way from making a profit. Gaines and Feldstein were cautiously feeling their way, changing the names of the new comics in response to the shifts they perceived in the marketplace. *Saddle Justice* lasted just six issues before becoming *Saddle Romances*. After eight issues, *Moon Girl* segued into *A Moon, A Girl... Romance*. EC wasn't the only comic publisher doing the name-change mambo. Fox Features Syndicate's *Western Killers* suddenly mutated into *My True Love*; Marvel's *Cindy Smith* grew hair on her chest and was reborn as *Crime Can't Win*; Fawcett's *Captain Midnight* got an attitude adjustment and reemerged as *Sweethearts*. There's only one American institution that could cause such an outbreak of Marx Brothers silliness—the U.S. Post Office.

Working closely together, Al and Bill bonded almost immediately, both in the office and outside it. The two shared meals and confidences, and indulged their mad passion for roller derby and the Brooklyn Dodgers together. They shared alter egos as "Adrienne," "Amy," and "Chuck," composing replies to the lovelorn when EC's upstart replicas of Dear Abby began running in the romance titles. This was more than ironic, since Feldstein was having marital troubles at the time and the shy, divorced Gaines was living an all-but-celibate life with his mother in Brooklyn.

Gaines gave Feldstein a lift home every night on the way to his mother's house. It was during one of these rides that Al begin to noodle on why EC wasn't doing better. "You know, Bill," he began, "we're really fools for following the crowd. Crime comics...westerns...romances...This is an industry where everybody follows and very few take the lead.... But it's the guys who are the innovators who really prevail. All the imitators fail eventually."

Gaines and Feldstein discovered that among the common interests they shared was a love of spine-tingling tales of fright. Both had come of age in the heyday of radio thrillers, when families gathered 'round the crystal set the way they now congregate in front of the tube. Three years younger than Gaines, Feldstein had been too little to be permitted to listen in, but he crept out of bed and perched on the top of the stairs while his older brother shivered along with *Inner Sanctum* and Arch Oboler's *Lights Out*, especially "The Old Witch's Tale." "I talked to Bill about the old horror stories and how much we'd loved them," recalls Feldstein. I said, "Why don't we put this stuff in the comics?"

In the 1930s, kids gathered around the crystal set to listen to radio thrillers in much the same way as they huddle around the television today.

Comics were shipped second class and required a $2,000 permit for each new title. To avoid the fee, publishers sent new titles out on existing permits. If they snuck up on the name change, usually they got away with it. It wasn't until Gaines tried to metamorphose *A Moon, A Girl... Romance* into *Weird Fantasy* that the Post Office caught him.

The Descent into the Crypt

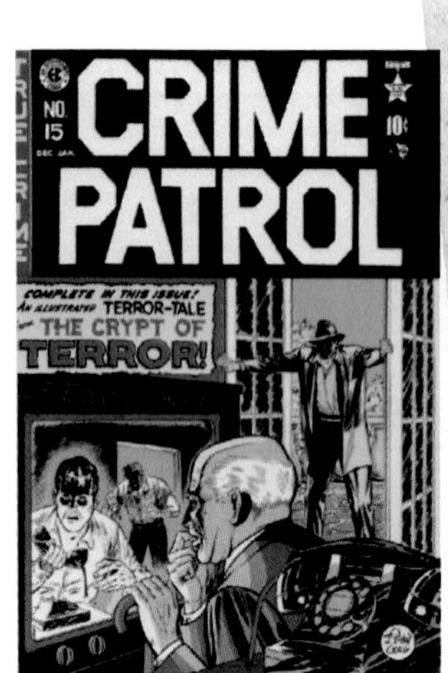

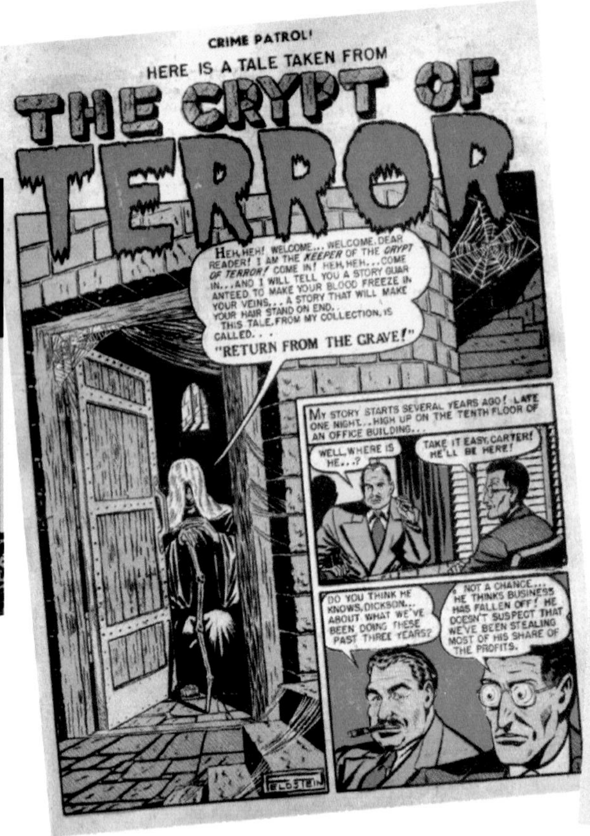

In addition to providing the debut of the Crypt Keeper, "Return from the Grave" in *Crime Patrol* #15 marks the first in a long parade of Gaines/Feldstein corpses who come back from the dead. Ambulatory cadavers were one of the most popular and enduring EC house plots.

Gaines thought he was onto something, and soon Al was helping Bill take Max's legacy in a direction his father had never dreamed of—horror. They dropped early hints of their intentions into the non-horror titles *Crime Patrol* and *War Against Crime*, both to test the market and to establish a transition that avoided payment of the second-class mailing permit fees.

Gaines was enamored of the new material, and even more delighted when he learned how well it was selling.

EC's distibutors employed "road men" who functioned a bit like a Nielsen rating service for comic books. Road men hit the newsstands and went into the mom and pop stores to make sure their comics were properly displayed. They also counted how many magazines were still on the racks. One good barometer of how well a comic was doing was the "ten-day checkup." After ten days on the stands, the road men counted how many were left. If only ten of the original fifty copies had been sold, the magazine was selling at twenty percent and that comic was a dog. If forty of the fifty were gone, the comic was selling at eighty percent and was a big hit. Bill Gaines had not inherited much of his father's personality, but he did inherit some of Max's business acumen. When the ten-day checkups of the revamped *Crime Patrol* with horror started showing vast improvement over previous sales, Bill pressed his advantage.

One feature that had appealed to Feldstein about the old radio thrillers was the presence of a host—a ghoulish ancestor of Alistair Cooke of *Masterpiece Theatre*. Al told Bill that he wanted to have a continuing character to present his scary stories, which is how the Crypt Keeper was born. He made his debut in *Crime Patrol* #15 in a story called "Return from the Grave," and returned for a curtain call in *Crime Patrol* #16 in "The Spectre in the Castle."

The Crypt Keeper was a bona fide personality from the very beginning. He was

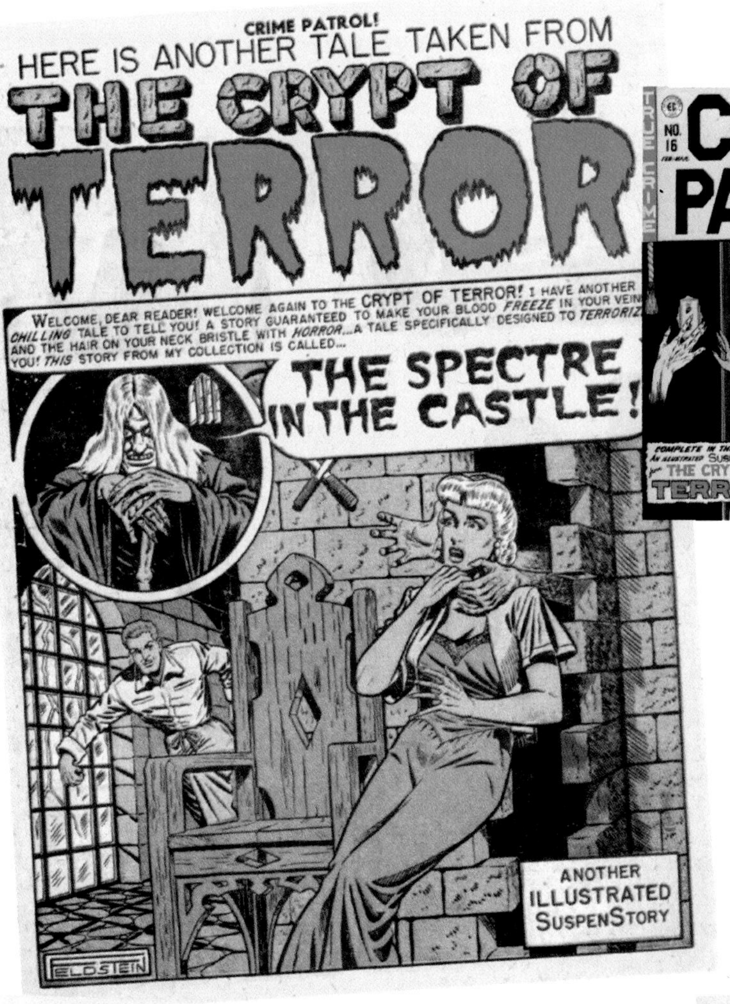

also a wisecracking smartass. Feldstein developed him as a sort of sarcastic color commentator on the ghoulish goings-on, and used him to highlight the fact that EC horror, however grisly it became, was always written with tongue firmly planted in cheek.

At about the same time, Feldstein's eight-page story "Buried Alive" appeared in Issue #10 of *War Against Crime*. This tale was hosted by the Vault Keeper, and marked his first appearance in print. The Vault Keeper, like the Crypt Keeper, commented on the stories from a vantage point outside the proceedings. In the same issue was a Johnny Craig story called "The Idol's Revenge." In the following issue, *War Against Crime* #11, Feldstein brought the Vault Keeper back to preside over a story entitled "The Mummy's Curse."

As it turned out, *Crime Patrol* #16 and *War Against Crime* #11 were the twilight of the old order. With Issue #17 and Issue #12, the Crypt Keeper and the Vault Keeper each got his own show, as it were, and the titles of their comics were changed to *The Crypt of Terror* and *The Vault of Horror*. Gaines and Feldstein

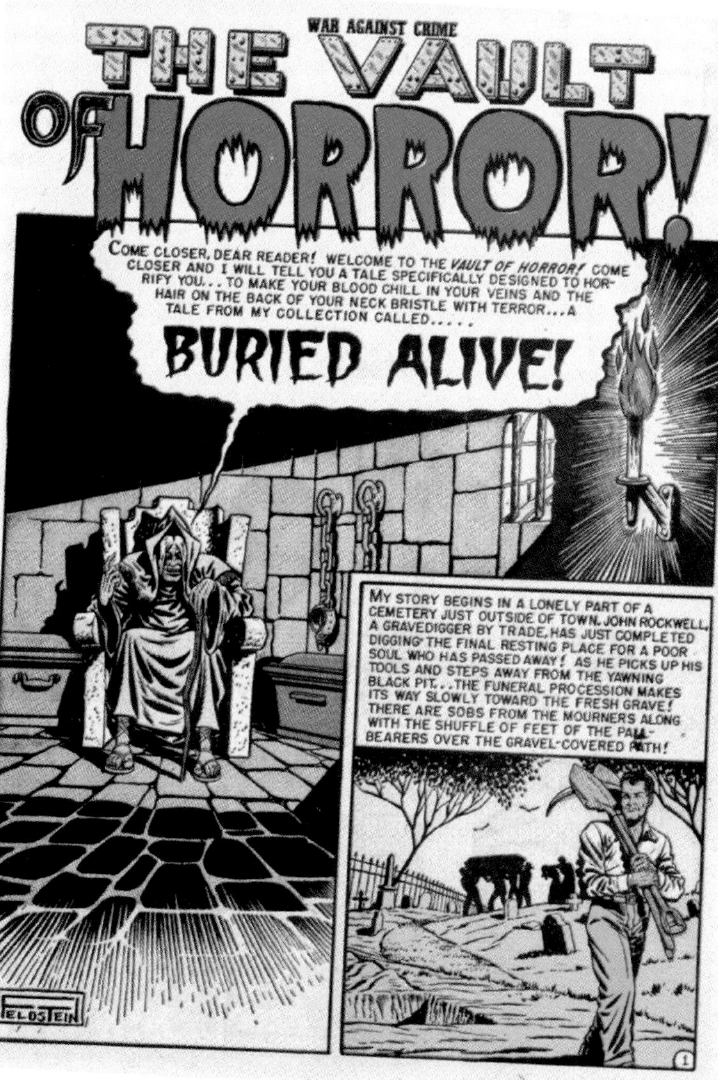

made the switch in January of 1950, premiering the new titles with the April/May issues. They also added a companion title, *The Haunt of Fear* (hosted by the Old Witch, another Feldstein GhouLunatic). With Gaines' announcement of the debut of his *New Trend* in comics, he left other publishers scrambling to respond to his innovation.

The final leap into the Crypt from *Picture Stories from the Bible* was a bit much for Sol Cohen, Max's former circulation manager, who went to Avon Comics. Rather than hire someone to replace him, Gaines and Feldstein assumed command of EC.

The first issues of EC's three horror titles all appeared in 1950. The title *The Crypt of Terror* was used on issues #17, 18, and 19. With Issue #20 (Oct./Nov. 1950), the title was changed to *Tales from the Crypt*, but it was not until Issue #22 (Feb./Mar. 1951) that the now famous trademark logo appeared.

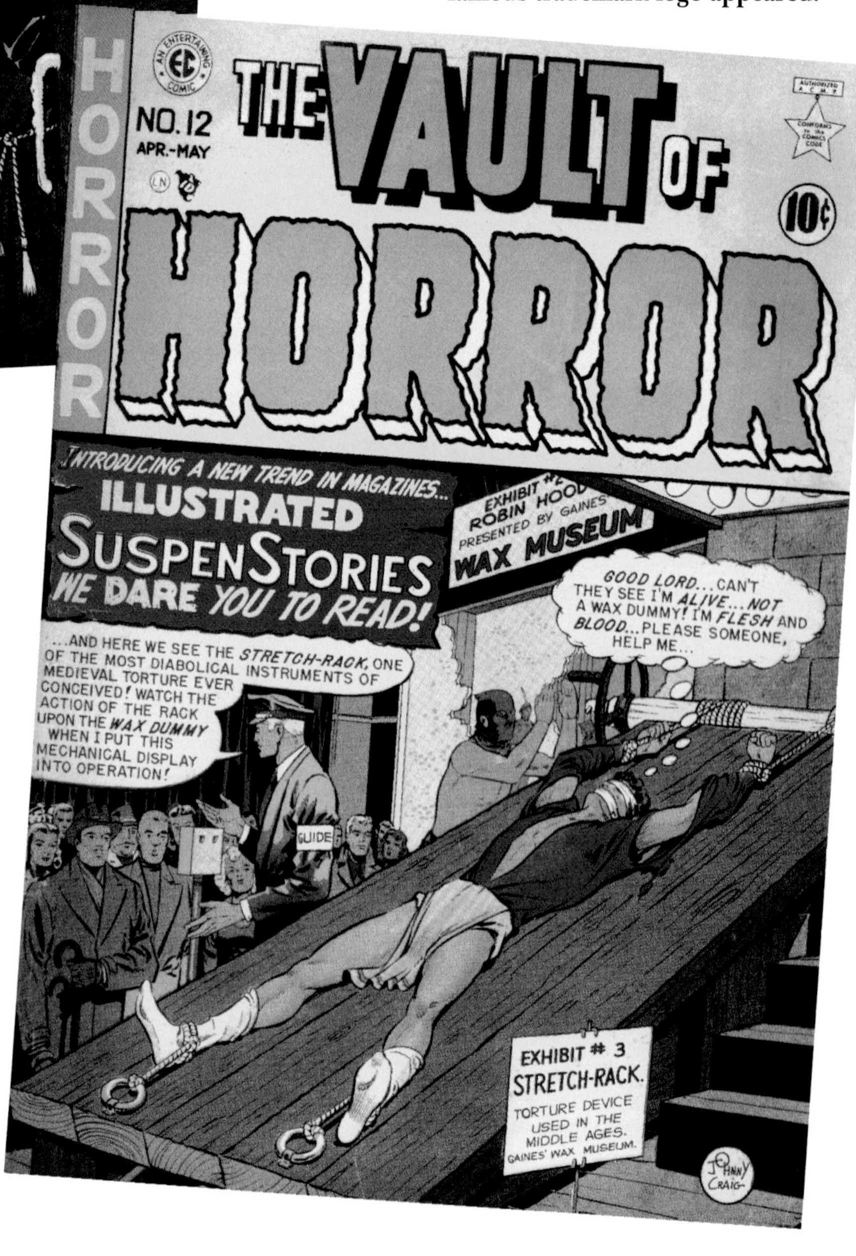

Now that those idiots are done with all this deadly history, we finally get to me! Here comes the real meat of the story. Heh, heh, heh.

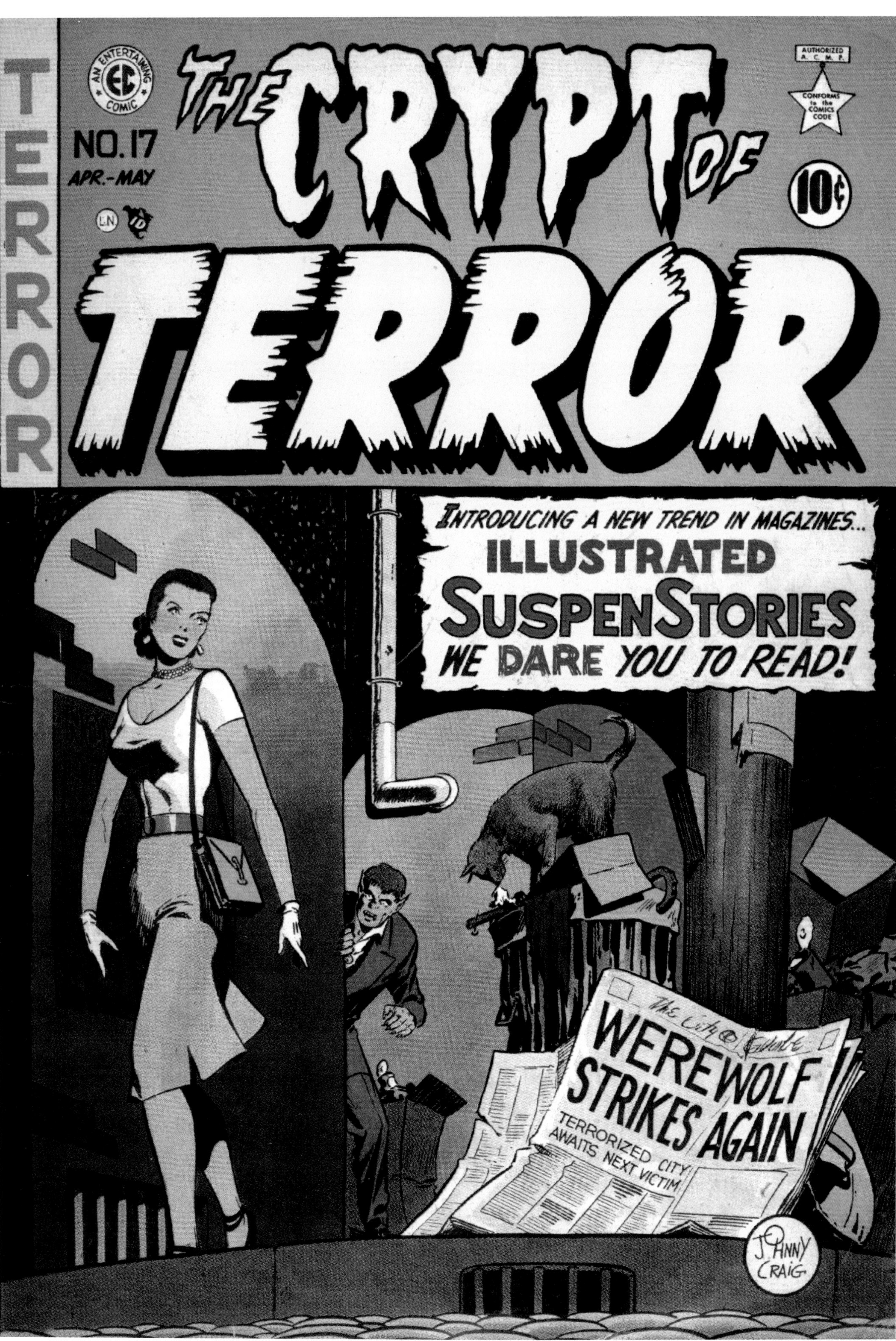
TERROR
AN ENTERTAINING EC COMIC
THE CRYPT OF TERROR
NO. 17
APR.-MAY
AUTHORIZED A. C. M. P.
CONFORMS to the COMICS CODE
10¢
INTRODUCING A NEW TREND IN MAGAZINES...
ILLUSTRATED
SUSPENSTORIES
WE DARE YOU TO READ!
WEREWOLF STRIKES AGAIN
TERRORIZED CITY AWAITS NEXT VICTIM
JOHNNY CRAIG

EC Splatters America with

With their horror tales, Feldstein and Gaines struck a nerve deep in the national psyche.

On September 3, 1949, the Soviet Union exploded its first A-bomb, ending the U.S. atomic monopoly and raising the spectre of global nuclear war. Kids were ducking under desks in school rooms all over America in preparation for the seemingly inevitable mushroom cloud.

Atop the Bone Pile

Frankenstein, Dracula, and the Phantom of the Opera had sprung from the nightmare conditions of the early days of the Industrial Revolution. Horror comics of the 1950s appealed to teens and young adults who were trying to cope with the aftermath of even greater terrors—Nazi death camps and the explosion of the atomic bombs at Hiroshima and Nagasaki.

Fifties kids came of age in a booming, button-down America during an era punctuated by outbursts of national paranoia. School duck-and-cover drills nourished the fear that at any moment a nuclear attack could send us into shelters to live on Ritz crackers for years. As high school graduates were getting shipped off to Korea, the McCarthy hearings and the Rosenberg spy trial reinforced the idea that America's enemies were everywhere—without constant vigilance we would be destroyed from within. For the good of the country it was necessary to ferret out the sinister Commies who had camouflaged themselves as red-blooded patriots and infiltrated the high school faculty.

It was difficult for adolescents to deal with these deep-seated fears for survival, rational or otherwise, when everything looked so rosy at home. Times were good; the factories were humming. With the advent of Levittown, everyone could safely aspire to be Ozzie and Harriet. Millions of young Americans, who had no frame of reference to judge how far the times were out of joint, were whipsawed by the dichotomy between mortal terror and creature comforts. Cultural historian David J. Skal states the case vividly in *The Monster Show:*

The new American prosperity of the early 1950s was won atop the largest bone pile in human history. World War II had claimed the lives of over 40 million soldiers and civilians, and had introduced two radical new forms of mechanized death—the atomic bomb and the extermination camp—that seriously challenged the mind's ability to absorb, much less cope with, the naked face of horror at mid-century....If America in 1950 was filled with the smell of new cars, it was still permeated by the stench of mass death, and the threat of more to come.

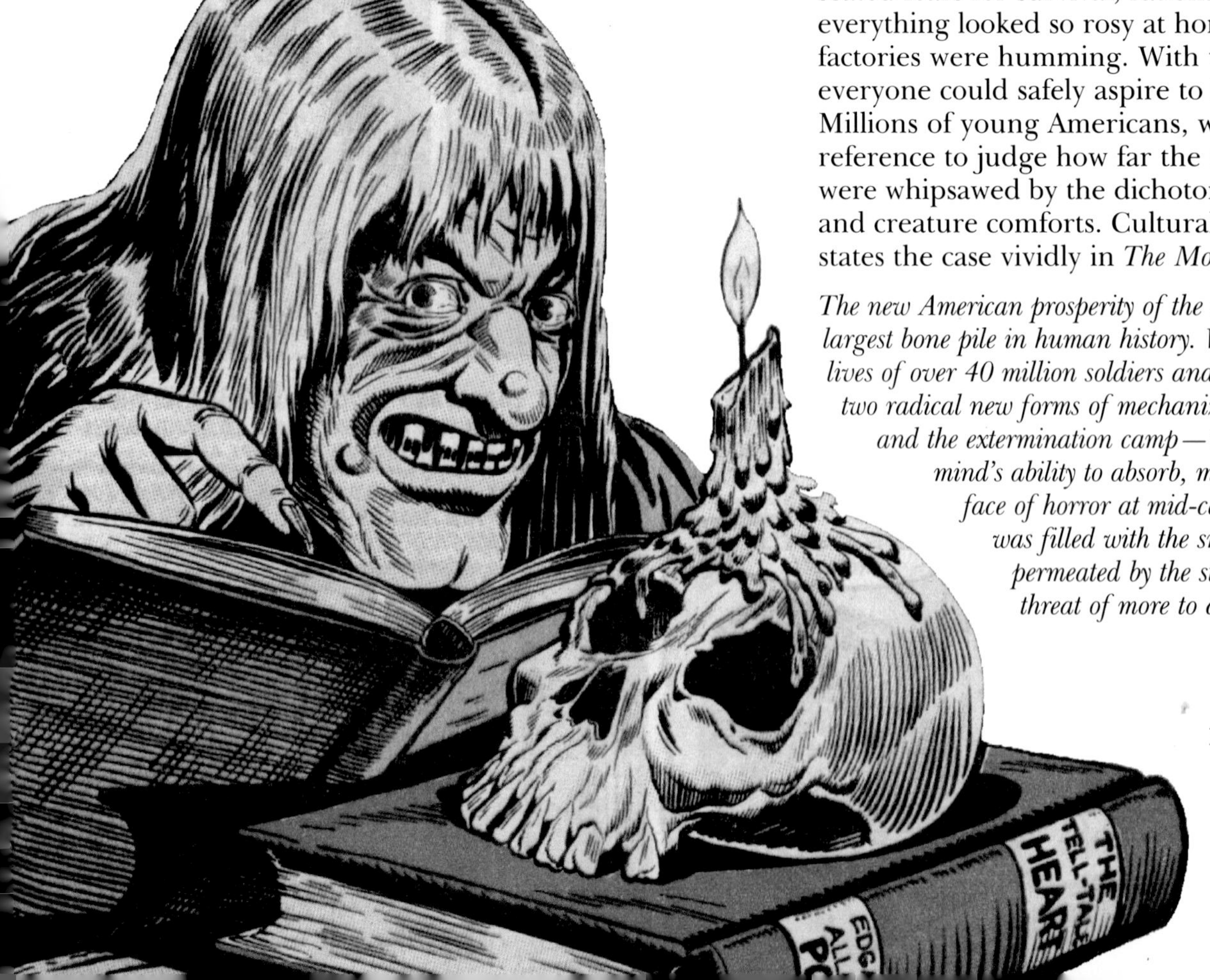

Feldstein called his rendition of the Crypt Keeper a "gnarled old creature...with pimples and hair growing out of his nose."

AN EXPLOSION OF HORROR

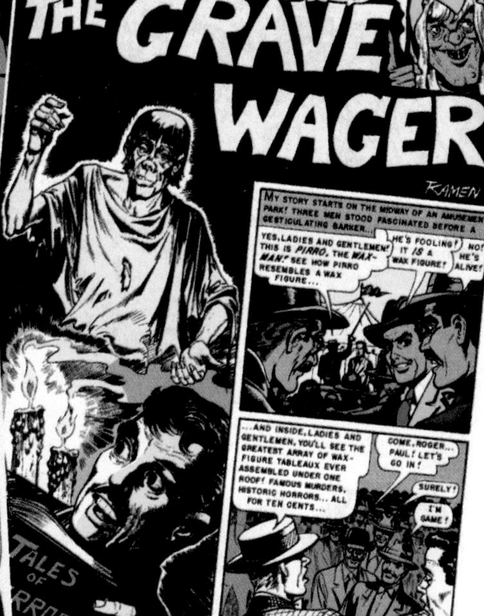

The Time of His Life

Bill Gaines was not looking for the underlying reasons why his horror comics were taking off in the marketplace. Perhaps for the first time in his life, he was simply jazzed about what he was doing. He had made the creative decision to pioneer a new genre that appealed to him personally. Now in 1950 he was putting out comics that *he* wanted to read, and his innovation was being handsomely rewarded. Although they didn't match DC or Marvel in overall sales volume,

New Trend comics began to outsell almost everything else

on a percentage basis, and Gaines started whittling down the debt he'd inherited from his father.

Appropriately dubbed "splash pages" in the jargon of the comic book industry, the opening spreads of these early stories grabbed the reader with superb dramatic images.

Al Feldstein was the key ingredient from the beginning.

Like one of EC's own stories where one person is trapped inside the body of another, Gaines rapidly discovered that within the body of his friend the artist beat the heart of a writer—and a pretty terrific writer at that. Although a few other writers had been involved early on in the horror magazines, it was apparent to Bill that Feldstein's stuff was superior and he quickly jettisoned the rest.

Horror Haikus

Building on their friendship, the two men developed a close working relationship that was responsible for most of the EC horror story lines. Feldstein was the engine; Gaines was the spark plug; Dexedrine was the inadvertent catalyst. In a cycle that no doubt fed on itself (as it were), the perpetually Pooh-shaped Gaines, a binge eater, was constantly dieting. He took an appetite suppressant as part of this effort, and the appetite suppressant of choice at that time was a form of speed called

Dexedrine. It was also used by many students (both then and later) to help them stay awake and cram for exams. Gaines' use of the drug was not uncommon, nor was it considered substance abuse; it was liberally prescribed by doctors who were either oblivious to or unconcerned about its side effects. Because the Dex would keep Bill up at night, he read—and what he read was horror stories. It was enough to give the phrase "speed reading" a whole new connotation. "I read like a maniac," recalled Gaines in a 1983 *Comics Journal* interview. "I would read every science fiction and horror story I could get my hands on. They couldn't publish them fast enough."

Bill would return to the office in the morning with the germ of an idea for a story—or rather, several germs for several stories—culled from his night's reading. Gaines called his ideas "springboards," the basic rudiments of a plot from which Feldstein could take off and write the complete tale. Often these springboards were no more than a small slip of paper containing a hastily scribbled brief note or sentence fragment—little horror haikus that Feldstein rapidly fleshed out into complete stories.

Gaines' biggest hurdle in the morning was to "sell" Feldstein a springboard. In his 1973 biography (written by *MAD* staffer Frank Jacobs), Gaines recalled, with slight exaggeration, how the springboard pitch process worked. "After Al had rejected the first thirty-three on general principles, he *might* show a little interest in Number 34. Then I'd give him the hard sell.... He'd normally write a story in three hours, but during those three hours I'd have a nervous stomach, wondering if Al was going to come in screaming, 'I can't write that goddamn plot!'"

Gaines kept and recycled his little paper springboards. Often what Feldstein didn't "buy" from Gaines on one morning he bought the next day—or the next week. Sometimes Gaines was able to add a new twist that made a rejected idea more salable. Sometimes they were writing for a different artist whose style was more suited to the material. And sometimes they were just more desperate.

Since Al had to write the story quickly, he was a tough audience. "I used to drive him nuts because we would plot these together and I would say, 'No, no, no, Bill, that just doesn't work,'" recalled Feldstein.

"Terror in the Swamp" begins with a guest appearance by the Old Witch in the Vault Keeper's magazine (*Vault of Horror* #15). This is a 1950 "first generation" Old Witch, drawn by Al Feldstein. "Ghastly" Graham Ingels had not yet made her his own. Even after he no longer drew them for their stories, Feldstein versions of the Crypt Keeper, Vault Keeper, and Old Witch remained on the covers until 1953.

This Feldstein story from the first issue of *Vault of Horror* (#12, Apr./May 1950) is unusual because it is not introduced by any of the GhouLunatics.

"The truth was that Bill was just anxious to get to lunch." Gaines' love of food was legendary, and the legend (as well as Bill's girth) grew over time. Hunger was about the worst thing that could happen to a person, and heaven forbid EC's head writer should have to work on an empty stomach.

"We'd plot in the morning," Feldstein reminisces, "then go to Patrissy's, the local Italian restaurant. We'd gorge ourselves on spaghetti and manicotti and bread. I got fat. In a very short time I ballooned from 150 to 180 pounds." Rather than follow Gaines on the Dexedrine diet plan (which Al could plainly see was not working), Feldstein began passing up Patrissy's, opting instead for melba toast and cottage cheese at the drawing board.

His choice may have had as much to do with deadlines as with dieting. The artists couldn't work without the story, and he was keeping the entire staff busy virtually single-handedly. Having determined with Gaines not just the plot but whether the story would take up six, seven, or eight pages, Feldstein then got right to it after lunch.

"I would go into the back room and write the stories directly onto the illustration board," recalls Feldstein.

"I knew what the layout and the timing of the story were going to be. This came naturally to me, and I was amazed because I was an artist; I was never a writer. I started writing two lines below the top of the panel to give our letterer space to work in. He could letter in the caption and at the same time still be able to read the rest of what I'd written. When he was finished, he would erase out my hand lettering. It disappeared, and all that remained was the lettered panels. There are no existing original scripts of anything I wrote."

The idea of a convict escaping from prison hidden in a coffin that becomes his tomb reoccurs in "The Substitute" (*Tales from the Crypt* #45).

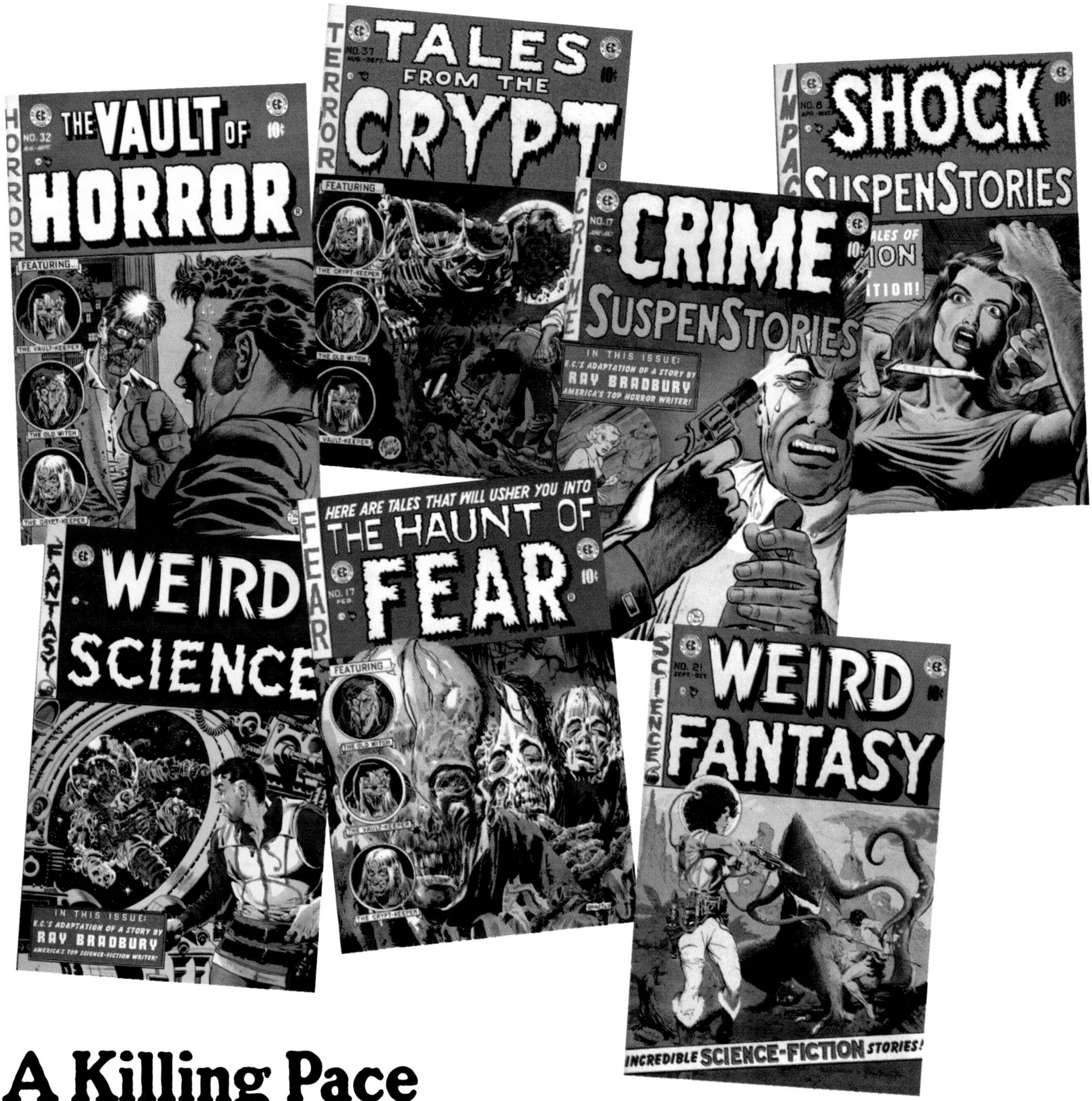

A Killing Pace

By day's end, Feldstein's story was complete, and his emergence with the finished draft was a special time in the office. Because much of the plot was conveyed through dialogue, Feldstein's stories were almost little mini-dramas, like the old radio thrillers. When Al had set down his tale panel by panel, he brought it to Bill, who'd give a dramatic reading of it to whoever was around, often cackling gleefully as he did so. "This was the fun part," Gaines told Maria Reidelbach in *Completely MAD: A History of the Comic Book and Magazine*. "We always thought of our work as being theatrical, and it had to read right." The next day the two started all over on another story.

Al and Bill were frighteningly prolific. The EC production schedule was grueling, and Feldstein in particular kept up a pace that was absolutely aerobic—in hindsight it's astonishing that Gaines, not Feldstein, was the one on stimulants. At maximum output in 1953, Al was writing four stories a week—*and* editing seven magazines—*Tales from the Crypt*, *Haunt of Fear*, *Vault of Horror**, *Crime SuspenStories*, *Shock SuspenStories*, *Weird Science*, and *Weird Fantasy*.

*Johnny Craig wrote and drew the Vault Keeper's lead story, and held the title of editor, but Feldstein wrote the other three stories in the magazine and prepared the Vault Keeper's dialogue.

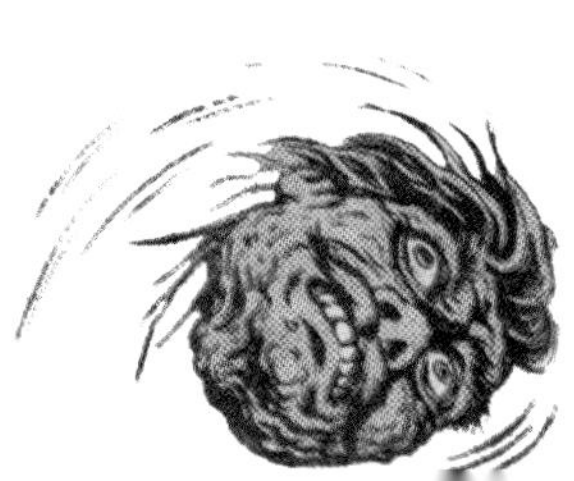

It Came from Outer Space

Gaines tried hard to boost EC's science fiction comics, enlisting the successful hosts of his horror magazines to promote them.

If *Tales from the Crypt, Vault of Horror,* and *Haunt of Fear* were Gaines' successful offspring who became the wealthy doctor, lawyer, and business tycoon, *Weird Science* and *Weird Fantasy* were his two favorite sons who grew up to be eccentric but ne'er-do-well professors. They were introduced in May of 1950, close on the heels of the horror magazines, and any other publisher besides Gaines would have killed them off after a couple of issues. They never generated anything like the revenues of other EC titles, and by 1953 they were barely paying for themselves, if not flat out losing money.

The fans of *Weird Science* and *Weird Fantasy* may not have been legion, but they were devoted. Gaines and Feldstein assiduously set out to cultivate them in the same manner that they established a personal relationship with their horror fans. What the science fiction comic lacked, however, was a host character. (With benefit of hindsight, some have speculated that *Weird Science* and *Weird Fantasy* would have been more commercially successful if they'd featured s-f interpretations of the Crypt Keeper.)

Perhaps in response to the impending threat of nuclear war, readers soon expressed a preference for the "ultimate catastrophe yarn"—Feldstein's "Destruction of the Earth" was an early favorite. Not surprisingly, other favorites were tales of alien beings from outer space—the early 1950s were the heyday of reports of flying saucers—and stories of extraterrestrial invaders (both benign and deadly) were popular fodder, not just in comic books, but in movies as well, including *Invaders from Mars* (1953) and most notably Robert Wise's *The Day the Earth Stood Still* (1951).

Working with Gaines springboards, Feldstein wrote *Weird Science* and *Weird*

Fantasy, just like he wrote the stories for horror comics. Even after his writing and editing duties mounted and he no longer had time to draw his own stories, Feldstein struggled to make time to keep doing cover art. Al enjoyed doing covers—it was virtually the only opportunity he had to draw. For his part, Gaines was delighted to oblige his artistic desires—his sales data showed that issues with Feldstein covers, whether they were horror comics or science fiction, generally outsold those with other artists' work on the cover.

Science fiction was Gaines' passion before it was Feldstein's, but he too became enamored of it. Each of the horror magazines trumpeted, "EC is proudest of its two science fiction comics," and Gaines and Feldstein kept producing them because they loved them, even if the customers did not.

Ray Bradbury & EC

"The first Buck Rogers comic strip I saw in 1929 changed my life forever," says distinguished science fiction author and futurist Ray Bradbury, "because he was going into the future and I wanted to go there." With works such as **The Martian Chronicles**, **Fahrenheit 451**, and **The Illustrated Man**, Bradbury's writings took him—and all of us—into the future, and into the scary recesses of fantasy. They also took him into the pages of EC comics.

Born in Waukegan, Illinois, in 1920, Bradbury began writing as an adolescent, penning his own sequels to the works of Edgar Rice Burroughs on a toy typewriter. By age fifteen, he was submitting his works to magazines, and he collected six years of rejection slips before his works began selling to the pulp magazines in the early 1940s. Quickly thereafter, however, they began appearing in magazines such as **The New Yorker**, **Collier's**, and **The Saturday Evening Post**.

What began as an exchange of letters with Bill Gaines over EC's "borrowing" of "The Emissary" (which appeared uncredited as "What the Dog Dragged In" in **Vault of Horror** #22) blossomed into an affection between Bradbury and Bradbury fans Gaines and Feldstein, and many of Bradbury's stories were adapted by Feldstein into comic form.

"I thought the adaptations were very good," says Bradbury. "They were very accurate. They quoted from me directly. You can't ask for more than that."

Asked to explain our fascination with horror stories, Bradbury suggests: "As I was growing up, my friends and I all loved to be frightened. It's a rehearsal of death. We know it's out there, so you've got to practice ahead of time in order to make do with it."

EC'S Ray Bradbury Adaptations

Comic Title	Comic/Issue#	Artist
"What the Dog Dragged In"	**Vault of Horror** #22	Jack Kamen
"Home to Stay"	**Weird Fantasy** #13	Wally Wood
"The Coffin"	**Haunt of Fear** #16	Jack Davis
"There Will Come Soft Rains"	**Weird Fantasy** #17	Wally Wood
"The Long Years"	**Weird Science** #17	Joe Orlando
"Let's Play Poison"	**Vault of Horror** #29	Jack Davis
"There Was an Old Woman"	**Tales from the Crypt** #34	Graham Ingels
"The Small Assassin"	**Shock SuspenStories** #7	George Evans
"The Screaming Woman"	**Crime SuspenStories** #15	Jack Kamen
"Zero Hour"	**Weird Fantasy** #18	Wally Wood
"Mars Is Heaven!"	**Weird Science** #18	Wally Wood
"The Black Ferris"	**Haunt of Fear** #18	Jack Davis
"King of the Grey Spaces"	**Weird Fantasy** #19	John Severin/ Will Elder
"The One Who Waits"	**Weird Science** #19	Al Williamson
"The Lake"	**Vault of Horror** #31	Joe Orlando
"The Handler"	**Tales from the Crypt** #36	Jack Kamen
"The October Game"	**Shock SuspenStories** #9	Jack Kamen
"Touch and Go"	**Crime SuspenStories** #17	Johnny Craig
"I, Rocket"	**Weird Fantasy** #20	Al Williamson
"Surprise Package"	**Weird Science** #20	Jack Kamen
"The Million Year Picnic"	**Weird Fantasy** #21	John Severin/ Will Elder
"Punishment without Crime"	**Weird Science** #21	Jack Kamen
"The Silent Towns"	**Weird Fantasy** #22	Reed Crandall
"Outcasts of the Stars"	**Weird Science** #22	Joe Orlando
"The Flying Machine"	**Weird Science-Fantasy** #23	Bernie Krigstein
"A Sound of Thunder"	**Weird Science-Fantasy** #25	Al Williamson

Source: Ray Bradbury bibliographer Donn Albright

Jolts of Social Conscience in Comic Book Disguise

Crime SuspenStories debuted in October 1950; *Shock SuspenStories* followed in February of 1952. Both offered different kinds of "horror" stories, those that proved that some of the scariest stuff around wasn't necessarily from outer space or the mummy's tomb—sometimes it was from around the corner or down the street. Often it was from city hall, as stories in these magazines often dealt with corruption of public officials. Gaines himself summarized how these magazines differed from his horror titles: "*Shock SuspenStories* do not contain supernaturalism. We want shock endings to wind up plain, logical suspense stories. *Crime SuspenStories* contain no shock. These are logical stories in which the villain tries to get away with murder—and probably does."

Neither of the *SuspenStories* magazines featured a host. Instead, *Shock SuspenStories* offered up a Whitman's Sampler approach—often combining a crime story, a science fiction story, a horror story, and a shock story in the same issue. Some fans were disappointed by this type of smorgasbord (for example, those who liked horror but didn't care for science fiction), feeling they were guaranteed at least one or two "duds" in each issue.

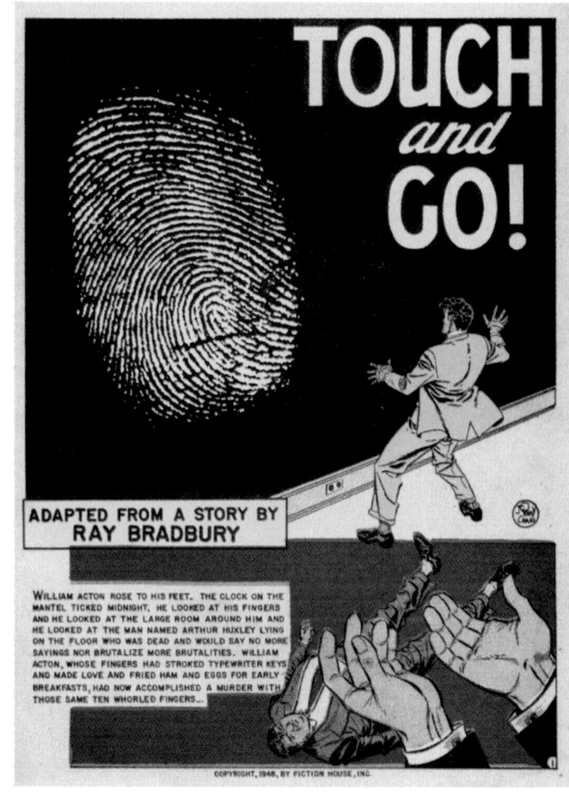

Feldstein's adaptations of Bradbury in the *SuspenStories* include "Touch and Go!," "The Small Assassin," "The Screaming Woman," and perhaps the best of all, "The October Game."

Feldstein produced a comic book version of film noir in *Crime SuspenStories*, as he cleverly worked in themes from James M. Cain, Cornell Woolridge, and Mickey Spillane.

EC was fearless in its presentation of sensitive social issues, which—predictably—triggered more criticism of the comics.

Increasingly Gaines and Feldstein used these two venues to take on some of the most explosive issues of the day. They called their tales "Preachies," and used *Shock* in particular to tackle themes such as racism ("The Guilty," *Shock SuspenStories* #3, Feldstein/Wood), drug addiction ("The Monkey," *Shock SuspenStories* #12, Feldstein/Orlando), and anti-Semitism ("Hate!" *Shock SuspenStories* #5, Feldstein/Wood). Not surprisingly, this determination resulted both in fine work and public controversy.

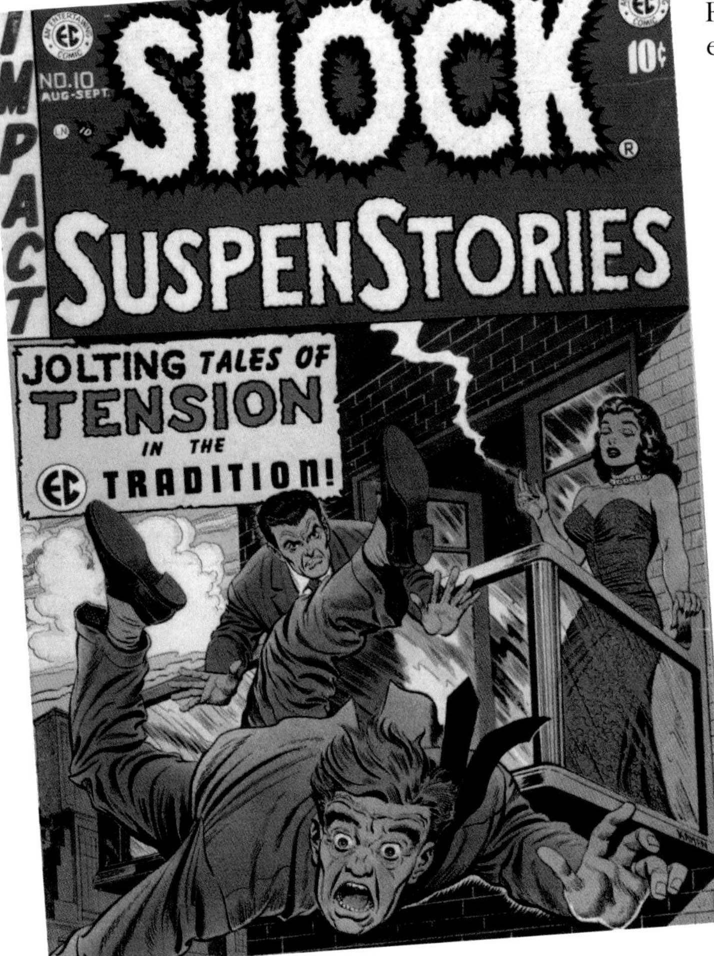

Jack Kamen's murderous couple on the cover of #10 was more in the *Shock SuspenStories* mold than Feldstein's stunning image of a man struck by lightning on the cover of #7, which is clearly in the horror tradition.

The Just Desserts Cookbook

Although Gaines and Feldstein didn't target any particular segment of the population (other than themselves) with their stories, the loyal core of their clientele was teen and young adult males. Others have speculated that perhaps Bill Gaines was himself a pudgy Peter Pan, a perpetual pubescent out to shock adults, but the fact remains that the EC horror stories had a consistent, readily identifiable style that appealed to their adolescent and postadolescent readership.

The most obvious common thread was the ironic twist of fate at the end. Unlike the old days of the superheroes, the good guys didn't always save the day in the EC comics—often there were no good guys, and if there were, their survivorship was not guaranteed. Virtue did not always triumph, but on the other hand, the bad guys usually got what was coming to them. In the tradition of Edgar Allan Poe, Ambrose Bierce, and O. Henry, Feldstein's stories concluded with one grisly form of retribution or another, and one of the tasks of morning story meeting between Al and Bill was to come up with the comeuppance *du jour*.

The grotesque recipes they concocted for just desserts gave the EC stories the resonance of little morality plays—demonstrations that what goes around, comes around—usually in some fiendishly clever way, almost always with fatal consequences.

By the time "None But the Lonely Heart" was published, Graham Ingels had placed his distinctive imprimatur on the Old Witch and had perfected his gothic horror style. Like many EC rogues who come to a bad end, Howard's greed propelled him to his demise, despite numerous omens and portents that something was amiss (including the whining of his dog, King).

"If somebody did something really bad," Gaines said, "he usually 'got it.' And of course the EC way was he got it the same way he gave it."

In "None But the Lonely Heart" (*Tales from the Crypt* #33, Dec. '52/Jan. '53, Feldstein/Ingels), a gold-digging man (bearing a striking resemblance to Vincent Price) who has married and bumped off seven rich but ugly widows falls for the beautiful picture of an eighth, and his ardor is further enhanced by her description of her mansion. Planning to keep this one rather than kill her, he drives to her posh estate, only to discover that the hardwoods and bronze trims she wrote about grace her coffin, which is lodged inside a fine stone mausoleum with stained glass windows. Naturally, he's doomed to share living quarters with her from then on.

Yum, yum.... That Old Crone tells a tasty tale, but she does carrion, if you gruesome groupies get my drooling drift.... Heh, heh, heh. I'm a much better Master of Scare-a-Monies than that croak in a cloak!!!

'HOW LONG WAS IT AFTER OUR WEDDING, KING? SIX MONTHS? NOT MUCH MORE! POOR MATILDA! SHE NEVER EVEN KNEW WE'D LOOSENED THE TOP CELLAR STAIR...'
EEEEEAAAAHH!
MATILDA! WHAT IS IT?
'THE FALL DIDN'T KILL HER, DID IT? WE HAD TO GO DOWN AND FINISH THE JOB! MESSY BUSINESS...'
HOWARD...GASP...I'M HURT... GASP...I...I...
HOWARD!
'HOW MUCH DID WE MAKE ON THAT DEAL, KING? LET'S SEE! WE SOLD THE HOUSE FOR TEN THOUSAND... AND...OH, YES! ALL TOLD, ABOUT FIFTEEN GRAND...'
YOU'RE... LEAVING US, MR. CROWN?
WHY...YES, MRS. SENTINE! I...I JUST CAN'T STAY HERE...WITH ALL THESE MEMORIES...
'HEH, HEH! SO WE MOVED ON, EH, KING? AND ABOUT THREE MONTHS LATER, WE CONTACTED OUR SECOND VICTIM! SHE'D ADVERTIZED IN A PERSONAL COLUMN, HADN'T SHE? YEP...IT BEGAN AGAIN...'
WELL, AT LEAST SHE'S BETTER THAN THE LAST ONE, EH, KING? LORD! AREN'T THERE ANY PRETTY RICH WIDOWS?
'TOOK US SIX MONTHS OF ARDENT LOVE-MAKING VIA THE U.S. MAIL TO CONVINCE THAT ONE, HUH, KING! WHAT WAS HER NAME? OH...YES...'
HOWARD! SWEET...
EPHIE...MY DEAR...
'WE DIDN'T WASTE MUCH TIME WITH HER, EH, KING? SHE WASN'T AS WEALTHY AS WE THOUGHT! SOMETIMES IT'S HARD TO TELL, ISN'T IT? AND YOU CAN'T VERY WELL ASK! HOW LONG DID EPHIE LAST BEFORE SHE FELL FROM HER APARTMENT WINDOW?...'
YAAAAAAGGHH!
'THE FRESH-AIR-FIEND! HEH, HEH! IT WAS SO EASY TO PUSH HER! SHE HAD JEWELRY, THOUGH! HOW MUCH DID WE GET? FIVE GRAND OR SO, WASN'T IT?'
WE HATE TO SEE YOU GO, MR. PRINCE!
THE APARTMENT...WELL... IT'S SO BIG AND... EMPTY NOW!
3

'WE COULDN'T RESIST, COULD WE, KING? WE HAD TO WRITE! AND THEN HER ANSWER CAME...'
'DEAR MR. THRONE, YOUR LETTER ARRIVED TODAY, AND I READ IT WITH MUCH INTEREST! YOU SOUND VERY CULTURED AND WELL TRAVELED! I WOULD ENJOY CORRESPONDING WITH YOU! JANET LANE
HOWARD PUT HIS PIPE DOWN AND SMILED! HE SHUFFLED THROUGH A SHEAF OF PAPERS...
SO WE STARTED WRITING, EH, KING! LET'S SEE! HERE'S HER SECOND LETTER...
'DEAR HOWARD... IF I MAY BE SO SO BOLD, I RESIDE IN A STURDILY BUILT STONE HOUSE. THE PROPERTY IS VERY LARGE... ALMOST TWELVE ACRES...AND VERY WELL KEPT! BUT FOR A WOMAN SUCH AS MYSELF, BEING ALONE AS I AM...WITHOUT ANYONE LIVING FOR MILES AROUND... LIFE CAN BE VERY HARD. YOUR LETTERS ARE A GREAT COMFORT...
CAN'T YOU SEE HER, KING? THIS RAVISHING WOMAN LIVING ALONE ON THIS PALATIAL ESTATE IN A HUGE FIELDSTONE HOUSE! WHY... IT SOUNDS ALMOST TOO GOOD TO BE TRUE...
LISTEN TO THIS LETTER! 'MARBLE FLOORS...' SAY! 'FURNISHED IN EXQUISITE TASTE'... 'HARD WOODS'...'BRONZE TRIMS'...'SATIN DRAPERIES'...'STAINED GLASS WINDOWS'...
KING, M'BOY! I THINK IT'S TIME THAT YOU AND I WERE SETTLING DOWN! WE'RE NOT GETTING ANY YOUNGER, YOU KNOW! AND IF JANET...
HOWARD PICKED UP THE PHOTOGRAPH OF THE LOVELY WOMAN...
...IF JANET LOOKS LIKE THIS, I THINK WE'VE FOUND THE RIGHT ONE, THIS TIME! WHY, YOU'LL HAVE THAT BIG ESTATE TO ROMP AROUND IN... WITH THE HAND-WROUGHT-IRON GATES! AND THE GARDENERS...AND TREES... FLOWERS...AND A BIG STONE HOUSE...
5

HOWARD PICKED UP A PEN...
I'M GOING TO PROPOSE TO HER, KING! SHE SPEAKS OF HOW LONELY SHE IS... AND SHE HAS MY PICTURE! MAYBE... MAYBE SHE'LL SAY 'YES'!
THREE DAYS LATER, JANET'S ANSWER CAME...
SHE'S ACCEPTED, KING! SHE'LL MARRY ME! OH, I WOULDN'T LET MYSELF HOPE...BUT NOW I'M SO HAPPY!
HOWARD PACKED HIS BAGS...
NO MORE WANDERING AROUND FOR US, BOY! NO MORE ALIASES... NO MORE FALSE LOVE-MAKING! WE'RE SETTLING DOWN... FOR GOOD...
HOWARD SENT A TELEGRAM ON AHEAD ANNOUNCING HIS EXPECTED ARRIVAL DATE, AND HE AND KING SET OUT BY CAR FOR JANET'S HOME...
ONLY FIFTY MORE MILES, BOY! WE'LL BE THERE BEFORE MIDNIGHT!
HOWARD CHECKED JANET'S ADDRESS WITH A POLICEMAN IN THE TOWN...
BAYBERRY ROAD? WHY IT'S STRAIGHT ON SOUTH ABOUT TWO MILES! YOU CAN'T MISS IT! WHAT NUMBER WAS THAT?
THAT'S ALL RIGHT OFFICER! I'LL FIND IT! THANKS!
BAYBERRY ROAD WAS A LONG NARROW TREE-LINED LANE OFF THE MAIN HIGHWAY! THERE WERE FEW HOUSES ALONG IT! FINALLY...
THERE'S THE WROUGHT-IRON GATE, KING! WE'RE HERE!
AS HOWARD'S CAR SWUNG IN AT THE GATE, HIS HEADLIGHTS FELL ACROSS...
WHAT THE..?
6

THE LETTERS WERE RUSTED AND OLD, BUT VERY CLEAR...
A CEMETERY!
CEMETERY
KING BEGAN TO WHINE SOFTLY...
STEADY, BOY! STEADY! WE MUST HAVE MADE A MISTAKE...
SUDDENLY, THE CAR DOOR SWUNG OPEN! KING YELPED...
YI-YI-YI-YI!
GOOD LORD!
THE ROTTED, DECAYED THING GRINNED...REACHING OUTWARD! ITS FLESH CRAWLED WITH THE SLIME OF DEATH! ITS VOICE RASPED LIKE A WORN OUT GRAMAPHONE CYLINDER...
HOWARD...DA-A-ARLING!
JANET! GASP! NO! NO!
KING LEAPED FROM THE CAR, HOWLING! THE THING CLOSED ITS FLESH-TATTERED BONEY FINGERS AROUND HOWARD'S WRIST IN A VICE-LIKE GRIP AND DRAGGED HIM FROM THE CAR TOWARD THE OPEN MAUSOLEUM...
I'M SORRY I DIDN'T HAVE A MORE RECENT SNAPSHOT, MY DEAR! AREN'T THE GROUNDS JUST AS I DESCRIBED THEM?
THE FEMALE-THING DRAGGED THE SCREAMING MAN INTO THE SATIN DRAPED MAUSOLEUM WITH THE STAINED GLASS WINDOW... ACROSS THE MARBLE FLOOR AND INTO THE HARD-WOOD, BRONZE-TRIMMED COFFIN! AND ALL THE WHILE, AS IT CLOSED THE LID DOWN, IT KEPT MURMURING... SPEWING ITS FOUL-SMELLING BREATH UPON HIS TERROR-STRICKEN FACE...
IT'S BEEN SO LONELY HERE... MY DEAR! BUT NOW... THAT'S ALL OVER!
HEE, HEE! WHAT A LOVE AFFAIR, EH, KIDDIES? 'ALL OVER, NOW' IS RIGHT... FOR HOWIE, THAT IS! OH, BY THE WAY! IN CASE YOU'RE WONDERING WHAT HAPPENED TO KING, REST YOUR FIENDISH MINDS! JANET HAD A DOG... NAMED QUEENIE! AND NOW, IT'S TIME TO CLOSE THAT THIEVING CRYPT-KEEPER'S MAG! WE'LL ALL SEE YOU NEXT IN THE VAULT-KEEPER'S MESS, THE VAULT OF HORROR! BYE NOW! AND IF YOU GET ANY LOVE LETTERS SIGNED 'JANET' OR 'HOWIE' ... HEE, HEE...WELL...
THE END

Jack Davis took Feldstein's concept of the Crypt Keeper and embellished it. "When Jack Davis walked in," recalls Al Feldstein, "I took him on immediately because I thought his style would be perfect for horror stories."

In EC science fiction, even insects have feelings and can seek revenge against the cruelties of human injustice.

Weird Science and *Weird Fantasy* were where Gaines and Feldstein placed many of their moralistic tales of extraterrestrial reprisal, where giant cockroaches and other alien civilizations from outer space punished insensitive or perverted humans who showed a flagrant disregard for basic human and animal rights.

Gaines once confessed to being a closet vegetarian, and any number of EC stories in both the horror and the science fiction comics are animal activist anthems in which torture and mistreatment of nonhumans results in similar treatment of their tormentors. In "Half Baked" (*Tales from the Crypt* #40, Feb./Mar. '54, Feldstein/Ingels) restaurateur Calvin Dugan, a man who revels in broiling live lobsters, meets his end in a fiery car crash and is himself broiled alive. "Survival or Death" (*Tales from the Crypt* #31, Aug./Sept. '52, Feldstein/Davis) is the story of two bored officers on a banana boat who amuse themselves by watching rats fight one another for survival on a small platform in a water-filled barrel. When the officers' ship sinks, the two fight off other crewmen as they reach the lifeboat and finally do in one another by squabbling over a piece of driftwood to cling to. "The Trophy" (*Tales from the Crypt* #25, Aug./Sept. '51, Feldstein/Davis), deals with the fate of Clyde Franklin, a wealthy big game hunter who wantonly kills animals for sport, keeping only the heads for his collection. He finds himself the quarry of a madman, and his disembodied head panics as it too becomes a trophy.

By the logic of EC justice, restaurateur Dugan deserved his fate not only for torturing lobsters, but for murdering an impoverished fisherman whose pots he was raiding.

SLOWLY, THE RAT APPROACHES THE CHEESE...
THE TEETER-BOARD TIPS...
...AND THE RAT PLUNGES INTO THE WATER...
...AND CLIMBS OUT ONTO THE PLATFORM WHICH IS JUST LARGE ENOUGH TO HOLD HIM!
I DON'T GET IT, GENTLEMEN! I...
YOU'LL SEE, CAPTAIN! ALL RIGHT, GREG! THERE'S ANOTHER ONE! WHICH ONE DO YOU WANT?
I'LL TAKE THE FIRST ONE! SHALL WE MAKE IT $100?
THE SECOND RAT EDGES OUT ON THE TEETER-BOARD TOWARD THE CHEESE...
ALL RIGHT, GREG! IT'S A BET!
THE TEETER-BOARD TIPS UP AND THE RAT PLUNGES INTO THE WATER...
COME, CAPTAIN! NOW YOU'LL SEE SOMETHING!
DON'T FORGET, CHARLES! THE FIRST ONE'S MINE!
PLOP!
THE THREE MEN WATCH, FASCINATED, AS THE SECOND RAT SWIMS TOWARD THE PLATFORM! THE FIRST RAT CROUCHES UPON IT, FANGS BARED, READY TO DEFEND HIS PLACE OF SAFETY...
SEE? HEH, HEH! SEE? THERE'S ONLY ROOM FOR ONE RAT ON THAT PLATFORM!
GOOD LORD!
THE FIGHT TO THE DEATH BEGINS! THE CAPTAIN TURNS AWAY IN DISGUST...
MINE'S WINNING! MINE'S WINNING!
NOT YET! THERE'S STILL SOME FIGHT LEFT IN MINE!
COUGH!
THAT NIGHT, THE MACY-WARNER CARGO VESSEL RAN INTO A STORMY SEA! MOUNTAINOUS WAVES LASHED AT THE SHIP, TOSSING IT ABOUT! TWO OF ITS THREE LIFEBOATS WERE TORN FROM THEIR MOORINGS AND LOST...
TOWARDS MORNING, AS A FOG DESCENDED...
CAPTAIN HESTON! THERE'S A CRACK IN THE AFT HULL! WE'RE TAKING ON WATER!
PREPARE TO ABANDON SHIP!
CAPTAIN! WHAT'S GOING ON? WE'RE LISTING!
WE'RE SINKING, MR. WARREN! GET INTO YOUR LIFE-JACKET AND MAKE FOR THE REMAINING LIFEBOAT!
GOOD LORD!
HURRY, CHARLES! HURRY!
THE TWO SHIP OWNERS CLIMBED INTO THE LIFEBOAT AS THE MEMBERS OF THE CREW POURED ONTO THE DECK! IN A FEW SECONDS, THE CROWDED LIFEBOAT WAS LOWERED AWAY...
CAPTAIN! THERE ARE TWO MEN MISSING!
WE'RE ALL GOING TO DIE!
CALM DOWN, MR. MACY!
WHEN THE OVER-CROWDED LIFEBOAT REACHED THE WATER, IT BEGAN TO ROCK AND ROLL LIKE A MATCHSTICK...
WE'LL BE SWAMPED! THERE'S TOO MANY OF US HERE! THE BOAT'S LOADED DOWN TOO MUCH! LOOK!
CAN'T YOU SHUT HIM UP, MR. WARNER?
HE'S RIGHT! THE WATER'S ALMOST UP TO THE EDGES!
SUDDENLY, A FIGURE BOBBED UP NEAR THE PITCHING LIFEBOAT...
IT'S JENSEN! HERE, JENSEN! HERE! OVER THIS WAY!
NO! WE'VE NO ROOM! ONE MORE AND WE'LL SURELY BE SWAMPED!
FOR GOD'S SAKE, MR. MACY!
JENSEN REACHED THE LIFEBOAT AFTER A HARD STRUGGLE! AS HIS HANDS CLASPED ITS SIDES...
NO MORE ROOM! NO MORE...
SIT DOWN, MR. MACY! SIT...
GREGORY'S HEEL CAME DOWN ON THE EXHAUSTED CREW MEMBER'S FINGERS! AGAIN AND AGAIN HE STAMPED...
NO MORE ROOM! GO AWAY! WE'LL... WE'LL ALL DROWN!
FINALLY JENSEN'S RAW AND BLOODY FINGERS SLIPPED FROM THE GUNNELS AND HE DISAPPEARED BELOW THE SURFACE! CAPTAIN HESTON SCREAMED AT MACY...
A GENTLEMAN IS ALWAYS A GENTLEMAN, EH, YOU MURDERER?
THIS IS DIFFERENT! IT WAS OUR LIVES OR HIS! MANY... FOR ONE!
ANOTHER FIGURE APPEARED AT THE LIFEBOAT'S SIDE! CHARLES SEIZED AN OAR...
IT'S GILPEN...
LOOK OUT!
VAP!
THE OAR SPLINTERED AS IT STRUCK GILPEN'S HEAD! CHARLES TEETERED, THEN LOST HIS BALANCE! THE LIFEBOAT TIPPED! WATER POURED OVER ITS SIDE! SUDDENLY...
YAAAAAAAAAH!
WE'RE GOING OVER!
CHARLES WARREN, GASPING FOR BREATH, FINALLY REACHED THE SMALL PIECE OF FLOATING DEBRIS...
GASP... THANK GOD! I...I COULDN'T HAVE LASTED MUCH LONGER!
SUDDENLY ANOTHER SWIMMING FIGURE MOVED OUT OF THE FOG TOWARDS HIM...
CHARLES! GASP! IT'S ME! GREG!
KEEP AWAY, GREG! KEEP AWAY! THIS IS MY PIECE OF WOOD! IT'S NOT BIG ENOUGH TO HOLD TWO OF US!
CHARLES! PLEASE! I'M...I'M EXHAUSTED!
NO! GO FIND YOUR OWN!
ALL RIGHT! I...I... WILL!
GREGORY MACY LUNGED AT HIS PARTNER! HIS FINGERS CLOSED ABOUT CHARLES'S THROAT...
I'VE...GASP... FOUND IT! I'M... GOING... TO TAKE IT... AWAY... FROM YOU!
OOURRGHHHHH!
THE STRUGGLE LASTED FOR FIVE MINUTES... MAYBE MORE! FINALLY, CHARLES'S BODY WENT LIMP! IT SLIPPED FROM GREG'S FINGERS AND SUNK BELOW THE WAVES! GREG LOOKED AROUND...
OH, LORD! THE PIECE OF DRIFTWOOD! IT... IT'S GONE!
YES! WHILE GREGORY AND CHARLES WERE FIGHTING, THE PIECE OF DRIFTWOOD HAD FLOATED OFF INTO THE THICK FOG! POOR GREG WAS TOO TIRED TO EVEN TRY TO LOOK FOR IT! HE JUST GURGLED A LITTLE... AND SANK FROM SIGHT! EVEN THE RATS HAD A BETTER DEAL THAN GREG! AT LEAST, WHEN THEY WON, THE PLATFORM WAS STILL THERE! AND I SEE THAT THE VAULT-KEEPER IS STILL THERE, WAITING TO TELL HIS HORROR STORY! BUT I WON'T DIG YOU LATER, AS USUAL! INSTEAD, THOSE TWO IDIOTS, MY EDITORS, HAVE COMMANDEERED MY SPACE FOR THEIR OWN USE! HMMPH! 'BYE! OOOOH, I'M SO MAD!

THE OLD WITCH

Part of the appeal of the Crypt Keeper, the Vault Keeper, and the Old Witch was that they were not the least bit penitent about being reprehensible.

Send in the Ghouls

Franklin's end was macabre, and it was often the very gruesome nature of the retribution that delighted the readers, vengeance that frequently came from beyond the grave. This black justice generated the exceptionally black humor provided by the GhouLunatics, who adored commenting upon the hideously appropriate nature of the demise. Interestingly, the EC horror comics were the first "hit" comic books without continuing heroes or positive role model characters. The only constants from one issue to the next were the Crypt Keeper, the Vault Keeper, and the Old Witch. Other horror publishers tried to imitate them, but none of the wannabes ever came close to the mystique of the GhouLunatics.

The most endearing quality about them was that they had no endearing qualities. Completely irreverent, they dissed EC, the characters in the stories, each other, and the readership. Jerry Weist, former editor of the fanzine *Squa Tront* and currently consultant to Sotheby's on collectible comics, summarized their ongoing appeal. "Gaines and Feldstein created these cult personalities in the hosts. They had the capacity to make the darker side of human nature absurdly humorous. The GhouLunatics were like wild, unrestrained Lenny Bruces walking around the magazines." The Crypt Keeper, the Vault Keeper, and the Old Witch got to mouth off in a way that was not yet common among adolescents. (Father still knew best in the early 1950s; the societal onset of full-on teen rebellion was still a few years off.) The kids ate it up.

The sarcastic use of bogus sponsor Nightmare Mattress, who lets you "snore with gore," presages *MAD*'s commercial spoofs.

These photos are actually a shot of Vault Keeper artist Johnny Craig in full ghoul regalia, with makeup by Al Feldstein. Over a relatively short span of time, EC comics developed a devoted following that years later played a major part in the Crypt Keeper's triumphant resurrection.

Although EC comics may have shocked some adults, the Crypt Keeper's over-the-top dialogue was never taken seriously by the readership.

The GhouLunatics also performed another very important function. They provided a continuing external point of view that kept the reader outside the story. Like the chorus in a Greek tragedy or the proscenium in a theater, their presence was bizarrely reassuring, a reminder to the reader that it was "just a story."

Part of Feldstein's editing duties included coming up with the snappy repartee that made the Crypt Keeper, the Vault Keeper, and the Old Witch so appealing (and appalling), and breathing life into the GhouLunatics was an assignment he pulled off with great panache. He had them each address the "audience" directly, freely sprinkling their dialogue with beastly bons mots, painful puns and awful alliterations. As morbid as they were (not to mention corny), you couldn't help laughing.

Until the GhouLunatics came along, there hadn't been much to laugh at about horror, certainly not for adolescents. Now there was.

Much in the same way that Al and Bill had collaborated on responses to the "advice to the lovelorn" columns in the pre-*Trend* comics, the two now colluded on answers to letters from EC's growing legion of fans, written in the personas of the GhouLunatics.

It didn't take long for Gaines and Feldstein to realize they had a popular character in the Crypt Keeper. By Issue #23 (April/May '51), they were offering photos for a dime apiece. The Crypt Keeper reached out to the readership, asking their input on such grisly endeavors as "The Horror Hit Parade." EC devotees came up with such Top 40 candidates as a Patti Page near-miss called the "Tennessee Vaults," that accordion favorite "Lady of Pain (I Will Gore You)," and a deadly deviation on Gene Autry's theme song, "I'm Back in the Coffin Again (Out Where a Fiend Is a Fiend)."

The primary distinction among the Crypt Keeper, the Vault Keeper, and the Old Witch was visual. The GhouLunatics were quite similar in their demeanor, their punning, and the way they introduced their stories.

There really was a genuine relationship between the staff and the fans. Gaines, the biggest fan of all, wanted his readers to appreciate his publications as much as he did. His raucous read-aloud sessions were largely responsible for the recommendation by the GhouLunatics that fans read the stories out loud to one another.

"Writers are God's creatures. Without the writer you have no theater, you have no television, you have no radio, you have no movies, you have no books, you have no magazines—you have *nuthin*'! The artist can enhance a good story, but he can't save a bad one. He's very important, but he's not as important as the writer. We never thought so."

—Bill Gaines

In the Beginning Was the Word

Like the snap ending and the GhouLunatics, another hallmark of EC stories was a love of language, often over and above the pictures that accompanied them. Among other sources for Gaines' "springboards" were back issues of *Weird Tales*, a pulp magazine, in which many of Ray Bradbury's early stories had appeared.

There were occasions when Gaines' "springboards" did not "spring" quite far enough from Bradbury's originals,

and in 1952 EC got a letter from Bradbury, by then a noted best-selling author.

Bradbury, a comic book fan from way back, got a big kick out of what Gaines and Feldstein had done with his work. He was not upset that EC had used his material, only that they'd done so without asking. Fittingly, Bradbury's accusation of plagiarism was couched in tongue-in-cheek humor. "I notice that you've overlooked sending me royalty payments for

"The Coffin" (*Haunt of Fear* #16, Nov./Dec. '52) was the first "authorized" EC Bradbury adaptation.

In early '53 Bradbury was stung by criticism that he was ruining his literary reputation by "writing for" comic books. His relationship with EC remained more than cordial, but at about the time that these stories appeared, he asked Gaines to stop using his name on the covers.

The Ray Bradbury–EC Mutual Admiration Society

April 18, 1952

Dear Bill:

By all means please show this letter to Jack Davis and Joe Orlando. I want to thank them for the painstaking work they did on "The Coffin" and "The Long Years." I got a great deal of pleasure lookng at the silver prints of the adaptations. Thanks so much for sending them on! And please thank Al for the fine layout work, and the adaptations themselves! This is a real adventure for me!…I've nothing but the kindest regard and love for you, Al, Mr. Orlando, and Mr. Davis for work beautifully and handsomely and cleverly thought out and completed. Long may we all work together! My blessings to you all!

Yours, Ray

use of my stories." Gaines sent off a check and a letter of apology *tout de suite*. All was forgiven and soon thereafter Bradbury's stories began appearing regularly in EC comics. Bradbury's compensation was the princely sum of $25 for each one.

Bradbury eventually gave his permission for Feldstein to adapt all of his stories from *Golden Apples of the Sun*, *The October Game*, and *The Martian Chronicles*, a process that prompted Al to go back and read more of Bradbury's work. "Because I was so impressed with his writing, I was trying to capture as much of it as I could in the captions. The more of Bradbury's work I read, the more flowery I became in my own writing," Feldstein admits with a smile. This created something of a production problem in the shop. "I started to use more and more narrative captions to move the story along, and then break into the dialogue. The artists were complaining that I

wasn't leaving them any room to draw. Pretty soon the characters in the magazines had hunchbacks because they were ducking under the heavy copy."

Feldstein's stories are indeed much wordier than other comics of the time, and there have been any number of readers (not just artists) who found this to be a flaw rather than an asset. Whenever this "problem" was brought to his attention, Gaines was monumentally unsympathetic. Feldstein's stories were "very text-heavy," he conceded in 1983, adding a big so-what, "and that's because Al and I both got enamored with his words. He wrote so beautifully."

With a lot of text it was quite a problem for the artist to squeeze in a drawing, but many found creative solutions to this challenge—including the use of forehead space for dialogue.

THE LEROY QUESTION

At Gaines' direction, EC letterer Jim Wroten used the Leroy mechanical lettering system for **Tales from the Crypt** and the other horror comics. It gave the text great uniformity, but the stiff Leroy format was not a good stylistic match with the magazines. When Harvey Kurtzman began editing EC's war comics **Frontline Combat** and **Two-Fisted Tales**, he went with hand lettering instead—a choice Feldstein in hindsight would have preferred.

Leroy lettering appears formal and regular.

Hand lettering is looser, allowing use of much bolder inking for emphasis.

Why was Leroy lettering used? Because Bill had inherited both the system and its operator from his father. Wroten had started out as a salesman for a drafting company named Keuffel & Esser, which made slide rules and Leroy lettering templates. "My father, when he did **Wonder Woman**, used Leroy lettering," Gaines recalled.

Gaines also maintained that Leroy was the only way that Al's text-heavy stories would fit in the panels. "Because Al used so many words, we found we could do it more clearly with Leroy lettering. If we had wanted a hand letterer to work that small, to get all that copy in, it would have been very difficult for him," Gaines told **Comics Journal**.

The Star System

Even before the debut of *New Trend*, Gaines had shown a knack for hiring quality artists. Graham Ingels was already in residence when Al Feldstein arrived in March of 1948, working first in the old western comics *Gunfighter* and *Saddle Justice*. Johnny Craig was another early arrival. At a time when there was a formulaic, assembly line mentality in most comic book houses, EC under the leadership of Gaines and Feldstein adopted a hands-on approach that in short order produced a reputation for quality that endures to this day. Word got out quickly within the small community of comic book artists in New York that EC was a congenial shop. Not surprisingly, many of the best gravitated to EC during the *New Trend* era, including such legends in the business as Jack Davis, Jack Kamen, Wally Wood, George Evans, Harvey Kurtzman, Al Williamson, Joe Orlando, and Will Elder.

Each of these men had a remarkable career in his own right, but as a team, they nurtured each other's creative talents and all contributed to the Crypt mix. Life in the office was a sort of creative bedlam, presided over by Gaines, now the *enfant terrible* not just of his family but of the comic world. "Everybody knew everybody..." recalled Gaines of his *New Trend* artists in the 1983 interview in *Comics Journal*. "They had a tremendous admiration for one another. Wally Wood would come in with a story and three artists would crowd around him and *faint*, just poring over every brushstroke and panel, and of course Wally, who's

Every panel was a monsterpiece, a real Pablo Pi-corpse-so. When it came to art, ole Bill Gaines wouldn't put up with any hatchet work, heh, heh. Who could axe for anything more?

This EC family portrait by colorist Marie Severin shows the spirit of horseplay that existed among the artists and staff.

Each story was written with a specific artist in mind. Gaines announced who the target was at each morning springboard meeting, telling Feldstein, "Today we're writing an eight-page lead for Ingels for *Haunt of Fear*. As soon as I'd say that, both our minds were in a certain frame of reference for Ingels. With Ingels, you know what we're looking for: Yuchh! Rotting corpses, moors..."

getting this adulation, sits there and loves it. Next time around it's his turn to adulate someone. Everybody tried to outdo each other, which is one of the reasons we got such incredibly good art. They were all in a friendly competition....And it was wonderful. Just a nice, warm place."

They were also trying to impress Gaines, who gushed appreciatively over each effort, praising every nuance. The EC ambience of camaraderie and high-spirited one-upmanship made each artist strive to do his best. This work environment was deliberately cultivated by Gaines, who went out of his way to make sure it was the direct opposite of the constant criticism he'd heard throughout his own childhood. He cherished his role as paterfamilias to his merry band of artists (a precursor to *MAD*'s "usual gang of idiots"), and relished the idea that they vied with one another for his favor.

As Joe Orlando recalled, "I enjoyed working on the stories, living with them for a week or two. It was almost a sexual thing. The climax was delivering a job and Bill laughing. When Bill liked it and Al liked it, it was the end

"We always knew exactly who we were writing for," says Feldstein. "A Jack Kamen story was almost the polar opposite of Ingels. For Kamen we developed stories that were lighter and more humorous—pretty women, a little sex, a little double entendre." Kamen stories rarely showed actual bloodshed.

"Bill Gaines was to EC Comics as Louis B. Mayer was to MGM."

—Russ Cochran

of the whole process and you lived for it. Nothing else mattered—nothing."

"Bill Gaines was to EC Comics as Louis B. Mayer was to MGM movies," notes Russ Cochran, publisher of the complete series of EC reprints. "Just as Metro-Goldwyn-Mayer had the lion's share of the greatest Hollywood stars of the 1930s and 1940s, Gaines had as his goal the building of a 'star-system' for the best comic book artists in the business. He gradually built up his stable of artists and he knew exactly which artist to cast in a given part."

Feldstein could not write all the stories, put puns and wisecracks into the mouths of the Crypt Keeper, the Vault Keeper, and the Old Witch, *and* produce his share of the artwork. Johnny Craig took over the Vault Keeper and assumed responsibility for the lead story in the *Vault of Horror* (Gaines and Feldstein continued to collaborate on the rest.) Graham Ingels, who had really found his métier with horror, was given the job of limning the Old Witch. And Jack Davis, who had joined EC after arriving from Atlanta, took on the Crypt Keeper.

Two Heads Are Stranger Than One

Siamese twins were one of Gaines and Feldstein's favorite themes, and they show up in various guises throughout the *New Trend* series. Feldstein's first was "The Hunchback" (*Haunt of Fear* #4, Nov./Dec. 1950), followed by "Heads Up" (*Crime SuspenStories* #4), "The Basket" (*Haunt of Fear* #7), and "The Ventriloquist's Dummy (*Tales from the Crypt* #28). Others include "People Who Live in Brass Hearses" (*Vault of Horror* #27), "Chess-Mate" (*Haunt of Fear* #22), and of course the Crypt Keeper origin tale, "Lower Berth" (*Tales from the Crypt* #33, Feldstein/Davis). Feldstein speculated to fanzine editor John Benson that the affection he and Gaines shared for the twins stories might have reflected "Bill's and my interdependence upon each other, that we were like Siamese twins in the way we worked together." Another possibility, however, is that they mirrored society's burgeoning concern about genetic mutation as a result of nuclear disaster. Toward the end of the *New Trend* run, two other Siamese twin stories, "My Brother's Keeper" (*Shock SuspenStories* #16) and "About Face" (Haunt of Fear #27), appeared. These, however, were written by latecomer Carl Wessler.

In most twin stories, like "My Brother's Keeper" (top, Wessler/Evans) and "The Basket" (Feldstein/ Davis), there is one good head and one evil head, but in "Chess-Mate" (directly above, Feldstein/Evans) and "People Who Live in Brass Hearses" (right, Feldstein/Davis), both are good.

This Grim Fairy Tale introduction by the Crypt Keeper acknowledges that he was poaching on what was normally the Old Witch's terrain.

Grim Fairy Tales

Rocky & Bullwinkle had their *Fractured Fairy Tales*; EC had its *Grim Fairy Tales*. Because Jack Kamen's specialty was "horror lite," he was a logical choice to draw them. "I liked them," he told Sam Kingston in a 1994 interview, "because Al Feldstein would put humorous touches in them. A typical one was 'The Sleeping Beauty,' when she turns out to be a vampire. And the little guy telling the story looks like [bespectacled '50s nerd and Milton Berle's "stagehand"] Arnold Stang."

Kamen had a regular slot in *Haunt of Fear*, and many of the *Grim Fairy Tales* appeared there. "Hansel & Gretel" portrayed the two lost children as obnoxious brats who were quite literally eating their parents out of house and home. "Snow White and the Seven Dwarfs" has the Wicked Queen getting the bad news about who is the fairest of them all not from a mirror but from a TV screen bearing the likeness of Howdy Doody. She learns that the executioner didn't kill Snow White from another TV image—this time it's rubber-faced Joe E. Brown. Snow White herself is eventually done in by the Seven Dwarfs themselves, who tire of her compulsive neatness. (This was something of an EC in-joke, since Bill Gaines, contrary to his rumpled demeanor, was compulsively tidy.)

In the Grim Fairy Tales, the characters we knew as good from the originals often turned evil, and vice versa.

The Arnold Stang lookalike dwarf named "Stupid" brings up the rear, carrying a book by "Melvie Splane," a parody on the name of popular '50s tough guy crime novelist Mickey Spillane.

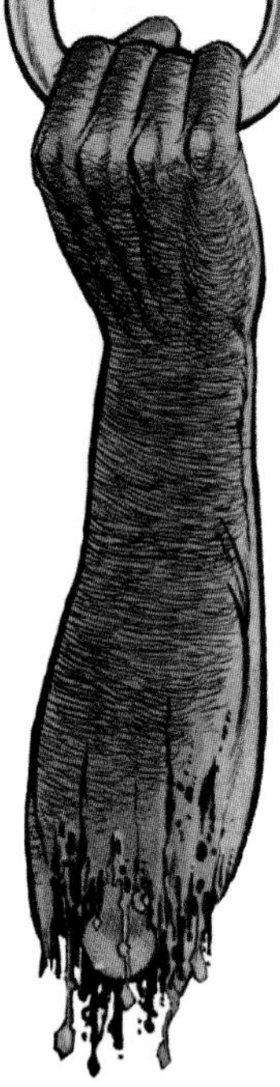

Let the Artists Create

Once Gaines had provided the springboard, he knew enough to get out of the way. The rest of his time was taken up with the minutiae of running a business—paying bills, dealing with printers and distributors, haggling on the phone. Feldstein worked with his team of artists the way he himself liked to work—in short, he told them what the art was supposed to convey, and then let them execute it however they thought best served the storyline.

"One of the things that I insisted upon from the very beginning was that every artist had his own signature, his own style," says Feldstein emphatically.

"I did not ask them to imitate [*Captain America* creator and comics legend] Jack Kirby or to mimic whatever was popular at the time. We had a stable of artists doing their stuff. We tailor-made stories for each of these guys. They got the artboard with the lettering already on it; all they had to do was draw."

Feldstein sat down with each artist and went over the story. "We'd talk, but I'd never tell anyone how to do it," recalls Feldstein. "If the story called for a truck plunging over a cliff, he could draw the scene from any perspective he wanted. The artist could depict this looking down from an aerial view, or assume a position standing under the truck looking up as it came over. I didn't want to inhibit him in any way. I never insisted on layouts because I think it takes away some of the creativity."

Feldstein's approach was diametrically opposed to that of Harvey Kurtzman. The difference was roughly the same as that between one film director who sees movies as a collaborative medium and welcomes input from actors and techies, and another who views himself as the *auteur* and feels the movie is his own. Either approach can yield quality work. Harvey put out two scrupulously researched and edited war/antiwar comics called *Two-Fisted Tales* and *Frontline Combat*, but unlike Al was almost pathologically unable to delegate any creative decision-making whatsoever to his artists. Kurtzman did his own layouts and insisted that his artists follow them meticulously. Some rebelled (George Evans among them), and took to deliberately altering small details in the background just to get Harvey's goat.

GIs made up a substantial portion of EC's adult readership, and their war and horror comics were especially popular with troops in Korea. In *Two-Fisted Tales* and *Frontline Combat*, Kurtzman was determined that all drawings of rifles, helmets, and other military paraphernalia be completely accurate. When Jack Davis brought him artwork depicting an Army corpsman's kit, he groused, "No, Jack, the gauze pad goes to the *right* of the sulfa!"

The EC Constellation of Comic Book Artists

During the **New Trend** era, EC became a magnet for talented artists, and Bill Gaines' stable was the envy of the comic book world. Other publishers coveted Gaines' stars, but were not willing to match either EC's pay scale or the artistic freedom that Gaines and Feldstein so deliberately cultivated. All the men—and they were men, with the exception of colorist Marie Severin—thrived in the genteel lunacy of the EC hothouse. For many their time at EC marked a personal best—not only did they do better work than other artists were doing for other houses, they also did better work than they had ever done elsewhere.

"Comic books were printed with metal plates on the cheapest paper you could get — it was like one grade above toilet paper. If you look at the original artwork, you will see that artists who worked at EC put in tiny details, little minute scratches of the pen or brush, into their drawings that they knew would not show up with cheap comic book reproduction. I couldn't figure out why these guys went to all the trouble to do that, knowing it wouldn't reproduce, until I realized that they were doing it for each other. There was a mutual admiration society among the artists at EC. They were always trying to impress one another. It was a labor of love."

— Russ Cochran

AL FELDSTEIN

Born in October 1925, Al Feldstein is the son of a Russian immigrant father and first-generation Polish mother, and was an early graduate of the school of hard knocks. In 1938, his father's dental laboratory went under. At age fourteen he took on an after-school job to help the family make ends meet. While still enrolled in Manhattan's High School of Music and Art, he found work at Eisner & Iger, a large comic "factory." Al started as little more than a gofer, running errands and cleaning up pages. Eisner & Iger worked on an assembly line system, and the work was passed from hand to hand. Eventually Feldstein was permitted to do background work, first just inking, then drawing and inking, and finally he was given responsibility for inking figures.

For Al it was all marking time, however. He wanted to be an art teacher, and began taking education courses at Brooklyn College by day and art classes at the Art Students League at night. In 1943, he joined the Army Air Corps and spent the rest of the war doing artwork (painting signs and murals and decorating aviator jackets) at various airfields, beginning in Blytheville, Arkansas. After he was mustered out in '45, Feldstein decided to return to school to finish getting his credential as an art teacher. While waiting for the new semester to begin at Columbia, however, he returned to his old studio, now called simply S. M. Iger. (Will Eisner had left to go off on his own.)

Iger's shop did work for a variety of publishers, including Fiction House, Fox Features Syndicate, and Quality House. Jerry Iger had industrialized the comic book process and was making a bundle. His "bullpen" included Bob Webb (**Sheena, Queen of the Jungle**), and two eventual EC regulars, Reed Crandall (**Blackhawk**) and Jack Kamen. "Iger made a lot of money on them," recalls Feldstein. "He would pay the artists $75 a week. For that they'd do two pages a day, which he was selling for $30 a page. When I got wise to what he was up to, I decided to freelance."

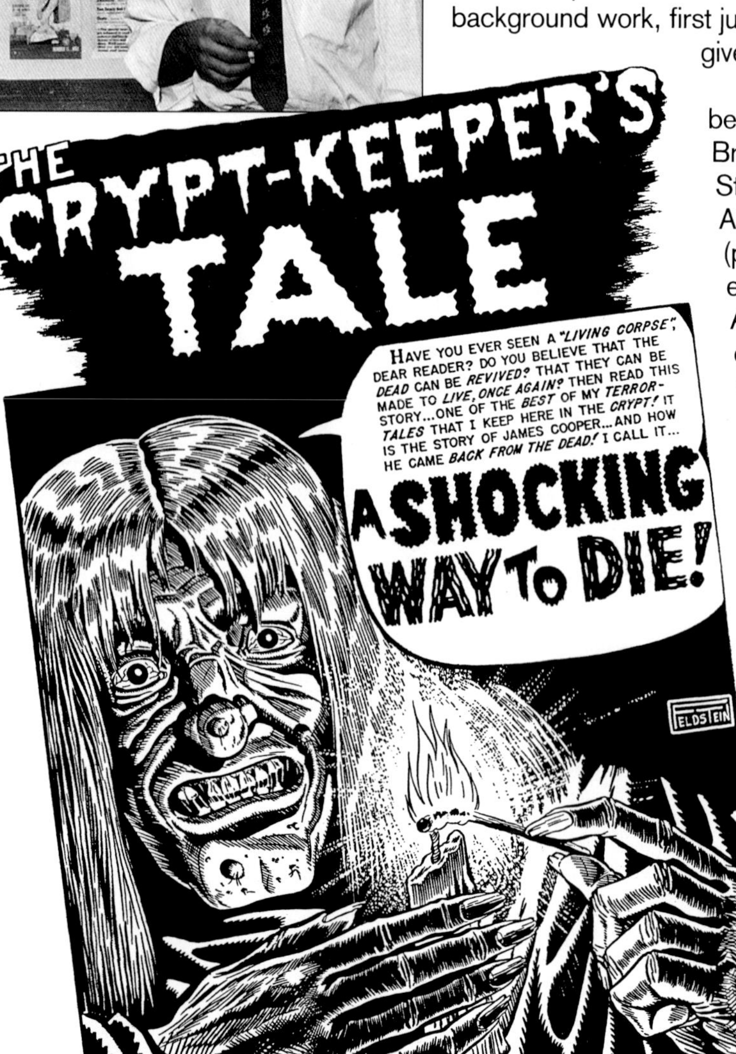

Feldstein drew the original Crypt Keeper, and often had him looking straight out at the reader.

Walking corpses and things returned from the dead — as well as people's astonished reactions to them — were a particular Feldstein specialty.

As a freelancer, Feldstein worked on several hardly memorable comics, including **Hap Hazard**, **Aggie Mack**, and **Seven Seas**. Feldstein was freelancing for Victor Fox at Fox Features Syndicate, contributing to **Western Outlaws**, **Western Thrillers**, and **Western Killers**. He was also working on three teen comics, **Junior**; **Sunny, America's Sweetheart**; and **Meet Corliss Archer** (which soon became **My Life**), when he was asked to show his portfolio to Bill Gaines.

With the exception of a brief lapse between the demise of **New Trend** and his return to edit **MAD**, Feldstein worked at EC continuously from 1948 till his retirement in 1985. During that time he wrote and edited the EC horror and science fiction comics, the short-lived **New Direction** and **Picto-Fiction** series, the **MAD** clone **Panic**, and eventually **MAD** itself.

After his long busy stint in comics, Al fled the sidewalks of New York for the Big Sky country of Montana, where he indulges his passion for painting and fly fishing.

FELDSTEIN

Feldstein has self-deprecatingly called his style "rigid and hard"; fans disagree. His stiffness and bold outlines capture the paralysis and petrification that comes with a moment of fear or pain (not to mention rigor mortis), and his cover artwork is much sought after by collectors.

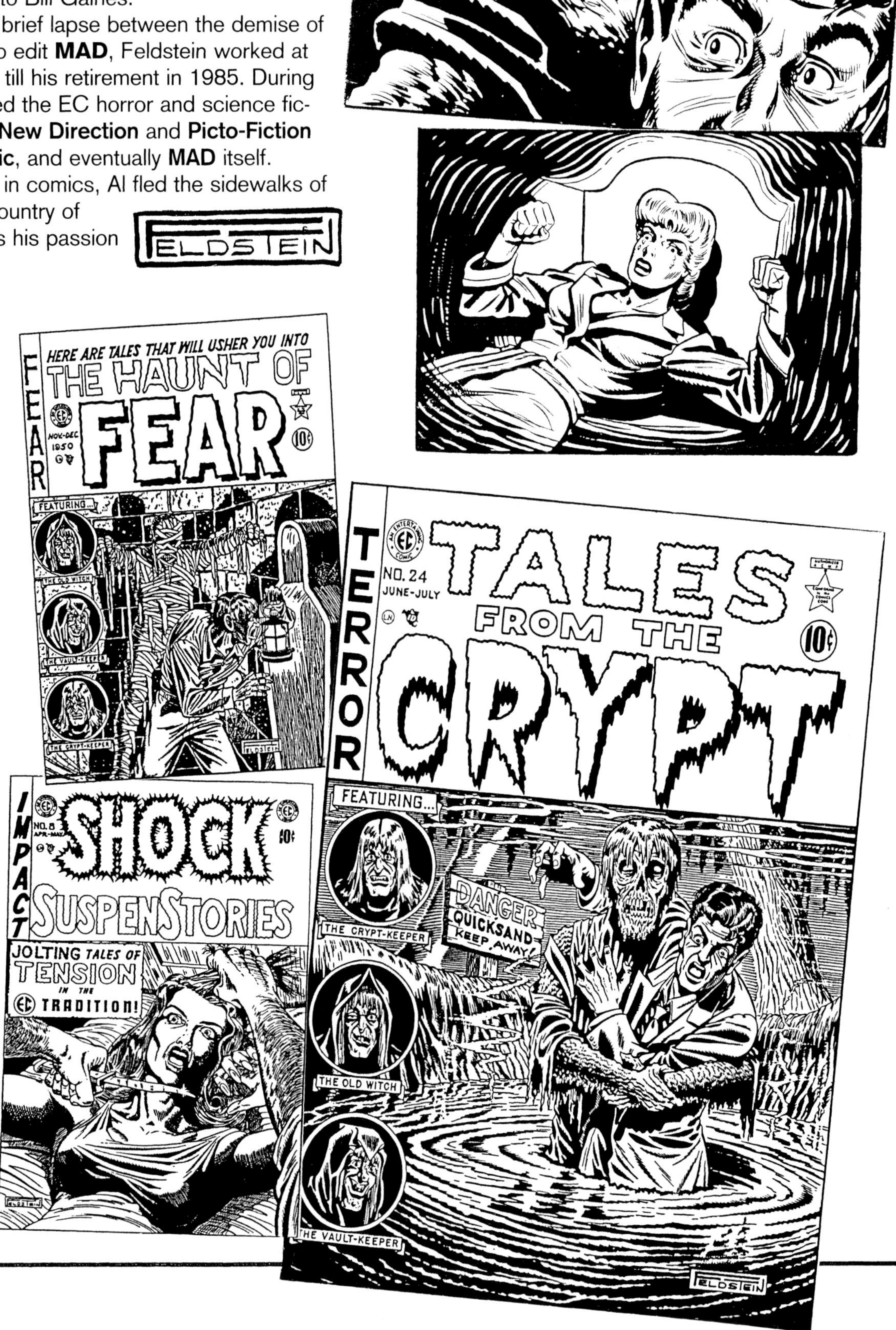

Even after Al Feldstein stopped doing story art, he continued drawing covers. Issues with his covers sold especially well.

Orlando's rounded forms and buxom women reminded many of the work of his friend and mentor, Wally Wood.

Orlando resented attacks on EC comics but was most concerned about the reaction from friends and family. "'I was worried about my mother saying, 'I hear you're doing material that's destroying the minds of kids — and your friends are all a bunch of Commies.'"

JOE ORLANDO

Born in Bari, Italy, in 1927, Orlando came to New York as a toddler. After serving with the Army in World War II, he studied at the Art Students League before forming a small studio with Wally Wood and another comic book artist named Harry Harrison. It was Wood who coaxed him into bringing his portfolio to EC in 1952.

Orlando fit in with the EC "family" right away. "Bill and I had a lot in common," he recalls. "We'd both had very bad relationships with our fathers which certainly affected our personalities. It produced a certain rebelliousness."

Other artists in the EC stable may have been a bit squeamish about doing horror comics. Not Joe. "I got my emphasis on horror from going to church every Sunday. As I sat there listening to the sermon, I concentrated on those bloody wounds of all the saints — arrows in the chest, blood pouring out, all the rest."

As Wertham and other critics of EC comics closed in, Orlando's rebellious nature vented. "Bill didn't have the chutzpah to do this, but when they were trying to put us out of business I wanted to get even with all those self-righteous religious hypocrites. I told Bill, 'Let's do the Bible in the real way, come in close on the spikes in the hands and the lions ripping the Christians apart. The next cover should be Christ on the cross, bleeding. They think we did horror? We'll show 'em what horror really is!'"

When Bill Gaines stopped publishing, Orlando found work at Marvel Comics under Stan Lee. By 1957, however, Al Feldstein had lured him back as a regular contributor to **MAD**. Nine years later he became an editor at DC Comics (National Periodical Publications), which by this time owned **MAD** magazine, where he is now an Associate Publisher.

Joe Orlando

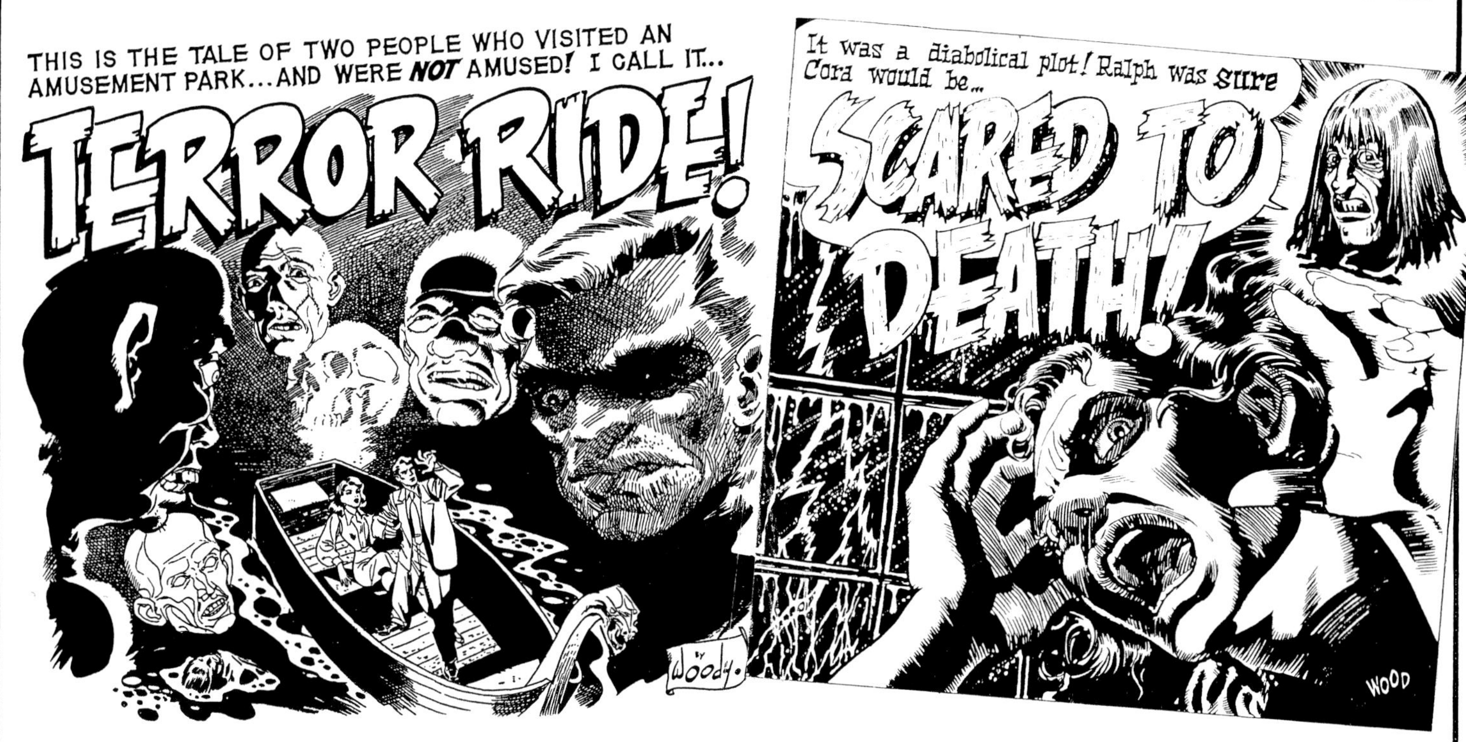

Wood's work was characterized by a dramatic use of light and shadow.

WALLY WOOD

Born in Minnesota in 1927, Wally Wood kicked around in a series of odd jobs until World War II. He was still underage when he enlisted in the military, serving both in the merchant marine and as a paratrooper. After the war he finished his education at New York's School of Visual Arts, and began his comic book career working on Milton Caniff's **Terry and the Pirates** and Will Eisner's **The Spirit**.

In 1950 he joined EC, and became known as the "Dean of Comic Book Science Fiction," working frequently on **Weird Science** and **Weird Fantasy**. Wood was one of Harvey Kurtzman's favorites, and worked with him on **MAD**, where his ability to imitate the styles of other artists fit well with the magazine's penchant for parody. Wood was the man who drew **Superduperman** in a style close enough for **Superman**'s owners to bring suit.

Behind his skill as a mimic was a strong personal style of his own, highlighted by deft use of detail and a rounded, realistic anatomical representation of the human form. His work was characterized by a dramatic use of light and shadow, giving his drawings almost a chiaroscuro effect. In failing health beginning in the late 1970s, Wood took his own life rather than face dependency on kidney dialysis. He passed away in 1981.

By Woody.

Wally Wood drew the classic "My World" about what it's like to work in science fiction, but the story was actually written by Al Feldstein.

JACK DAVIS

Jack Davis was the Norman Bates of EC Comics. Born in 1926, he spent most of World War II in the Navy (drawing for the **Navy News**). Following the war he attended the University of Georgia on the GI Bill, where he and some fraternity brothers put out a shoot-from-the-hip campus magazine called **Bullsheet**.

Davis joined EC in 1951, after having studied at New York's Art Students League. He walked into Al Feldstein's office one day and never really left. Davis had a scratchy kind of style with a great deal of line work, and a bit of his country boy naivete crept into his art. When Gaines and Feldstein were matching a story to his capabilities, we gave him the "yokel stories or small town stories," recalls Feldstein, "stories with kids, either robbing graves or carrying a coffin down the street."

A mild-mannered, soft-spoken southerner from Atlanta, there was nothing in his demeanor that suggested a knack for horror. However, he turned out freaks, monsters, and ghouls that had a grisly appeal all their own. Unlike Ingels' dripping cadavers, which had long since ceased being **Homo sapiens**, Davis' creations were scary precisely because they were almost human. He knew just which parts of the anatomy to torque in order to turn just folks into just ogres. As Al Feldstein became increasingly burdened with his writing duties, he tapped Davis to take over drawing the Crypt Keeper. Davis was quick and efficient, a quality that pleased the overburdened Feldstein but troubled the finicky Harvey Kurtzman, who once remarked, "The one fault I found with Jack was that he worked too fast."

Davis could draw everything from tearful children to homicidal maniacs, but the giblet-laced "Foul Play" (above) is one story he'd rather forget.

Davis had a scratchy kind of style with a great deal of line work.

One of Davis' many strong points was his mastery of facial expressions. Both the oaf and the pixilated convict demonstrate how Davis could effortlessly shift from horror into **MAD**.

Although their features were distorted, the human lineage of Davis' werewolves, vampires, and other monsters was always evident.

HARVEY KURTZMAN

Harvey Kurtzman was born in New York in 1924, and attended the High School of Music and Art with Bill Elder. He was taking courses at Cooper Union when he was drafted into the Army in 1942. At the end of the war, he did **Hey Look**, a one-page humor strip, for Stan Lee at Timely/Marvel. Harvey came to EC in 1949, essentially by mistake. Bill Gaines was already taking EC into its "Entertaining" mode, but the phone book still listed the company as "Educational Comics." Kurtzman arrived for an interview hoping to do nonfiction work, but his first EC job was an assignment that only **MAD** might come up with. Bill's uncle, David Gaines, was putting out educational handbooks in comic book form, and Bill sent Kurtzman to David to draw **Lucky Fights It Through**, a comic book about gonorrhea.

He worked on the horror comics before editing **Two-Fisted Tales** and **Frontline Combat**, gutty, realistic war comics that did not glamorize mortal combat. Kurtzman loved the fighting man, but hated the fighting, and many of his stories vividly convey this philosophy.

In 1952 he began editing **MAD**, drawing on campus humor magazines for inspiration. After an acrimonious tussle with Gaines, Kurtzman left in 1956 to start **Trump** for Hugh Hefner, plus **Humbug**, **Help!**, and **Little Annie Fanny** with Bill Elder. He passed away in 1993.

H. Kurtz

Kurtzman was never fond of the horror genre, but his knack for satire and his cartoon figures were ideally suited to MAD.

Kurtzman had to rein in his gift for caricature and parody to work in horror, but he later inspired a whole new generation of underground cartoonists.

Elder was and is a master at mimicking the styles of other artists.

BILL (WILL) ELDER

Bill Elder (he didn't become Will until later in his career) was born William Wolf Eisenberg in the Bronx in 1922. The son of Polish immigrants, he attended New York's High School of Music and Art (as did many comic book artists). He had been an ardent comics fan in his youth, and was particularly fond of **Li'l Abner** and the **Katzenjammer Kids.** During World War II, Elder served in the Army Air Corps as a map designer. Believing his assignment would keep him behind the lines, he was horrified to find himself ahead of the rest of the troops, gathering information, and was in the thick of things during the Battle of the Bulge.

Elder was a high school chum of Harvey Kurtzman, and the two shared many aspects of their careers. He was something of a class clown. He was also something of an "anarchist." Like the Marx Brothers, he enjoyed creating art that made large tears in the "fabric of society," and exposing hypocrisy wherever he found it. It was a life philosophy tailor-made for **MAD**.

Elder's drawing of a "just divorced" St. Nick for Al Feldstein's **Panic** kicked off legal battles both in Massachusetts and New York. Like Wally Wood, Elder was and is a master at mimicking the styles of other artists. It was Elder who drew **MAD**'s withering takeoffs on Mickey Mouse (**Mickey Rodent**), and Archie (**Starchie**) — in a style blisteringly close to the original. After leaving **MAD** with Kurtzman in 1956, he was involved with subsequent Kurtzman ventures including **Trump**, **Humbug**, and **Help!** In 1962 the two began collaborating on Playboy's ribald **Little Annie Fanny**, ending in 1988.

Bill Elder

Elder's comic sensibilities are visible even in his horror drawings.

Crandall's use of fine shading and cross-hatching was admired by other artists, and gave his work an etchinglike quality.

REED CRANDALL

Reed Crandall was born in Indiana in 1917 and educated at the Cleveland School of Art. In 1940, he began with the Eisner-Iger shop (where the very young Al Feldstein also worked), then moved on to Quality comics, where he worked on **Hit Comics** and **Crack**. Although he was not the originator of the characters, he drew the very successful **Blackhawk** and **Doll Man** in the late 1940s.

Like virtually all the other artists in Gaines' stable, Crandall was not "recruited." In a **Comics Journal** interview, Gaines recalled, "Crandall was the last EC artist to arrive. He walked in and said, 'I'm Reed Crandall.' I said, 'So what took you so long?? We've been sitting here waiting for you!'"

Crandall arrived in 1953 with his highly regarded portfolio, and was looked up to by the rest of the EC staff. Feldstein fed him assignments right away, putting him to work on the three horror titles, and especially on **Shock SuspenStories** and **Crime SuspenStories**. He also drew a Ray Bradbury adaptation, "The Silent Town," for **Weird Fantasy**. When Gaines was forced to fold the **New Trend**, Crandall worked on **New Direction** titles and began doing cover work for the ill-fated **Picto-Fiction** line.

Following the collapse of EC, he continued to work in comics on such publications as **Eerie**, **Creepy**, and **Classics Illustrated**. He passed away in 1983.

Crandall's skillful use of fine line shading gave his work a film noir sensibility evocative of Dashiell Hammett and Raymond Chandler.

Johnny Craig edited Vault of Horror and drew all its covers. Like Feldstein, he was a master of the single bold image that grabbed readers from across the room.

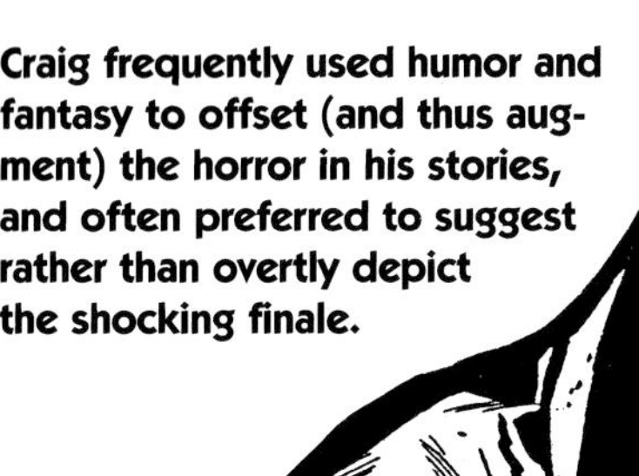

With a clean and extremely commercial style, Johnny Craig's figures are somewhat reminiscent of Milt Caniff (Terry & the Pirates).

Craig frequently used humor and fantasy to offset (and thus augment) the horror in his stories, and often preferred to suggest rather than overtly depict the shocking finale.

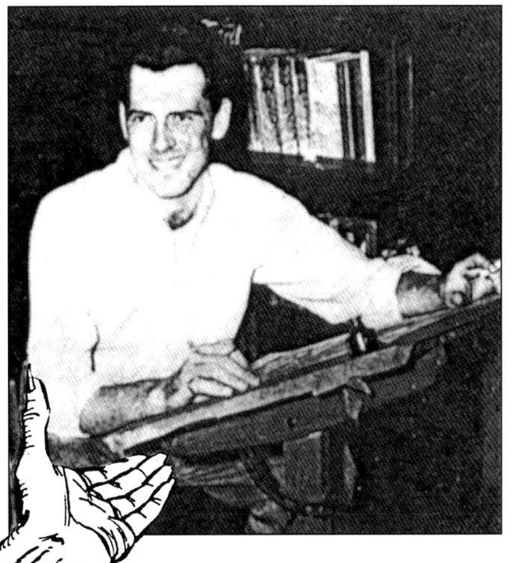

JOHNNY CRAIG

Born in Pleasantville, New York, in 1926, Craig joined EC in 1947 after attending the Art Students League and a stint in the Army during World War II. Craig's style of artwork was clean and uncluttered and extremely commercial. His figures could just as well have been modeling clothing or selling soap, which made their vile and violent behavior all the more shocking. Many of his horror stories are tales of domestic tranquillity gone fatally awry.

Craig was hired by Max Gaines and was the senior member of the EC staff. When Bill took over, he assigned Craig to draw the first EC horror story, which appeared in **Moon Girl** #5. After Feldstein turned his attention to writing, Craig took the lead on **The Vault of Horror**. He became the man behind the Vault Keeper, drew all of the **Vault** covers, and the lead story. Unlike the other EC artists, Craig wrote his own stories, working directly with Gaines to formulate the plot. A meticulous craftsman, he worked slowly, writing his story in a week and taking another three weeks to draw it.

Artists like Kamen excelled at suggesting the terror that occurred "offstage," but Ingels made it quite visible, so much so that his liquid style epitomized the gothic horror genre.

GHASTLY GRAHAM INGELS

Born in 1915, Graham Ingels was one of the first artists to come to work for EC, joining the company in 1947 just after Bill Gaines had taken over following the death of his father. Although he worked on western, crime, and romance stories, he found his true metier in horror. He became the alter ego of the Old Witch, signing his drawings with his moniker, "Ghastly," a nickname that was richly deserved. Although others portrayed horror as just a step or two around the corner from real life, Ingels took it to the extreme. He was, as it were, a master of decomposition, and had his own personal fan following.

He was always uneasy with his talent for the macabre. A devout Catholic, his conscience was increasingly troubled by the horror genre, and even more so, presumably, by his special knack for it. He developed a dependency on alcohol which led to missed deadlines. To compensate, Feldstein took to dissembling about when the artwork was really needed, pushing up the deadline by a few days so that when Ingels was "late," he was still on time.

Once Gaines dropped the EC horror comics line under pressure from critics, Ingels had a particularly difficult time. Since he was so well known as a horror expert, publishers had trouble believing he could draw anything else. Eventually he found work teaching at the Famous Artists School in Westport, Connecticut, then moved to Florida to give art lessons out of his home. Once in Florida he deliberately cut himself off from his former life. Gaines had to seek him out to pay him royalties on his work — money which he at first rejected. Before he died in 1991, however, he reconciled with his conscience, and painted a number of oils of the Old Witch to be sold at auction.

GHASTLY

His style is fluid and almost cinematic

AL WILLIAMSON

Al Williamson was the baby of the EC family of artists. When he joined the company in 1952, he was just twenty-one years old, and in many ways was like the 'kid brother'; the others were already family men. Born in Bogota, Colombia, he was the only member of the staff who'd been too young to serve during World War II. Williamson was working with Richard Hughes on **Forbidden Worlds** when he brought his portfolio to EC at the suggestion of Wally Wood.

Once taken into the EC fold, he frequently worked in collaboration with Frank Frazetta, Roy Krenkel, and Angelo Torres, even though his was the only signature that appeared on the panels. Williamson loved pencil work but was "deathly afraid" of inking, a task that Frazetta often undertook for him. His style is fluid and almost cinematic — Williamson liked to use movie stills for reference, and many of his heroes bear a striking resemblance to Stewart Granger. Although Williamson worked on **Tales from the Crypt** and **Vault of Horror**, he came to specialize in science fiction, both at EC and later on after **New Trend** folded. A graduate of Pratt Institute, Williamson was inspired to be a comic artist by Alex Raymond's **Flash Gordon**, and eventually went on to follow in Raymond's footsteps, working on **Flash Gordon** in the 1960s, as well as **Secret Agent Corrigan** and the **Star Wars** comic strip.

Williamson's fluid, cinematic style was apparent even in his first assignment (above), and became increasingly evident in his later horror and science fiction work (below) — as did the influence of mentor Alex Flash Gordon Raymond.

GEORGE EVANS

A Pennsylvania native, George Evans was born in 1920. He took night classes at the Art Students League and jumped right into the comic book field following his stint as an Air Force mechanic in World War II. Perhaps it was this up-close-and-personal relationship with aircraft that gave his illustrations of machinery such power.

Evans credits (or blames) Al Williamson for bringing him into the EC fold, and the two share a friendship that dates back to 1945. Evans was working full time at Fawcett when that firm lost its legal battle with DC Comics, effectively putting them out of business. DC had alleged that **Captain Marvel** was nothing more than a clone of **Superman**, and won. Williamson, who had begun working at EC, encouraged Evans to join the team. He was hired right away. (Evans paid him back by memorializing his name in many of his stories, naming a store "Williamson & Co." or putting up a billboard advertising "Williamson's Hair Tonic."

George Evans' poor eyesight grounded him during World War II, but he was able to draw aircraft as if he'd been a barnstorming aviator.

With his technical knowledge and his ability to render machinery accurately, Evans was a Kurtzman favorite, but he chafed under Kurtzman's tissue overlays, which specified the exact placement of each figure. Even alterations in the name of greater accuracy (which was a particular Kurtzman trademark) were not appreciated. "Harvey would never say a thing when he saw my changes," recalled Evans, "but after it was published he'd reveal that I'd desecrated his story."

George vastly preferred the freedom of working with Feldstein on the horror magazines. "I loved Bradbury's stories and Al's adaptations because he knew how to keep the Bradbury feeling in his scripts," said Evans in a 1992 interview with Paul Wardle (published in **Comics Journal**, May 1995). He also felt buoyed by the appreciation that abounded at EC. "This was the joy of working for Al. When you brought in the finished art, he would say, 'Oh geez, I never imagined a picture like that! Look at this, Bill!' And Bill would look and say, 'Holy cripes! Here's another one, Al.' This was a delight. You'd work for them for free."

Evans' work has a stop-action quality — like a moment frozen in time, or a frame clipped from a reel of motion picture film.

Evans' puckish sense of humor prompted him to christen billboards and commercial establishments after pal Al Williamson, in appreciation for Williamson's boost in bringing him to EC. (Note the small sign which reads "Bookie Inside.")

Nice guy Jack Kamen specialized in placing clean-cut guys and curvaceous girls in shocking situations, and frequently drew the lead story in **Shock SuspenStories.**

JACK KAMEN

Jack Kamen was another member of the EC "stable" who was an alumnus of the Art Students League. (Others included Johnny Craig, Jack Davis, Al Feldstein, and George Evans.) Born in Brooklyn in 1920, he broke into comic book illustration through a "back door" — work in the pulp magazines. Perhaps it was through this experience that he became known for his ability to render comely, seductive, large-bosomed women.

From this proficiency it naturally followed that he became the acknowledged EC expert in stories dealing with infidelity or the battle of the sexes. Bill Gaines called them "Buster" stories, because sooner or later the fed-up young woman always said, "Look, Buster! I've had it!!" Often as not, homicide followed shortly thereafter. Kamen once confessed that he specialized in these types of stories not just because of his unquestionable skill in rendering sexy women, but because he lacked the savoir faire of an Ingels or a Davis in dealing with in-your-face gore. After leaving EC, Kamen first switched to advertising and eventually left the field of illustration altogether. He became a prosperous entrepreneur, with both a medical supply and a helicopter business.

Jack Kamen

"We gave Jack Kamen the Marcus Welby stories," Al Feldstein laughs, "you know — where the nice All-American girl and guy are married and then chop each other to pieces."

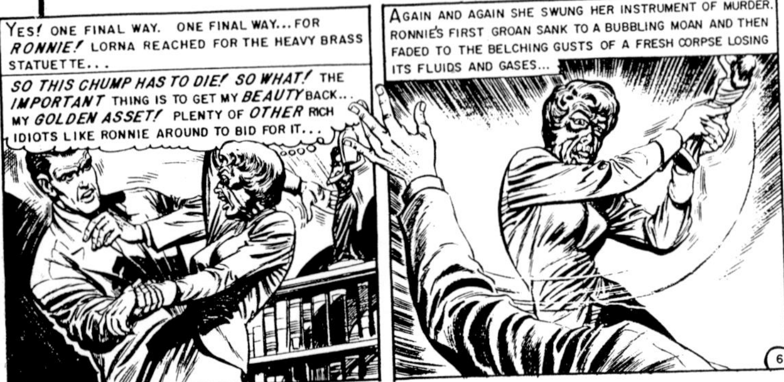

In Kamen's stories, violence and bloodshed were almost invariably implied rather than overt. With his use of unusual angles and dramatic contrast of light and shadow, however, Kamen invited readers to imagine the worst.

MARIE SEVERIN

Marie Severin was one of the few women admitted to what was very much the boys' clubhouse among the comic book artists.

She was also the last person to touch the artwork before it went off to the printer. Severin was EC's colorist—it was her selection of bright pure hues that added an extra layer of fright to the artists' panels. She also added a layer of continuity that was sometimes lacking. Some artists would include a belt or piece of jewelry or other article of clothing in one panel, but omit it thereafter. This kind of detail might be missed when the art was black & white, but Severin would be able to pick it up.

Al Feldstein only half-jokingly referred to Marie Severin as the "conscience" of EC. Gaines and Feldstein both allege that she subdued any panel she found overly gory by using dark blues or purples rather than her customary brighter colors, an assertion Severin denies, saying, "I would have no right to obliterate art."

After leaving EC, Severin enjoyed a lengthy career at Marvel, working on **The Hulk** and a Marvel superhero parody entitled **Not Brand Echh**.

Severin added color and gave instructions to printers for matching her hues (above). Today her hand-colored silver prints (left) are prized by collectors. A 1955 self-caricature (below) that shows her wielding a brush (as well as a bucket of whitewash) supports the theory that she was the office censor.

Credit Where It's Due

Freelance artists will tell you that it takes a lot more than just artistic elbow room to make them gravitate toward a certain publisher. Baldly put, it takes money, and money for artists was something that Gaines (otherwise a notorious tightwad) was quite willing to part with. Almost from the beginning he paid his artists better than most other comic book publishers. Knowing all too intimately the financial perils of freelancing, Feldstein saw to it that they got paid promptly. Whenever an artist came in to deliver a job, he also picked up a check and his next assignment.

In return Gaines kept the rights to the artwork (as did most comic book publishers). What was unusual was that Gaines also kept the artwork itself, even though it cost him money to do it. When the art overflowed the files of the old offices at 225 Lafayette, he wrapped it in brown butcher paper and stockpiled it in a vault on Second Avenue.

"I saved all the art. I just did it because I loved the stuff and I felt that's what you're supposed to do,"

Gaines told EC collectibles expert Grant Geissman (author of *Collectibly Mad*) in a 1990 interview. "My father didn't do that, and I was always quite angry....If he'd been on the ball we would have had twelve copies of *Action Comics #1* [pristine copies are now worth more than $100,000 apiece], and I think he blew it. I was a kid when that stuff came out, but I remember they were all around the house and we used to sweep them up every once in awhile and throw 'em all away."

Respecting both the art and the storyline was yet another way that Bill Gaines was trying to escape from his father's shadow, even as he ran what had been his father's business. Although he was the founding father of the genre, comics patriarch Max Gaines had been notoriously unappreciative of the artistic merit of the material he published. If it kept the presses running and it sold, it was good. His editor Sheldon Mayer recalled, "We slapped the books together. Max wasn't concerned with the literary or entertainment part of it. I had to argue to get him to run story strips like *Terry and the Pirates* in chronological order."

Bill's admiration for both the art and the artists led to regular "artist spotlights" in the three horror magazines. The "EC Artist of the Issue" depicted the cartoonist at his drafting table and provided a thumbnail biography. It was yet another means of boosting reader identification with the magazines, and the first EC Fan Addict Club was born in 1953.

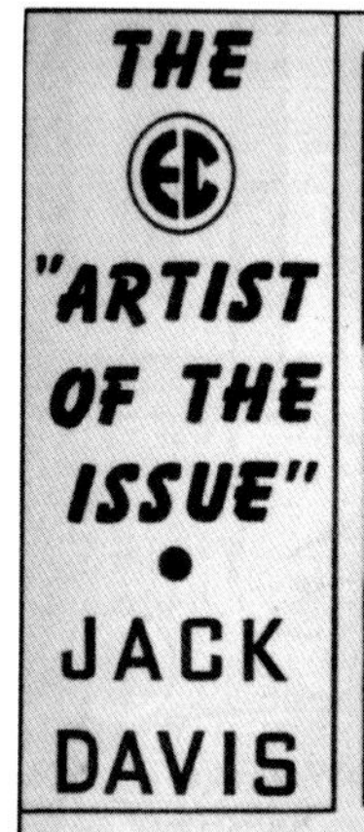

THE EC "ARTIST OF THE ISSUE" • JACK DAVIS

This 6 foot, 3 inch long drink of water was born in Atlanta, Georgia, 26 years ago and subsequently christened Jack Burton Davis, Jr. Since then he's picked up a little weight . . . today he tips the scales, wringing wet, at a wiry 155 pounds! By the time he reached grammar school, Jack was deep in art work . . . using text-books and writing tablets as sketch-pads for his budding talent. Jack's first published work appeared when he was twelve years old in Georgia Tech's college humor magazine! (Seems Jack's uncle was a professor there, and "convinced" the editor . . . who happened to be failing at the time . . . of Jack's genius!) He continued drawing through high school for the school annuals and newspaper. In 1943, Jack entered the Navy and was sent to Pensacola, Florida, where he did art work for Navy publications in the public relations department. From there he was shipped to Norfolk . . . then overseas to Guam, where they still couldn't stop him from drawing. In Guam, he created a character called BOONDOCKER for the Navy News, which was distributed over the Marianas daily. In 1946, Jack was discharged and entered the University of Georgia on the G.I. Bill. He did considerable work for the college paper and humor magazine. During his summer vacations, he did a sports strip for an Atlanta newspaper. Then Jack's big chance came. He received an important assignment from the Coca-Cola Company which netted him enough moola to buy a car and finance a trip to the big city of New York. With plenty of encouragement from his parents, he left Atlanta to try his luck, thinking he was the "only cartoonist"! After pounding the pavements for six months, and having his car stolen, he was ready to heave his brushes and samples in the river! Then he got a job with the New York Herald Tribune which kept him in New York long enough for E.C. to discover him. A few highly satisfactory and well-received jobs for us won him a permanent spot in the E.C. family. But all work and no play made Jack a dull life, so he headed south to fetch himself a wife. And he fetched a beauty too! Name's Deena! Today, Jack and Deena have a lovely little apartment in Westchester. Jack is an ardent golfer, shooting in the 80's. He's quite a home movie fan, too. (By the way, the police found his car!)

Jack works exclusively for E.C., and has a big future here. He draws The Crypt of Terror feature in all E.C. horror mags, appears in every issue of Frontline Combat and Two-Fisted Tales (usually doing the leads), and occasionally appears in Crime SuspenStories. Jack is well-liked by everybody here at E.C. and apparently by all of you fans as well. (The fan mail which Jack "jus' luhves t' geht" attests to that!)

All EC regulars eventually were spotlighted as "artist of the issue."

EC was all by itself in this endeavor. Other publishers, who generally viewed their artists and writers as so many interchangeable parts, did not have any desire to have their readers identify with particular individuals. EC, on the other hand, wanted the fans to know each artist by name. In the Crypt

One of the reasons for the Crypt Keeper's Corner was that postal regulations required second-class mail to have a certain number of pages with nothing but print in each issue.

"Kamen's Kalamity" (*Tales from the Crypt* #31), was an EC insider spoof that showed incorrigible Mr. Nice Guy Jack Kamen finally joining his ghoulish confreres Ingels, Craig, and Davis in depravity. Feldstein and Gaines also appear in the story, which was drawn by Kamen himself.

Keeper's Corner, the Keeper ran a most unscientific popularity poll, keeping tabs issue by issue, as if the artists were race horses, or political candidates. From this popularity poll, however, may have sprung the misconception among the readers that the artists not only drew the stories but wrote them as well. Here is a sample from Issue #28 (Feb./Mar. '52):

> *"Madame Bluebeard" by Oozing Joe Orlando wins first place (by a shave)! This, incidentally, wins for Joe the right to have his biog appear on the inside front cover of this issue! Second place goes to Jack Drooling Davis for his savory "Well-Cooked Hams!" Ghastly Graham Ingels' "Horror! Head...It Off!" takes third niche. Jack Creepy Kamen follows closely with his "Return!"*

Eventually, the staff artists resorted to self-parody. The EC penchant for self-mockery began early, and the first of it was perpetrated by Gaines and Feldstein on themselves. In "Horror Beneath the Streets" (*Haunt of Fear* #17, Sep./Oct. '50), Al lampooned both Bill and himself as they literally descended into horror—in the sewers of New York. It was another demonstration of the spirit of camaraderie mixed with hijinks that existed at EC. In "Undertaking Palor" (*Tales from the Crypt* #39, Dec. '53/Jan. '54), Jack Davis caricatured Harvey Kurtzman as a murderous undertaker who generated his own clientele.

Since they were on the outside of so much of what went on in the adult world, kids loved sharing these inside jokes. These pranks in print, plus the lively give-and-take of the Crypt Keeper's Corner, reflected a capacity to laugh at oneself that foreshadowed the advent of *MAD*.

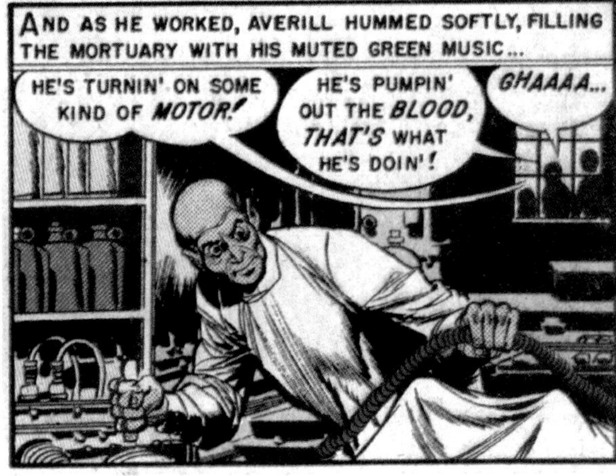

Davis and Kurtzman shared a warm personal relationship, but Jack's caricature may be an elbow-in-the-ribs jest at Harvey's nit-picky perfectionism.

EC's MAD Magazine

MAD was born in 1952—largely because Harvey Kurtzman needed a raise.

In the time that the perfectionist Kurtzman lovingly produced his two war comics, Feldstein was churning out seven. Because Gaines paid on a per-issue basis, there was a considerable disparity in their income. Increasingly, it rankled Kurtzman, who felt that his punctilious attention to detail merited further compensation. Issue-for-issue, however, Al's magazines were also bringing in substantially more money than Harvey's; Bill wasn't about to pay more for craftsmanship that wasn't helping the bottom line.

As a means of solving the dilemma, he suggested to Kurtzman that he start another magazine. That way, reasoned Gaines, his income would go up by 50 percent. *MAD* debuted in the summer

Steven Spielberg owns the original artwork for *MAD* #1.

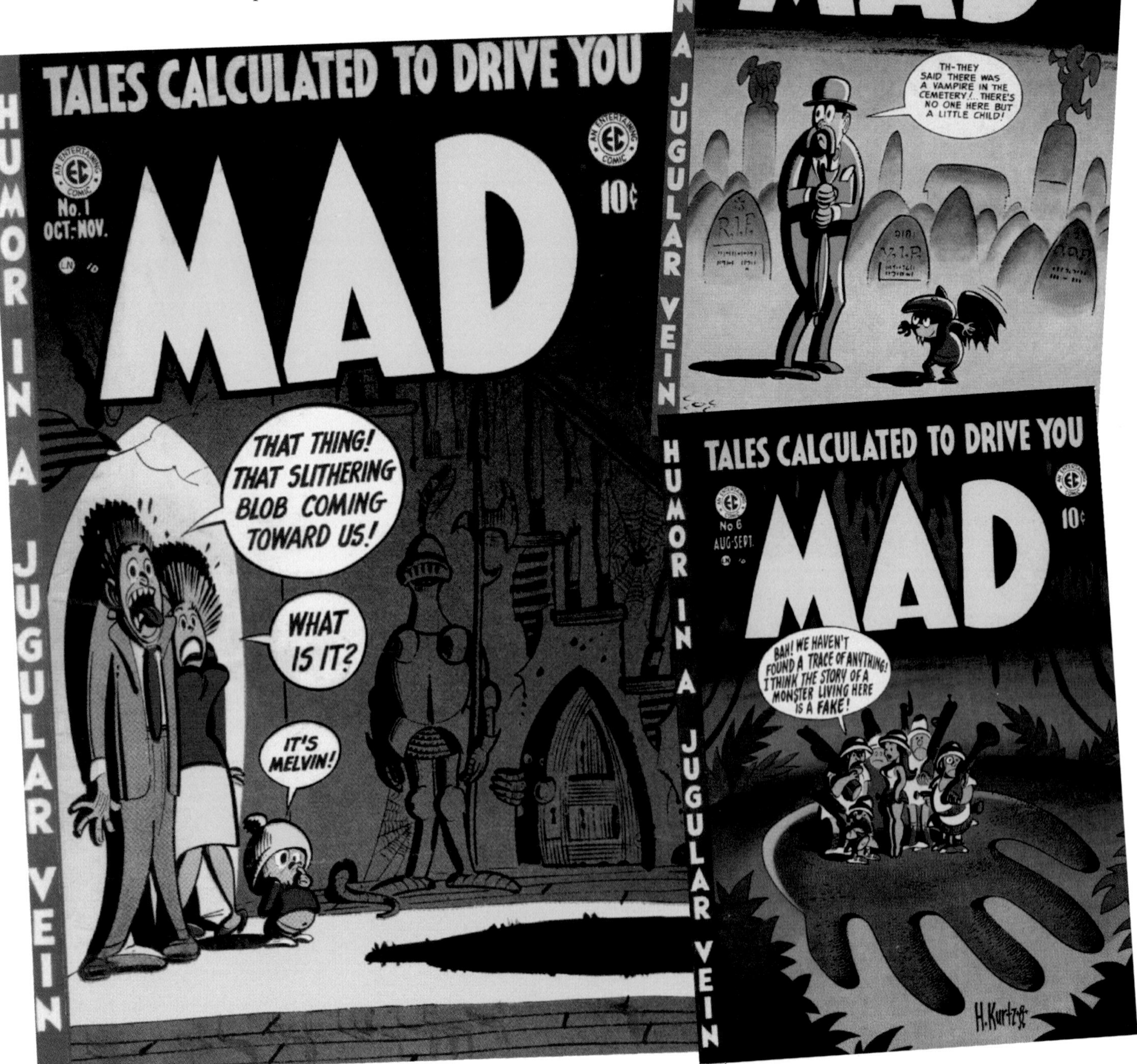

of 1952. Originally patterned on campus humor magazines, its first targets were other comic books. To prove that buffoonery started at home, issue #1 skewered EC's own horror comics, which Kurtzman had never really cared for. (Harvey had worked on some of them, but stopped almost as soon as he began editing *Two-Fisted Tales*.) Sales of issues #1–3 were, to put it mildly, disappointing. Because he liked what Kurtzman was doing, however, Gaines was willing to stick with it for awhile, letting the profits from the horror magazines carry *MAD*, even as they carried *Weird Science* and *Weird Fantasy*.

It soon became clear, however, that *MAD* had no need for a crutch. With Wally Wood's "Superduperman," in issue #4, sales of *MAD* began to soar. Kurtzman came up with withering parodies of some of comics' most hallowed icons—Mickey Mouse became Mickey Rodent; happy-go-lucky Archie was transmogrified into Starchie, an armed-and-dangerous juvenile delinquent; there was Woman Wonder, the Lone Stranger, Poopeye, and all the Melvins—Little Orphan Melvin, Smilin' Melvin, and Melvin of the Apes. Then he expanded into the world at large, taking on advertising, TV, movies, and one of the key underpinnings of fifties consumerism, planned obsolescence. There was no cow too sacred for *MAD*.

Gaines and Feldstein prodded Kurtzman to broaden his targets beyond EC, first to other comics and then to the world at large. At the same time, however, Kurtzman honed his focus, taking deadly aim at a particular comic or advertisement as representative of the genre. "*Superduperman* and *Mickey Rodent*," he said, are stories that are "engraved on my memory, because they sum up what *MAD* was all about: trying to make the truth visible."

A Million Kids, a Million Flashlights, Under a Million Blankets

Tales from the Crypt and the horror magazines were a financial and cultural phenomenon. After bedtime a million kids armed with a million flashlights huddled under a million blankets, eagerly devouring each new bimonthly issue. Adolescent boys bonded over shared horror stories. As the Crypt Keeper had recommended, they read them aloud to one another. Copies were passed from hand to hand, if need be in secret.

Bill, Al, and new EC business manager Lyle Stuart at first tried to hide the fact that the horror comics were profitable, but the horrible truth was that they were doing fabulously well.

Issues frequently sold out; there were many letters from readers complaining that they couldn't find the magazines in the stores (they were encouraged to subscribe by mail). "Break even was 36 or 37 percent," recalls Stuart. "Our magazines were coming in at 89 percent...93 percent...even *Life* wasn't doing that well." With the cooperation of Gaines' distributor, Leader News, nobody outside EC knew what the real circulation numbers were; in fact many inside the EC "family" (including the artists) were kept in the dark, for about a year. After that, the news leaked out and everyone wanted a piece of the action.

Few of the horror knockoff comics had the sense of humor or the sense of ironic justice that made EC stories so distinctive.

The Copycat Brigade

Once the financial success of EC's *New Trend* was apparent, all of the other comic book publishers hurried to produce imitations. Gaines called them "the copycat brigade." The same lemmings who rushed to duplicate successful teen comics, romances, and westerns now jumped into horror, getting as close to EC titles as they dared. Avon was one of the first publishers to make the leap with *Strange Worlds* in 1950. Atlas came out with *Adventures into Terror* (formerly *Joker*) in 1950, and *Mystic*, *Astonishing* (formerly *Marvel Boy*), and *Strange Tales* in 1951. ACG began putting out *Forbidden Worlds* in July of that same year. Harvey introduced *Witches Tales* in January 1951 and *Chamber of Chills* six months later. *Tomb of Terror* followed in 1952. Also in 1952, Fawcett debuted *Strange Stories from Another World* and *Worlds of Fear*, and Star published *Startling Terror Tales*.

In a continuation of the post office name-change follies (designed to avoid paying for a $2,000 second-class mail permit) Star turned *Jungle Thrills* into *Terrors of the Jungle*. Ajax's *Rocketman* became *Strange Fantasy*. The word "weird" began popping up ubiquitously. There was *Weird Terror*, *Weird Thrillers*, *Weird Worlds*, *Weird Horrors*, *Weird Adventures*, *Weird Mysteries*, and *Weird Tales of the Future*.

And that was just the beginning. By 1953, approximately one quarter of the comic book industry was following Gaines into the horror field. By one estimate, there were about 150 horror titles in print. Grown-ups rather than children were in the vanguard. According to one study, 54 percent of the comic book buying public was over twenty-one, and more American adults were reading horror comics than were reading *Reader's Digest* or *The Saturday Evening Post*.

Further into Horror

From George Evans' oversized Whitman sampler filled with Irwin's fat wife in "An Ample Sample" (*Vault of Horror* #32) to the tub full of flesh-eating *piranha* fish in "The Bath" (*Tales from the Crypt* #42), an array of off-stage gore began to take center stage.

It took a lot of guts to illustrate my dreadtime gories, but those EC artists were just dying to do it...heh, heh, heh, heh.

Soon the press of competition, plus the cumulative effects of writing four stories a week, began to tell on Gaines and Feldstein. The stress of daily collaboration took its toll on their relationship, and though they were still cordial, their friendship cooled. As Feldstein began pedaling faster and faster just to stay in one place, Gaines started to spend much more time with Lyle Stuart.

As exhaustion set in, Bill and Al began having story problems. With all the imitators, it was now much more difficult to maintain EC's quality and originality, but in his voracious reading, Gaines had already consumed most of the better and more obvious sources for springboards. As they reached deeper and deeper into the bottom of the springboard barrel, the stories got bloodier and bloodier. In the early stories, much of the gore took place "offstage," and more was left to the reader's imagination. With the later tales, however, the unseen terrors declined and the visible human giblet count rose markedly.

Finally Gaines hollered for help from outside freelance writers in the February 1954 issue of *Writer's Digest*:

> *We give up. For five years my editors and I have been writing an average of a comic book every six days: five a month, sixty a year. Each magazine contained four stories. That's 240 plots a year, 1200 in five years. Now we're written out. Bone dry.*

Gaines went on to specify what kinds of stories he wanted from writers, and in so doing set down as good a definition of the do's and don'ts of horror, EC style, as has ever been published.

His advice to writers and the content of his magazines stood in stark contrast to the guidelines his father had published by. In *Tales from the Crypt*, *Vault of Horror*, and *Haunt of Fear*, it appeared as if the rebellious Bill had methodically gone out of his way to violate his father's publishing shibboleths—and to do so in as flamboyant a manner as possible. By late 1953, he hadn't missed a one.

Bill Gaines' Do's and Don'ts of Horror

We have no ghosts, devils, goblins, or the like.
We tolerate vampires and werewolves, if they follow tradition and behave the way respectable vampires and werewolves should.
We love walking corpse stories.
We'll accept the occasional zombie or mummy.
And we relish the **contes cruels** story.

Note: **Contes cruels** are tales of sadism.

The Gospel According to Max Gaines

In 1942, the New York **World Telegram** published an article about violence in comics headlined "Youngsters Want Blood, Thunder in Their Comics." After complaining that "publishers keep feeding death to the kids through villains now pictured as Nazis, Japs [sic] and sundry enemies to society," the article went on to describe the strictures that Max Gaines and Sheldon Mayer, his editor, placed on artists and writers at All-American Comics who worked on **Wonder Woman**, **Flash**, and the other superhero comic magazines.

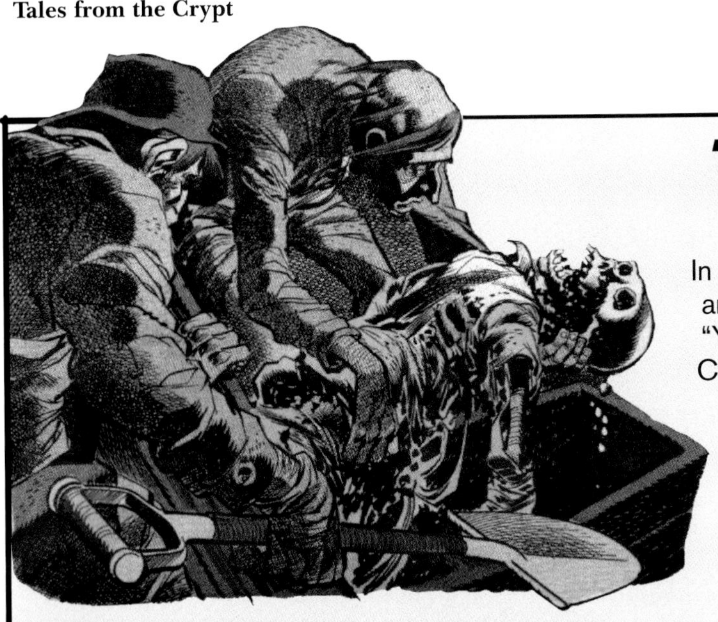

"Never show a coffin, especially with a corpse in it."

"Don't chop the limbs off anybody."

"Don't roast anybody alive."

"Never show an electric chair or a hanging. If you must, do it in silhouette or with the lights dim."

"Never show a hypodermic needle."

"Don't put anybody's eyes out."

"Never show anybody stabbed or shot. Make killings in two panels: In one, the villain approaching with the weapon; In two, the villain leaving the body with the smoking gun. Never show the kill."

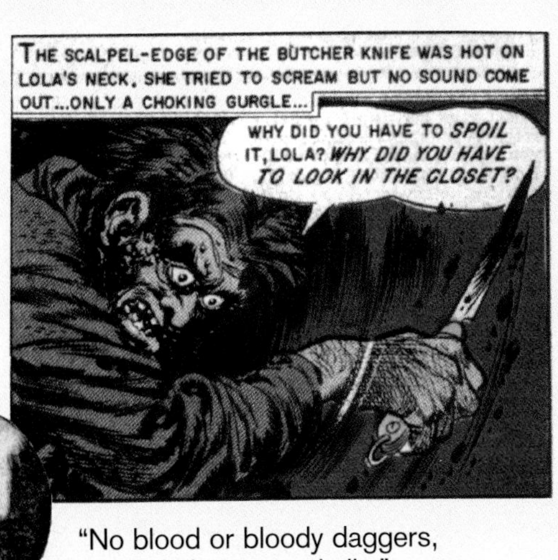

"No blood or bloody daggers, no skeletons or skulls."

"Show no torture scenes; show no whippings."

A "can you top this?" atmosphere prevailed in the later issues of the horror titles, as can be seen in: Reed Crandall's slimy "Swamped" (*Haunt of Fear* #27), Davis' rotted sailor in "Forever Ambergis" (*Tales from the Crypt* #44), and Craig's apocalyptic ending to "Surprise Party" (*Vault of Horror* #37).

When other writers were brought in to help Feldstein write horror stories in the last year, no definitive records were kept of authorship. Jack Oleck, Carl Wessler, and Otto Binder each contributed several stories. The material was probably suggested by Gaines/Feldstein and certainly edited by Feldstein. According to John Benson, the authorship of the 72 stories in the last six issues of the horror titles has been positively identified for all but 17 stories.

Dead Man's Curve

Despite all the imitators, EC's horror magazines were still the top sellers. Bill Gaines now had to cope with something his father had assured him over and over would never happen—he was "amounting to something." Like the ugly duckling that turned into a swan, with the success of the *New Trend*, all those character traits that had been considered flaws and defects by his father had become strengths and advantages. Max Gaines had bequeathed Bill just enough propensity for hard bargaining to be a good contract negotiator. Everything else that was paying off—his creativity, his taste for practical jokes, his laissez faire attitude toward regular hours, his generosity with praise for the efforts of others—was unique to Bill.

Gaines, who had been troubled from time to time by nightmares about his father, was now a success because of who he was, not because of who his father had been. It was as if he had taken the keys to his dad's Hudson Hornet—without permission—souped it up, painted flames on the hood, taken it down to the strip, and gone drag racing with the big boys from uptown. When the smoke cleared, he was headed home with everyone else's pink slips in his back pocket. It was a very long way from *Bouncy Bunny in the Friendly Forest* to *Ooze in the Cellar*, but ooze was selling and bouncy bunnies had not.

A change was in the wind, however, as voices of concern began to be raised in protest to the amount of horror available on the newsstands. As 1954 dawned, Bill's Hornet, flames and all, was headed for Dead Man's Curve.

PREMATURE DEATH OF TALES

The Gathering Storm

Even when Max Gaines was still publishing *Superman* and *Green Lantern*, there were those who maintained that comic books were having a harmful effect on America's youth. In May of 1940, *Chicago Daily News* editor Sterling North condemned comic books as "a poisonous mushroom growth" and claimed that publishers were "guilty of a cultural slaughter of the innocents."

North's early crusade was interrupted by World War II. Whatever momentum he had gathered was defused by the fact that comic book publishers, Max Gaines included, enlisted their superheroes in the war against fascism. It was difficult to attack the actions of *Wonder Woman* and the Man of Steel without appearing to be for the Nazis and against "Truth, Justice, and the American Way." Once the war was over and the superhero vogue had passed its peak, however, public concern about the effect of comics on children resurfaced.

In a transition that echoed the rise of film noir in Hollywood, crime comics climbed to prominence with the end of the war, such that by 1948 they were by far the most popular type of comic. However, the self-appointed guardians of social morality were much tougher on the comics than they were on the movies. At the same time that moviegoers flocked to see *The Big Sleep*, *Key Largo*, and *The Postman Always Rings Twice*, critics alleged that crime comics glorified villainy and violence. News stories appeared about youths who had committed violent felonies that duplicated crimes they had read about in the comics. These accounts frequently described the young perpetrators not only as juvenile delinquents but as "comic book addicts." FBI Director J. Edgar Hoover warned that "Crime books, comics, and newspaper stories crammed with anti-social and criminal acts, the glorification of un-American vigilante action, and the deification of the criminal are extremely dangerous in the hands of the unstable child."

The foremost critic of comic books was a psychiatrist named Fredric Wertham. A senior psychiatrist for twenty years with the New York Department of Hospitals and director of the Lafargue Clinic, the first psychiatric clinic in Harlem, Wertham began hammering on comic books as early as 1948, when he realized that the reading of comic books was a common habit among his young maladjusted patients.

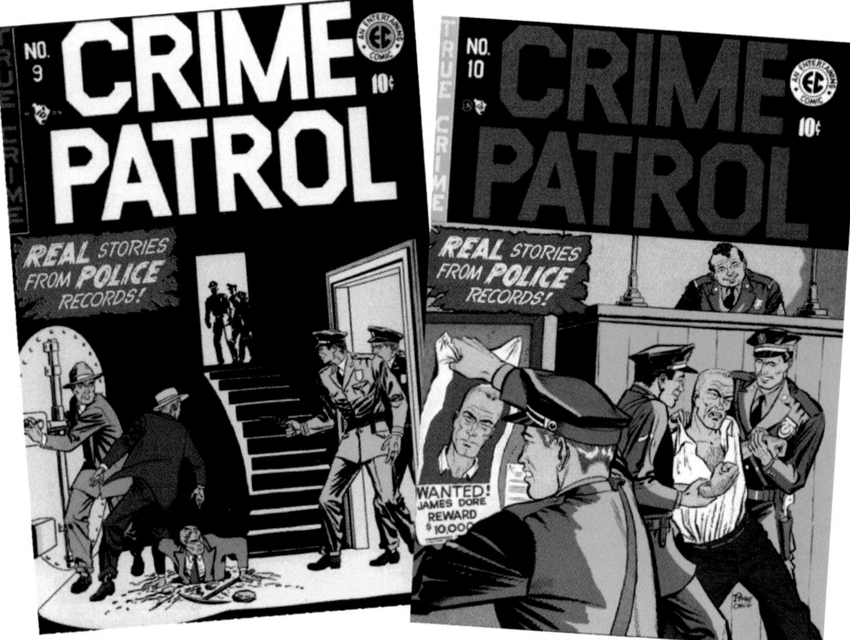

By attacking covers such as these, Wertham was able to rally women's groups and religious organizations, notably the Catholic Legion of Decency, to his cause.

Wertham committed one of the classic desecrations of the scientific method.

Since all his budding sociopaths read comics (even as they wore pants and drank Coca-Cola), he concluded that therefore the comics must be the cause of their deviance. He then generalized his findings to deduce that crime comics were the root cause not just of his patients' troubles, but of America's blossoming incidence of juvenile delinquency (an "increase" more supported by headlines than by statistics).

Wertham then worked overtime to sell his allegations to the public. He was nothing if not tenacious, writing articles in popular magazines, lecturing, and appearing on radio programs. With a genius for garnering headlines that predates the term "sound bite," whatever Wertham was lacking in scientific method he made up for in hucksterism and salesmanship. In a clipped Teutonic accent that would remind later generations of Peter Sellers' portrayal of apocalyptic Dr. Strangelove, he was able to generalize on a grand scale, maintaining that comic book reading was "definitely and completely harmful and was a distinct influencing factor in every single delinquent or disturbed child we studied."

Paradoxically, he alleged that the happy, well-adjusted kids who were filling new elementary schools all over suburbia were the most at risk. Despite the fact that almost all his experience was in working with children with emotional problems, Wertham contended that it was primarily the normal child who was harmed by crime and horror comics, claiming "the most morbid children are least affected because they are wrapped up in their own fantasies."

His particular target was crime comics, but for Wertham, that covered a lot of ground. He defined "crime comics" as those dealing with "crime, murder, detailed descriptions of all kinds of felonies, torture, sadism, attempted rape, flagellation, and every imaginable kind of violence." Not surprisingly, Wertham believed that "an overwhelming majority of comic books are crime comics," and did not distinguish among westerns, detective stories, space comics, and ghost or horror stories, saying, "If a girl is raped, she's raped whether it's on a space ship or a prairie. If a man is killed, he is killed whether on Mars or here." Even squeaky clean funny animal comics were not immune. "Ducks shoot atomic rays and threaten to kill rabbits," he complained.

Wertham identified standard but abhorrent themes that he found to be common threads running through what he defined as "crime comics." These elements included injury to the eye, blood sucking, desecration of the dead, violence against the police,

Wertham was certainly correct that horror comics wallowed in the exploitation of gore. Axe murders, electrocutions, acid baths, live burials, and worse abound in these pages. Many of the images are shocking and horrific, but often the scenes are so extreme, so "over-the-top," that the underlying graveyard humor is obvious. Wertham never dealt with the fact that the stories were almost always presented in a comedic context by both the GhouLunatics and the publisher.

branding, stoning of victims, and tying up of females. Although Wertham generally avoided singling out any comic publication by name, his allegations left little doubt that he had EC in his crosshairs.

Wertham was particularly offended by the treatment of women in comic books. He objected to the way they were portrayed "in a smutty, unwholesome way, with emphasis on half-bare and exaggerated sex characteristics." Comics, he maintained, were "sexually aggressive in an abnormal way."

When the complaints of Wertham and others first started surfacing, comics publishers made a halfhearted attempt at self-censorship. Founded in 1948, the Association of Comic Magazine Publishers (ACMP) went through the motions of adopting a code, but had a hard time gaining and keeping member publishers. Although EC was one of the founding members, Gaines pulled out in 1950 after Henry Schultz, the Executive Director, had denied the ACMP seal of approval to some of his publications. (Amazingly, however, Schultz had okayed all of EC's work until that time.) "I used to go up to Schultz and yell and scream and pull my hair and talk him out of almost anything," Gaines recalled. "If you look at my old books with the seal on them you'll see what we could publish with the Association's approval, because Schultz was just getting a salary." Comic book publishers, as always, were guided far more by the demands of the marketplace than by the strictures of the code. By the time of the Kefauver hearings in 1954, only three comic book publishers were still members. Schultz admitted to the senators that the ACMP seal was "meaningless," and that "some publishers make up their own seals of approval and place them on their comic books."

The 1954 publication of Fredric Wertham's book *Seduction of the Innocent* turned up the heat on the issue of comics and juvenile delinquency.

(Note the similarity between Wertham's title and Sterling North's original 1940 condemnation, "slaughter of the innocents.") From the fears of nuclear annihilation in the Cold War to advertising products that ended domestic anxiety about spotted glassware, bad breath, and waxy yellow buildup, much about the 1950s preyed on people's insecurities. The general public looked for strong, confident leadership, and in their vulnerability sometimes found demagoguery instead. From FBI Director J. Edgar Hoover to Senator Joseph McCarthy to Dr. Fredric Wertham, people who had the confidence of their convictions — however wrongheaded they might be — were held in esteem, at least for a time. Faith in the integrity of physicians and the infallibility of science still ran high, and the fact that Wertham contended that his conclusions were based on eight years of "scientific" clinical studies heightened alarm among insecure parents across the country. At the EC shop, Gaines and Feldstein may have been working too hard to pay much attention.

In matters of sex, EC is relatively innocent of Wertham's claims. Despite regular appearances by attractive women, there is no nudity and no sexual activity in the pages of EC. The shapely ladies keep their clothes on (with the rare exception of a two-piece bathing suit), and a passionate embrace is the closest we get to lovemaking. These comics hardly seem to be the "sexually aggressive" publications that Wertham described.

The Weird Science of Dr. Fredric Wertham

Seldom in contemporary history have the bizarre beliefs and quasi-scientific assertions of one twisted physician been accepted at face value by so much of the populace. Dr. Fredric Wertham was a psychiatrist with a mission. Firmly convinced that comic books were largely responsible for juvenile delinquency in America, he began a one-man crusade to eliminate them. He especially singled out horror and crime titles—the life blood and cash cow of EC Comics.

Seduction of the Innocent had a huge impact—akin to Tipper Gore's attack on rap lyrics, and Senator Bob Dole's characterization of certain films as "nightmares of depravity." In one chapter entitled "I Want to Be a Sex Maniac," Wertham attempted to prove that comic books were the primary contributing factor to sexual deviance among children.

Wertham declared, "If a boy sees a girl in a comic book being whipped, and the man who does it looks very satisfied and on the last page there is an advertisement of a whip with a hard handle, surely the maximum of temptation is given to the boy at least to have fantasies about these things.... The difference between surreptitious pornographic literature for adults and children's comic books is this: in one it is a question of attracting perverts; in the other of making them."

Wertham did not feel constrained to remain within the bounds of his area of expertise. He attacked comic books not just for their content but for their deleterious effect on children's reading habits. Wertham contended that "the balloon print pattern (in comics) makes it harder for children to learn to read from left to right." According to Maria Reidelbach in **Completely MAD**, he also found onomatopoeia harmful, and objected to such sound-effects words as "yeow, arghh, thunk, blam, glurg, and kurrack."

Wertham rejected the now commonly accepted idea that comics are modern fairy tales. He believed that crime comics, with their realistic settings and preoccupation with violent anti-social behavior, adversely affected children because they were unable to distinguish real life from the world of make-believe. On April 21, the same day that Gaines testified before the Senate subcommittee, Wertham warned the legislators, "The children see these things over and over again. They see how women are beaten up, how people are shot and killed, and finally they become, as St. Augustine said, 'unconsciously delighted.'"

Comics historian Les Daniels reports that "research teams have yet to uncover a library copy of Seduction in an unmutilated condition. In every case, some of the good Doctor's carefully selected illustrations have been removed by some student of suppression who felt obliged to study it more intimately."

This is the infamous panel of "Foul Play" (Haunt of Fear #19) in which human bones and entrails are used as sporting equipment. Drawn by Jack Davis, it was trumpeted by Wertham as emblematic of what was wrong with comic books. Wertham lifted this and other individual comic book panels out of context to "prove" his points, whether or not the story supported his allegations.

Unconsciously delighted... What big ears you have, Dr. Freud. In delving into Wertham's psyche, Les Daniels in **Comix: A History of Comic Books in America**, has revealed a great deal about Wertham that leads one to suspect that Wertham himself may have derived the same "unconscious delight," the same vicarious thrill from comics that millions of other readers did, but unlike the rest of us, he believed that this titillation was sinful.

In a prior work called **The Show of Violence**, Wertham discussed a number of lurid cases of individuals he had examined, people who had either committed homicide before coming under his care or who did so later in life. There was a man who had strangled a ten-year-old girl and then eaten her. When X-rayed, medical teams discovered that he had inserted a total of twenty-seven needles into his scrotum. Another fellow was a sculptor who had garroted a model and her mother, then stabbed their lodger with an ice pick. Before committing these acts, he'd half-succeeded in amputating his own genitalia.

The bizarre gruesomeness of the cases far exceeds anything in **Tales from the Crypt**. But the most important facet of **The Show of Violence** is the loving attention to detail that Wertham bestowed on these cases. He went on and on about the sculptor — for a total of 84 pages — in a way that suggests not just "unconscious delight," but perhaps "conscious delight" as well.

Calling comics "the new pornography of violence," his own fears and hang-ups are revealed in some of his more off-the-wall allegations, among them:

- Batman & Robin were a homosexual couple
- Wonder Woman was a lesbian sadist
- Ads for binoculars in comics encourage children to spy on their neighbors

At the time, however, no one was looking too closely at Wertham's own background to find the wellspring of his allegations. In a fearful and uncertain age, it was in a way comforting to parents and politicians that one single source for juvenile delinquency had been "scientifically" identified and could hence be eliminated, especially since no one was blaming **them** for the problem. Comic books were brazenly displayed on the newsstands of every drugstore and corner grocery in the country. All that had to happen was to eliminate the worst of them and clean up the rest. As Wertham said during the Kefauver hearings, "I think Hitler was a beginner compared to the comic book industry... As long as the crime comic book industry exists in its present form, no American home is safe."

Wertham groused that the suggestive display of legs, thighs, and garters aroused prurient interest in children, but he also believed kids who read comics were further corrupted by bad grammar.

Wertham claimed that children told him what the man (left) was going to do with that hot poker, and believed that kids would imitate what they read in the comics. He complained, "Children, often with comic books sticking out of their pockets, play massacre, hanging, lynching, torture."

The Santa Claus Affair

The first real shot across the EC bow in the censorship battle did not come from Wertham. It came from Holyoke, Massachusetts. In 1953, in addition to his horror duties, veritable one-man-band Al Feldstein was also editing a *MAD* clone called *Panic*. *MAD* had already spawned a host of imitators, including *Crazy*, *Unsane*, *Whack*, and *Nuts*, put out by other publishers, so Gaines decided to jump on his own bandwagon. *MAD* was "humor in a jugular vein"; *Panic* was "humor in a varicose vein." The premier issue came out in December '53 (bearing a March '54 publication date—comics were always dated several months in advance), and had a Feldstein cover showing Santa's black boot emerging from the chimney flue, headed straight for an industrial-strength bear trap. A leering Grinch-faced little boy peeked around the mantel, waiting for the denouement. The issue featured a Will Elder sendup of Clement Moore's old chestnut, *The Night Before Christmas*. No one messed with Moore's doggerel, but Elder's illustrations were decidedly nontraditional. Instead of visions of sugarplums, little tots conjured up images of Marilyn Monroe, and Jane Russell (*and* lifetime subscriptions to EC Comics.) Dasher, Dancer, Donner, Blitzen, and the rest of Santa's reindeer appeared in various incarnations as a ballet dancer, a horse, and a sprinter. The artwork that seemed to generate the most ire was Elder's unorthodox drawing of Santa's sleigh. A sign reading "Just Divorced" dangled from the stern; a meat cleaver, a garbage can, and two daggers trailed in tow behind.

This sort of parody is the stock-in-trade of much of the contemporary Christmas greeting card industry today, but in December 1953, some of the more devout folks in Massachusetts were not amused. Where Elder and Feldstein saw the mockery of the commercialized symbol of the most sacred season in retailing, the Bay State sanctimonious bluenoses saw blasphemy and sacrilege. Commercialized or not, Santa Claus was St. Nicholas, and a religious figure was not a proper subject for ridicule. Acting on complaints from the well-connected Patrick J. McDonough of the Governor's Council, Massachusetts

With "The Night Before Christmas," Feldstein and Elder eclipsed Ernest Hemingway. Hemingway's *A Farewell to Arms* was outlawed in the city of Boston; *Panic* was banned in the entire state of Massachusetts.

Attorney General George Fingold moved to prohibit the statewide sale of *Panic* on the grounds that it "desecrated Christmas" by depicting the night before Christmas in a "pagan manner."

References to sleighs and reindeer are hard to come by in the Bible, so McDonough's outcry put Fingold on shaky theological ground.

He was on unstable legal ground as well, since the Attorney General could not ban distribution of any publication on his own say-so. Explaining that his tirade was meant to encourage voluntary compliance, Fingold then urged retailers to pull the magazine from their shelves. There was sufficient hue and cry among McDonough's supporters that distributors recalled existing copies and sent unopened batches back to New York.

To Bill Gaines, it was as if the gauntlet of censorship had been flung down right before him. Acting through his attorney, the very able Martin Scheiman, he struck back in print, telling the *New York Times* that Fingold's action was a "gross insult to the intelligence of the Massachusetts people." Scheiman offered up arguments that rang like a demented version of the courtroom scene in *Miracle on 34th Street*. "Every reasoning adult knows that there just isn't any Santa Claus," he thundered. He then alleged that Fingold's actions had inflicted "wanton damage" on Gaines, and that it was unthinkable that censors would "come to the rescue of a wholly imaginary, mythological creature rarely believed to exist by children more than a few years old." If anyone found it ironic that the Catholic McDonough and the atheist Gaines were going *mano a mano* over Kris Kringle through two Jewish lawyers, Fingold and Scheiman, it was never mentioned in the press.

Lyle Stuart, who replaced Frank Lee as EC's business manager, suggested that Gaines retaliate by pulling all issues of *Picture Stories from the Bible* out of Massachusetts. It was a move borne of frustration, but a few days later Gaines was embarrassed by the revelation that *Picture Stories from the Bible* had not been sold anywhere in Massachusetts since 1948.

The upshot of the Santa Claus Affair in Massachusetts was a copycat wave of complaints in Manhattan, and a visit to EC offices by the New York Police Department. The officers bought a copy of the same issue of *Panic* from the EC mailroom, then came looking for Gaines. Gaines was shaking so badly that Stuart was afraid he would not bear up well under incarceration. He squirreled Bill away in the men's room, then confronted the cops.

"Do you have to arrest the publisher, Officer?" Stuart asked. "How about taking me? I'm the business manager." After the gendarmes got the okay from headquarters (ironically it was the same precinct that had just booked mobster Frank Costello), Stuart then allowed himself to be taken into custody for selling "disgusting" literature. This time the offending work was apparently not Elder's spoof of Santa Claus, but rather a Feldstein/Davis lampoon of Mickey Spillane called *My Gun Is the Jury*. When the police realized that they hadn't actually purchased the magazine from Stuart himself, they returned to arrest the "vendor," EC's black receptionist, Shirley Norris, who walked all the way to the Elizabeth Street station, laughing and joking with the officers, before Stuart, already in custody, told her she was about to be booked.

Critics of comic books used *Panic* to "prove" their case. New York Assemblyman James A. Fitzpatrick reads aloud from the first issue at a 1954 hearing on juvenile delinquency.

The prosecutor expressed outrage at the thigh-hiked dress in Davis' Spillane spoof, but ignored the violence of the belly-button gun blast.

Stuart's arrest was no laughing matter; he faced a possible year in prison if convicted. Although Gaines remained deeply opposed to censorship throughout his life, he was concerned for the welfare of Stuart. Thus when Bill was offered a chance to resolve the case quietly in the judge's chambers, he was tempted to accept. He was forcefully dissuaded by Lyle, who said it would be the end of their friendship. "You know, Bill, if you do this," he threatened, "I'm never going to speak to you again."

Because of the gravity of the charges, Scheiman went to court loaded for bear. A very fidgety NYPD officer took the stand and was compelled to identify exactly what it was that was "disgusting" about Volume 1, Number 1 of *Panic*. When the embarrassed officer nervously singled out a drawing of a woman showing off her legs in the Spillane parody, the judge asked the cop if he'd ever seen hosiery ads in the subway. After a few more minutes of interrogation, he turned to the officer and said, "I want you to deliver a message to the police attorney. Tell him that if he ever brings a flimsy case like this before me again, I'm going to arrest him."

Despite the legal victory, the Santa Claus Affair and Stuart's arrest kicked up a lot of negative press for EC. The potshots from PTAs, church groups, mothers' clubs, and Catholic Legions of Decency continued. The New York legislature passed numerous bills outlawing horror comics, only to have Governor Thomas Dewey veto them. Dewey's popularity was not affected.

Rivalry in the comic book industry had always been fierce. Other publishers reacted to the attacks on Gaines as if just EC's end of the horror comic boat was sinking. Atlas (Marvel), and DC Comics had been trying to play catch-up with EC in the horror genre, but EC, with Feldstein's sophisticated stories and a stable of quality artists, was still the acknowledged sales leader by far.

The Secret Life of Walter Winchell

There is considerable evidence that the New York "raid" on EC offices was a put-up job engineered by gossip columnist Walter Winchell. In addition to his duties as EC business manager, Lyle Stuart also edited a monthly tabloid called **Exposé**. In 1951 he'd run a story called "The Truth About Walter Winchell," which detailed the seamier side of Winchell's private life and public hypocrisy. Stuart's piece engendered a twenty-four-part series in the **New York Post** (for which Stuart provided the sources), and which apparently prompted Winchell to suffer a nervous breakdown early in 1952. Shortly thereafter, Stuart was hired to write a book called **The Secret Life of Walter Winchell**. The gossip columnist retaliated with scathing attacks on Stuart in print. He also spread the word that friendship with Stuart would be reflected badly in Winchell's column; he was successful to the extent that Stuart found himself a pariah among many of his former friends. Winchell had good connections with the New York Police Department and, although no "smoking gun" exists as proof, it's more than likely that the raid was orchestrated at Winchell's behest as one more way of avenging himself on Stuart.

Panic #9 (June/July '55) skewered Winchell with "Does Walter Winchell read comics?"

Lyle Stuart's book revealed sordid facets of Winchell's life, disclosures that may have provoked a vendetta against EC Comics.

While Gaines and EC were taking a pounding in the media, the other comic book publishers sat on their hands, happy to see a rival brought down. Stuart recalls Gaines' description of this phenomenon. "The only way these guys are happy," Gaines had told him, "is not if they hear that a competitor is dying, but if he's dying particularly painfully."

The Kefauver Hearings

The Kefauver hearings became what Gaines called "a headline-seeking carnival" that gave "fuel to those in our society who want to tar with the censor's brush."

Connecticut Senator William Purtell called for an investigation of comic books.

His request dovetailed with the efforts of the Senate Subcommittee to Investigate Juvenile Delinquency and its "star," mediagenic Senator Estes Kefauver. Three years earlier, the New York hearings of Kefauver's committee investigating organized crime were broadcast "nationally"—that is, to about twenty cities in the East and Midwest. The confrontation between Kefauver and mobster Frank Costello (who would allow his hands, but not his face, to be shown) gripped the country in much the same way that the Watergate hearings did many years later. Because Costello's nervous hands and tightly clenched fingers belied the bland assurances coming out of his mouth that he was just an ordinary businessman, Kefauver emerged as a national political figure and a viable presidential hopeful. Thus when hearings by Kefauver's committee investigating juvenile delinquency were scheduled for the same New York courthouse in Foley Square, it had all the makings of another media circus, especially since most of the witnesses lined up to speak were known foes of comic books. With Lyle Stuart's encouragement, Gaines volunteered to appear before the committee. After a parade of witnesses, including Fredric Wertham, had lambasted comics as a bad influence on youth, Gaines read a statement he had prepared with Stuart, then submitted to questioning from the senators and committee investigators. Bill got no support from other comic book publishers. They were more than content to leaving him twisting in the wind.

Comics were under attack at all levels of government. New York State Assemblyman James Fitzpatrick, Chairman of the State Joint Legislative Committee to Study the Publication of Comics, and New Jersey Senator Robert Hendrickson, Chairman of the Senate Juvenile Delinquency Subcommittee, confront "the enemy."

Bill Gaines' Statement to the U.S. Senate Subcommittee to Investigate Juvenile Delinquency

April 12, 1954

My name is William Gaines. I am a graduate of the School of Education of New York University. I have the qualifications to teach in secondary schools—high schools.

What then am I doing before this Committee?

I am a comic magazine publisher. My group is known as EC—Entertaining Comics. I am here as a voluntary witness. I asked for and was given this chance to be heard.

Two decades ago, my late father was instrumental in starting the comic magazine industry. He edited the first few issues of the first modern comic magazine, **Famous Funnies**.

My father was proud of the industry he helped found. He was bringing enjoyment to millions of people. The heritage he left, the vast comic book industry, employs thousands of writers, artists, engravers, printers. It has weaned hundreds of thousands of children from pictures to the printed word. It has stirred their imaginations, given them an outlet for their problems and frustrations...but **most** important, given them millions of hours of entertainment.

My father before me was proud of the comics he published. My father saw in the comic book a vast field for visual education. He was a pioneer. Sometimes he was ahead of his time.

He published **Picture Stories from Science**, **Picture Stories from World History**, and **Picture Stories from American History**. He published **Picture Stories from the Bible**.

Since 1942, we have sold more than five million copies of **Picture Stories from the Bible** in the United States. These copies are used widely by churches and schools to make religion interesting, more vivid, more real. **Picture Stories from the Bible** is now published throughout the world in dozens of translations. But make no mistake about it, it is nothing more and nothing less than a comic magazine.

I publish many comic magazines in addition to **Picture Stories from the Bible**.

For example, I publish horror comics. I was the first publisher in these United States to publish horror comics. I'm responsible! I started them!

Some may not like them. That's a matter of personal taste. It would be just as difficult to explain the harmless thrill of a horror story to a Dr. Wertham as it would be to explain the sublimity of love to a frigid old maid.

My father was proud of the comics he published, and I'm proud of the comics I publish. We use the best writers, the finest artists. We spare nothing to make each magazine, each story, each page, a work of art.

As a result, we have the largest percentage of sales in independent distribution.

The comic magazine is one of the few remaining pleasures that a person can buy for a dime today.

Pleasure is what we sell. Entertainment. Reading enjoyment.

Entertaining reading has never harmed anyone....

Our American children are, for the most part, normal children. They are bright children. But those who want to prohibit comic magazines seem to see instead dirty, twisted, sneaky, vicious, perverted little monsters who use the comics as blueprints for action....

What are we afraid of? Are we afraid of our own children? Do we forget that they are citizens too, and entitled to the essential freedom to read?

Or do we think our children so evil, so vicious, so single-minded, that it takes but a comic magazine story of murder to set them to murder — of robbery to set them to robbery?

[Former New York Mayor] Jimmy Walker once remarked that he never knew a girl to be ruined by a book.

And no one has ever been ruined by a comic. As has already been pointed out by previous testimony, no healthy normal child has ever been made the worse for reading comic magazines....

I do not believe that anything that has ever been written can make a child hostile, over-aggressive, or delinquent. The roots of such characteristics are much deeper.

The truth is that delinquency is a product of the real environment in which a child lives—and not of the fiction he reads.

Gaines added further remarks to his prepared testimony, a postscript which not surprisingly was not picked up by the local papers.

I would like to add something based on what I have heard here today.

No one has to buy a comic book to read horror stories. Anyone, any child, any adult—can find much more extreme descriptions of violence in the daily newspaper....

In today's edition of the **Daily News**—which more children will have access to than they will to any comic magazine—there are headlines and stories like these:

WAKES TO FIND HE HAS KILLED WIFE WITH GUN...

COPS PLEA IN COCKTAIL POISONINGS—a 20 year old youth who reads poetry but not comic magazines pleaded guilty to second degree murder. He helped poison the mother and father of a friend....

I'm not saying it's wrong. But when you attack comics, when you talk about banning them as they do in some cities, you are only a step away from banning crime news in the newspapers....

[In America] we print our crime news. We don't think that crime news or any news should be banned because it is "bad for the children."

Once you start to censor, you must censor everything. You must censor comic books. And magazines. And radio and television and newspapers. Then you must censor what people may say.

And then you will have turned this country into a Spain [governed at that time by Fascist dictator Generalissimo Francisco Franco] or a Russia.

Kefauver vs. Gaines, or The Affair of the Severed Head

The exchange during the Foley Square hearings between Bill Gaines and presidential wannabe Senator Estes Kefauver (D-Tennessee)—with interjections by "the Herberts" (Tweedle Dum/Tweedle Dee Senate Subcommittee investigators Herbert Beaser and Herbert Hannoch)—has become legendary in the annals of comic book history. It is an archetypal interchange between an advocate of free speech and a politician seeking to capitalize on the hot topic of the hour to further his own ambitions.

Mr. Beaser: Is there any limit you can think of that you would not put in a magazine just because you thought a child should not see or read about it?

Mr. Gaines: No, I wouldn't say that there is any limit for the reason you outlined. My only limits are the bounds of good taste, what I consider good taste.

Mr. Beaser: Then you think a child cannot in any way, in any way, shape, or manner, be hurt by anything that a child reads or sees?

Mr. Gaines: I don't believe so.

Mr. Beaser: There would be no limit actually to what you put in the magazines?

Mr. Gaines: Only within the bounds of good taste.

Mr. Beaser: Your own good taste and salability?

Mr. Gaines: Yes.

Sen. Kefauver: (holding up magazine) Here is your May 22 issue. This seems to be a man with a bloody ax holding a woman's head up which has been severed from her body. Do you think that is in good taste?

Mr. Gaines: Yes, sir; I do, for the cover of a horror comic. A cover in bad taste, for example, might be defined as holding the head a little higher so that the neck could be seen dripping blood from it and moving the body over a little further so that the neck of the body could be seen to be bloody. [see postscript, below]

Sen. Kefauver: You have blood coming out of her mouth.

Mr. Gaines: A little.

Sen. Kefauver: Here is blood on the ax. I think most adults are shocked by that.... Here is the July issue. It seems to be a man with a woman in a boat and he is choking her to death here with a crowbar. Is that in good taste?

Mr. Gaines: I think so.

Mr. Hannoch: How could it be worse?

POSTSCRIPT
In one of Bill Gaines' last interviews (with Steve Ringgenberg in **Gauntlet** in 1992), Gaines revealed one small insight about the Johnny Craig severed head cover that had generated so much controversy. "What Kefauver didn't know, and I did know, was that when Craig originally brought that cover in, there **was** blood dripping from the neck. I myself had suggested that he raise the bottom of the cover up to cover the neck, so the neck was cut off before it was shredded. When Kefauver asked, do I think it's in bad taste, knowing what it had been originally, I said, 'No, this is in good taste.'"

Aftermath

At EC offices, opinion was divided about how well Gaines' statements had gone over. Lyle Stuart felt he'd done just fine. "I thought he read his statement very well. He was very sincere; he thought he'd delivered a good anticensorship appeal."

Al Feldstein was somewhat more pessimistic. "Bill wasn't ready for this," he says. "He wasn't as sharp as he could have been. When they got into the issue of the ax and the severed head, Senator Kefauver really trapped him."

Gaines himself admitted that he'd been taking diet pills during the hearings, and that midway through the session they began to wear off. "Dexedrine keeps you hyper, but when it wears off it leaves you like a limp rag," Gaines told Mark Voger. "Halfway through, it wore off and I sat there like a punch-drunk fighter, getting pummeled."

Feldstein also thinks that Gaines may have been affected by something much deeper in his personality. A piece of the rebellious little boy who defied his father, Max, never really left Bill. In the early days after he took control of EC following his father's death, he used to have nightmares. In them, Max would appear before him and demand that his son return "his" business to its rightful owner. Feldstein believes that at the hearings, Bill may again have been troubled by visions of his father.

"I think Bill saw his father standing there talking to him, telling him what a bad boy he was for doing all those terrible things."

The televised Senate hearings demonstrated the burgeoning power of the fledgling medium to shape public opinion. The press was in a frenzy and powerful forces were brought to bear on the wholesalers who were distributing comic books. Protests and boycotts were staged across the country, and grandstanding politicians jumped on the bandwagon. There were public burnings of comic books, which reminded many of Nazi book bonfires before the Second World War. Municipalities were attempting to ban sales of crime and horror comics. Even New York's mayor Robert Wagner asked his DAs to ban them under obscenity laws. As Gaines had foreseen, however, some officials were reluctant, fearing that the works of Arthur Conan Doyle and Edgar Allan Poe would be outlawed together with *Tales from the Crypt*.

"When Kefauver died, I said no prayers for him. I hope they have a pit in hell hot enough for him. Everybody remembers what a bastard McCarthy was, and nobody remembers what a bastard Kefauver was. Well, maybe it's just as well. Nobody should remember him."

— George Evans

And whatever happened to Fredric Wertham? He spent his declining years denying that his work had been the impetus for the decline of comic books. "I've got a delightful picture of him reading a copy of *Shock SuspenStories*," chortled Gaines in one of his last interviews. "When he died, it went up on the wall at *MAD*."

Through it all, bundles of EC comics were being returned to the office, unopened. Gaines was having trouble finding wholesalers who would carry them.

Gaines had always believed that the horror genre, like the superhero genre before it, would die of natural causes, declining in popularity as kids moved onto the next new craze. It was not to be. *Tales from the Crypt* and its siblings had become the lightning rod for the entire comic book industry. At social events, Orlando, Davis, Craig, and many of the other artists began describing themselves as "commercial illustrators."

Judge Charles Murphy, with "before" unsavory comic and new improved "after" version. Murphy wielded a $100,000 budget and took his mandate to "clean up" comics seriously.

EC comics had literally become too hot to handle.

In 1954, confessing that one drew horror comics for a living was only marginally more socially acceptable than confessing that one was a Communist or a full-time pornographer.

Realizing that his business was on the line, Gaines tried to rouse his fellow publishers to defend their medium. In an effort to quell the storm, Gaines proposed a new comic publishers association to fight censorship. It was his intention that they fund an independent study conducted by educators and psychologists to determine once and for all whether there really was any connection between comics and delinquency. He was also prepared to propose a concerted public relations counterattack to reassure parents that comics were not harmful to their children.

The New Association and the New Comic Code

Representatives of eight other publishing houses showed up at the meeting Gaines called, and the Comics Magazine Association of America (CMAA) was formed. As their first act they banned the use of the words "crime," "horror," and "terror" in comics. Even "weird" got the ax. "This isn't what I had in mind," said Gaines, as he turned on his heel and stomped out of the meeting.

John Goldwater, the publisher of **Archie** comics, became CMAA president, a sinecure he held for the next twenty-five years. Jack Liebowitz of DC Comics, Max Gaines' former partner-cum-adversary, became vice president. Shortly thereafter, the CMAA instituted a censorship process that required a seal of approval for all comics before distribution. At Goldwater's suggestion, the publishers recycled former ACMP legal counsel Henry Schultz to draft a Code of Ethics. Those complying with the code would receive the CMAA seal of approval. Both advertising and editorial matter were to be subjected to scrutiny by the censors. The Code forbade "all scenes of horror, excessive bloodshed, gory or gruesome crimes, depravity, lust, sadism, and masochism," as well as the "walking dead, torture, vampires, ghouls, cannibalism and werewolfism." Judge Charles F. Murphy became the first Code Administrator — in effect the comics czar. Murphy was not the first choice. The czar's chair was initially offered to Fredric Wertham.

Bowing to the Inevitable

Gaines was disgusted and his business was in ruins. On September 14, 1954, he reluctantly announced that he would cease publication of his five horror and crime comics.

Gaines' disillusionment with the new CMAA was complete when he realized that there was a double standard (and not inconsiderable double-dealing) involved. It had been clear when the CMAA was founded and the Code was established that all crime and horror would be *verboten*. However, the Code as adopted permitted the word "crime" in a comic title, provided that the word was used "with restraint." Gaines pulled out of the CMAA as he had from the ACMP, its predecessor.

"Naturally, with comic magazine censorship now a fact, we at EC look forward to an immediate drop in the crime and juvenile delinquency rate in the United States. We trust there will be fewer robberies, fewer murders, and fewer rapes!"

— Bill Gaines

The New Direction

To save his company, Gaines had killed off his favorite "children," his horror comics. In their stead he and Feldstein developed a new "clean, clean" line. EC's *New Direction* comics, including *Aces High*, *Impact*, *Piracy*, *Valor*, *Extra!*, *MD*, and *Psychoanalysis*, debuted in January 1955. Even though Gaines was no longer a CMAA member, the comics met the letter of the code. However, because these comics did not carry the CMAA seal, they too were returned unopened by the distributors.

With revenues plummeting, Gaines was forced by economic necessity to swallow his pride and rejoin the CMAA. Gaines stayed with the CMAA for about ten months, reluctantly submitting his publications to Murphy and his staff. He didn't have a great deal of respect for the CMAA or the people who ran it, and his contempt for the process was more than likely ill-disguised. "This is what our forefathers came to America to escape," he wrote to his distributors. His position did not waver over time.

"I've never believed in any kind of censorship against anything in any way for anybody nohow,"

he told Steve Ringgenberg in a 1992 *Gauntlet* interview. "The Comics Code group was run by three or four old ladies who were shocked by almost anything," he continued. "Murphy headed it, but I don't think he read anything. This staff of old ladies read everything and it wasn't hard to shock them."

During the months that Gaines tried to behave himself and remain in the CMAA, Judge Murphy's "little old ladies" eviscerated every EC story they scrutinized. Even with the censor's seal, however, unopened bundles of *New Direction* comics were still being returned. It was apparent that EC was being blackballed by the rest of the comic book industry. With the Code seal or without it, *Aces High*, *Piracy*, *Valor*, *Extra!*, *MD*, and *Psychoanalysis* lumbered toward failure throughout 1955. They failed in part not because readers rejected them but because the EC boycott was so pervasive that they were never given a fair chance to hold their own in the marketplace.

Here Comes the Judge

One famous instance of censorship involved an issue of *Incredible Science Fiction* (formerly *Weird Science/Fantasy*), and a particular story called "Judgment Day." The story was one of Feldstein's "preachies," an allegory about a planet populated by orange robots and blue robots, and the space galaxy investigator who came to see if they were advanced enough to join the galactic empire. After determining that the blues and oranges had not sufficiently progressed in ending prejudice between them, the investigator returned to his space ship. Once inside, he removed his helmet, revealing himself to be a man with distinctly African features. This proved that although the orange and blue robots were still trapped in their biases, the great galactic empire had achieved equality and harmony and was now one people. On the man's brow, some drops of perspiration glistened like the stars outside in deep space.

This really made 'em go bananas in the Code czar's office. "Judge Murphy was off his nut. He was really out to get us," recalls Feldstein. "I went in there with this story and Murphy says, 'It can't be a black man.' But...but that's the whole point of the story!" Feldstein sputtered.

When Murphy continued to insist that the black man had to go, Feldstein put it on the line. "Listen," he told Murphy, "you've been riding us and making it impossible to put out anything at all because you guys just want us out of business."

Al reported the results of his audience with the czar to Gaines, who was furious. Bill immediately picked up the phone and called Murphy. "This is ridiculous!" he bellowed. "I'm going to call a press conference on this. You have no grounds, no basis, to do this. I'll sue you."

Murphy made what he surely thought was a gracious concession. "All right. Just take off the beads of sweat."

At that, Gaines and Feldstein both went ballistic. "Fuck you!" they shouted into the telephone in unison. Murphy hung up on them, but the story ran in its original form.

To Feldstein it was just the lowest example of the petty vindictiveness and cutthroat competition in the comic book industry. "I firmly believe that the *Archie* crowd and the DC crowd wanted us out of business because our sales were great and we were very innovative," he says emphatically. "Even though we weren't doing horror anymore, they didn't know what else we'd come up with next so they wanted us gone."

Recent statements by longtime CMAA president and *Archie* executive John Goldwater certainly suggest that Feldstein's suspicions are well founded. In 1992, Goldwater looked back on his years as Archie's godfather in an excerpt from *My Life with Archie, the Comic Book* in *History of the Comics* and recalled the beginning of the CMAA

"Judgment Day" was substituted for another story which Murphy had already rejected. Gaines may have felt empowered to challenge him because *Incredible Science Fiction* #33 was EC's last color comic.

code. "Those of us in the industry saw these trends—both the publication of the offensive comic books and the reaction—as a threat to everything we had worked so hard to create. Lord knows the themes and content of these comics were totally antithetical to the themes and content of the *Archie* series. ...We had certain moral obligations to guarantee that 'comic books are reasonably acceptable to reasonable people.'...I doubt that we could have made a finer choice than that of Judge Charles F. Murphy [as Code Administrator]. He performed an outstanding service to all parties concerned with comic magazines...."

"A threat to everything...totally antithetical...moral obligations to guarantee that 'comic books are reasonably acceptable to reasonable people'..." Goldwater's words were all but a declaration of war on everything that Gaines stood for. Virtually from that point forward, every contract Gaines entered into had a clause custom-designed for him by his attorneys, Marty Scheiman and Jack Albert; "This agreement is not subject to the criterion of reasonableness." Henceforth from a legal standpoint Gaines could be as crazy as he wanted to and get away with it—it was right there in black and white.

Editorial statement which appeared in the last issue of the five horror and crime comic titles

HORROR COMICS: IN MEMORIAM

You may never read this magazine. For that matter, this magazine may never be printed. If it is printed, it may never be distributed. If it is distributed, it may be kept in a bundle behind the counter and never see the light of day. But if, through some miracle, it **does** reach the newsstand, this will probably be the last issue of this magazine you will ever read.

As a result of the hysterical, injudicious, and unfounded charges leveled at crime and horror comics, many retailers and wholesalers throughout the country have been intimidated into refusing to handle this type of magazine.

Although we at EC still believe, as we have in the past, that the charges against horror and crime comics are utter nonsense, there's no point in going into a defense of this kind of literature at the present time. Economically our situation is acute. Magazines that do not get onto the newsstand do not sell. We are forced to capitulate. **We give up**. WE'VE HAD IT!

Naturally, with comic magazine censorship now a fact, we at EC look forward to an immediate drop in the crime and juvenile delinquency rate of the United States. We trust there will be fewer robberies, fewer murders, and fewer rapes!

We would like to say in passing...passing away that is!...that if you have enjoyed reading EC's horror and crime efforts over the past five years half as much as we have truly enjoyed creating them for you, then our labors of love have not been in vain.

But enough mush! This is not only an obituary notice; it is a birth announcement!

BOY...WHAT WE GOT IN STORE FOR YOU! (Ya didn't think EC was gonna die with the books did ya? We got talent we ain't even used yet!)

EC is planning the NEW NEW TREND. In January of 1955, we hit! In fact, we hit with five (5) sensational new titles. They won't be horror magazines...they won't be crime magazines! They'll be utterly new and different – but in the old reliable EC tradition! Naturally, we can't tell you what they'll be YET...we can feel the hot breath of our floundering competitors who followed us into horror on our necks. When the mags are ready to go, they'll be announced in MAD, PANIC, WEIRD SCIENCE-FANTASY, PIRACY, and TWO-FISTED TALES!

We feel it's gonna be a HAPPY NEW YEAR with our NEW NEW TREND!

Your grateful editors

And Then There Was One

With the failure of Gaines' *New Direction*, the world had finally been made safe for *Archie*. There was only one profitable piece of Gaines empire still standing: *MAD* magazine.

CORPSES & COVERS

Covers sell comics. News racks were overflowing with comic books in the early 1950s, and it took a strong graphic image to make a comic grab a kid's attention amidst the jumble of competing titles. A cover had to stand alone, usually without caption, sort of a mute single-frame snapshot of one of the stories in the issue.

At EC, the cover artwork was not necessarily drawn by the same artist who drew the story inside the comic. Thus fans were sometimes treated to different visions of the same tales. On the cover of *Shock SuspenStories* #13, Jack Kamen captured the frozen terror of a young woman thrown from a roller coaster who has not yet hit the ground, but science fiction master Frank Frazetta drew the story, "Squeeze Play." Wally Wood showed the shocked reaction of spectators to a guillotine in action on the cover of *Tales from the Crypt* #27. The story, entitled "Horror! Head...It Off!" was drawn by Ghastly Graham Ingels.

Jack Davis' covers had a funhouse macabre feeling to them, a grisly glee that was perfectly attuned to the mood set by the GhouLunatics. Al Feldstein said he "never really cared" for own artwork, but thought it "worked pretty well on covers," which is quite an understatement. With great economy of style, he repeatedly came up with dramatic cover images that are still riveting today.

These freeze frames often convey horror, not at what has already happened, but helplessness at what is about to occur. Alternatively, they show clandestine activity observed, a secret as yet unrevealed. These kinds of drawings were what made readers plunk down their dimes for EC comics— because they couldn't wait to see what happened next.

THE VAULT OF HORROR
NO.12 APR-MAY
10¢
INTRODUCING A NEW TREND IN MAGAZINES... ILLUSTRATED SUSPENSTORIES WE DARE YOU TO READ!
WAX MUSEUM
EXHIBIT # 3- STRETCH-RACK

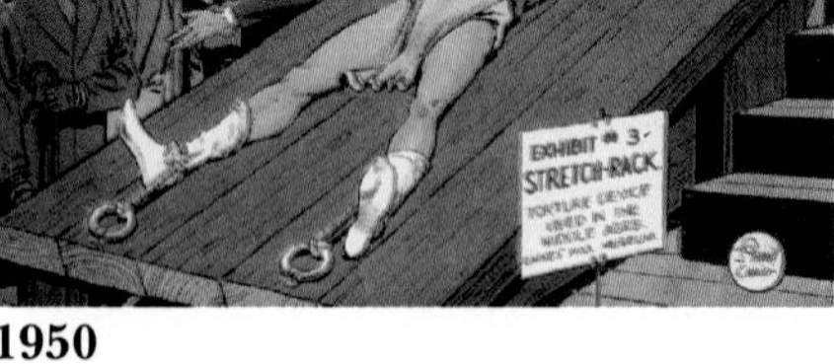

THE CRYPT OF TERROR
NO.17 APR-MAY
10¢
INTRODUCING A NEW TREND IN MAGAZINES... ILLUSTRATED SUSPENSTORIES WE DARE YOU TO READ!
WEREWOLF STRIKES AGAIN

HERE ARE TALES THAT WILL USHER YOU INTO THE HAUNT OF FEAR
NO.15 MAY-JUNE
10¢
INTRODUCING A NEW TREND IN MAGAZINES... ILLUSTRATED SUSPENSTORIES WE DARE YOU TO READ!

1950

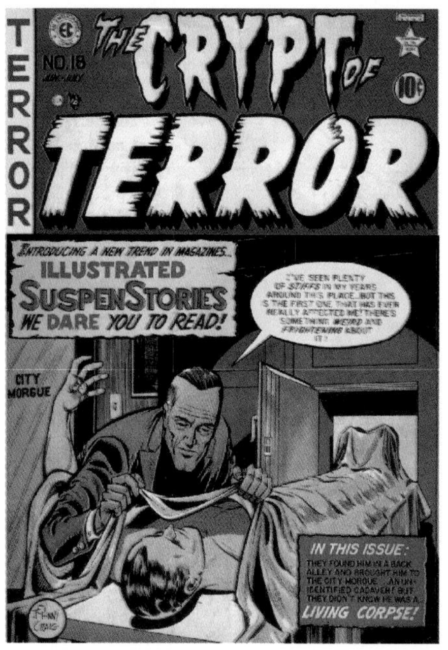
THE CRYPT OF TERROR
NO.18 AUG-SEPT
10¢
INTRODUCING A NEW TREND IN MAGAZINES... ILLUSTRATED SUSPENSTORIES WE DARE YOU TO READ!
CITY MORGUE
IN THIS ISSUE:
LIVING CORPSE!

HERE ARE TALES THAT WILL USHER YOU INTO THE HAUNT OF FEAR
NO.16 JULY-AUG.
10¢
INTRODUCING A NEW TREND IN MAGAZINES... ILLUSTRATED SUSPENSTORIES WE DARE YOU TO READ!

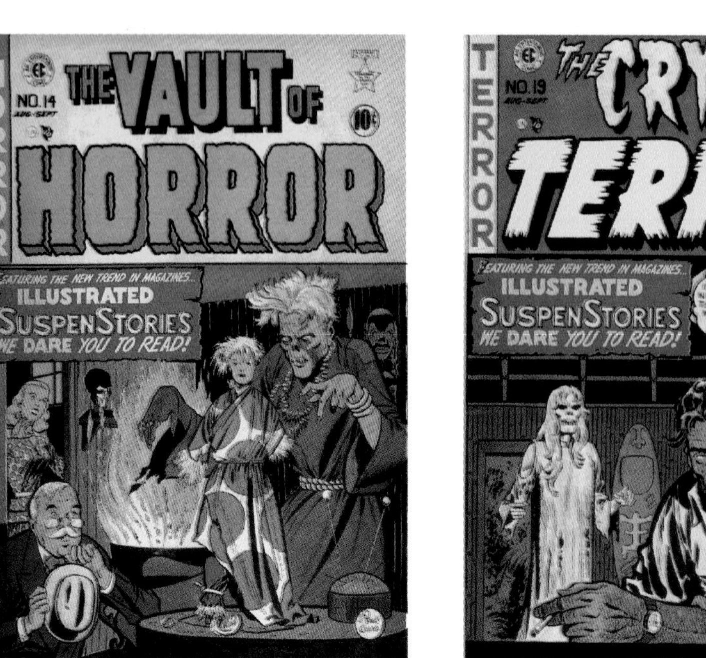
THE VAULT OF HORROR
NO.14 AUG-SEPT
10¢
FEATURING THE NEW TREND IN MAGAZINES... ILLUSTRATED SUSPENSTORIES WE DARE YOU TO READ!
THE CRYPT OF TERROR
NO.19 AUG-SEPT
10¢
FEATURING THE NEW TREND IN MAGAZINES... ILLUSTRATED SUSPENSTORIES WE DARE YOU TO READ!

HERE ARE TALES THAT WILL USHER YOU INTO THE HAUNT OF FEAR
NO.17 SEPT-OCT
10¢
FEATURING THE NEW TREND IN MAGAZINES... ILLUSTRATED SUSPENSTORIES WE DARE YOU TO READ!
the Haunt of Fear
the Vault of Horror
the Crypt of Terror

HORROR
THE VAULT OF HORROR
NO.15
OCT.-NOV.
10¢
ABNER DOON
BORN 1888
DIED 1885
REST
THE VAULT-KEEPER

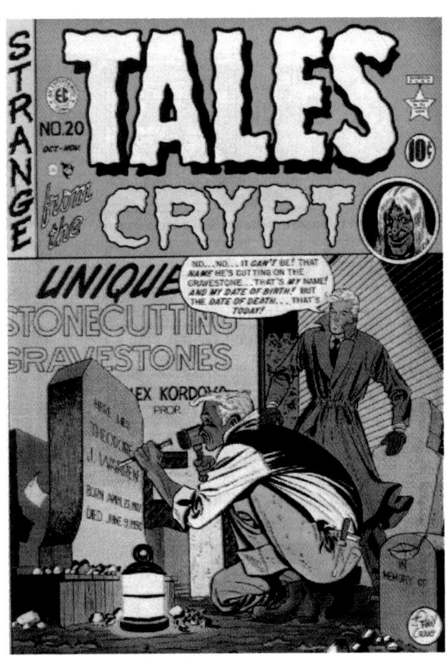
STRANGE
TALES from the CRYPT
NO.20
OCT.-NOV.
10¢
NO...NO...IT CAN'T BE! THAT NAME HE'S CUTTING ON THE GRAVESTONE...THAT'S MY NAME! AND MY DATE OF BIRTH! BUT THE DATE OF DEATH...THAT'S TODAY!
UNIQUE
STONECUTTING
GRAVESTONES
EX KORDOV
PROP.

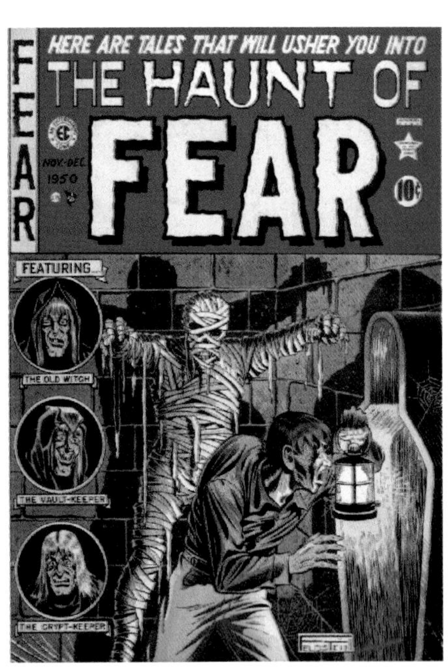
HERE ARE TALES THAT WILL USHER YOU INTO
THE HAUNT OF FEAR
FEAR
NOV.-DEC.
1950
10¢
FEATURING...
THE OLD WITCH
THE VAULT-KEEPER
THE CRYPT-KEEPER

HORROR
THE VAULT OF HORROR
NO. 16
DEC.-JAN.
10¢
THE VAULT-KEEPER
THE OLD WITCH

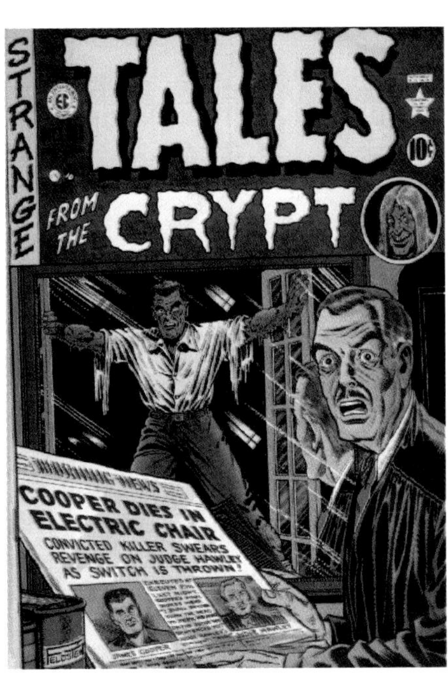
STRANGE
TALES FROM THE CRYPT
10¢
COOPER DIES IN ELECTRIC CHAIR
CONVICTED KILLER SWEARS REVENGE ON JUDGE HAWLEY AS SWITCH IS THROWN!

HERE ARE TALES THAT WILL USHER YOU INTO
THE HAUNT OF FEAR
FEAR
NO. 5
10¢
FEATURING...
UGH! WHAT A...MESS! BUT THEY'LL NEVER THINK OF LOOKING FOR A FRESH CORPSE IN THE COFFIN OF A MAN WHO DIED IN 1867!
THE OLD WITCH
THE VAULT-KEEPER
THE CRYPT-KEEPER

HORROR
THE VAULT OF HORROR
NO.17
FEB.-MAR.
10¢
FEATURING...
GOOD LORD...WHAT'S HAPPENING TO MY HANDS? THEY'RE CHANGING! THEY LOOK...LIKE AN ANIMAL'S!
CDL
THE VAULT-KEEPER
THE OLD WITCH
THE CRYPT-KEEPER

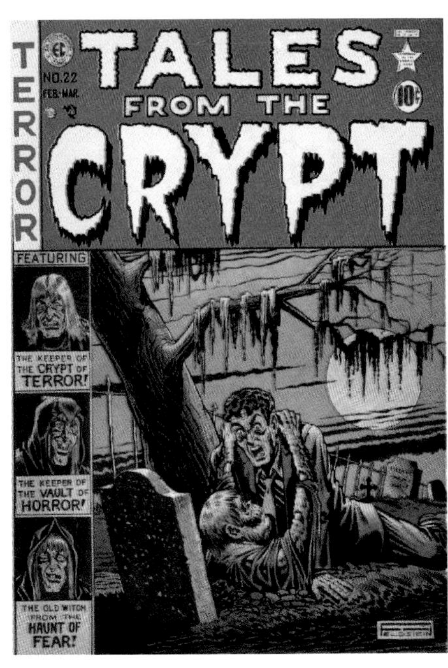
TERROR
TALES FROM THE CRYPT
NO.22
FEB.-MAR.
10¢
FEATURING
THE KEEPER OF THE CRYPT OF TERROR!
THE KEEPER OF THE VAULT OF HORROR!
THE OLD WITCH FROM THE HAUNT OF FEAR!

HERE ARE TALES THAT WILL USHER YOU INTO
THE HAUNT OF FEAR
FEAR
NO. 6
10¢
FEATURING...
THE OLD WITCH
THE VAULT-KEEPER
THE CRYPT-KEEPER

1951

THE VAULT OF HORROR
HORROR
NO. 18
APR-MAY
10¢
FEATURING...
THE VAULT-KEEPER
THE CRYPT-KEEPER
THE OLD WITCH
WISHING WELL

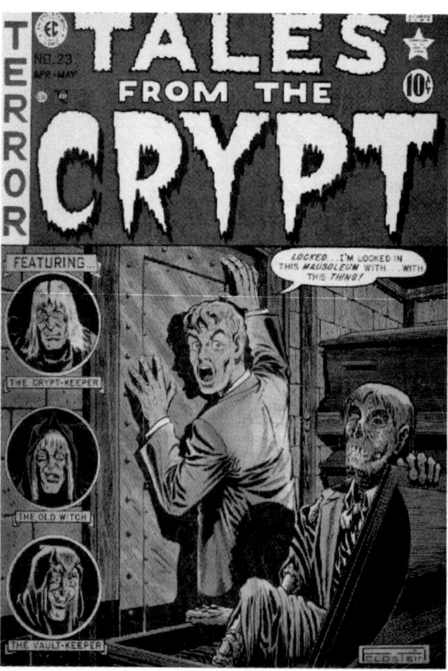
TALES FROM THE CRYPT
TERROR
NO. 23
APR-MAY
10¢
FEATURING...
LOCKED... I'M LOCKED IN THIS MAUSOLEUM WITH... WITH THIS THING!
THE CRYPT-KEEPER
THE OLD WITCH
THE VAULT-KEEPER

HERE ARE TALES THAT WILL USHER YOU INTO
THE HAUNT OF FEAR
FEAR
NO. 7
10¢
FEATURING...
HEH, HEH! I MUST BE GETTING PRETTY JUMPY SINCE I BURIED ROBERT DOWN HERE! I THOUGHT I HEARD A NOISE!
THE OLD WITCH
THE VAULT-KEEPER
THE CRYPT-KEEPER

THE VAULT OF HORROR
HORROR
10¢
FEATURING...
OH, RALPH... RALPH! I MISS YOU SO! WHY DID YOU HAVE TO DIE? IF ONLY YOU COULD COME BACK TO ME!
THE VAULT-KEEPER
THE CRYPT-KEEPER
THE OLD WITCH

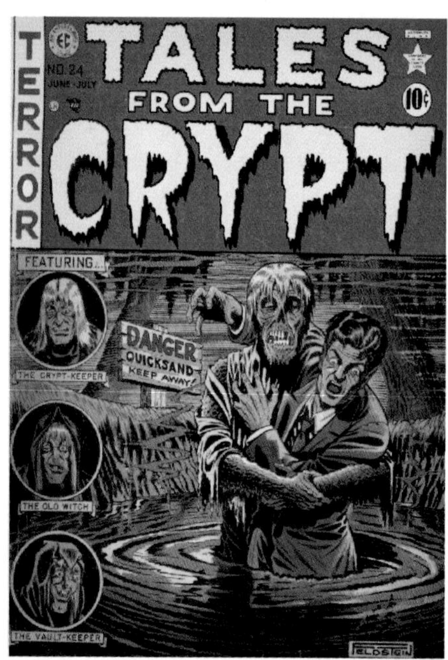
TALES FROM THE CRYPT
TERROR
NO. 24
JUNE-JULY
10¢
FEATURING...
DANGER
QUICKSAND
KEEP AWAY!
THE CRYPT-KEEPER
THE OLD WITCH
THE VAULT-KEEPER

HERE ARE TALES THAT WILL USHER YOU INTO
THE HAUNT OF FEAR
FEAR
NO. 6
10¢
FEATURING...
THE OLD WITCH
THE VAULT-KEEPER
THE CRYPT-KEEPER

THE VAULT OF HORROR
HORROR
NO. 20
10¢
FEATURING...
THAT'S IT! THAT'S IT! DRIVE THE STAKE THROUGH HIS VAMPIRE HEART!
THE VAULT-KEEPER
THE CRYPT-KEEPER
THE OLD WITCH

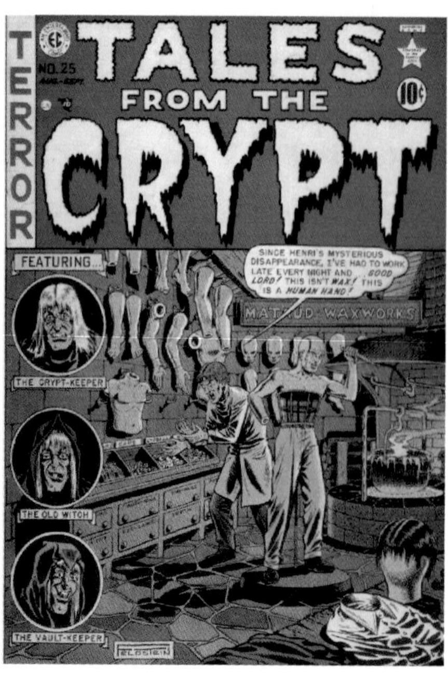
TALES FROM THE CRYPT
TERROR
NO. 25
10¢
FEATURING...
SINCE HENRI'S MYSTERIOUS DISAPPEARANCE, I'VE HAD TO WORK LATE EVERY NIGHT AND... GOOD LORD! THIS ISN'T WAX! THIS IS A HUMAN HAND!
WAXWORKS
THE CRYPT-KEEPER
THE OLD WITCH
THE VAULT-KEEPER

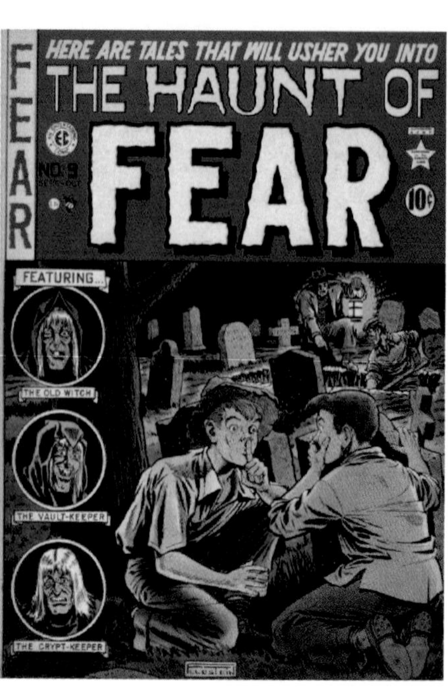
HERE ARE TALES THAT WILL USHER YOU INTO
THE HAUNT OF FEAR
FEAR
NO. 9
10¢
FEATURING...
THE OLD WITCH
THE VAULT-KEEPER
THE CRYPT-KEEPER

HORROR
THE VAULT OF HORROR
NO. 21
10¢
FEATURING...
ALLIGATOR PIT
HEH, HEH! BY NOW, MY PETS SHOULD HAVE ELIMINATED ALL TRACES OF THE BODY I FED THEM! I WONDER WHO THEIR NEXT VICTIM WILL BE!
THE VAULT-KEEPER
THE CRYPT-KEEPER
THE OLD WITCH

TERROR
TALES FROM THE CRYPT
NO. 26
10¢
FEATURING...
QUICKLY! LIFT OUT HIS COFFIN! HE DOESN'T BELONG IN OUR SACRED GRAVEYARD! HE DESECRATES THE VERY GROUND IN WHICH HE'S BURIED!
THE CRYPT-KEEPER
THE OLD WITCH
THE VAULT-KEEPER

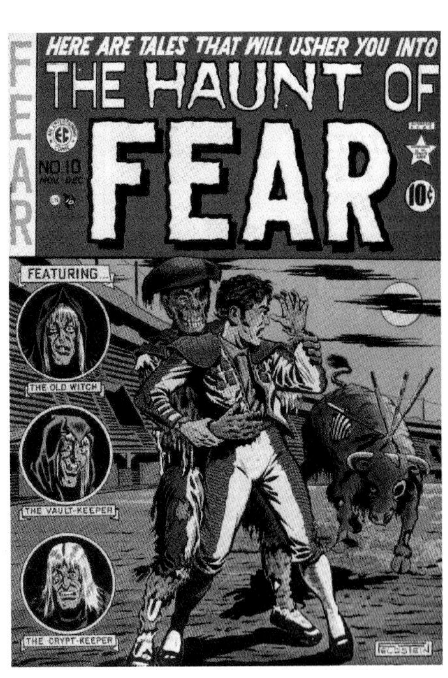
HERE ARE TALES THAT WILL USHER YOU INTO
THE HAUNT OF FEAR
FEAR
NO. 10
NOV.-DEC.
10¢
FEATURING...
THE OLD WITCH
THE VAULT-KEEPER
THE CRYPT-KEEPER

HORROR
THE VAULT OF HORROR
NO. 22
DEC.-JAN.
10¢
FEATURING...
THE VAULT-KEEPER
THE CRYPT-KEEPER
THE OLD WITCH
IN THIS ISSUE, THE OLD WITCH REVEALS THE STARTLING REDISCOVERY OF THE AUTHENTIC FRANKENSTEIN MONSTER!

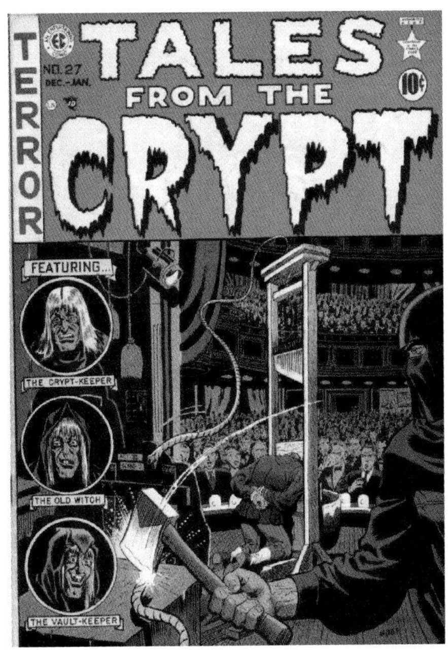
TERROR
TALES FROM THE CRYPT
NO. 27
DEC.-JAN.
10¢
FEATURING...
THE CRYPT-KEEPER
THE OLD WITCH
THE VAULT-KEEPER

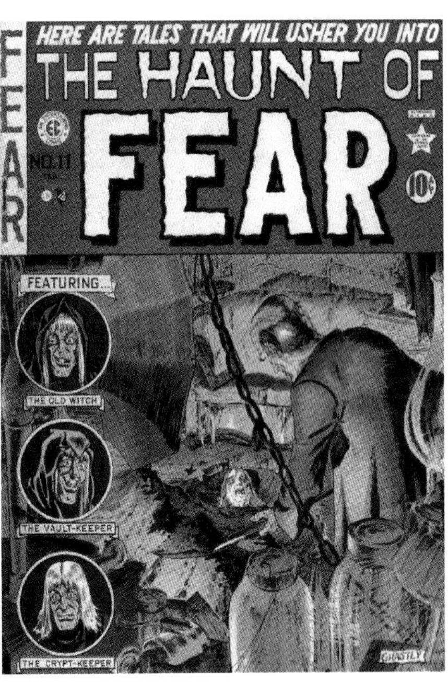
HERE ARE TALES THAT WILL USHER YOU INTO
THE HAUNT OF FEAR
FEAR
NO. 11
10¢
FEATURING...
THE OLD WITCH
THE VAULT-KEEPER
THE CRYPT-KEEPER
GHASTLY

HORROR
THE VAULT OF HORROR
NO. 23
FEB.-MAR.
10¢
FEATURING...
THE VAULT-KEEPER
THE OLD WITCH
THE CRYPT-KEEPER

TERROR
TALES FROM THE CRYPT
NO. 28
FEB.-MAR.
10¢
FEATURING...
THE CRYPT-KEEPER
THE OLD WITCH
THE VAULT-KEEPER

IMPACT
SHOCK SUSPENSTORIES
NO. 1
FEB.-MAR.
10¢
JOLTING TALES OF TENSION IN THE EC TRADITION!

1952

FEAR
HERE ARE TALES THAT WILL USHER YOU INTO
THE HAUNT OF
FEAR
NO. 12
APR.
10¢
FEATURING
THE OLD WITCH
THE VAULT-KEEPER
THE CRYPT-KEEPER

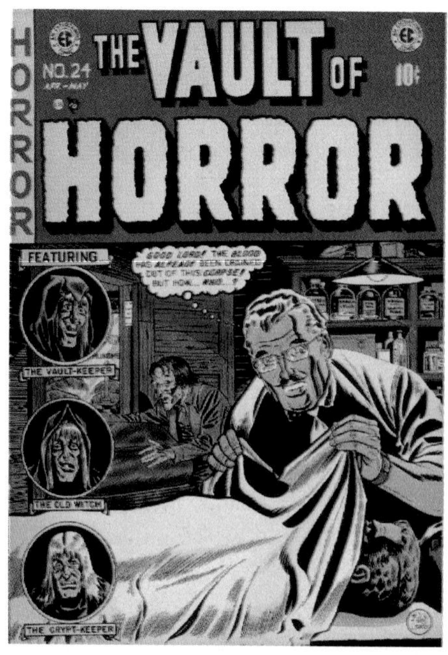
HORROR
NO. 24
APR.-MAY
THE VAULT OF
10¢
HORROR
FEATURING
THE VAULT-KEEPER
THE OLD WITCH
THE CRYPT-KEEPER

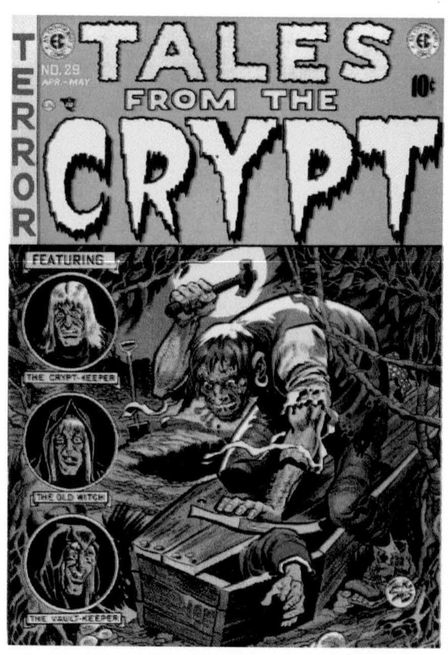
TERROR
TALES
NO. 29
APR.-MAY
10¢
FROM THE
CRYPT
FEATURING
THE CRYPT-KEEPER
THE OLD WITCH
THE VAULT-KEEPER

IMPACT
NO. 2
APR.-MAY
SHOCK
10¢
SUSPENSTORIES
JOLTING TALES OF
TENSION
IN THE
EC TRADITION!

FEAR
HERE ARE TALES THAT WILL USHER YOU INTO
THE HAUNT OF
FEAR
NO. 13
JUNE
10¢
FEATURING
THE OLD WITCH
THE VAULT-KEEPER
THE CRYPT-KEEPER

HORROR
NO. 25
JUNE-JULY
THE VAULT OF
10¢
HORROR
FEATURING
THE VAULT-KEEPER
THE OLD WITCH
THE CRYPT-KEEPER

TERROR
TALES
NO. 30
JUNE-JULY
10¢
FROM THE
CRYPT
FEATURING
THE CRYPT-KEEPER
THE VAULT-KEEPER
THE OLD WITCH

IMPACT
NO. 3
JUNE-JULY
SHOCK
10¢
SUSPENSTORIES
JOLTING TALES OF
TENSION
IN THE
EC TRADITION!

FEAR
HERE ARE TALES THAT WILL USHER YOU INTO
THE HAUNT OF
FEAR
NO. 14
AUG.
10¢
FEATURING
THE OLD WITCH
THE VAULT-KEEPER
THE CRYPT-KEEPER

HORROR
THE VAULT OF HORROR
NO. 26
AUG.-SEPT.
10¢
FEATURING...
THE VAULT-KEEPER
THE OLD WITCH
THE CRYPT-KEEPER

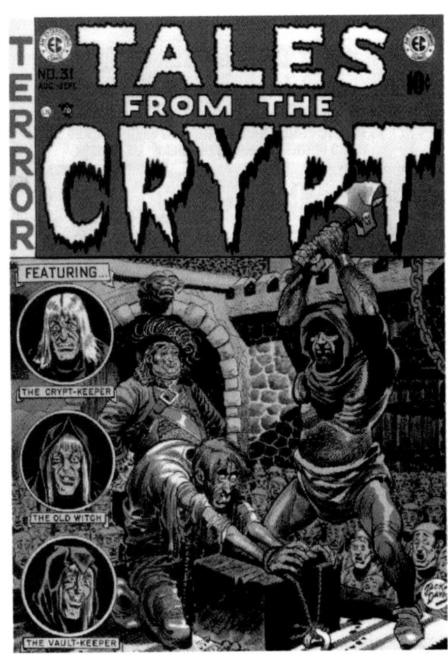
TERROR
TALES FROM THE CRYPT
NO. 31
AUG.-SEPT.
10¢
FEATURING...
THE CRYPT-KEEPER
THE OLD WITCH
THE VAULT-KEEPER

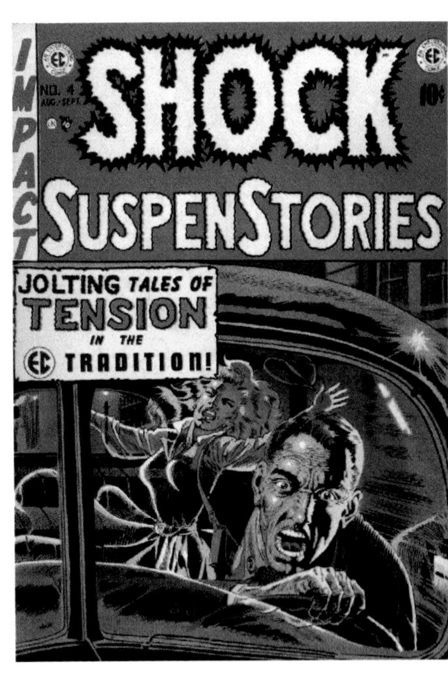
IMPACT
SHOCK SUSPENSTORIES
NO. 4
AUG.-SEPT.
10¢
JOLTING TALES OF TENSION IN THE EC TRADITION!

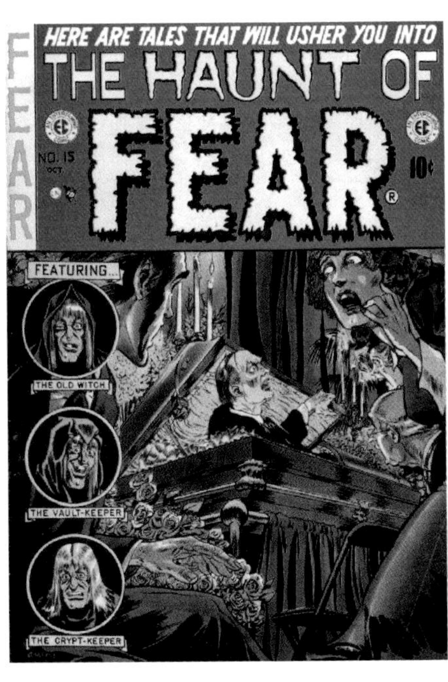
HERE ARE TALES THAT WILL USHER YOU INTO
THE HAUNT OF FEAR
FEAR
NO. 15
OCT.
10¢
FEATURING...
THE OLD WITCH
THE VAULT-KEEPER
THE CRYPT-KEEPER

HORROR
THE VAULT OF HORROR
NO. 27
OCT.-NOV.
10¢
FEATURING...
THE VAULT-KEEPER
THE OLD WITCH
THE CRYPT-KEEPER

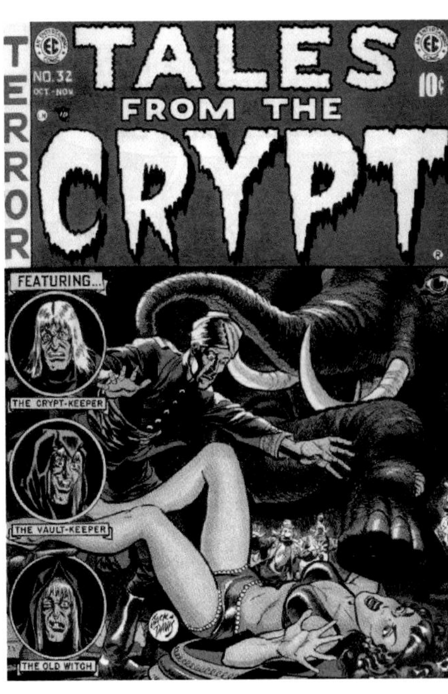
TERROR
TALES FROM THE CRYPT
NO. 32
OCT.-NOV.
10¢
FEATURING...
THE CRYPT-KEEPER
THE VAULT-KEEPER
THE OLD WITCH

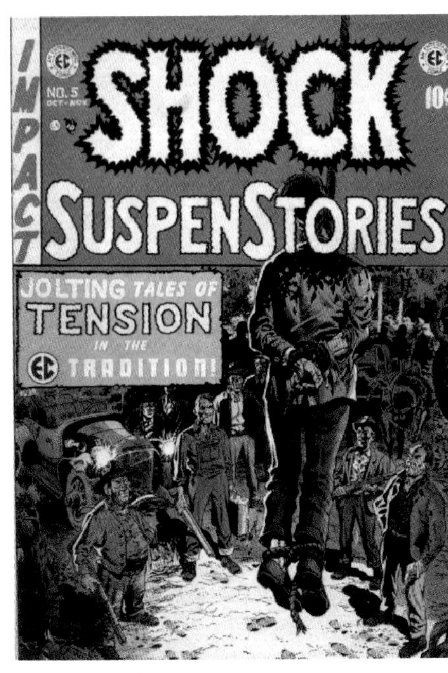
IMPACT
SHOCK SUSPENSTORIES
NO. 5
OCT.-NOV.
10¢
JOLTING TALES OF TENSION IN THE EC TRADITION!

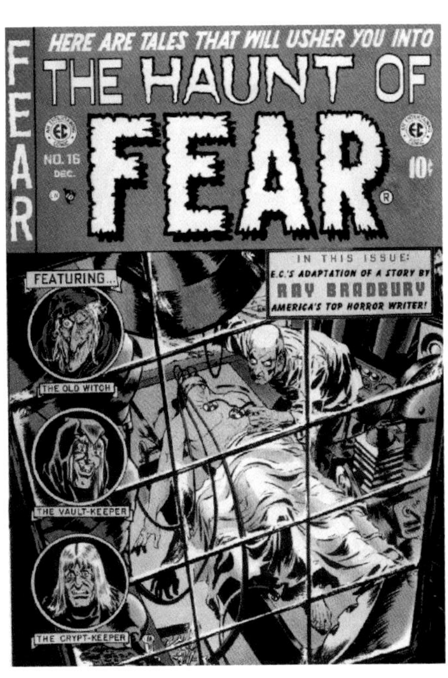
HERE ARE TALES THAT WILL USHER YOU INTO
THE HAUNT OF FEAR
FEAR
NO. 16
DEC.
10¢
IN THIS ISSUE!
E.C.'S ADAPTATION OF A STORY BY
RAY BRADBURY
AMERICA'S TOP HORROR WRITER!
FEATURING...
THE OLD WITCH
THE VAULT-KEEPER
THE CRYPT-KEEPER

HORROR
THE VAULT OF HORROR
NO. 28
DEC.-JAN.
10¢
FEATURING...
THE VAULT-KEEPER
THE OLD WITCH
THE CRYPT-KEEPER

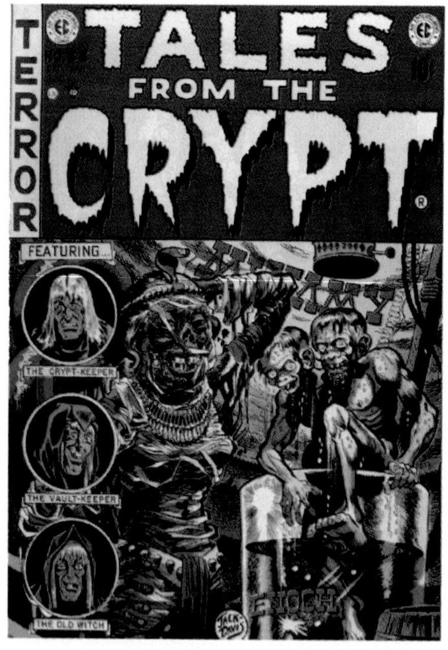
TERROR
TALES FROM THE CRYPT
FEATURING...
THE CRYPT-KEEPER
THE VAULT-KEEPER
THE OLD WITCH

IMPACT
SHOCK SUSPENSTORIES
JOLTING TALES OF TENSION IN THE EC TRADITION!

FEAR
HERE ARE TALES THAT WILL USHER YOU INTO
THE HAUNT OF FEAR
NO. 17 FEB.
10¢
FEATURING...
THE OLD WITCH
THE VAULT-KEEPER
THE CRYPT-KEEPER

HORROR
THE VAULT OF HORROR
FEATURING...
THE VAULT-KEEPER
THE OLD WITCH
THE CRYPT-KEEPER
IN THIS ISSUE:
E.C.'S ADAPTATION OF A STORY BY
RAY BRADBURY
AMERICA'S TOP HORROR WRITER!

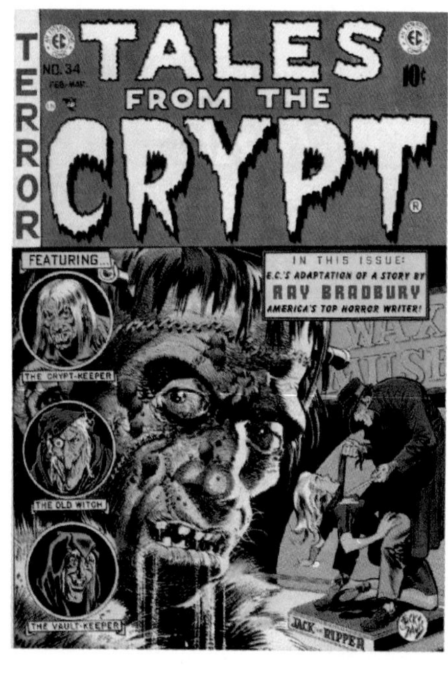
TERROR
TALES FROM THE CRYPT
NO. 34
10¢
FEATURING...
IN THIS ISSUE:
E.C.'S ADAPTATION OF A STORY BY
RAY BRADBURY
AMERICA'S TOP HORROR WRITER!
THE CRYPT-KEEPER
THE OLD WITCH
THE VAULT-KEEPER
JACK THE RIPPER

IMPACT
NO. 7 FEB.-MAR.
SHOCK
10¢
SUSPENSTORIES
JOLTING TALES OF TENSION IN THE EC TRADITION!
IN THIS ISSUE:
E.C.'S ADAPTATION OF A STORY BY
RAY BRADBURY
AMERICA'S TOP HORROR WRITER!

1953

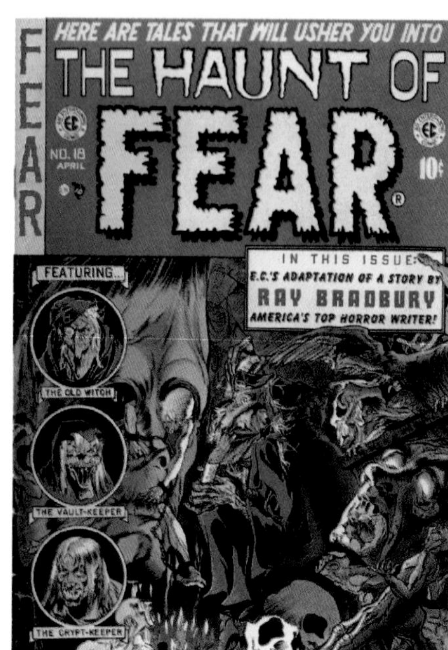
FEAR
HERE ARE TALES THAT WILL USHER YOU INTO
THE HAUNT OF FEAR
NO. 18 APRIL
10¢
FEATURING...
IN THIS ISSUE:
E.C.'S ADAPTATION OF A STORY BY
RAY BRADBURY
AMERICA'S TOP HORROR WRITER!
THE OLD WITCH
THE VAULT-KEEPER
THE CRYPT-KEEPER

HORROR
NO. 30 APR.-MAY
THE VAULT OF HORROR
10¢
FEATURING...
THE VAULT-KEEPER
THE CRYPT-KEEPER
THE OLD WITCH
STOMACH UPSET?

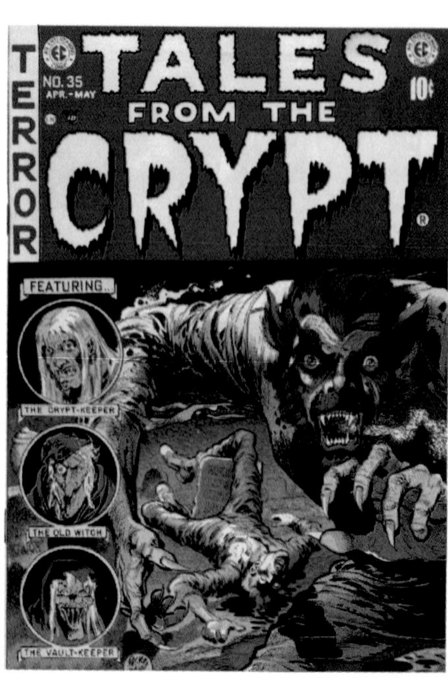
TERROR
NO. 35 APR.-MAY
TALES FROM THE CRYPT
10¢
FEATURING...
THE CRYPT-KEEPER
THE OLD WITCH
THE VAULT-KEEPER

IMPACT
SHOCK
NO. 8 APR.-MAY
10¢
SUSPENSTORIES
JOLTING TALES OF TENSION IN THE EC TRADITION!

HERE ARE TALES THAT WILL USHER YOU INTO
THE HAUNT OF
FEAR
NO. 19 JUNE
10¢
FEAR
FEATURING...
THE OLD WITCH
THE VAULT-KEEPER
THE CRYPT-KEEPER

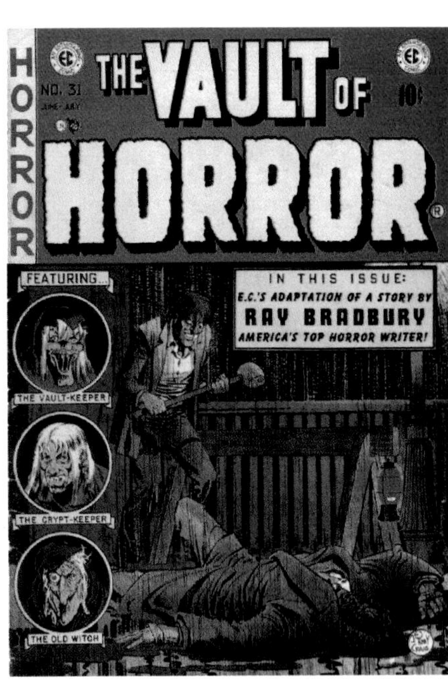
HORROR
THE VAULT OF
HORROR
NO. 31 JUNE-JULY
10¢
FEATURING...
IN THIS ISSUE:
E.C.'S ADAPTATION OF A STORY BY
RAY BRADBURY
AMERICA'S TOP HORROR WRITER!
THE VAULT-KEEPER
THE CRYPT-KEEPER
THE OLD WITCH

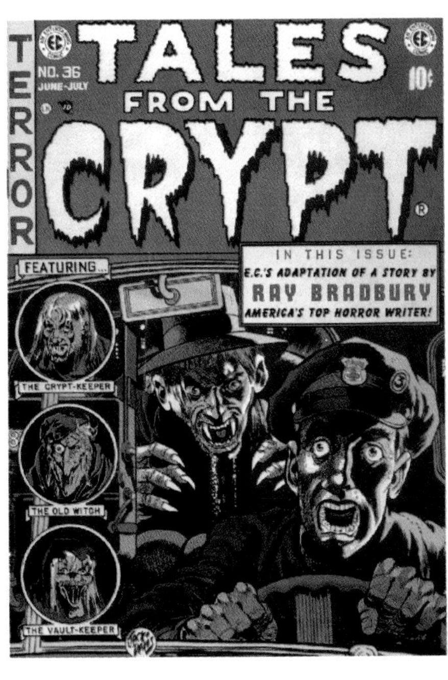
TERROR
TALES FROM THE CRYPT
NO. 36 JUNE-JULY
10¢
IN THIS ISSUE:
E.C.'S ADAPTATION OF A STORY BY
RAY BRADBURY
AMERICA'S TOP HORROR WRITER!
FEATURING...
THE CRYPT-KEEPER
THE OLD WITCH
THE VAULT-KEEPER

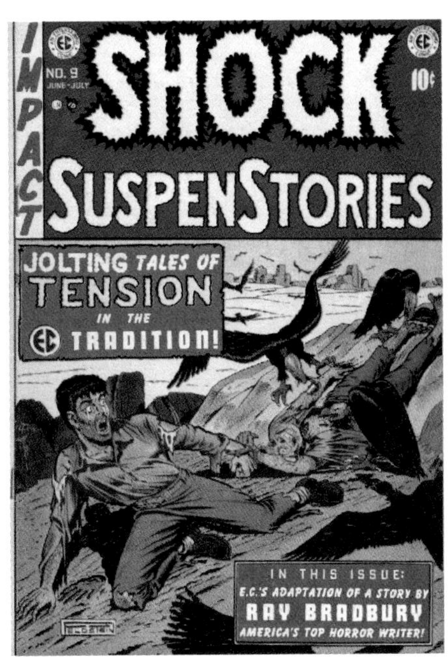
IMPACT
SHOCK
NO. 9 JUNE-JULY
10¢
SUSPENSTORIES
JOLTING TALES OF TENSION IN THE EC TRADITION!
IN THIS ISSUE:
E.C.'S ADAPTATION OF A STORY BY
RAY BRADBURY
AMERICA'S TOP HORROR WRITER!

HERE ARE TALES THAT WILL USHER YOU INTO
THE HAUNT OF
FEAR
NO. 20 AUGUST
10¢
FEAR
FEATURING...
THE OLD WITCH
THE VAULT-KEEPER
THE CRYPT-KEEPER

HORROR
THE VAULT OF
HORROR
NO. 32
10¢
FEATURING...
THE VAULT-KEEPER
THE OLD WITCH
THE CRYPT-KEEPER

TERROR
TALES FROM THE CRYPT
NO. 37 AUG.-SEPT.
10¢
FEATURING...
THE CRYPT-KEEPER
THE OLD WITCH
THE VAULT-KEEPER

IMPACT
SHOCK
NO. 10 AUG-SEPT
10¢
SUSPENSTORIES
JOLTING TALES OF TENSION IN THE EC TRADITION!

HERE ARE TALES THAT WILL USHER YOU INTO
THE HAUNT OF
FEAR
FEAR
10¢
FEATURING...
THE OLD WITCH
THE VAULT-KEEPER
THE CRYPT-KEEPER

HORROR
THE VAULT OF
HORROR
10¢
NO. 33
FEATURING...
THE VAULT-KEEPER
THE CRYPT-KEEPER
THE OLD WITCH

TERROR
TALES
FROM THE
CRYPT
10¢
NO. 38
FEATURING...
THE CRYPT-KEEPER
THE OLD WITCH
THE VAULT-KEEPER

IMPACT
SHOCK
SUSPENSTORIES
10¢
NO. 11
JOLTING TALES OF
TENSION
IN THE
EC TRADITION!
NOAH'S

HERE ARE TALES THAT WILL USHER YOU INTO
THE HAUNT OF
FEAR
FEAR
10¢
NO. 22
DECEMBER
FEATURING...
THE OLD WITCH
THE VAULT-KEEPER
THE CRYPT-KEEPER

HORROR
THE VAULT OF
HORROR
10¢
NO. 34
DEC.-JAN.
FEATURING...
THE VAULT-KEEPER
THE CRYPT-KEEPER
THE OLD WITCH

TERROR
TALES
FROM THE
CRYPT
10¢
NO. 39
DEC.-JAN.
FEATURING...
THE CRYPT-KEEPER
THE OLD WITCH
THE VAULT-KEEPER

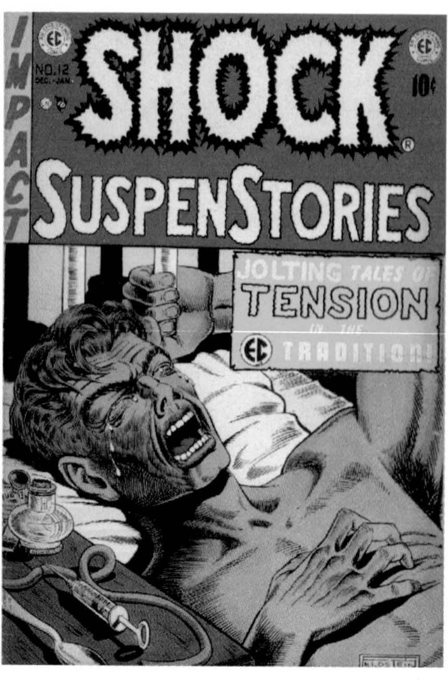
IMPACT
SHOCK
SUSPENSTORIES
10¢
NO. 12
DEC.-JAN.
JOLTING TALES OF
TENSION
IN THE
EC TRADITION!

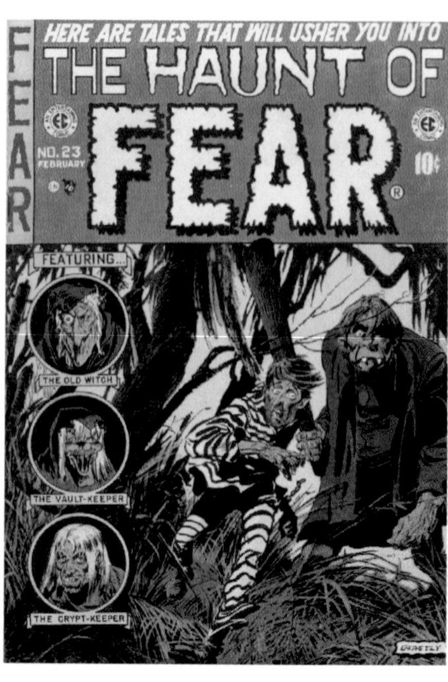
HERE ARE TALES THAT WILL USHER YOU INTO
THE HAUNT OF
FEAR
FEAR
10¢
NO. 23
FEBRUARY
FEATURING...
THE OLD WITCH
THE VAULT-KEEPER
THE CRYPT-KEEPER

HORROR
THE VAULT OF
NO. 35
MARCH
10¢
HORROR
FEATURING...
THE VAULT-KEEPER
THE CRYPT-KEEPER
THE OLD WITCH

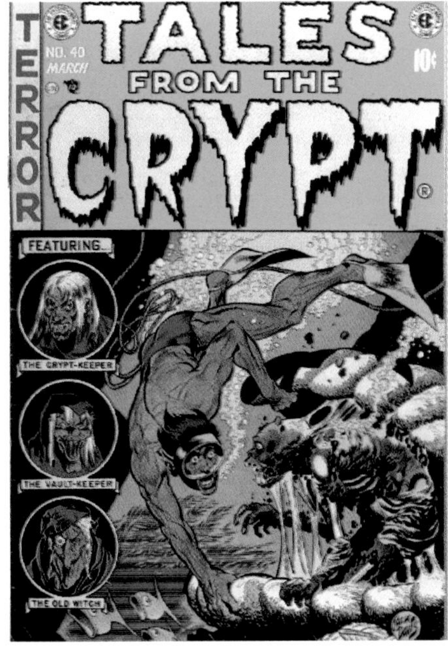
TERROR
TALES FROM THE
NO. 40
MARCH
10¢
CRYPT
FEATURING...
THE CRYPT-KEEPER
THE VAULT-KEEPER
THE OLD WITCH

IMPACT
SHOCK
NO. 13
MAR.
10¢
SUSPENSTORIES
JOLTING TALES OF
TENSION
IN THE
EC TRADITION!

1954

HORROR
THE VAULT OF
NO. 36
MAY
10¢
HORROR
FEATURING...
THE VAULT-KEEPER
THE CRYPT-KEEPER
THE OLD WITCH

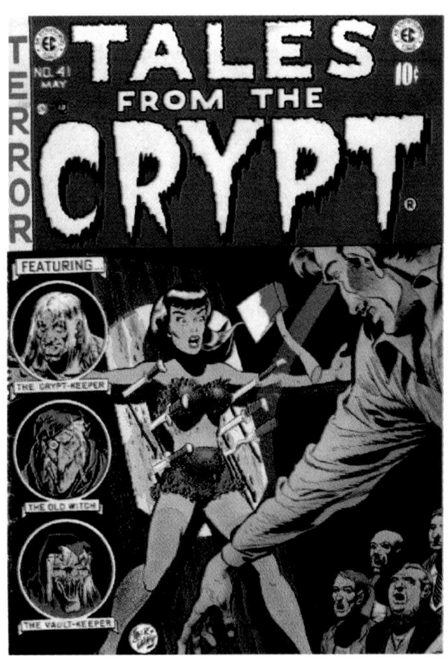
TERROR
TALES FROM THE
NO. 41
MAY
10¢
CRYPT
FEATURING...
THE CRYPT-KEEPER
THE OLD WITCH
THE VAULT-KEEPER

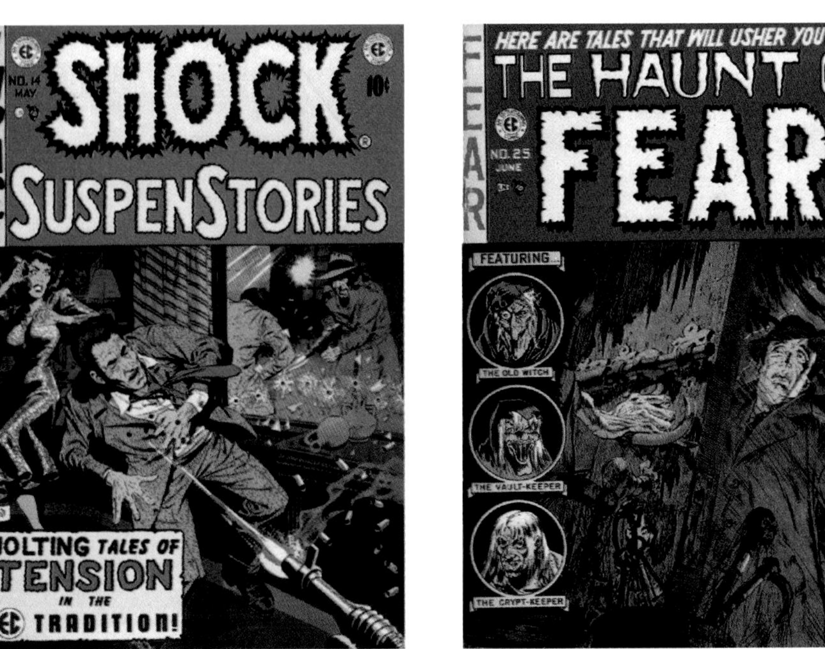
IMPACT
SHOCK
NO. 14
MAY
10¢
SUSPENSTORIES
JOLTING TALES OF
TENSION
IN THE
EC TRADITION!

FEAR
HERE ARE TALES THAT WILL USHER YOU INTO
THE HAUNT OF
NO. 25
JUNE
FEAR
10¢
FEATURING...
THE OLD WITCH
THE VAULT-KEEPER
THE CRYPT-KEEPER

HORROR
THE VAULT OF
NO. 37
JULY
10¢
HORROR
FEATURING...
THE VAULT-KEEPER
THE CRYPT-KEEPER
THE OLD WITCH

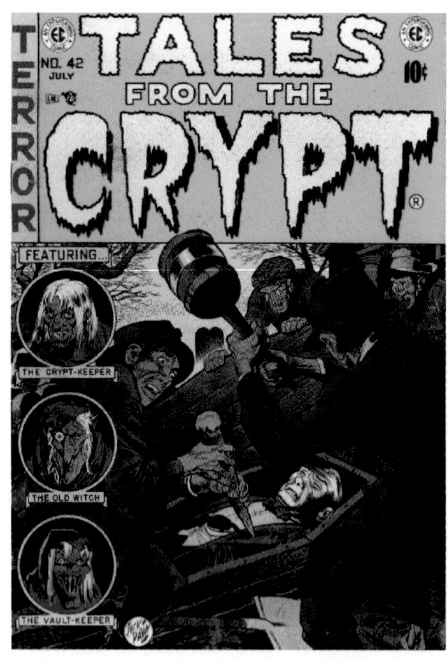
TERROR
TALES FROM THE CRYPT
NO. 42 JULY
10¢
FEATURING...
THE CRYPT-KEEPER
THE OLD WITCH
THE VAULT-KEEPER

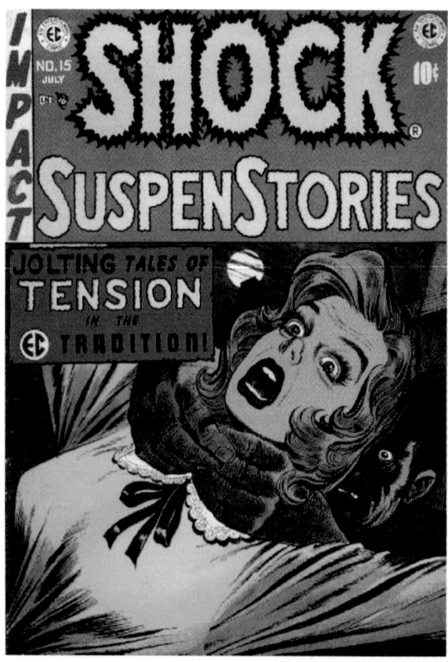
IMPACT
SHOCK SUSPENSTORIES
NO. 15 JULY
10¢
JOLTING TALES OF TENSION IN THE EC TRADITION!

FEAR
HERE ARE TALES THAT WILL USHER YOU INTO
THE HAUNT OF FEAR
NO. 26 AUGUST
10¢
FEATURING...
THE OLD WITCH
THE VAULT-KEEPER
THE CRYPT-KEEPER

HORROR
THE VAULT OF HORROR
10¢
FEATURING...
THE VAULT-KEEPER
THE CRYPT-KEEPER
THE OLD WITCH

TERROR
TALES FROM THE CRYPT
NO. 43 SEPTEMBER
10¢
FEATURING...
THE CRYPT-KEEPER
THE OLD WITCH
THE VAULT-KEEPER

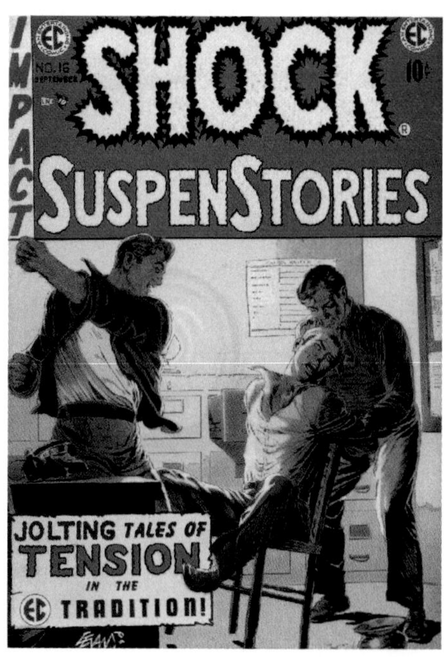
IMPACT
SHOCK SUSPENSTORIES
NO. 16 SEPTEMBER
10¢
JOLTING TALES OF TENSION IN THE EC TRADITION!

FEAR
HERE ARE TALES THAT WILL USHER YOU INTO
THE HAUNT OF FEAR
NO. 27
10¢
FEATURING...
THE OLD WITCH
THE VAULT-KEEPER
THE CRYPT-KEEPER

HORROR
THE VAULT OF HORROR
NO. 39 NOV.
10¢
FEATURING...
THE VAULT-KEEPER
THE CRYPT-KEEPER
THE OLD WITCH

TERROR
TALES FROM THE CRYPT
NO. 44 NOV.
10¢
FEATURING...
THE CRYPT-KEEPER
THE OLD WITCH
THE VAULT-KEEPER

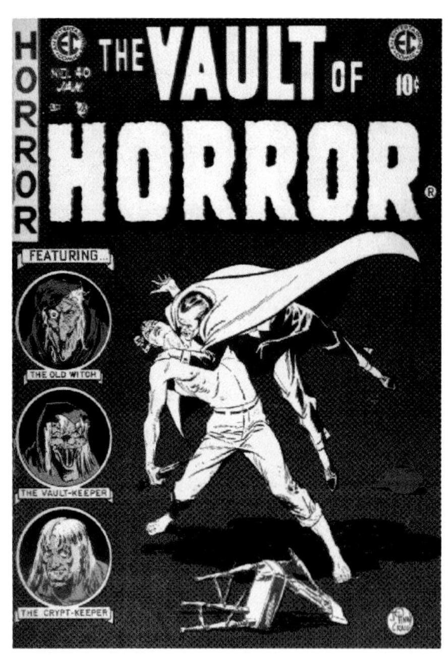

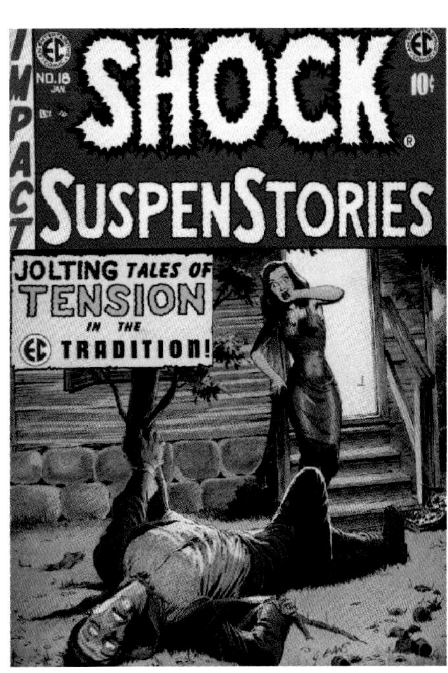

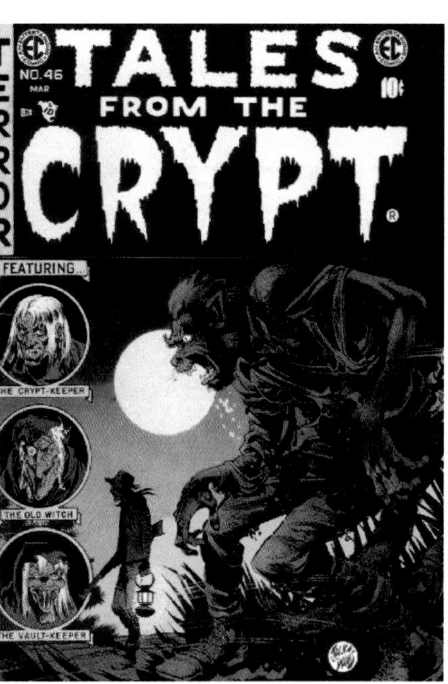

EC published three volumes of collected favorites entitled *Tales of Terror*.

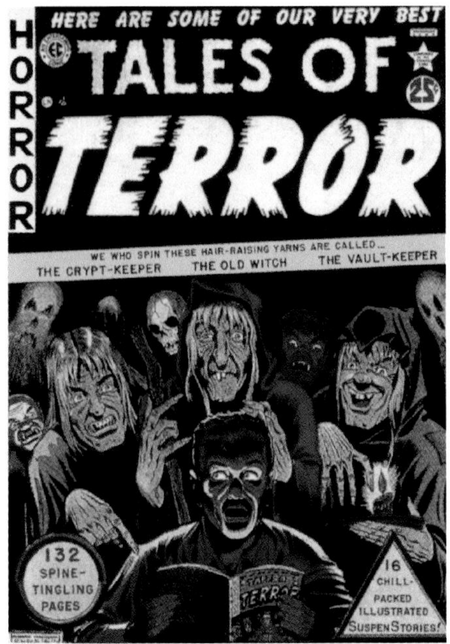

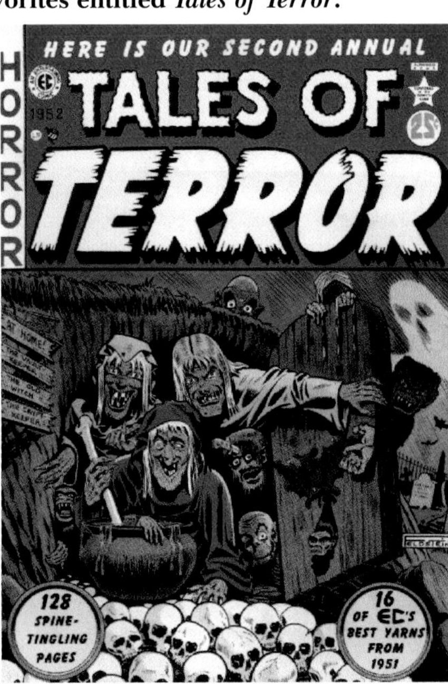

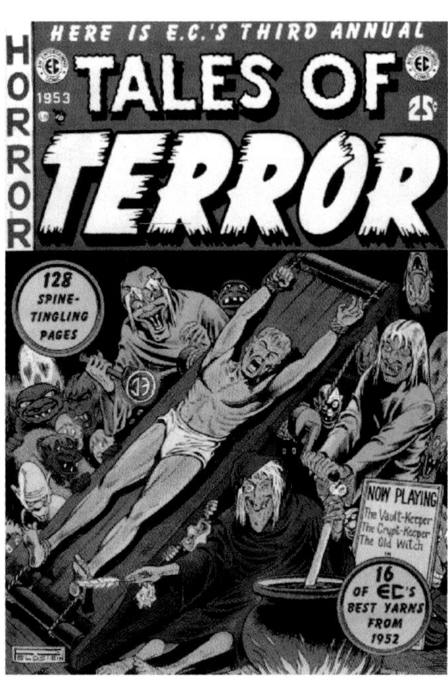

FOUR FOUL TALES

Whether it is for their artwork or their storyline, many stories in EC's *New Trend* are considered "classics." The four included in this section all display a strong story mixed with dynamic illustration, plus a little something extra that enhances their historic interest.

"Lower Berth," the tongue-in-cheek tale of the origin of the Crypt Keeper, is an excellent example of the synergy between Feldstein's stories and Jack Davis' masterful illustration (*Tales from the Crypt* #33). The story culminates in the birth of the infant Crypt Keeper.

When the crush of his editorial and writing duties started to overwhelm him, Al Feldstein reluctantly retired from illustrating stories. "The Thing from the Grave" (*Tales from the Crypt* #22), is an early Feldstein story from the sixth issue of *Tales* (and the first to use all three GhouLunatics on the cover). It reveals his exemplary use of stark contrast between light and shadow, and highlights his ability to render a moment of horror frozen in time.

"Horror We? How's Bayou?", illustrated by "Ghastly" Graham Ingels, is the quintessential "dripping" story (*Haunt of Fear* #17), and a long-time favorite of EC Fan-Addicts. (Attendees at the 1972 Convention voted it best horror artwork in an individual story.) The title confuses many, especially those who are unaware that it spoofs "How's by you?", a vintage New York salutation.

In "The October Game," Jack Kamen illustrated one of Feldstein's finest adaptations of a Ray Bradbury story (*Shock SuspenStories* #9). Kamen captured the mood flawlessly, with its innocent spooky Halloween patina overlaid on a deadly tale of marital discord and retribution. "The October Game" also accentuates Kamen's prowess at portraying horror without gore or bloodshed, a powerful skill that became his trademark.

TERROR

AN ENTERTAINING COMIC

NO. 33 DEC.-JAN.

TALES FROM THE CRYPT ®

10¢

ARE YOU A RED DUPE?

- HERE IN AMERICA, WE CAN **STILL** PUBLISH COMIC MAGAZINES, NEWSPAPERS, SLICKS, BOOKS AND THE BIBLE. WE DON'T **HAVE** TO SEND THEM TO A CENSOR FIRST. NOT **YET...**
- BUT THERE ARE SOME PEOPLE IN AMERICA WHO WOULD **LIKE** TO CENSOR... WHO WOULD **LIKE** TO SUPPRESS COMICS. IT ISN'T THAT THEY DON'T LIKE COMICS FOR **THEM!** THEY DON'T LIKE THEM FOR **YOU!**
- THESE PEOPLE SAY THAT **COMIC BOOKS** AREN'T AS GOOD FOR CHILDREN AS **NO** COMIC BOOKS, OR SOMETHING LIKE THAT. SOME OF THESE PEOPLE ARE NO-GOODS. SOME ARE DO-GOODERS. SOME ARE WELL-MEANING. AND SOME ARE JUST PLAIN MEAN.
- BUT WE ARE CONCERNED WITH AN AMAZING REVELATION. AFTER MUCH SEARCHING OF NEWSPAPER FILES, WE'VE MADE AN ASTOUNDING DISCOVERY:

THE GROUP MOST ANXIOUS TO DESTROY COMICS ARE THE COMMUNISTS!

- WE'RE SERIOUS! NO KIDDIN'! **HERE! READ THIS:**

THE [COMMUNIST] "DAILY WORKER" *OF JULY 13, 1953 BITTERLY ATTACKED THE ROLE OF:*

"...SO-CALLED 'COMICS' IN BRUTALIZING AMERICAN YOUTH, THE BETTER TO PREPARE THEM FOR MILITARY SERVICE IN IMPLEMENTING OUR GOVERNMENT'S AIMS OF WORLD DOMINATION, AND TO ACCEPT THE ATROCITIES NOW BEING PERPETRATED BY AMERICAN SOLDIERS AND AIRMEN IN KOREA UNDER THE FLAG OF THE UNITED NATIONS."

THIS ARTICLE ALSO QUOTED **GERSHON LEGMAN** *(WHO CLAIMS TO BE A GHOST WRITER FOR* **DR. FREDERICK WERTHAM**, *THE AUTHOR OF A RECENT SMEAR AGAINST COMICS PUBLISHED IN* **"THE LADIES HOME JOURNAL"**). *THIS SAME* **G. LEGMAN**, *IN ISSUE #3 OF* **"NEUROTICA,"** *PUBLISHED IN AUTUMN 1948, WILDLY CONDEMNED COMICS, ALTHOUGH ADMITTING THAT:*

"THE CHILD'S NATURAL CHARACTER... MUST BE DISTORTED TO FIT CIVILIZATION... FANTASY VIOLENCE WILL PARALYZE HIS RESISTANCE, DIVERT HIS AGGRESSION TO UNREAL ENEMIES AND FRUSTRATIONS, AND IN THIS WAY PREVENT HIM FROM REBELLING AGAINST PARENTS AND TEACHERS... THIS WILL SIPHON OFF HIS RESISTANCE AGAINST SOCIETY, AND **PREVENT REVOLUTION.**"

- SO THE **NEXT** TIME SOME JOKER GETS UP AT A P.T.A. MEETING, OR STARTS JABBERING ABOUT THE "NAUGHTY COMIC BOOKS" AT YOUR LOCAL CANDY STORE, GIVE HIM THE **ONCE-OVER.** WE'RE NOT SAYING HE **IS** A COMMUNIST! HE MAY BE INNOCENT OF THE WHOLE THING! HE MAY BE A **DUPE!** HE MAY NOT EVEN **READ** THE "DAILY WORKER"! IT'S JUST THAT HE'S **SWALLOWED** THE **RED BAIT... HOOK, LINE,** AND **SINKER!**

HEH, HEH! GOT A *COLLECTORS' ITEM* FOR YOU FIENDS! GOT A *REAL GREAT CHILLER-DILLER! GIVE* THE MAN YOUR *GRIMY LITTLE DIME* IF YOU HAVEN'T *DONE SO ALREADY,* AND COME INTO *THE CRYPT OF TERROR!* THIS IS THE *CRYPT-KEEPER,* READY WITH ANOTHER OF MY *TALES OF HORROR!* SO SIT DOWN ON THE *TANBARK FLOOR,* AND I'LL BEGIN THE *BLOOD-CURDLING YARN* I CALL...

LONG BEFORE THE ADVENT OF RADIO, MOVIES, TELEVISION AND COMIC BOOKS, THE ONLY ENTERTAINMENT FOLKS THROUGHOUT THE COUNTRY ENJOYED WERE THE TRAVELING CARNIVALS, WHICH SET UP THEIR GAILY COLORED TENTS ON VACANT TRACTS OF LAND AT THE OUTSKIRTS OF THEIR TOWNS! ABOUT 80 YEARS AGO, ONE OF THESE CARNIVALS CAME TO A SMALL TOWN IN THE OZARK MOUNTAINS...

THE SIDE SHOW OF THIS PARTICULAR CARNIVAL WAS OWNED BY A MAN NAMED ERNEST FEELEY! PATIENTLY, OVER THE YEARS, HE HAD ASSEMBLED A FABULOUS COLLECTION OF ODDITIES AND FREAKS! HE HAD THE USUAL ATTRACTIONS...
SEE FANNY, THE FAT LADY, FOLKS! FOUR HUNDRED AND FIFTY POUNDS OF FEMALE PULCHRITUDE! SEE HADNAR, THE SWORD-SWALLOWER... SKULL-FACE, THE LIVING SKELETON...FEGO, THE FIRE-EATER...
FANNY

BUT ERNEST FEELEY HAD ONE ATTRACTION... A HEADLINE ATTRACTION... THAT NEVER FAILED TO DRAW THE CROWDS... TO SEPARATE THE CURIOUS FROM THEIR QUARTERS...
AND LAST BUT NOT LEAST, FOLKS... THE STAR ATTRACTION OF FEELEY'S SIDE-SHOW... THE MOST UNUSUAL ODDITY EVER TO BE PUT ON DISPLAY ANYWHERE... ANYTIME! INSIDE... IN ITS ORIGINAL SARCOPHAGUS... IS MYRNA, THE ONLY FEMALE EGYPTIAN MUMMY IN EXISTENCE! TWENTY-FIVE CENTS, FOLKS! RIGHT THIS WAY...
25¢

MYRNA, THE EGYPTIAN MUMMY, WAS OWNED BY ZACHARY CLING, A RETIRED ARCHEOLOGIST! ERNEST FEELEY PAID ZACHARY CLING A VERY LARGE SALARY FOR THE PRIVILEGE OF EXHIBITING MYRNA...
... AND NOW, FOLKS... IF YOU WILL STEP THIS WAY... DOCTOR CLING, WHO FOUND MYRNA THE EGYPTIAN MUMMY, WILL TELL YOU ALL ABOUT HER AND SHOW HER TO YOU...

FIVE TIMES A DAY, ZACHARY CLING WOULD NARRATE HOW HE DISCOVERED MYRNA, AND THEN SHOW HER TO THE GAPING CUSTOMERS! HE'D EVEN UNDO PART OF HER WRAPPINGS...
MYRNA, THE ONLY FEMALE EGYPTIAN MUMMY IN AMERICA WAS FOUND IN THE VALLEY OF THE KINGS BY MY EXPEDITION! HER TOMB WAS DEEP IN THE CLIFFS THAT TOWER OVER THE NILE RIVER...

'ON THE TOMB WALLS, WE FOUND THE INSCRIPTIONS DESCRIBING HER INCARCERATION! IT SEEMS THAT MYRNA, OR MYRANAH, AS THE EGYPTIANS CALLED HER, WAS A LADY-IN-WAITING TO THE PHARAOH'S WIFE...'
BRING ME MY PERFUME, MYRANAH!
YES, MISTRESS!

'MYRANAH WAS VERY BEAUTIFUL, AND SOON CAUGHT THE PHARAOH'S FANCY! BUT LOYAL MYRANAH, FAITHFUL TO HER MISTRESS, REPELLED THE PHARAOH'S ADVANCES...'
DO NOT STRUGGLE, MY PET! I AM YOUR KING! YOU MUST DO AS I WISH!
NO! NO! I WILL NOT! NEVER! NEVER!

'THE PHARAOH, IN ANGER, ORDERED THAT SHE BE BURIED ALIVE AS PUNISHMENT! MYRANAH WAS FORCIBLY WRAPPED IN THE CEREMONIAL BURIAL WINDINGS...'
SHE FIGHTS LIKE A CAT, SIRE!
SHE WILL FIGHT NO MORE! HURRY!
EEEMMMMPH!
2

... AND SO, FOR FOUR THOUSAND YEARS, THIS POOR GIRL LAY IN HER TOMB UNTIL I UNCOVERED HER! AND NOW... I GIVE YOU...

MYRNA!
GASP!
CHOKE!

THE MUMMIFIED BODY OF THE UNFORTUNATE SERVANT GIRL STOOD IN ITS SARCOPHAGUS, ITS ARMS FOLDED ACROSS ITS CHEST! THE CARNIVAL CUSTOMERS NEVER FAILED TO GASP AND SCREAM WHENEVER DOCTOR CLING WOULD UNCOVER IT...
AND NOW... I WILL REMOVE SOME OF THE WRAPPINGS!

IF THE SIGHT OF THE MUMMY WAS REVOLTING, HER UNWRAPPED FACE WAS EVEN MORE SO! THE WRINKLED DRIED FLESH CLUNG TO HER SKULL LIKE WET TISSUE PAPER! HER EYES HAD RECEDED DEEP INTO THEIR SOCKETS! LIPS WERE DRAWN TIGHTLY BACK IN A LEERING GRIN! SOME CRIED OUT...SOME TURNED AWAY...
GOOD LORD!

BUT THERE WERE ALWAYS MORE THE NEXT NIGHT! MORE OF THE CURIOUS! WORD TRAVELED FAST IN SMALL TOWNS! THEY FLOCKED TO SEE MYRNA... SHE WELL EARNED HER KEEP! ERNEST FEELEY PAID ZACHARY CLING HIS SALARY HAPPILY! AND THEN, WHEN THE CARNIVAL HIT THAT SMALL OZARK TOWN...
YOU MR. FEELEY? MY NAME'S JEB SICKLES! I UNNERSTAN' YOU OWN THIS HERE SIDE-SHOW, MR. FEELEY! I THINK MEBBE YOU MIGHT BE INTERESTED IN WHAT I GOT!
WHAT'S THAT, MR. SICKLES?

I'M THE DOC 'ROUND THESE PARTS, MR. FEELEY! AIN'T GOT NO LICENCE OR NUTHIN', BUT FOLKS LIKE WHAT I DO FOR 'EM SO THEY COME T'ME! 'BOUT TWO YEARS AGO, THIS HERE CRONE COME DOWN FROM THE MOUNTAINS! I'D NEVER LAID EYES ON 'ER B'FORE! SHE BEGGED ME T'COME BACK WITH HER...
LOOK, MR. SICKLES! I'M A BUSY MAN! GET TO THE POINT! WHAT IS IT YOU'VE GOT THAT I'D BE INTERESTED IN?

I'LL GET TO IT, MR. FEELEY! TAKE IT EASY! ANYWAY, THIS OLD CRONE BEGGED ME SO BAD I WENT! SHE TOL' ME HER SON WAS SICK... TERRIBLE SICK! SHE SAID HE WAS A-DYIN'! SHE TOOK ME UP INTO THE MOUNTAINS TO THIS HERE CAVE! I NEARLY THROW'D UP AT WHAT I SAW!
WHAT WAS IT, MR. SICKLES?
3

'IT WAR HER *SON*, MR. FEELEY! HER SON HAD *TWO HEADS!* IT WAS *HORRIBLE...*'
CHOKE!
KIN YUH... KIN YUH DO ANYTHING FOR ENOCH?

'HE WAS TOO FAR GONE FOR ME T'SAVE! HE DIED 'BOUT AN HOUR AFTER WE GOT T' THE CAVE...
I'M *SORRY*, MA'AM! I *DONE* ALL I *COULD! ENOCH* IS *DEAD!*
TAKE 'IM *AWAY!* TAKE 'IM...SOB... *OUT OF MY SIGHT!*

HE MUSTA BEEN *TWENNY-TWO*, MR. FEELEY! I TOOK HIS BODY BACK *DOWN* THE MOUNTAIN AND PUT IT IN A *MOONSHINE STILL!* I DIDN'T WAN' *NOBODY* T' *SEE* IT!
AND YOU STILL *HAVE* IT... THE TWO-HEADED BODY?

IT'S *BEEN* IN THE STILL FOR *TWO YEARS*, MR. FEELEY! THE *MOONSHINE* SEEMS T'HAVE *PRESERVED IT!* YOU...
TAKE ME TO IT! *QUICKLY!*

MR. FEELEY AND THE QUACK DOCTOR PUSHED THEIR WAY THROUGH THE CROWD OGLING AT MYRNA, THE MUMMY! OUTSIDE THE CARNIVAL GROUNDS, A HORSE AND WAGON WAITED! THEY DROVE TO A HIDDEN STILL...
THAR SHE *IS*, MR. FEELEY!
C'MON!

THE LIGHT FROM THE LANTERN CAST AN ORANGE GLOW INTO THE HUGE WOODEN STILL-VAT! BELOW THE SURFACE OF THE MOONSHINE, THE PULPY WHITE FACES OF THE TWO-HEADED CORPSE STARED UP AT ERNEST FEELEY...
THAT'S *HIM*...
GULP!

ERNEST TURNED TO JEB SICKLES...HIS EYES WIDE...HIS FACE FLUSHED...
HOW WOULD YOU LIKE TO JOIN MY *SHOW*, JEB? DO WHAT OLD *DOC CLING DOES! EXHIBIT* THIS HERE *ENOCH!* TELL HOW YOU *GOT* HIM! I'LL PAY YOU A *GOOD SALARY!*
JOIN UP WITH YOU FELLERS, EH? WAL, *I DUNNO!* I...I *GUESS* I'D LIKE *THAT!*

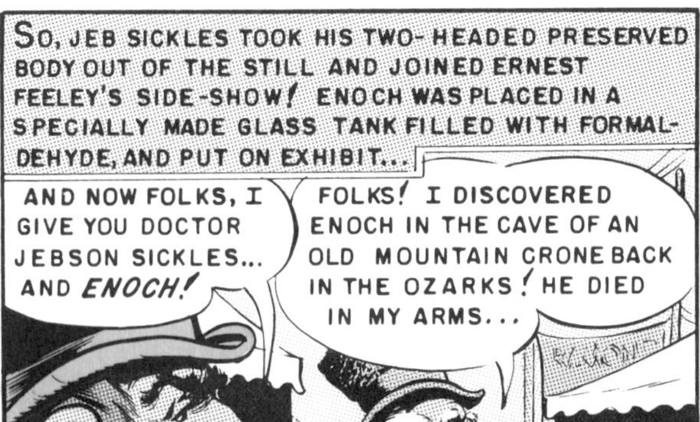

It didn't take long for Ernest Feeley to realize that the thing in the huge glass tank was a really valuable exhibit and deserved star billing, like Myrna...

That's right, Jeb! I'm movin' you up to *star attraction!* You'll *share* it with *Doc Cling,* here!

Thanks, Mr. Feeley!

Hmmph.

THE CARNIVAL MOVED ON FROM TOWN TO TOWN! THE CROWDS FLOCKED TO SEE ENOCH AND MYRNA! AND JEALOUSY BETWEEN ZACH CLING AND JEB SICKLES FLAMED...
WHAT DO YOU MEAN YOU'RE CUTTING MY SALARY? IF IT WASN'T FOR MYRNA...
ENOCH PULLS 'EM IN TOO, ZACH! I'VE BEEN UNDERPAYING JEB! HE AND YOU GET THE SAME FROM NOW ON! I'M LOWERIN' YOUR PAY, AND RAISIN' HIS!

THE BLOATED BODY WITH THE STARING PAIRS OF EYES SWAYED IN THE FORMALDEHYDE! THE DRIED REMAINS IN THE ROTTED WRAPPINGS STOOD SILENTLY! FIVE TIMES A DAY THEY GAZED UPON EACH OTHER...
...ENOCH...
... MYRNA...

THEN ERNEST FEELEY...ALWAYS THE BUSINESS MAN...ANNOUNCED...
I'M MOVIN' YOU AND MYRNA OUT FRONT, CLING! WE NEED A DRAW FOR THE ADMISSIONS! JEB AND ENOCH ARE THE STARS NOW...

AND SO, WHEN THE ROTTED WRAPPINGS WERE REMOVED FROM MYRNA'S SUNKEN, MUMMIFIED EYES, SHE LOOKED OUT ACROSS THE CROWD AND SAW NOTHING...
I GIVE YOU... MYRNA...

AND WHEN THE CURTAIN WAS PULLED BACK UNCOVERING ENOCH'S TANK, HE LOOKED OUT ACROSS THE CROWD AND SAW NOTHING...
I GIVE YOU... ENOCH!

THUS, IN THE BLACK OF NIGHT, WHEN THE CARNIVAL FOLK LAY ASLEEP, A DRIED AND BONEY HAND MOVED... SLOWLY... HESITANTLY... PULLING AWAY ITS ROTTED BROWN WRAPPINGS...

...WHILE A BLOATED, PALE HAND SLID UPWARD AND OVER THE TANK-RIM, PULLING ITS CHALKY, PULPY BODY AFTER IT...

THE MORNING HEARD THE SIDE-SHOW TENT ECHO WITH ANGRY VOICES...
HE STOLE ENOCH!
HE STOLE MYRNA!
CALM DOWN, YOU TWO!

ERNEST QUIETED THE RAGING ODDITY OWNERS...
USE YOUR HEADS, YOU FOOLS! IF BOTH ARE MISSING, NEITHER OF YOU COULD HAVE DONE IT!

OLD DOC CLING KNELT TO THE TAN-BARK AND PICKED UP A MUSTY-SMELLING FRAGMENT...
A PIECE OF MYRNA'S WRAPPINGS!
DROPS OF FORMALDEHYDE! THEY GO THAT WAY!

THE THREE MEN FOLLOWED THE FRAGMENTS OF MUMMY WRAPPINGS AND THE DROPLETS OF FORMAL-DEHYDE OUT OF THE SIDE-SHOW TENT AND INTO THE MORNING SUNLIGHT! THE TRAIL WAS CLEAR... VERY CLEAR...
IT LEADS TO THAT HOUSE!
LOOK AT THE SIGN!
GASP! JUSTICE OF THE... GOOD LORD!
JUSTICE OF THE PEACE

THE JUSTICE OF THE PEACE WAS VERY FRIENDLY! HE TOLD THE SIDE-SHOW MEN ALL HE KNEW...
COUPLE CAME LAST NIGHT! YEP! WANTED TO GET MARRIED! I DID IT! I PERFORMED THE CEREMONY!
WASN'T THERE ANYTHING... ER... STRANGE ABOUT THEM?

SHUCKS! ALL I CAN SAY IS THEY MUST'VE BEEN DRINKING! SMELLED MIGHTY BAD... LIKE AS IF THEY'D BEEN! BUT FIVE BUCKS IS FIVE BUCKS!
DIDN'T YOU SEE...?

DIDN'T SEE NUTHIN'! CAN'T SEE! I'M BLIND, Y'KNOW!
BLIND!
GOOD LORD!

HEH, HEH! CAREFUL NOW! *DON'T PEEK!* HERE COMES THE *FINISH! BRACE* YOURSELVES! FIRST, LET ME SAY THAT MR. FEELEY, JEB, AND ZACH LOST MYRNA AND ENOCH'S TRAIL AFTER THEY LEFT THE J.P.! JUST COULDN'T FIND 'EM! IN FACT, IT WASN'T TILL A YEAR LATER, WHEN THE CARNIVAL RETURNED TO THE VERY OZARK TOWN WHERE ENOCH HAD FIRST JOINED THE SIDE-SHOW...

...THAT MR. FEELEY HEARD ABOUT THE STRANGE DOIN'S UP IN THE MOUNTAINS...

SOMEBODY SAID THEY *SEEN 'EM,* BUT I DON'T *BELIEVE* 'EM! WHO EVER HEERD OF A *LIVIN' MUMMY* AND A *TWO-HEADED CORPSE...*

WHERE? WHERE DID THEY *SEE* 'EM?

UP IN THE *OLD CRONE'S CAVE!* SHE'S *DEAD* NOW! BUT THE *FOLKS* 'ROUND HERE ARE *MIGHTY SUPERSTITIOUS!* IF'N YOU ASK *ME,* THEY'RE *SEEIN' THINGS!* NOW...

JEB'LL TAKE ME THERE! HE KNOWS WHERE IT IS!

THEY WENT! JEB AND ZACH... WHO'D STAYED ON WITH THE CARNIVAL AS HANDY MEN... AND MR. FEELEY! THEY WENT UP THE MOUNTAIN TO THE OLD CRONE'S CAVE...

AND THE THREE CARNIVAL MEN DRAGGED THEIR LONG-LOST ODDITIES BACK DOWN THE MOUNTAIN...

BUT THE THREE MEN WERE OUT OF EARSHOT WHEN THE *WAIL* DRIFTED OUT FROM DEEP IN THE BOWELS OF THE CRONE'S CAVE! THEY NEVER *SAW* THE *INFANT-THING* CRAWL OUT INTO THE SUNLIGHT... ITS EYES STREAMING WITH TEARS... *CRYING FOR ITS PARENTS...*

HEH, HEH! YEP! THAT'S *IT,* KIDDIES! THAT'S *MY STORY!* YEP! *ENOCH* OF THE *DOUBLE DOMES* WAS *MY OLD MAN,* AND *MYRNA* THE *MUMMY* WAS *MY OLD LADY!* YOU *MIGHT* SAY, THE *MUMMY* WAS MY *MOMMY!* BY THE WAY! I UNDERSTAND THAT THERE'S A CARNIVAL *TODAY... EIGHTY YEARS LATER...* THAT *STILL EXHIBITS* A *MUMMY* AND A *TWO-HEADED PRESERVED CORPSE!* IF ANY OF YOU *SEE THEM... WRITE ME!* I WANT TO SEND A *CARD!* IT'S THEIR *ANNIVERSARY* NEXT MONTH!

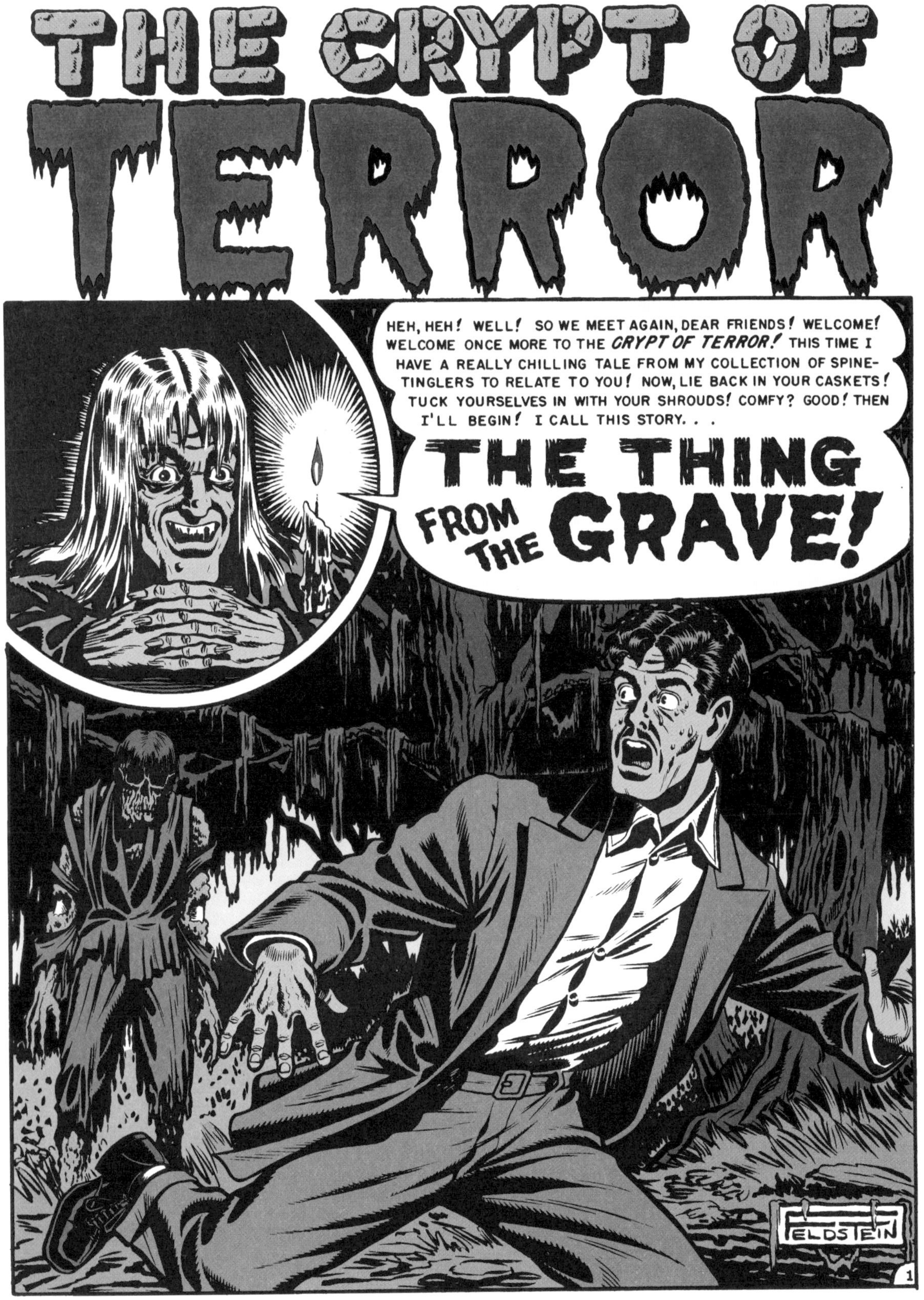

HEH, HEH! WELL! SO WE MEET AGAIN, DEAR FRIENDS! WELCOME! WELCOME ONCE MORE TO THE *CRYPT OF TERROR!* THIS TIME I HAVE A REALLY CHILLING TALE FROM MY COLLECTION OF SPINE-TINGLERS TO RELATE TO YOU! NOW, LIE BACK IN YOUR CASKETS! TUCK YOURSELVES IN WITH YOUR SHROUDS! COMFY? GOOD! THEN I'LL BEGIN! I CALL THIS STORY. . .

THE THING FROM THE GRAVE!

FELDSTEIN

1

JAMES BARRY AND WILLIAM FERTH WERE BOTH IN LOVE WITH THE SAME GIRL, LAURA MASON! JIM WAS KIND... CONSIDERATE... A GENTLEMAN! BILL WAS BRAZEN... FUN-LOVING... AND AT TIMES, LAURA WAS ALMOST AFRAID OF HIM! AND SO WHEN JIM ASKED THE INEVITABLE QUESTION...

MARRY ME, LAURA? I KNOW I CAN MAKE YOU HAPPY!
BUT, JIM! WHAT ABOUT BILL? I...I'M AFRAID OF WHAT HE'LL DO WHEN HE FINDS OUT!

DON'T WORRY, LAURA! BILL WILL HAVE TO TAKE IT LIKE A MAN! ALL'S FAIR IN LOVE AND WAR, Y'KNOW!
YES! BUT BILL ISN'T THE TYPE TO GIVE UP EASILY!

LAURA DIDN'T KNOW HOW RIGHT SHE WAS WHEN SHE SPOKE THOSE WORDS! YES! BILL WAS NOT THE TYPE TO GIVE UP SO EASILY! HE WANTED LAURA!
...AND I'LL HAVE HER, TOO! EVEN IF I HAVE TO KILL YOU, JAMES BARRY!

SOON, LAURA AND JIM WERE MARRIED! THEY WERE VERY HAPPY THOSE FIRST FEW WEEKS... BUT THEN, BUSINESS CALLED JIM OUT OF TOWN FOR A FEW DAYS...
I'LL BE BACK THURSDAY NIGHT, DEAREST!
OH, JIM! I'M AFRAID! I DON'T WANT TO BE LEFT ALONE! BILL MIGHT...

BILL WON'T DO ANYTHING TO YOU, LAURA! BUT, IF YOU EVER ARE IN DANGER, NO MATTER WHERE I AM, SOMEHOW, I'LL GET TO YOU... AND SAVE YOU!
YOU'RE JOKING WITH ME, JAMES BARRY... BUT I'VE BEEN SERIOUS!

SO HAVE I, LAURA! SO HAVE I! 'BYE!
'BYE, JIM! HURRY BACK!
2

JIM'S CAR SPED ALONG A DARK COUNTRY ROAD TOWARDS THE MAIN HIGHWAY! THE HEADLIGHTS, KNIFING THROUGH THE VELVETY BLACKNESS, SUDDENLY FELL UPON...
A MAN! STANDING IN THE ROAD...

JIM PRESSED HARD ON HIS BRAKES AND THE CAR SCREECHED TO A STOP...
CRAZY FOOL! I COULD HAVE KILLED YOU! WHO ARE YOU...ANYWAY?
BILL! IT'S ME... BILL!

THE SHADOWY FIGURE MOVED TOWARDS THE CAR...AND AS HE PASSED THE HEADLIGHT, A GLINT OF SHINY STEEL CAUGHT JIM'S EYE...
HE... HE'S GOT A KNIFE! HE'S...GOING TO KILL ME!

THE SOUND OF A STRUGGLE SHATTERED THE SILENCE HANGING OVER THE DESERTED ROAD AND THE HEAVY WOODS FLANKING IT! THEN THERE WAS A THUD AND A PIERCING SHRIEK...
...AND NOW, LAURA WILL BE MINE! ALL MINE!

BILL FERTH PICKED UP THE BODY OF THE MURDERED JAMES BARRY AND DRAGGED IT INTO THE WOODS...
...GOT TO GET RID OF THE BODY SO NO ONE WILL EVER FIND IT! GOT TO BURY IT DEEP IN THESE WOODS!

AGAIN THE THICK SILENCE OF THE WOODS WAS BROKEN! THIS TIME BY THE SOUND OF A SPADE STRIKING THE SOFT EARTH BELOW TOWERING TREES...
SORRY TO GIVE YOU SUCH A CRUDE BURIAL, JIM OL' BOY, BUT IT'S THE BEST I CAN DO UNDER THE CIRCUMSTANCES!
3

SOON, A GAPING HOLE WAS OPENED AND THE STIFF BODY OF JAMES BARRY WAS DROPPED INTO IT...
NOW TO COVER IT UP, DITCH THE CAR, AND GET BACK HOME! THEN ALL I DO IS WAIT! IF I PLAY MY CARDS RIGHT, SHE'LL BE MINE!
A LITTLE LATER, THE SLEEK FORM OF JAMES BARRY'S AUTOMOBILE HURTLED OVER A CLIFF INTO A DEEP LAKE...
THEY'LL NEVER FIND THE CAR! IT'LL SINK INTO THE MUD AT THE BOTTOM OF THE LAKE!
AND SO THE JOB WAS DONE! BILL FERTH HAD PLANNED EVERYTHING CAREFULLY! THE WEEKS WENT BY, AND THEN THE TIME CAME FOR HIM TO GO AND SEE LAURA...
YES, LAURA! BUT IT'S OVER A MONTH NOW! HE'S LEFT YOU! HE'S PROBABLY FOUND ANOTHER WOMAN!
I CAN'T BELIEVE THAT, BILL! SOMETHING'S HAPPENED TO HIM! I KNOW IT! I FEEL IT!
BILL COULD WAIT! HE HAD PLENTY OF TIME! SHE'D COME AROUND! HE WAS SURE! AFTER ANOTHER MONTH...
IF ANYTHING HAD HAPPENED TO HIM, YOU WOULD HAVE KNOWN BY NOW, LAURA! CAN'T YOU SEE? HE'S LEFT YOU...DESERTED YOU!
I'LL WAIT FOR HIM... TO COME BACK!
HE'LL NEVER COME BACK! NEVER!
THEN I'LL WAIT FOR HIM FOREVER! I'LL NEVER STOP LOVING HIM, BILL! JIM WAS MY LIFE! WITHOUT HIM...
THEN... IT'S ALL WASTED! THE PLANNING...THE WORK...THE WAITING... WASTED!
WHAT DO YOU MEAN? WHAT ARE YOU SAYING?
4

I'M GOING TO SET FIRE TO THE CABIN! THEY'LL NEVER FIND WHAT'S LEFT OF YOU...NEVER! IT'LL BE ASHES...ALL ASHES!

SLOWLY, THE EARTH GAVE WAY, AS THE THING PUSHED UPWARD, CLAWING! THE CLEAN FRESH AIR SEEPED DOWN INTO ITS SHALLOW GRAVE...

IT GOT TO ITS FEET CLUMSILY... STOOD ERECT IN THE MOONLIGHT! IT LIFTED ITS HEAD... LISTENING! IT HAD HEARD A SCREAM... A SCREAM THAT HAD MADE IT SEEK THE OPEN AIR...

IT MOVED FORWARD AT A STUMBLING GATE! ITS ROTTED LEGS... ITS SIGHTLESS EYES... THE DECAYED FLESH THAT CLUNG HERE AND THERE TO WHITENED BONE... MOVED THROUGH THE UNDERBRUSH...

BACK AT THE CABIN, BILL POURED THE CAN OF KEROSENE AROUND THE OUTSIDE WALLS...
GO AHEAD... SCREAM, YOU FOOL! NO ONE WILL HEAR YOU!
EEEE

BUT OUT IN THE DEEP SHADOWS OF THE WOODS, THE THING HEARD THE SCREAM... AND STUMBLED FORWARD... TOWARDS IT...
EEEEE

THE CABIN WAS ON FIRE NOW! INSIDE LAURA CRINGED AGAINST THE DOOR AS THE FLAMES LICKED AT HER... WHITE... HOT...
OH... SAVE ME, JIM! WHEREVER YOU ARE... YOU PROMISED... OOOOH!

OUTSIDE, BILL WATCHED AS THE FLAMES LEAPED HIGHER AND HIGHER! THEN, FROM THE FRINGE OF THE TREES, HE SAW THE THING COMING... STUMBLING... STAGGERING...
GOOD LORD!
6

THE THING DID NOT SEE BILL! IT WAS LOOKING AT THE BURNING CABIN! BILL PUT HIS HAND OVER HIS MOUTH! HE WAS SICK! HE WHIMPERED...
J-JIM...

THE THING WENT INTO THE FIRE! IT DID NOT FEEL THE FLAMES LICKING AT ITS TATTERED CLOTHES...ITS ROTTED FLESH! IT WAS DEAD! IT COULD FEEL NOTHING...

AFTER A FEW MOMENTS IT CAME OUT! ITS HAIR WAS SINGED! ITS DECAYED FLESH WAS CHARRED! WHERE THE FIRE HAD TOUCHED THE BONE, IT WAS BLACK AND SCORCHED! IT CARRIED THE GIRL...

BILL WAS SCREAMING NOW! HE BEGAN TO RUN WILDLY INTO THE WOODS... SCREAMING...SCREAMING.
A-A-A-A-A-A-H

THE THING PUT LAURA DOWN ON THE COOL GRASS FAR FROM THE BURNING CABIN! SHE WAS UNCONSCIOUS! SHE HAD FAINTED BEFORE THE THING HAD REACHED HER! SHE HAD NOT SEEN IT...

THEN THE THING TURNED...TOWARDS THE HYSTERICAL SHRIEKING THAT CAME FROM THE NEARBY WOODS...

SLOWLY IT SHAMBLED TOWARDS THE SCREAMING BILL AS HE CRASHED MADLY THROUGH THE THICK UNDER-GROWTH...
HE'S COMING ...AFTER ME!

AND THAT'S MY STORY, DEAR READER! JIM CERTAINLY *KEPT* HIS *PROMISE* TO LAURA, DIDN'T HE? LUCKY FOR HER SHE *FAINTED BEFORE* HE GOT THERE, THOUGH! SHE'LL ALWAYS REMEMBER HIM IN A *NICE* WAY, NOW! AND *POOR BILL!* NOW *JIM'S* GOT HIM FOR *COMPANY* ...DOWN THERE WHERE IT'S COLD AND BLACK! WELL, THEY CAN ALWAYS HOLD *GRAVE CONVERSATIONS* TOGETHER! HEH, HEH! NOW, IF YOU'RE NOT TOO BROKEN UP OVER *THIS* TALE... WHY NOT READ ON! MORE CHILLS AWAIT YOU!

HEE, HEE! I SEE YOU'RE *HORROR-HUNGRY* AGAIN... BACK FOR MORE *SAVORY SERVINGS* OF *SCREAMS* FROM MY *CAULDRON!* WELL, *GOOD!* WELCOME TO *THE HAUNT OF FEAR!* THIS IS YOUR *DELIRIUM-DIETICIAN, THE OLD WITCH,* COOKING UP ANOTHER *REVOLTING RECIPE!* READY? GOT YOUR *DROOL CUPS* FASTENED UNDER YOUR *DRIBBLING CHINS?* GOT YOUR *SHROUDS* TIED NEATLY AROUND YOUR *NECKS?* THEN I'LL BEGIN DISHING OUT THE *TERROR-TIDBIT* I CALL...

HORROR WE? HOW'S BAYOU?

THE MOSS-LADEN CYPRESS TREES THAT LINE THE RUTTED BAYOU ROAD SEEM TO PART... AND AN OLD PLANTATION HOUSE, WEATHERBEATEN AND FADED, LOOMS UP IN THE CAR'S HEADLIGHT BEAMS! ITS COLUMNED PORTICO LEERS OMINOUSLY, LIKE SOME GIGANTIC FANGED MONSTER SQUATTING IN THE ROAD, BLOCKING THE AUTOMOBILE'S FURTHER PROGRESS! OFF IN THE DISTANCE A SWAMP BIRD SCREAMS INTO THE NIGHT, AS IF LAUGHING AT THE DRIVER'S DISCOMFORT...

THE CAR DOOR SWINGS OPEN AND A YOUNG MAN STEPS OUT! HE STRIDES TOWARD THE RUN-DOWN MANSION...
THERE'S A LIGHT SHINING THROUGH ONE OF THOSE SHUTTERED WINDOWS! THAT MEANS SOMEONE'S LIVING THERE! PERHAPS THEY CAN GIVE ME DIRECTIONS...
GREY FORMS SCATTER AS THE LOST STRANGER MOUNTS THE STEPS OF THE COLUMNED PORCH...
WHEW! SWAMP RATS! UGH! HOW COULD ANYONE LIVE OUT IN THIS GOD-FORSAKEN COUNTRY?
THE LARGE BRASS DOOR-KNOCKER RESOUNDS HOLLOWLY INSIDE THE ONCE GLORIOUS HOUSE! FOOTSTEPS APPROACH AND THE HEAVY OAK FRONT DOOR CREAKS OPEN...
YES?
HOW DO YOU DO? MY NAME IS FORMAN...MAX FORMAN! I MUST HAVE MADE A WRONG TURN A FEW MILES BACK...
THE DOOR OPENS WIDE, REVEALING A SMALL, SAD-EYED, MIDDLE-AGED MAN...
COME IN, MR. FORMAN! COME IN! MY! I'D GONE TO BED! I'D GIVEN UP FOR TONIGHT!
GIVEN UP? I...I DON'T UNDERSTAND!
GIVEN UP WAITING FOR SOMEONE LIKE YOU TO COME ALONG, MR. FORMAN! YOU SEE, I SWITCHED THAT SIGN DOWN THERE SO YOU'D MAKE THE TURN INTO OUR ROAD...
YOU... YOU DID THAT... ON PURPOSE! WHY?
FOR EVERETT, MR. FORMAN! EVERETT...MY BROTHER! EVERY SO OFTEN HE GETS DIFFICULT... AND I HAVE TO PROMISE HIM THINGS...
BUT WHAT'S THAT GOT TO DO WITH ME?
EVERETT IS MAD, MR. FORMAN! THAT'S WHY WE LIVE OUT HERE IN THE BAYOUS! HE IS DANGEROUS! HE IS A HOMICIDAL MANIAC...
BUT... WHY... WHY... ME? CHOKE...

EVERETT HAS A STRONG DESIRE TO KILL, MR. FORMAN! THIS DESIRE CANNOT GO UNSATISFIED FOR ANY LENGTH OF TIME! IF IT DOES... HE MAY TURN ON ME!
YOU'RE...YOU'RE JOKING! THIS IS SOME SORT OF GAG!
IF YOU WILL LOOK BEHIND YOU, YOU WILL SEE THAT THIS IS NO JOKE, MR. FORMAN!
GASP!
UH-HUHH! ...FOR EVERETT? FOR ME?
YES, EVERETT FOR YOU...
UH-HUHH! UH-HUHH!
K-KEEP AWAY...
UH-HUHH! UH-HUHH!
KEEP AWAY!
KEEP AWA-A-A EEGGGGHHHHH!
THE SCREAMING PROTESTS OF THE YOUNG MAN DIE IN A CHOKING GURGLE AS THE LUMBERING MANIAC'S VICE-LIKE FINGERS CLOSE AROUND HIS NECK...
UH-HUHH! UH-HUHH!
TAKE HIM AWAY, EVERETT! TAKE HIM DOWN INTO THE CELLAR! I DON'T WANT TO SEE!
THE ELDER MAN WATCHES AS HIS YOUNGER MAD BROTHER SWINGS THE PROSTRATE FORM OF THE STRANGER OVER HIS MASSIVE SHOULDERS AND MOVES OFF THROUGH THE MUSTY OLD MANSION...
I DON'T WANT TO SEE YOU DISMEMBER HIS BODY!
UH-HUHH... UH-HUHH...
3

LATER, THE DOOR TO THE OLD PLANTATION HOUSE OPENS AND THE ELDER BROTHER COMES OUT...
NOW TO GET RID OF THE CAR...
THE CAR LEAPS FORWARD WITH A LOUD GRINDING OF GEARS, DOWN AN OVERGROWN PATH, FINALLY STOPPING BEFORE A SHIMMERING YELLOW POOL...
THE QUICK-SAND POOL WILL SWALLOW UP ALL TRACES OF IT...
RELEASING THE EMERGENCY BRAKE, THE ELDER BROTHER LEAPS OUT, AND THE CAR ROLLS FORWARD INTO THE SUCKING BOG.. SINKING SLOWLY FROM SIGHT! BEYOND, FROM THE MANSION, A SICKENING SHRIEK OF LAUGHTER ECHOES INTO THE BAYOU NIGHT...
POOR EVERETT. WELL, PERHAPS THIS WILL SATISFY HIM... FOR A WHILE, AT LEAST!
FINALLY THE CAR HAS DISAPPEARED BELOW THE SURFACE OF THE ROLLING QUICKSAND POOL! THE ELDER BROTHER MOVES BACK THROUGH THE BAYOU OVERGROWTH TO THE MANSION! EVERETT STANDS IN THE OPEN DOORWAY, BREATHING HEAVILY! HIS HANDS ARE BLOTCHED RED...
I'M...FINISHED, SIDNEY! COME...SEE!
N-NO, THANK YOU, EVERETT! JUST PUT WHAT'S LEFT OF HIM IN THE SACK, AS USUAL...
EVERETT LUMBERS OFF AND RETURNS SHORTLY AFTER, A LARGE BLOOD-STAINED SACK SWUNG OVER HIS SHOULDERS...
HE...HE WAS A DOCTOR, SIDNEY! I FOUND HIS CARD! I DON'T LIKE DOCTORS!
THROW WHAT'S LEFT OF HIM IN THE QUICKSAND POOL, EVERETT... WITH THE OTHERS!
EVERETT'S STUPID FACE BRIGHTENS! HE GRINS IDIOTICALLY...
REMEMBER THE OTHERS, SIDNEY? THE FAT SALESMAN... AND THE WOMAN...
YES, EVERETT! I REMEMBER! GO AHEAD, NOW! IN THE QUICK-SAND POOL...
THE WOMAN WAS NICE! HER FLESH WAS SO SOFT! WHEN I CUT...
EVERETT!
4

EVERETT SCURRIES OFF TOWARD THE QUICKSAND POOL WITH HIS GORY CARGO! SIDNEY WATCHES HIM GO! YES! THE WOMAN! SHE WAS THE FIRST! HE REMEMBERED HER...
I'M AFRAID I'VE LOST... MY WAY! COULD YOU HELP ME GET BACK TO THE... THE HIGHWAY!
UH-HUHH! UH-HUHH!
EVERETT? WHO IS IT?
I BEG YOUR PARDON, MA'AM! MY BROTHER IS NOT TOO BRIGHT! COULD I HELP YOU?
I... I WANTED TO REACH HOUMA BY DARK! I MUST HAVE TURNED OFF THE MAIN ROAD...
YOU'LL NEVER MAKE HOUMA TONIGHT, MA'AM! YOU'RE WELCOME TO STAY THE NIGHT, THOUGH! YOU CAN START OUT FRESH IN THE MORNING!
WELL, I DON'T KNOW! I WOULDN'T WANT TO IMPOSE...
YES! THE WOMAN HAD BEEN THE FIRST! DURING THAT NIGHT, EVERETT HAD GONE TO HER ROOM AND...
EEEEEE...GGHH!
HUH? WHAT WAS THAT?
THE SCREAM HAD AWAKENED SIDNEY! HE'D RUSHED TO THE WOMAN'S ROOM...
EVERETT! CHOKE...
UH-HUHH! UH-HUHH!
SIDNEY HAD THROWN THE DISMEMBERED PARTS OF THE WOMAN'S BODY INTO THE QUICKSAND POOL! THAT HAD BEEN THE BEGINNING OF IT! AFTER THAT, EVERETT HAD GOTTEN WORSE AND WORSE! AND SIDNEY REALIZED THAT HE'D HAVE TO SUPPLY HIS MAD BROTHER WITH OTHER VICTIMS TO KEEP HIM SATISFIED...
ALL RIGHT, EVERETT! ALL RIGHT! I'LL THINK OF SOMETHING!
UH-HUHH... UH-HUHH...
SO SIDNEY'D THOUGHT OF ALTERING THE DIRECTIONAL SIGN DOWN AT THE ROAD, SO WANDERERS WOULD COME TO THE MANSION...
MY NAME'S JACKSON... ANTHONY JACKSON! I'M A TRAVELING SALESMAN! I SEEM TO HAVE GOTTEN ONTO YOUR ROAD BY MISTAKE!
COME IN, MR. JACKSON! COME IN!
5

AND NOW THE DOCTOR! SIDNEY WATCHES AS EVERETT LUMBERS BACK ONTO THE PORCH CARRYING THE EMPTY SACK...
DID YOU...?
YES, SIDNEY! I... I THREW THE PIECES IN THE POOL!
COME TO BED, EVERETT!
Y-YES...SIDNEY!
SOON, THE LIGHTS BLINK OFF ONE BY ONE IN THE RAMSHAKLE OLD PLANTATION HOUSE! SIDNEY AND HIS MAD BROTHER ARE ASLEEP! BUT DOWN IN THE BAYOU, THE QUICKSAND POOL ROLLS AND QUIVERS...
BENEATH ITS SUCKING SURFACE, THE DISMEMBERED PARTS OF THREE BODIES... A WOMAN'S, A SALESMAN'S, AND A DOCTOR'S... BUMP TOGETHER, TURNING LAZILY... MELTING... FUSING... REORGANIZING THEMSELVES... UNTIL...
...A PULPY HAND REACHES INTO THE BAYOU NIGHT...
A STRINGY-HAIRED ROTTED WOMAN'S HEAD BOBS TO THE SURFACE...
ANOTHER FOLLOWS...THE PLUMP SALESMAN'S FACE APPEARS...
...AND THEN THE RECENTLY MURDERED DOCTOR'S RISES.

IN HIS BEDROOM, SIDNEY STIRS UNCOMFORTABLY IN HIS SLEEP! SUDDENLY, THE DOOR TO HIS CHAMBER BURSTS OPEN AND THREE FIGURES ARE FRAMED IN IT, SWAYING UNSTEADILY...
WHO... WHO'S THERE? EVERETT? IS THAT... YOU? I THOUGHT I LOCKED YOU... IN... YOUR... GASP...
THE FIGURES MOVE FORWARD... INTO THE LIGHT! BUT THERE IS SOMETHING STRANGELY WRONG ABOUT THE FIGURES! SIDNEY STARES IN HORROR! A WHIMPER ESCAPES FROM HIS THROAT...
NO! NO! OH, LORD...
FOR THE DISMEMBERED PARTS OF EVERETT'S THREE VICTIMS HAVE FUSED INCORRECTLY! THE WOMAN'S HEAD RESTS UPON THE SALESMAN'S TORSO...
...WHILE DOCTOR FORMAN'S HEAD RESTS UPON THE WOMAN'S TORSO...
...AND MR. JACKSON'S, THE SALESMAN'S, HEAD HAS FUSED WITH THE DOCTOR'S BODY...
THE OTHER PARTS, THE ARMS AND LEGS OF EACH, ARE EQUALLY AS CONFUSED! THE CONGLOMERATIONS MOVE FORWARD... TOWARD THE HYSTERICALLY SCREAMING SIDNEY...
CLUTCHED IN ONE OF THE MIXED-UP-FIGURE'S HANDS IS A SMALL BLACK BAG... THE KIND USED BY DOCTORS TO CARRY THEIR SHINY LITTLE SHARP INSTRUMENTS...
EEEEEEEEAAAAAAAAGGGGHHHHHHHHHH!
7

LOCKED IN HIS BARRED-WINDOW ROOM, EVERETT LISTENS WITH GREAT PUZZLEMENT TO THE SHRIEKING THAT ECHOES THROUGH THE OLD HOUSE FOR THE NEXT TWENTY-FIVE MINUTES...
YAAAAEEEEEEEEEE!
FINALLY, THE SHRIEKING STOPS, AND ONLY A SOFT PITIFUL SOBBING IS HEARD! FROM THE BARRED WINDOW, EVERETT WATCHES AS THREE FIGURES TOTTER OUT OF THE MANSION...
...AND BACK INTO THE BAYOU TO THE QUICKSAND POOL...
SUDDENLY, A KEY RATTLES INTO THE LOCK OF THE HEAVY DOOR OF EVERETT'S ROOM! HE TURNS FROM THE BARRED WINDOW! SIDNEY, OR WHAT WAS ONCE SIDNEY BUT IS NOW NOTHING MORE THAN A CONFUSED REORGANIZATION OF SIDNEY'S DISMEMBERED BODY, STANDS BEFORE HIM... THE UPSIDE-DOWN HEAD HANGING FROM THE LEFT HIP, SOBBING... THE LEFT LEG, SEWN TO THE LEFT SHOULDER, CROOKED AWKWARDLY AROUND A MAKESHIFT CRUTCH... THE RIGHT LEG SWAYING FROM THE RIGHT SHOULDER... THE LEFT ARM, ERUPTING FROM THE NECK, GESTICULATING... AND THE RIGHT ARM SUPPORTING THE ENTIRE GRISLY SIGHT...
EVERETT! LOOK... WHAT THEY'VE... DONE TO ME!
UH-HUHH... CHOKE...
HEE, HEE! YEP, KIDDIES! EVERETT'S VICTIMS REALLY MESSED UP HIS BROTHER SIDNEY! YOU MIGHT SAY THEY GOT TOGETHER! OF COURSE, THE DOC WAS A SURGEON, SO HIS HEAD DIRECTED THE WHOLE OPERATION! WHAT A LAUGH, THOUGH! HE'D HAD NO ANAESTHETIC IN HIS BAG! SIDNEY THOUGHT IT WAS A SCREAM. WHAT HAPPENED TO SIDNEY AND EVERETT YOU ASK? OH, THEY'RE STILL DOWN THERE, DEEP IN THE BAYOUS OF LOUISIANA! NEXT TIME YOU'RE DRIVING IN THAT SECTION, JUST LOOK FOR THEM! THAT IS... IF THEY DON'T LOOK FOR YOU FIRST! AND NOW, THE VAULT-KEEPER AWAITS! SEE YOU LATER...

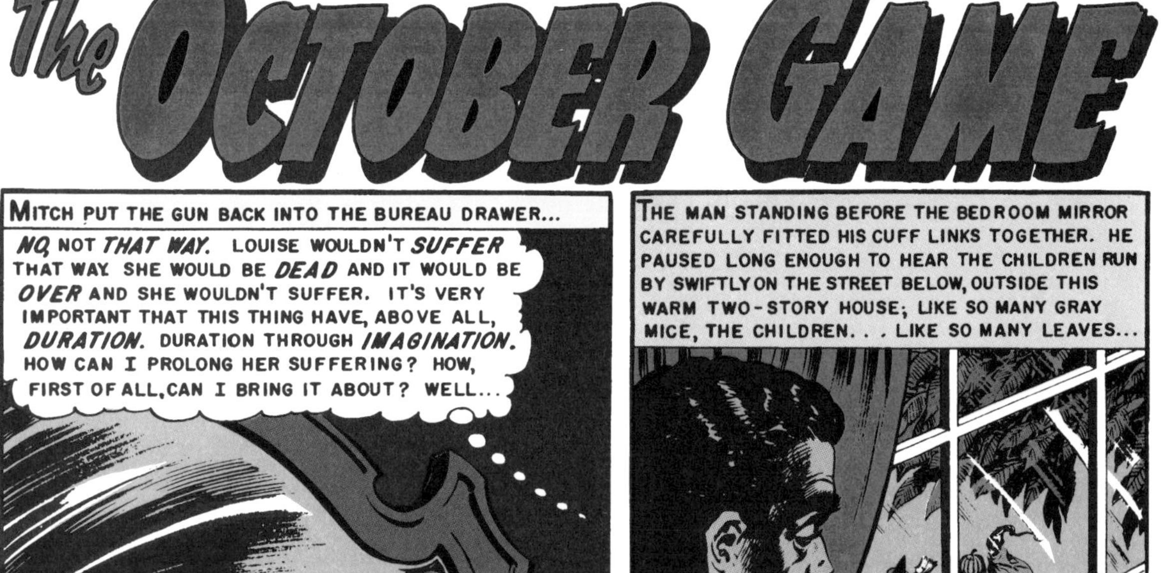

A HORROR SUSPENSTORY
ADAPTED FROM A TALE BY
RAY BRADBURY

NO. THINGS HADN'T BEEN RIGHT FOR SOME TIME. OCTOBER DIDN'T HELP ANY. IF ANYTHING, IT MADE THINGS WORSE. HE NODDED SLOWLY AT HIS IMAGE IN THE MIRROR... ADJUSTING HIS BLACK BOW-TIE...
IF... IF THIS WERE SPRING, THEN THERE MIGHT BE A CHANCE. BUT TONIGHT, ALL THE WORLD IS BURNING DOWN INTO RUIN. THERE'S NO GREEN OF SPRING, NONE OF THE FRESHNESS, NONE OF THE PROMISE...

MITCH HAD NEVER LIKED OCTOBER... EVER SINCE HE FIRST LAY IN THE AUTUMN LEAVES BEFORE HIS GRANDMOTHER'S HOUSE MANY YEARS AGO AND HEARD THE WIND AND SAW THE EMPTY TREES. IT HAD MADE HIM CRY... WITHOUT A REASON...
SOB... SOB...
AND A LITTLE OF THAT SADNESS RETURNED EACH YEAR TO HIM. IT ALWAYS WENT AWAY WITH THE SPRING.

BUT IT WAS DIFFERENT TONIGHT. THERE WAS A FEELING OF AUTUMN COMING TO LAST A MILLION YEARS. THERE WOULD BE NO SPRING. HE HAD BEEN CRYING QUIETLY ALL EVENING. IT DIDN'T SHOW ON HIS FACE. IT WAS ALL SOMEWHERE HIDDEN. BUT IT WOULDN'T STOP...
DADDY?
MARION?

THERE WAS A SOFT RUNNING IN THE HALL. IT WAS MARION, HIS LITTLE ONE. ALL EIGHT QUIET YEARS OF HER. NEVER A WORD. JUST HER LUMINOUS GRAY EYES AND HER WONDERING LITTLE MOUTH. MARION HAD BEEN IN AND OUT ALL EVENING, TRYING ON VARIOUS MASKS, ASKING HIM WHICH WAS MOST TERRIFYING, MOST HORRIBLE. THEY'D BOTH FINALLY DECIDED...
THE SKELETON MASK, DEAR. IT'LL 'SCARE THE BEANS' FROM PEOPLE!
ISN'T IT JUST AWFUL, DADDY? I LIKE IT, TOO!

AS HE FINISHED HIS BOW-TIE AND PUT ON HIS DARK COAT, MARION APPEARED IN THE DOOR, ALL SKELETONOUS IN HER DISGUISE...
HOW DO I LOOK, DADDY?
FINE!
FROM UNDER THE MASK, BLONDE HAIR SHOWED. FROM THE SKULL SOCKETS, SMALL BLUE EYES SMILED. MITCH SIGHED. MARION... AND LOUISE... THE TWO SILENT DENOUNCERS OF HIS VIRILITY, HIS DARK POWER...
COMING DOWN, DADDY?
IN A MOMENT...

WHAT *ALCHEMY* HAD THERE BEEN IN LOUISE THAT TOOK THE DARK OF A DARK MAN AND BLEACHED AND BLEACHED THE DARK BROWN EYES AND BLACK HAIR AND WASHED AND BLEACHED THE INGROWN BABY ALL DURING THE PERIOD BEFORE BIRTH UNTIL THE CHILD WAS BORN, MARION, BLONDE, BLUE EYES, RUDDY-CHEEKED...

SOMETIMES HE SUSPECTED THAT LOUISE HAD CONCEIVED THE CHILD AS AN IDEA, COMPLETELY ASEXUAL, A CONCEPTION OF CONTEMPTUOUS MIND AND CELL. AS A FIRM *REBUKE* TO HIM, SHE HAD PRODUCED A CHILD IN HER *OWN* IMAGE. HER EYES, THAT DAY IN THE HOSPITAL, WERE COLD. THEY'D SAID...

LOUISE HAD *NEVER WANTED* A CHILD. SHE'D BEEN *FRIGHTENED* OF THE IDEA OF BIRTH. HE'D *FORCED* THE CHILD ON HER. IT HAD BEEN VERY *EASY* FOR LOUISE TO *HATE* THIS HUSBAND WHO *SO WANTED A SON THAT HE'D GIVE HIS ONLY WIFE OVER TO A MORTUARY.* WHEN MITCH HAD PUT OUT A HAND TO TOUCH, THE MOTHER HAD TURNED AWAY TO CONSPIRE WITH HER NEW PINK DAUGHTER-CHILD, AWAY FROM THE DARK FORCING MURDERER...

AND IT HAD ALL BEEN SO BEAUTIFULLY IRONIC. HIS SELFISHNESS DESERVED IT. THE DOCTOR HAD SHAKEN HIS HEAD AND SAID...

NOW IT WAS OCTOBER AGAIN. THERE HAD BEEN OTHER OCTOBERS. HE'D THOUGHT OF THE LONG WINTERS, YEAR AFTER YEAR, THE ENDLESS MONTHS MORTARED INTO THE HOUSE BY AN INSANE FALL OF SNOW, TRAPPED WITH A WOMAN AND CHILD, NEITHER OF WHOM LOVED HIM...

DURING THE EIGHT YEARS, THERE HAD BEEN RESPITES. IN SPRING AND SUMMER HE GOT OUT, WALKED, WENT TO BALL GAMES; THERE WERE DESPERATE SOLUTIONS TO THE DESPERATE PROBLEM OF A HATED MAN...

BUT IN WINTER, THE HIKES AND GAMES AND ESCAPES FELL AWAY WITH THE LEAVES. LIFE, LIKE A TREE, STOOD EMPTY, THE FRUIT PICKED, THE SAP RUN TO EARTH. AND NOW, THE EIGHTH WINTER COMING, HE KNEW THINGS WERE FINALLY AT AN END. HE SIMPLY COULD NOT WEAR THIS ONE THROUGH . . .

THERE WAS AN ACID WALLED OFF IN HIM THAT HAD SLOWLY EATEN THROUGH TISSUE AND TISSUE OVER THE YEARS... AND NOW, TONIGHT, IT WOULD REACH THE WILD EXPLOSIVE IN HIM AND ALL WOULD BE OVER. DOWNSTAIRS, THERE WERE SHOUTS AND HILARITY. . . MARION, GREETING THE FIRST ARRIVALS... LOUISE, TAKING PARENTS' COATS. . .

A RICH SYRUPY SMELL OF CANDY FILLED THE BUSTLING HOUSE. LOUISE HAD LAID OUT APPLES IN NEW SKINS OF CARAMEL. THERE WERE VAST BOWLS OF PUNCH FRESH-MIXED...

... STRINGED APPLES IN EACH DOORWAY... SCOOPED, VENTED PUMPKINS PEERING TRIANGULARLY...

...AND A WAITING TUB OF WATER IN THE CENTER OF THE LIVING ROOM, WAITING WITH A SACK OF APPLES NEARBY FOR THE BOBBLING TO BEGIN . . .

MITCH WALKED TOWARD THE STAIRS. HE HESITATED...

HE DESCENDED THE STAIRS. LOUISE DIDN'T LOOK UP. THE CHILDREN SHOUTED AND WAVED AS HE CAME DOWN...

BY TEN O'CLOCK THE DOORBELL HAD STOPPED RINGING, THE APPLES WERE BITTEN FROM STRINGED DOORS, THE PINK CHILD FACES WERE WIPED DRY FROM APPLE BOBBLING, NAPKINS WERE SMEARED WITH CARAMEL AND PUNCH, AND HE, THE HUSBAND, HAD TAKEN OVER. HE TOOK THE PARTY RIGHT OUT OF LOUISE'S HANDS. HE RAN ABOUT, TALKING TO THE TWENTY CHILDREN AND THE TWELVE PARENTS, WHO WERE HAPPY WITH THE SPECIAL SPIKED CIDER HE'D FIXED THEM...

HE SUPERVISED *PIN THE TAIL ON THE DONKEY*...

...SPIN THE BOTTLE...

...MUSICAL CHAIRS...

...AND ALL THE REST, MIDST FITS OF SHOUTING LAUGHTER. THEN, IN THE TRIANGULAR-EYED PUMPKIN SHINE, ALL HOUSE LIGHTS OUT, HE CRIED...

HE TIPTOED TOWARD THE CELLAR. THE PARENTS COMMENTED TO EACH OTHER, NODDING AT THE CLEVER HUSBAND, SPEAKING TO THE LUCKY WIFE...

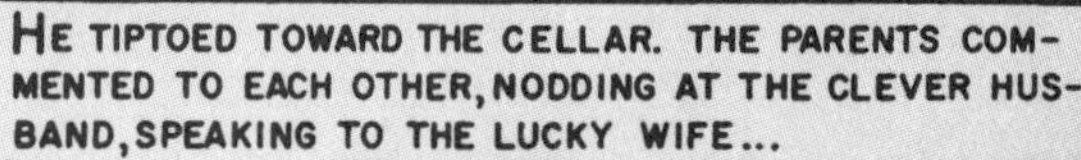

THE CHILDREN CROWDED AFTER THE HUSBAND, SQUEALING. HE MADE A MOCK SHIVER...

ABANDON *HOPE*... ALL YE WHO *ENTER HERE*.

THE PARENTS CHUCKLED...

ONE BY ONE, THE CHILDREN SLID DOWN A SLIDE, WHICH MITCH HAD FIXED UP FROM TABLE SECTIONS, INTO THE DARK CELLAR. HE HISSED AND SHOUTED GHASTLY UTTERANCES AFTER THEM. A WONDERFUL WAILING FILLED THE DARK PUMPKIN-LIGHTED HOUSE. EVERYBODY TALKED AT ONCE. EVERYBODY BUT MARION. SHE'D GONE THROUGH THE PARTY WITH A MINIMUM OF SOUND. IT WAS ALL INSIDE HER, ALL OF THE EXCITEMENT AND JOY...

NOW, THE PARENTS. WITH LAUGHING RELUCTANCE THEY SLID DOWN THE INCLINE, UPROARIOUS, WHILE MARION STOOD BY, ALWAYS WANTING TO SEE IT ALL, TO BE THE LAST. LOUISE WENT DOWN WITHOUT MITCH'S HELP. MARION STOOD BY THE SLIDE. MITCH PICKED HER UP...

THEY SAT IN A VAST CIRCLE IN THE CELLAR. WARMTH CAME FROM THE DISTANT BULK OF THE FURNACE. THE CHAIRS STOOD IN A LONG LINE DOWN EACH WALL, TWENTY SQUEALING CHILDREN, TWELVE RUSTLING RELATIVES, ALTERNATELY SPACED. THEY HAD ALL GROPED TO THEIR CHAIRS IN THE BLACKNESS. THE ENTIRE PROGRAM FROM HERE ON WAS TO BE ENACTED IN THE DARK, HE AS MR. INTERLOCUTOR...
NOW! QUIET!

THERE WAS A SMELL OF DAMP CEMENT AND THE SOUND OF THE WIND OUT IN THE OCTOBER STARS. EVERYBODY SETTLED. THE ROOM WAS BLACK BLACK. NOT A LIGHT, NOT A SHINE, NOT A GLINT OF AN EYE. THERE WAS A SCRAPING OF CROCKERY, A METAL RATTLE. THE HUSBAND INTONED...
THE WITCH... IS DEAD.
TEE-HEE...

THE WITCH IS DEAD, SHE HAS BEEN KILLED, AND HERE IS THE KNIFE SHE WAS KILLED WITH.
HE HANDED OVER THE KNIFE. IT WAS PASSED FROM HAND TO HAND, DOWN AND AROUND THE CIRCLE, WITH CHUCKLES AND LITTLE ODD CRIES AND COMMENTS FROM THE ADULTS...

THE WITCH IS DEAD, AND THIS IS HER HEAD.
...WHISPERED THE HUSBAND, AND HANDED AN ITEM TO THE NEAREST PERSON.

SOME LITTLE CHILD CRIED HAPPILY IN THE DARK...
OH, I KNOW HOW THIS GAME IS PLAYED. HE GETS SOME OLD CHICKEN INNARDS AND HE HANDS THEM AROUND SAYING 'THESE ARE HER INNARDS!', AND HE MAKES A CLAY HEAD AND PASSES IT FOR HER HEAD, AND PASSES A SOUP BONE FOR HER ARM, AND HE TAKES A MARBLE AND SAYS, 'THIS IS HER EYE!', AND SOME CORN FOR HER TEETH AND A SACK OF PLUMB PUDDING AND GIVES THAT AND SAYS, 'THIS IS HER STOMACH!' I KNOW HOW THIS IS PLAYED!
HUSH, YOU'LL SPOIL EVERYTHING.

MITCH SAID...
THE WITCH CAME TO HARM, AND THIS IS HER ARM.
TEE-HEE...

THE ITEMS WERE PASSED AND PASSED, LIKE HOT POTATOES, AROUND THE CIRCLE. SOME CHILDREN SCREAMED, WOULDN'T TOUCH THEM. SOME RAN FROM THEIR CHAIRS TO STAND IN THE CENTER OF THE CELLAR UNTIL THE GRISLY ITEMS HAD PASSED. ONE BOY SCOFFED...
AW, IT'S ONLY CHICKEN INSIDES. COME BACK, HELEN!

Shot from hand to hand with small scream after scream, the items went down the line, down, down, to be followed by another and another. The husband said...

Six or seven items moving at once through the laughing, trembling dark, Louise spoke up...

On and on the passing, the screams, the hilarity. The autumn wind sighed about the house. And he, the husband, stood in the dark cellar, intoning the words, handing out the items. Louise's voice came again from far across the cellar...

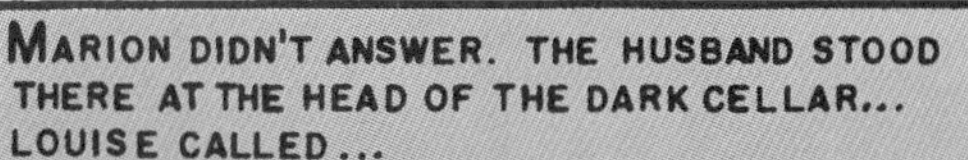

LOUISE CRIED OUT...
MARION... MARION...
TURN ON THE LIGHTS!
THE ITEMS STOPPED PASSING. THE CHILDREN AND ADULTS SAT WITH THE WITCHES' ITEMS IN THEIR HANDS.
THERE WAS A SCRAPING OF A CHAIR, WILDLY, IN THE DARK. LOUISE GASPED...
NO. NO, DON'T TURN ON THE LIGHTS, DON'T TURN ON THE LIGHTS, OH GOD, GOD, GOD, DON'T TURN THEM ON, PLEASE, PLEASE DON'T TURN ON THE LIGHTS, DON'T!
LOUISE WAS SHRIEKING NOW. THE ENTIRE CELLAR FROZE WITH THE SCREAM. NOBODY MOVED...

EVERYONE SAT SUSPENDED IN THE SUDDEN FROZEN TASK OF THIS OCTOBER GAME; THE WIND BLEW OUTSIDE, BANGING THE HOUSE. THE SMELL OF PUMPKINS AND APPLES FILLED THE ROOM WITH THE SMELL OF THE OBJECTS IN THEIR FINGERS WHILE ONE BOY CRIED...
I'LL GO UPSTAIRS AND LOOK!

...AND HE RAN UPSTAIRS HOPEFULLY AND OUT AROUND THE HOUSE FOUR TIMES, AROUND THE HOUSE, CALLING...
MARION, MARION, MARION!

...AND AT LAST COMING SLOWLY DOWN THE STAIRS INTO THE WAITING, BREATHING CELLAR AND SAYING TO THE DARKNESS...
I CAN'T FIND HER...

THEN... SOME IDIOT TURNED ON THE LIGHTS...
THE END

The Fans Keep the Flame Alive

Comic book history is littered with forgotten titles and abandoned characters. *Tales from the Crypt* and the Crypt Keeper could have easily been among them, but for one factor—the fans. High school kids and college students who loved them kept the flame alive—older readers didn't have the time. At times the loyal supporters were down to a mere handful, but at several points along the way history took a lucky bounce that ensured that *Tales from the Crypt* remained in the collective memory a little longer.

The period from 1955 to 1983 defines the low ebb in *Tales* history. EC horror comics had disappeared from newsstands and drugstores and were for the most part forgotten, at least by the general public. But diehard EC fans remembered, largely because they didn't have any alternative. For them, the choice between buying the lobotomized Code-approved new comics and re-reading old favorites was, as it were, a no-brainer.

Before the Fall

The National E.C. Fan-Addict Club (a name that surely gave Dr. Wertham the willies) had been founded in summer 1953 and grew rapidly—by March of 1954, there were 17,700 members. The national president's name was "Melvin," a *nom de joke* already well known to EC fans who read both the horror comics and *MAD* magazine. "National Headquarters"—i.e., EC offices on Lafayette Street in New York—sent off the pins and patches and ID cards, and encouraged readers to form local chapters, and many of them did. "Any group of five or more prospective members may join as an authorized chapter of the national organization. Each such chapter will be assigned a charter number. The name and address of the elected president of each authorized chapter will be made available to all members, so that those who are not already a member of a chapter will be able to join the one nearest them if they wish to."

The "National Headquarters" wasn't the least bit proprietary about being the only fan publication. The September 1954 *Fan-Addict Club Bulletin* listed four other fan publications: *Potrzebie*, *E.C. Fan Journal*, *E.C. Slime Sheet*, and

AN ENTERTAINING EC COMIC

The National
E.C. Fan-Addict Club

in solemn recognition of his/her/its stubborn, hopeless, and pitiful addiction to E.C. magazines, does hereby grudgingly bestow on

a Life Membership, together with such rights, privileges, and benefits (be they what they may) which ordinarily accompany such membership (be that what it may)

SIGNED Melvin*
PRESIDENT
NATIONAL E.C. FAN-ADDICT CLUB
ROOM 706
225 LAFAYETTE STREET
NEW YORK 12, NEW YORK

11961

The *MAD* sense of humor thoroughly permeated the EC sensibility—note that the membership card is "invalid if signed."

Failure to carry this card at all times will result...

This is to certify that

INVALID IF SIGNED

is a life member in good standing of
THE NATIONAL E.C. FAN-ADDICT CLUB
and is therefore entitled, upon presentation of this card, to purchase any 32 page E.C. magazine for the special membership newsstand price of 10c.

11961 Melvin*
PRESIDENT

If you find this card, kindly drop it...

In case of accident... tch, tch!

If this card is lost... tough!

E.C. Scoop. It also encouraged others who were also putting out fan publications to contact EC for a free plug in the *Bulletin*. Even then these fan magazines were called "fanzines."

One of them, published by "Bobby Stewart, Route 4, Kirbyville, Texas," actually predates the Fan-Addict Club itself. Comic book aficionados will better recognize "Bobby Stewart" as noted comics journalist Bhob Stewart.) Other EC fanzines soon followed, including *E.C. World Press*, *Good Lord!*, *Spoof*, *Scoop*, *Fanfare*, and *Concept*. There was also *Hoohah!*, considered by many to be the best of the "first generation" of EC fanzines—meaning those that were started by readers who could buy *Tales from the Crypt* off the news rack.

As EC came under attack by Dr. Wertham and the Senate subcommittee, Gaines tried to rally the readership in support of his beleaguered comics, using the *E.C. Fan-Addict Bulletin* as a bully-pulpit. Fans responded, but they were no match for the Wertham juggernaut. Indeed, their youth and their enthusiasm for horror comics ensured that their opinions would be disregarded. Gaines did not go gentle into that bad night—his *In Memoriam* in the final issues of the horror magazines left no doubt in any reader's mind that he'd been railroaded—a victim of injustice.

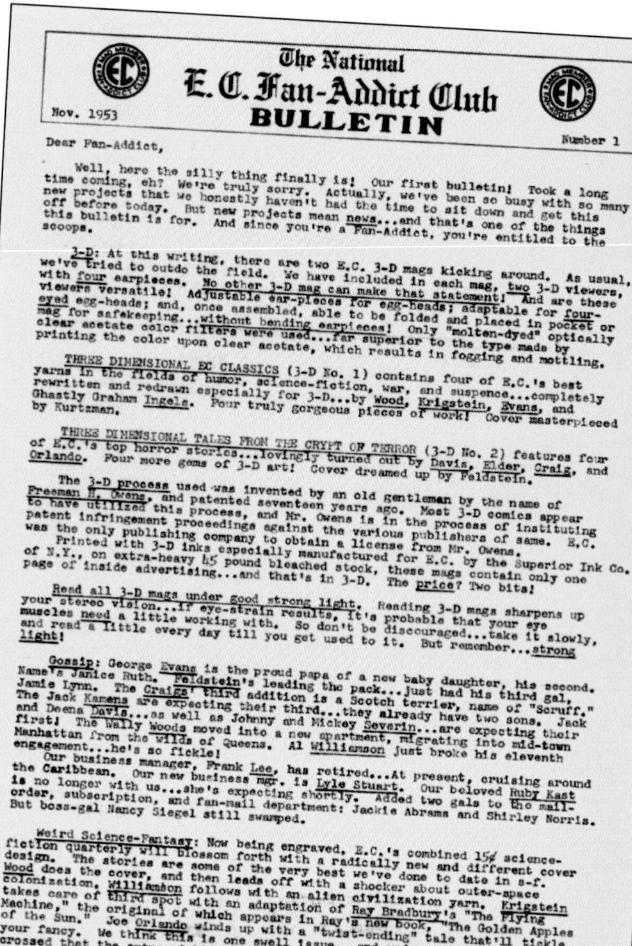

The National
E.C. Fan-Addict Club
BULLETIN

Nov. 1953

Number 1

Dear Fan-Addict,

Well, here the silly thing finally is! Our first bulletin! Took a long time coming, eh? We're truly sorry. Actually, we've been so busy with so many new projects that we honestly haven't had the time to sit down and get this off before today. But new projects mean news...and that's one of the things this bulletin is for. And since you're a Fan-Addict, you're entitled to the scoops.

3-D: At this writing, there are two E.C. 3-D mags kicking around. As usual, we've tried to outdo the field. We have included in each mag, two 3-D viewers, with four earpieces. No other 3-D mag can make that statement! And are these viewers versatile! Adjustable ear-pieces for egg-heads; adaptable for four-eyed egg-heads; and, once assembled, able to be folded and placed in pocket or mag for safekeeping...without bending earpieces! Only "molten-dyed" optically clear acetate color filters were used...far superior to the type made by printing the color upon clear acetate, which results in fogging and mottling.

THREE DIMENSIONAL EC CLASSICS (3-D No. 1) contains four of E.C.'s best yarns in the fields of humor, science-fiction, war, and suspence...completely rewritten and redrawn especially for 3-D...by Wood, Krigstein, Evans, and Ghastly Graham Ingels. Four truly gorgeous pieces of work! Cover masterpieced by Kurtzman.

THREE DIMENSIONAL TALES FROM THE CRYPT OF TERROR (3-D No. 2) features four of E.C.'s top horror stories...lovingly turned out by Davis, Elder, Craig, and Orlando. Four more gems of 3-D art! Cover dreamed up by Feldstein.

The 3-D process used was invented by an old gentleman by the name of Freeman H. Owens, and patented seventeen years ago. Most 3-D comics appear to have utilized this process, and Mr. Owens is in the process of instituting patent infringement proceedings against the various publishers of same. E.C. was the only publishing company to obtain a license from Mr. Owens.

Printed with 3-D inks especially manufactured for E.C. by the Superior Ink Co. of N.Y., on extra-heavy 45 pound bleached stock, these mags contain only one page of inside advertising...and that's in 3-D. The price? Two bits!

Read all 3-D mags under good strong light. Reading 3-D mags sharpens up your stereo vision...if eye-strain results, it's probable that your eye muscles need a little working with. So don't be discouraged...take it slowly, and read a little every day till you get used to it. But remember...strong light!

Gossip: George Evans is the proud papa of a new baby daughter, his second. Name's Janice Ruth. Feldstein's leading the pack...just had his third gal, Jamie Lynn. The Craigs' third addition is a Scotch terrier, name of "Scruff." The Jack Kamens are expecting their third...they already have two sons. Jack and Deena Davis...as well as Johnny and Mickey Severin...are expecting their first! The Wally Woods moved into a new apartment, migrating into mid-town Manhattan from the wilds of Queens. Al Williamson just broke his eleventh engagement...he's so fickle!

Our business manager, Frank Lee, has retired...At present, cruising around the Caribbean. Our new business mgr. is Lyle Stuart. Our beloved Ruby Kast is no longer with us...she's expecting shortly. Added two gals to the mail-order, subscription, and fan-mail department: Jackie Abrams and Shirley Norris. But boss-gal Nancy Siegel still swamped.

Weird Science-Fantasy: Now being engraved, E.C.'s combined 15¢ science-fiction quarterly will blossom forth with a radically new and different cover design. The stories are some of the very best we've done to date in s-f. Wood does the cover, and then leads off with a shocker about outer-space colonization. Williamson follows with an alien civilization yarn. Krigstein takes care of third spot with an adaptation of Ray Bradbury's "The Flying Machine," the original of which appears in Ray's new book, "The Golden Apples of the Sun." Joe Orlando winds up with a "twist-ending" tale that'll tickle your fancy. We think this is one swell issue...and we've got our fingers crossed that the extra nickle tariff won't scare away our regular readership... 'cause we'd like to continue publishing s-f.

The periodic *E.C. Fan-Addict Club Bulletin* helped followers keep tabs on the personal lives of the artists, reinforcing yet again the special sense of connection between the readers of the comics and those who created them.

The National
E.C. Fan-Addict Club
BULLETIN

June 1954

Dear Fan-Addict,

Number 3

THIS IS AN EMERGENCY BULLETIN!

This is an appeal for action!

THE PROBLEM: Comics are under fire...horror and crime comics in particular. Due to the efforts of various "do-gooders" and "do-gooder" groups, a large segment of the public is being led to believe that certain comic magazines cause juvenile delinquency, warp the minds of America's youth, and affect the development of the personalities of those who read them! Among these "do-gooders" are: a psychiatrist who has made a lucrative career of attacking comic magazines, certain publishing companies who do not publish comics and who would benefit by their demise, many groups of adults who would like to blame their lack of ability as responsible parents on comic mags instead of on themselves, and various assorted headline hunters. These people are militant. They complain to local police officials, to local magazine retailers, to local wholesalers, and to their congressmen. They complain and complain and threaten and threaten. Eventually, everyone gets frightened. The newsdealer gets frightened. He removes the books from display. The wholesaler gets frightened. He refuses shipments. The congressmen get frightened...November is coming! They start an investigation. This wave of hysteria has seriously threatened the very existence of the whole comic magazine industry.

WE BELIEVE: Your editors sincerely believe that the claim of these crusaders...that comics are bad for children...is nonsense. If we, in the slightest way, thought that horror comics, crime comics, or any other kind of comics were harmful to our readers, we would cease publishing them and direct our efforts toward something else!

And we're not alone in our belief. For example: Dr. David Abrahamsen, eminent criminologist, in his book, "Who Are The Guilty?" says, "Comic books do not lead to crime, although they have been widely blamed for it...In my experience as a psychiatrist, I cannot remember having seen one boy or girl who has committed a crime, or who became neurotic or psychotic...because he or she read comic books." A group led by Dr. Freda Kehm, Mental Health Chairman of the Ill. Congress of the P.T.A., decided that living room violence has "a decided beneficial effect on young minds". Dr. Robert H. Felix, director of the National Institute of Mental Health, said that horror comic books do not originate criminal behavior in children...in a way, the horror comics may do some good...children may use fantasy, as stimulated by the "comics" as a means of working out natural feelings of aggressiveness.

We also believe that a large portion of our total readership of horror and crime comics is made up of adults. We believe that those who oppose comics are a small minority. Yet this minority is causing the hysteria. The voice of the majority...you who buy comics, read them, enjoy them, and are not harmed by them...has not been heard!

The Senate Subcommittee to Investigate Juvenile Delinquency kept a separate running tally of those who mentioned the E.C. Fan-Addict Club in their letters. Their archives list 217 people who wrote them in support of horror comics.

WHAT YOU MUST DO: Unless you act now, the pressure from this minority may force comics from the American scene. It is members of this minority who threaten the local retailers, who threaten the local wholesalers, who have sent letters to the Senate Subcommittee on Juvenile Delinquency (now investigating the comic industry).

IT IS TIME THAT THE MAJORITY'S VOICE BE HEARD!

It is time that the Senate Subcommittee hears from YOU...each and every one of you!

If you agree that comics are harmless entertainment, write a letter or a postcard TODAY...to:

The Senate Subcommittee on Juvenile Delinquency
United States Senate
Washington 25, D. C.

and in your own words, tell them so. Make it a nice, polite letter! In the case of you younger readers, it would be more effective if you could get your parents to write for you, or perhaps add a P.S. to your letter, as the Senate Subcommittee may not have much respect for the opinions of minors.

Of course, if you or your parents disagree with us, and believe that comics ARE bad, let your sentiments be known on that too! The important thing is that the Subcommittee hear from actual comic book readers and/or their parents, rather than from people who never read a comic magazine in their lives, but simply want to destroy them.

It is also important that your local newsdealer be encouraged to continue carrying, displaying, and selling all kinds of comics. Speak to him. Have him speak to his wholesaler.

Wherever you can, let your voice and the voices of your parents be raised in protest over the campaign against comics.

But first...right now...please write that letter to the Senate Subcommittee.

Sincerely,
Your grateful editors
(for the whole E. C. Gang)

The E. C. Fan-Addict Club Bulletin
Room 706
225 Lafayette Street
New York City 12, N. Y.

GO MAD!
join the

From the old artist spotlights and fan-addict bulletins, EC readers were already familiar with the names and faces of their favorite artists. Fanzine editors kept in touch with them for interviews and "where are they now?" updates.

Jerry Weist on Becoming a Professional Fan

When I was in elementary school, a friend of mine in Battle Creek, Michigan, offered me seven EC comics for $1.50. I happened to be sick in bed with the flu the day they arrived. My mother brought me the package and it blew my mind. My friend Roger Hill and I began a methodical search. By not spending our lunch money, doing lawns and other odd jobs, within two and a half years, we had nearly everything. We were fanatical. I used to come home every day from grade school and run to get my mail, which was set at the end of the hall. At that time, I was looking for packages either from Claude Held in Ohio or Bill Thailing or Howard Rogofsky or Phil Seuling in New York. If there wasn't a manila envelope waiting for me, I'd take my schoolbooks and throw them the entire length of the hall.

Weist with Bill Gaines in 1987.

By the time Roger and I graduated from high school in 1967, we had complete collections, and were planning our first trip to New York City to visit Bill Gaines, who was our hero. We'd already called Harvey Kurtzman and Bill Elder and Johnny Craig.

If someone had said to me when I graduated from high school, "You're going to make your living doing one of two things: either you're going to become an astronaut and go to the moon, or you'll work for this venerable old English auction house called Sotheby's, and hold auctions of old comic books that bring in one to two million dollars a year," I would have said, "My God! I'm going to be an astronaut — I'm going to the moon!!"

When economic reality forced Gaines to drop *Tales* and the other horror titles, many readers were left with a profound feeling of loss. Fans who had been immersed in the EC family spirit mourned when the issues stopped coming—it was as if a member of the family had died. For the most fervent EC fans—and there were many—it was a bit like the death of Elvis.

Carrying the Torch

In withdrawal, EC fan-addicts reacted the way many fans do when a well-loved celebrity dies suddenly in his prime: they made shrines and venerated artifacts from the past. For several years after the end of *Tales from the Crypt*, the fanzines served as links among the faithful. Run off on mimeographs or hectographs, the homegrown fanzines revered not just EC's horror magazines but the science fiction titles as well. They were a place where fans could swap anecdotes and talk about their favorite stories and artists. In short, they were an ongoing printed wake. For EC that was appropriate, since in 1956 it was almost in the grave itself.

MAD was the only bright hope, and its sales were strong. Gaines was convinced that the key to *MAD*'s success was Harvey Kurtzman. At about the same time that Kefauver was bearing down on comic books, Kurtzman was offered a job with *Pageant* magazine, which had recently done a feature story on the *MAD* phenomenon. Harvey had coveted the idea of working for a "legitimate" magazine, or "slick" as it was known in the publishing business, and was about to defect. Fearing that he would lose Kurtzman, Gaines offered to change *MAD* from a comic book to a magazine if Harvey would stay at EC. Kurtzman accepted, and with issue #24 (July 1955), *MAD* changed format from a full-color comic book to a black-and-white magazine.

Bill was nervous about the transition, but the first issue of *MAD* as a magazine was so popular that they had to go back for a second printing —a rarity in magazine publishing.

Picto-Fiction

Coincidentally, by becoming a magazine rather than remaining a comic book, *MAD* escaped from Judge Murphy's little old ladies and their odious scissors. Gaines always maintained that he made the change to keep Kurtzman rather than to get out from under the CMAA code, but the idea that one could mutate a successful comic book into a successful magazine was not lost on him. In the summer of 1955 he started up four new magazines, dubbed *Adult Picto-Fiction*. He priced them at a quarter apiece (just like *MAD* magazine)

THE BASKET

The man was whistling softly as he trudged along.
Somewhere in the pines, a jay-bird screamed. A toad, invisible against the dust-dry background of the rutted road, leaped from under his hobnailed shoe in the nick of time. It startled him.
He stopped for a moment to study it. The toad waited, frozen, like a stone. He nudged it with his toe. The toad shot into the hot summer air. Once. Twice. It was lost in the high grass at the edge of the road.
The man moved on, still whistling.
The jay-bird screamed again, closer this time. A flash of blue streaked from the pines ahead and disappeared into the oaks on the other side of the road.
He hesitated. Something had scared that jay-bird. His knuckles paled as he grasped the basket perched on his right shoulder. He stopped whistling.
The boy came out of the pine grove. He pushed through the grass to the road. His head was down so he did not see.
When he looked up, his eyes widened, and his face paled. He froze there, like the toad, staring at the man with the basket.

GRAHAM INGELS

33

Then the boy turned and ran. Not in fear. In a kind of throbbing excitement. He sprinted down the road, his bare toes catching up dust and throwing it back behind him in little yellow clouds.
"He's coming! He's coming again!" he cried as he neared a small group of boys huddled over an engrossing game of marbles. "Mr. Cabez is coming into town again."

"Did you see him?" A freckled-faced boy got to his feet.
"He's up the road. Nearly scared me to death," the messenger gasped, breathlessly pointing in the direction from which he'd come.
"Has he got his basket with him?" Another boy stood up.
The boy on the ground took careful aim. "Did you ever see him *without* it?"

Four wide-eyed expectant faces turned in the direction of the distant sound of whistling. They waited, with only the rasps of their excited breathing. Their game was forgotten.
He rounded the bend in the road and came into sight. The man.
"See? What did I tell you? He never goes anywhere without that basket!"

They whispered among themselves as the strange figure with the round wicker basket perched on his shoulder approached.
"Always carries it on his right shoulder, too!"
"He's crazy, that's what he is!"
"Sh-h-h! He'll hear you!"
The man stopped whistling and smiled as he came up to where the group of boys stood waiting.

34

Al Feldstein wrote many of the *Picto-Fiction* stories, sometimes under the *nom de plume* Alfred E. Neuman. This story, "The Basket," was recycled from *Haunt of Fear* #7.

and printed them in black and white rather than in color. To further distinguish them from comics, narrative text ran at the top of each panel in lieu of dialogue balloons. The magazines featured stories and artwork by Feldstein and other veterans from the other horror comics. Called *Terror Illustrated*, *Shock Illustrated*, *Crime Illustrated*, and *Confessions Illustrated*, the titles of the magazines left no doubt that Gaines was aiming for the large market of horror lovers that the Code had forced him to abandon.

It wasn't a bad idea; it just didn't work. The *Adult Picto-Fiction* magazines were commercial failures. Early in 1956, it was clear that they would have to be abandoned. Indeed, it had been clear at Christmastime 1955 that they were doomed, but Gaines refused to give anyone the bad news during the holidays. As the new year dawned, Gaines with great sadness was forced to lay off much of his staff, including Al Feldstein and most of the artists—anyone who was not involved with *MAD*. Only a skeleton crew working with Harvey Kurtzman remained, and their future was in doubt. Reluctantly, Gaines also let his friend and business manager, Lyle Stuart, go. The creative but free-spending Kurtzman had a terminal personality conflict with Stuart, whose difficult job it was to guard the very endangered bottom line.

Flat Broke

It was not a good time to be without a business manager. The end of *New Direction* was followed closely by the failure of EC's distributor, Leader News. In January of 1956, Leader News went bankrupt, leaving Gaines holding an empty sack where $100,000 should have been. Worse yet, he owed this $100,000 that he did not have to his printer and friend, George Dougherty. The coffers were completely empty—there wasn't enough money to bind the 250,000-copy run of *Shock Illustrated* #3 that had already been printed. All 250,000 were destroyed, except for one or two hundred that were hand-bound for posterity. (*Shock Illustrated* #3 is now the Hope Diamond of EC collectibles.)

It was bitterly ironic that EC in 1956 was in exactly the same financial condition—$100,000 in the hole—that it had been

"*MAD* needed a mascot," says Al Feldstein. "Harvey had this character with the goofy grin, but he was just in the border on the cover. Norman Mingo painted his portrait, but I had to give him a name. Alfred E. Neuman was an EC house pseudonym. I put the name with the kid's picture and we ran him as a write-in candidate for president."

when Bill had taken over after his father's death in 1947. Without a cash transfusion, there was no way to print the next issue of *MAD*, which was now his only profit center. If they didn't print, there not only was no *MAD*, there was no EC either. In order to go to press, Bill and Harvey went hat in hand to see Jessie Gaines, Bill's mother, who owned 50 percent of EC. After the visit, she and Bill each put $50,000 of their own money into the business to keep it afloat.

The visit must have been more than a little uncomfortable for Kurtzman, who was once again flirting with departure. *Playboy* publisher Hugh Hefner wanted to start a comic humor magazine, and was courting

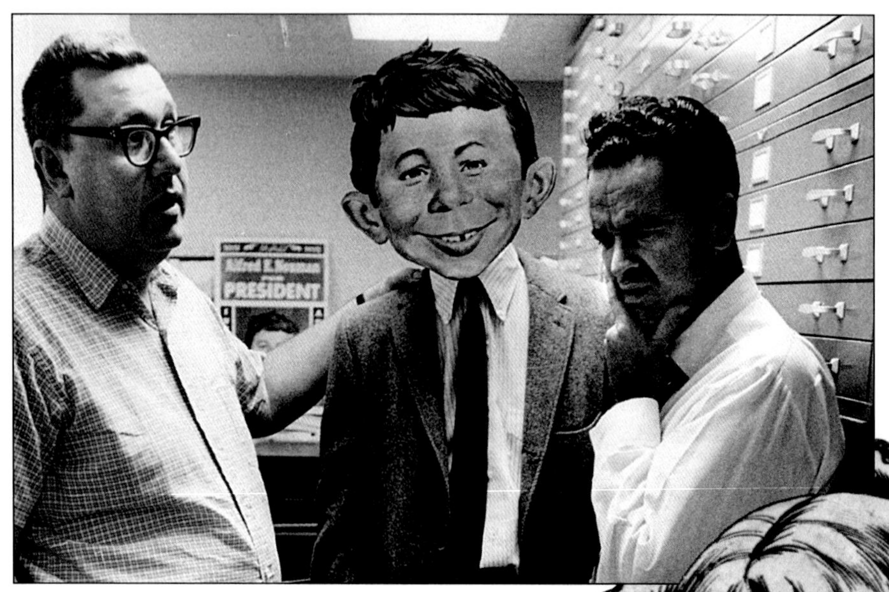

What, me gory? Gaines and Feldstein, the gruesome twosome, are okay, but that guy in the middle, Aldead E. Slewman, is a real stiff!

Kurtzman ardently. In April of 1956, after putting out five issues of *MAD* as a magazine and just a couple of months after helping convince Gaines *mère et fils* to throw $100,000 into EC, Harvey was sure enough of his future with Hefner that he risked a confrontation with Gaines over control of *MAD*.

Like a tenant who had lived in the building so long he thought he'd earned the deed to his own apartment, Kurtzman demanded a controlling interest in *MAD*. Gaines offered him 10 percent, but was offended not just by Kurtzman's power play but by its timing.

Fired by Bill Gaines, largely at Harvey Kurtzman's behest, Lyle Stuart was in Florida to escape the New York winter and the sting of his separation from EC. He still clearly recalls the emergency phone call he received from a sheepish but panicked Bill Gaines:

"Lyle, I'm in trouble," Bill said.

"What's wrong, Bill?" I asked.

"I know I don't have the right to ask you anything," Bill continued, "but..."

"Come on...but what?" I said.

"Well, Harvey Kurtzman is outside, and he said if I don't give him 51 percent of *MAD*, he's quitting."

So I said, "What floor are you on, the seventh or the eighth?"

Bill said, "The seventh."

"Good," I said. "You've got the big picture windows behind you. Open the window, go out, get Kurtzman, and throw him out the window."

Bill began laughing in spite of himself, then took a deep breath.

"Seriously, Lyle, what do I do?"

"Bill, I *am* serious," I replied. "Do what I tell you. Throw Kurtzman out the window!"

He said, "Then what do I do?"

"Get another editor."

"Who?"

"Get Feldstein back," I said.

"Do you think he can do it?" Bill asked.

"Why not? He did fine with *Panic—and* he was putting out seven other magazines at the same time."

Harvey left with Bill's foot propelling him from the rear.

What was particularly painful for Gaines was that Bill Elder and Jack Davis followed Harvey to work for Hefner. With the deadline for the next issue fast approaching, Gaines needed an editor for *MAD*.

Lyle Stuart was perhaps the first person to tell him to seek out Al Feldstein, but he wasn't the last. Bill's new bride, Nancy (who had worked in the subscription department of the old comics), gave him the same advice, as did artist Joe Orlando. Hearing the same counsel from three people he trusted, Bill sought out Al once again.

Feldstein had been out of work for about four months. He had spruced up his portfolio and had pounded the pavement looking to hook up with another comic book publisher. Now he was finally on the brink of landing a new position. He was one meeting away from clinching this new job when he got off the Long Island Railroad after having spent the day in Manhattan. Emerging from the train at his stop in Merrick, he saw Bill Gaines' familiar Michelin-man silhouette waiting for him on the platform.

The Bill & Al Show, Part II

Feldstein took up the reins at *MAD* with little if any loss of momentum. The major stumbling block was not the absence of Kurtzman, but the departure of Elder and Davis. Gaines and Feldstein set about building yet another stable of quality artists who, like the EC artists from the early days, would be given star billing in the magazine. Beginning with horror/science fiction survivors Wally Wood and Joe Orlando, the "usual gang of idiots" they assembled—Don Martin, Antonio Prohias, Sergio Aragones, Dave Berg, Norman Mingo, and Kelly Freas, among others—gave *MAD* its distinctive look and feel and brought it to its peak of popularity. In 1959 *MAD* was the favorite magazine of 58 percent of U.S. college students and 43 percent of high school kids.

By the early 1960s, as America headed into space and into JFK's "New Frontier," *MAD* under Feldstein was soaring, but the memory of the EC horror comics had faded—along with the controversy they engendered. Although the first generation of fanzines had petered out and most fan-addicts were in hibernation, the world climate was certainly similar to that in which *Tales from the Crypt* and the other EC comics had first flourished. Horror was making a strong showing in other media—Rod Serling's *Twilight Zone* and *Alfred Hitchcock Presents* were popular television shows, and Hitchcock's *Psycho* was one of the top films of 1960.

The horror comeback may have been due to the ongoing terrors of the Cold War, but every day there was horror on the daily news—fugitive Nazi war criminal Adolf Eichmann was captured in Argentina; Cuban exiles were massacred as they invaded their homeland at the Bay of Pigs; babies with flippers instead of arms were being born to women who took Thalidomide during pregnancy. We began being pulled into the Tar Baby that became Vietnam. But everyday horror was never more terrifying than the events of November 1963, when Americans got to watch the televised murder of a President and the strange events that followed—over and over and over in slow motion.

Then in 1964, two events occurred that rekindled interest in comics in general and EC comics in particular. The first comic book convention was held in New York City, bringing comic book aficionados and collectors together for the first time. Then in December of that year, New York publisher Ian Ballantine issued reprints of old EC comics. (Ballantine had previously reprinted early issues of the comic book version of *MAD*.) His first was *Tales from the Crypt*. Reprints from the EC science fiction comics, which Ballantine called *Tales of the Incredible*, followed four months later, and in August 1965, Ballantine brought out *The Vault of Horror*.

Although they were printed in black and white, the Ballantine reprints introduced a new generation of readers to EC comics.

Ballantine successfully published reprints of *MAD* comic book issues and other EC properties.

Weist established a high standard for EC scholarship and showed real flair as an editor in his issues of *Squa Tront*.

Passing the Torch

One of those who took up the torch was Jerry Weist, who learned of EC comics not from the Ballantine reprints, but from a friend who sold him a handful of them for the exorbitant sum of $1.50. Just a couple of months after graduating from high school in June of 1967, Weist started up *Squa Tront*, which remains by reputation the best second-generation fanzine. Weist put out four issues; with Issue #5 (1974) he relinquished the editor's chair to John Benson. Other second-generation fanzines included *Spa Fon* (1966–1969), and *The E.C. Fan-Addict* (later renamed *Seraphim*) (1967–1970).

Another torchbearer was Russ Cochran, one of the original EC Fan-Addicts. Now a tenured professor at Drake University, in 1965 he was set to attend a convention of physics teachers in New York. Fondly remembering his fan-addict days, Cochran wrote Bill Gaines, filling him in on what had happened to the members of Chapter #3 of the E.C. Fan-Addict Club, West Plains, MO. Among the E.C. alumni were two college professors, a physician, and a minister—not an axe murderer in the bunch. Gaines was tickled by the letter and wrote back inviting Cochran to drop in at the *MAD* offices and indulge in his favorite activity, breaking bread over a bottle of good wine. It was, as Bogey and Claude Rains said to one another at the end of *Casablanca*, the beginning of a beautiful friendship.

Derived from the exclamations of Martians in *Weird Science* stories, the titles *Squa Tront* and *Spa Fon* were also rumored to be scatological acronyms.

Russ Cochran: Leader of the West Plains Fan-Addict Club

Cochran with Buck, one of his three chimpanzees.

When I saw my first EC comic, I was fourteen. I lived in the small town of West Plains, Missouri, in the days before television. Comic books were what I existed on. I read the superhero comics, Captain Marvel, Superman, Batman, and the rest, and the crime comics that came out in the late '40s. By the time I was about 14, which was in 1951, I thought I had passed my comic reading stage until one day I happened upon an EC comic—I think the first one I ever saw was a copy of **Haunt of Fear**. I immediately recognized that the level of writing, the level of artwork, and the O. Henry type endings were very different from what I'd seen before. I loved it right away. I thought, "This is unique."

When the E.C. Fan-Addict Club was formed in 1953, my two younger brothers and I, together with about four other boys in the neighborhood, formed Chapter #3. In my capacity as president I went down to the hardware store and got a wooden shotgun shell box, a couple of hinges, a hasp, and a padlock. I made a locked wood box that held two stacks of EC comics perfectly. Every week we would have a meeting of our chapter. We would ceremoniously unlock the box, and take the comics out. We would sit in a circle, pass the comics around, and read and re-read and re-read them.

Tales from an English Crypt

In 1971 Amicus Films (a partnership between Max Rosenberg and Milton Subotsky) approached Bill Gaines about putting out a film version of *Tales from the Crypt*. He was charmed by Rosenberg's literate wit, and Gaines gave his approval for *Tales from the Crypt*, which was released in 1972. Amicus had already produced *Dr. Terror's House of Horrors* (1964) and *Torture Garden* (1967), both of which had been directed by British director Freddie Francis. Francis took on similar duties for *Tales from the Crypt*, working from a script by Subotsky. Before becoming a director, Francis had been an outstanding cinematographer, working on such highly regarded films as *Room at the Top* (1959) and *Saturday Night and Sunday Morning* (1960). He won an Oscar for cinematography for his work on the film adaptation of D. H. Lawrence's *Sons and Lovers* (1960).

***New York* magazine found the gore in *Tales from the Crypt* too graphic, making the movie fit only for "those with cast-iron stomachs and short memories."**

In keeping with the format of the comic book, the *Tales* movie was a group of stories that were linked together by the narration of the on-screen host, the Crypt Keeper. Starring as the Crypt Keeper was distinguished British actor Ralph Richardson (eventually to become Sir Ralph). Oddly enough, Richardson's first credited screen work was in a 1933 British film called *The Ghoul*, which starred William Henry Platt, whose stage name happened to be Boris Karloff. Unfortunately, Richardson in *Tales* looks much more like a dignified but eccentric old abbot than the GhouLunatic created by Feldstein and refined by Jack Davis. Indeed, the Keeper's "Crypt of Terror" is the sanctum sanctorum of an ancient monastery, and not nearly as sinister as the dark and scary crypt that many had conjured up in their imaginations while reading the comic book.

Sir Ralph's Crypt Keeper bore absolutely no resemblance to either the Feldstein or the Davis version.

The first story in the film is "And All Through the House" (originally depicted in *Vault of Horror* #35, Feb./Mar. '54, with story and art by Johnny Craig). The tale stars Joan Collins (taking her first steps to revive her career after her divorce from singer Anthony Newley, but very much pre–Alexis Carrington) as a woman who finds herself stalked by a psychopath after having murdered her husband on Christmas Eve. She is unwittingly done in when her child opens the door to the maniac, who has suited himself up as St. Nicholas. "Reflection of Death," the second story (*Tales from the Crypt* #23, Apr./May '51, Feldstein story and artwork), is the saga of a man who has forsaken his wife and children. On his way to rendezvous with his mistress, he is killed in an auto accident, becoming a grisly walking corpse. Or is he? The cad awakens in his car to find that this has all been a nightmare—except that his car is now hurtling headlong toward an inevitable crash. (Chalk up another behind-the-scenes credit for Ambrose Bierce.)

Joan Collins' first Christmas gift to herself, a dead husband, was also her last.

"Poetic Justice" (*Haunt of Fear* #12, Mar./Apr. '52, Feldstein/Ingels), featured horror megastar Peter Cushing as an elderly widower who hangs himself after being pressured to sell his property to the town's richest man and his son. He then rises from his grave on Valentine's Day to haunt his enemies as a ghastly spectre. The fourth story, "Wish You Were Here" (*Haunt of Fear* #23, Nov./Dec. '53, Feldstein/Ingels), is a reinterpretation of the "Monkey's Paw," or a takeoff on the old "three wishes" folktale. A woman is granted three wishes. Her first, for money, results in the death of her husband. Her second, for his return, brings her a zombie spouse. Her third, for his eternal

Makeup artists achieved a remarkable similarity between Peter Cushing in full regalia for the movie version of "Poetic Justice" and this Feldstein drawing in "Reflection of Death."

Cushing was one of horror's leading men, having achieved stardom in numerous Hammer productions in the 1950s.

Director Freddie Francis on the First Tales from the Crypt Movie

Academy Award winner Freddie Francis used his connections with the British film industry to bring noted actors and quality technical staff into what was essentially a low-budget production. "I insisted on key people with whom I'd worked previously. It was rather difficult because as a cameraman, the films that I'd photographed before were in a much more expensive category. It was often difficult to persuade people to work on these horror films, but we managed to get a few."

Tales from the Crypt was shot in about thirty days, and a lot of it was a bit more improvisational than Francis might have liked:

"Max [Rosenberg] and Milton [Subotsky] would budget a film and try to raise the money for it. Eventually somebody would offer them about half or two-thirds of what they needed and they would go ahead and begin production, then raise the rest as they went along. I was always presented with scripts that were about half as long as they should be, so I'd have to set about adding scenes, sometimes even as we were shooting. We had some fun doing **Tales**, but it was always a real shoestring operation."

Since the film was an anthology of short stories, each with a different cast, none of the actors was involved for more than a week.

"We had Ralph Richardson for two days and things were going slightly awry because the script was much too short. We made it up as we went along, and dear old Ralph didn't mind. I used to keep going along and apologizing to him, but he was quite happy in his dressing room, reading his books. We actually used just a half day of real shooting…to shoot just dialogue with Ralph didn't take any time at all."

Francis would have much preferred to keep more of the same sense of tongue-in-cheek humor in the **Tales** movie that made the EC comics so distinctive — but to do that he had to wait another twenty-four years. In a classic, EC-style, what goes around/comes around ending, in late 1995 Francis directed a segment of the **Tales from the Crypt** HBO series called "Last Respects." Working with actresses Emma Samms, Kerry Fox, and Julie Cox, Francis was finally able to be faithful to the campy humor of the originals. "I thought to myself, I deliberately don't do horror films now, but my God, if I could get a script like this and three actresses like these, I'd go back to doing them."

life, condemns him to perpetual dyspepsia as embalming fluid corrodes his innards. The role of the hapless, long-suffering husband was played by swash-buckling hero Richard Greene, perhaps best known to U.S. audiences as TV's Robin Hood. The final morality tale, "Blind Alleys" (*Tales from the Crypt* #46, Feb./Mar. '55, drawn by George Evans), is that of the retribution of a group of residents of a Dickensian home for the blind against their cruel overseer. The callous superintendent (Nigel Patrick) is literally backed onto the horns of a most distasteful dilemma by the vengeful inmates. To avoid being dismembered by his faithful slavering dog, Brutus, who has been starved by the men, he must walk or run down an exceedingly narrow corridor lined by the very finest double-edged razor blades Gillette can offer.

In the comic, Evans and Feldstein let the reader imagine the superintendent's gruesome fate. The film made it explicit.

Feldstein and Gaines were both present at the gala preview of *Vault of Horror*, but were disappointed by the result.

Bizarrely enough, none of the segments in the *Vault of Horror* film came from the *Vault of Horror* comic books.

In 1973, Amicus released a sequel entitled (of course) *Vault of Horror*.

It showcased a first-rate cast that included Terry-Thomas, Glynis Johns, Curt Jurgens, Denholm Elliot, and the Masseys, Daniel and Anna—the son and daughter of distinguished character actor Raymond (Dr. Gillespie to Richard Chamberlain's Dr. Kildare) Massey.

***Vault of Horror* director Roy Ward worked from Joe Orlando's panels in "Midnight Mess" to block out his scenes.**

In "Midnight Mess" (originally from *Tales from the Crypt* #35, Apr./May '53, Feldstein/Orlando), the first *Vault of Horror* tale, the sibling Masseys play (natch) brother and sister. After Daniel murders Sis, he dines out in a vampire restaurant and finds his jugular tapped as a beverage dispenser. "Neat Job" (*Shock SuspenStories* #1, Feb./Mar. '52, Feldstein/Kamen) has the fidgety Terry-Thomas as a compulsively tidy man (as was Gaines himself), whose obsession drives his spouse (Glynis Johns) to take extreme measures. After dispatching his soul to the great beyond, she fastidiously dismembers his parts and files them in well-labeled jars. "This Trick'll Kill You" (*Tales from the Crypt* #33, Dec./Jan. '52, Feldstein/Evans & Kamen) features a magician (Curt Jurgens) and his assistant (American starlet Dawn Addams, in her last screen appearance) whose quest to obtain a rope trick from a rival eventually results in their own grisly demise. In "Bargain in Death" (*Tales from the Crypt* #28 Feb./Mar. '52, Feldstein/Davis), a man who fakes his own death in order to bilk his insurance company discovers that the joke is on him when he finds himself permanently in the hereafter. In "Drawn and Quartered" (*Tales from the Crypt* #26, Oct./Nov. '51, Feldstein/Davis) an artist who had been cheated gets revenge on his enemies by using voodoo to disfigure their portraits, at least until turpentine is spilled on his own self-portrait and he's flattened by a truck.

Glynis Johns' role as a murderess and spouse dismemberer is a radical departure from her portrayal of Mrs. Banks, the sweet but ditzy suffragette mother in *Mary Poppins*.

Vault of Horror was directed by Roy Ward Baker, perhaps best known for *A Night to Remember* (1958), a documentary-style film of Walter Lord's book about the sinking of the *Titanic*. *Vault* was not as artistically or commercially successful as *Tales*, and Gaines, who had been particularly impressed by the photography of the first film (not surprising, considering Francis' background as a cinematographer), was reportedly unhappy with it. He did, however, share the proceeds he received from the production of both films with the artists and writers of that time—something he was under no legal obligation to do. He even sent money to Harvey Kurtzman, who'd worked very little in horror. Gaines, however, thought he owed him a percentage since he'd been third in command at EC at the time.

Bizarrely enough, *Tales from the Crypt* was not the first film made from an EC comic. In 1966, Al Feldstein went to an art movie house in New York and watched in fascination as one of his stories, "Gone Fishing" (*Vault of Horror* #22), unreeled as a French-produced short film called *The Fisherman*. Feldstein called Gaines and said, "Hey, Bill, we've been ripped off." Perhaps mindful of his early unauthorized adaptation experiences with Ray Bradbury, and Bradbury's gentlemanly response, Gaines contacted the producers—what he was after was less financial compensation than proper recognition. Eventually the producers added an "adapted from EC Comics" credit and gave both Feldstein and Gaines a copy of the film.

A Boondoggle Made in Heaven

The release of *Tales from the Crypt* and *Vault of Horror* corresponded with the crest of a tidal wave of new interest in EC comics, a wave generated in large measure by the activities of the fan-addicts.

Throughout the mid- to late 1960s, Russ Cochran and Bill Gaines played out their own version of *Same Time Next Year* as Cochran's junket to New York, ostensibly for the physics teachers convention, became an annual affair. Instead of attending lectures and seminars, Cochran the physics professor and Gaines the almost–chemistry teacher played hooky together. On one of these boondoggles, Cochran caught sight of some original EC artwork, which Gaines had pulled from the archives for the 1971 book *Horror Comics of the 1950s*, also called *The EC Horror Library* (Nostalgia Press), published by Woody Gelman and edited by Bhob Stewart (one of the earliest fan-addicts) and Ron Barlow. Cochran was struck by how much better the artwork looked in its original oversize form and asked permission from Gaines to put out a large portfolio, about the size of a tabloid newspaper, containing some of the most outstanding examples of EC artwork.

Gaines happily consented, and the physics professor was quickly in the publishing business. Cochran's *EC Portfolio* (the first of six) came out in 1971. By 1977, he had reproduced 27 covers and 29 stories. Selling them at comic book conventions all over the country, Cochran demonstrated a real market for EC artwork. In addition

In these Graphic Masters posters (above) and Cochran's portfolios (right), artists' details that had not been visible in the cheaply printed comic books emerged. These posters and portfolios are now collectors' items.

In 1973, the first East Coast Comix reprint was a comic which would have been the first issue of EC's fourth horror title. Gaines was planning to resuscitate *Crypt of Terror* (the original title of *Tales from the Crypt*), but when censorship problems became oppressive, he published the contents as the last *Tales from the Crypt* in 1955.

to Cochran's portfolios and the Nostalgia Press book, there was a *Haunt of Fear* poster reprint (published by Cochran), duplicate versions of the old E.C. Fan-Addict kits, put out by Dave Gibson (1971), more posters published by Graphic Masters (Bruce Hershenson and Ron Barlow), and *EC Classic Reprints* (1973–75), published by East Coast Comix —another Barlow and Hershenson venture.

Barlow and Hershenson also collaborated on an event that amounted to an EC reunion, 1972 E.C. Fan-Addict Convention. The enterprising pair rented a ballroom at New York's Hotel McAlpin for Memorial Day weekend and invited Gaines, Feldstein, all the EC artists, and anyone else who had been directly or tangentially involved with EC fandom. Amazingly enough, they all showed up (except Graham Ingels). A registration fee of $7.50 bought you access to the dealers' room, seminars with the artists, a screening of the new British *Tales from the Crypt* movie, and Harvey Kurtzman's home movies of the 1953 EC Halloween party and boat cruise.

What happened, of course, was true bonding—the hands that wrote the stories and drew the artwork shook the hands of the fans who loved it. People who had been speaking to one another by phone for years finally met face-to-face. As Russ Cochran recalls, "Everyone there was as nutty as I was. We all had a total immersion in EC comics for four days. It was fabulous."

The 1972 convention was the Woodstock of Tales from the Crypt.

The convention proved that old EC gospel—what goes around, comes around. With the Vault Keeper giggling over *Seduction of the Innocent* (long disregarded as a serious work), and new Wally Wood artwork for the brochure, the convention proved that Potrzebie's Revenge was at hand.

Russ Cochran resigned as head of the Drake University physics department and bought a vintage building in his old hometown of West Plains, which has become the capital of a bustling business in EC hardcover reprints.

The Complete Reprints

In 1978, after having successfully put out six portfolios, Russ Cochran was no longer content to publish merely highlights or bits and pieces of the EC *oeuvre*. He now wanted to go after the complete works. With Gaines' authorization, he began publishing the entire EC library, from the pre-*Trend* comics like *Crime Patrol*, *Moon Girl*, and *War Against Crime* through the horror and science fiction titles, *MAD* as a comic, its spinoff, *Panic*, the short-lived *New Direction* comics like *Aces High* and *Piracy*, all the way to the ill-fated *Adult Picto-Fiction*. The first volumes, the complete *Weird Science*, appeared in 1979; the last were published in 1995.

Cochran published his comics in handsomely bound hardcover volumes in an oversized format. Except for the covers, which were in full color, the interiors were in black and white so that the artists' line work, obscured in the original size by the smaller size and cheap printing quality, would be more visible. Gaines gave Cochran access to the originals in the Second Avenue vault in preparing the reprints.

Printed on quality paper, the comics appeared almost exactly as they had in the 1950s, with the addition of commentary and anecdotes by Cochran and other fan-addicts, including Bhob Stewart and *Squa Tront* editor John Benson, among others. Some of this explanatory text had originally appeared in *Squa Tront*; Cochran supplemented this information with additional material from Frank Jacobs' 1973 biography of Bill Gaines, which had been published by former EC business manager Lyle Stuart.

Cochran, however, did not print directly from the artists' originals. Instead, he and Gaines had the artwork meticulously photographed, and the books were prepared from slides. Once this task was accomplished, Bill Gaines felt that he could finally part with the now quarter-century-old original illustration boards.

The Comic Art Auctions

Gaines asked Cochran to handle the sales. His first EC comic book art auctions were held in 1979.

When they began, no one quite knew what to expect but Cochran's auctions demonstrated that a lively market existed for original comic art. Bill Gaines had caught another wave, this time one of nostalgia.

Why were the auctions so successful in the early 1980s? It was a time when the United States was taking its lumps internationally. The Ayatollah had taken the reins of power in Iran; terrorist incidents in the Middle East were frequent, and the U.S. seemed powerless to cope with them. The Sandinistas were thumbing their noses at us in Nicaragua. Americans in record numbers deserted Detroit for less expensive and better made Hondas and Toyotas. More prosperous car owners scorned Cadillacs and Chryslers in favor of Beemers and Mercedes. In household products, Sony and Panasonic trounced venerable American brands like RCA, GE, and Sylvania in everything from TVs to toaster ovens. We forsook hamburgers and roast beef for yuppie chow like radicchio, arugula, goat cheese, and raspberry vinaigrette, because "everyone knew" that the world's best cuisine came from France and Italy.

As it became tough to name more than five things that America still did better than anyone else in the world, naturally enough we began looking back to a simpler time, when U.S. preeminence was unquestioned. Although it had been a Broadway musical, the 1978 movie *Grease*, with John Travolta and Olivia Newton-John, epitomized the affection that people held for the Eisenhower era—even those who were too young to remember it firsthand. From the comparative safety of the early 1980s, it was easy to don rose-colored glasses and gloss over the duck and cover A-bomb drills and the communist witchhunts in order to recall the poodle skirts, the Chevies, do-wop, and *I Love Lucy*.

In the early '80s, Boomers and Pre-Boomers looked back fondly on their disappearing youth as they plucked their first gray hairs, and were prosperous enough to buy some of their childhood back. Yard sales, tag sales, and flea markets proliferated as the collectibles business mushroomed. Like Fiestaware and 3-D movies, comic books were part of the "good stuff" that people remembered about the 1950s. The film version of *Superman*, starring Christopher Reeve, came out in the same year as *Grease*, and demonstrated the enduring popularity of the Man of Steel. As comic book art prices began to skyrocket, eventually Sotheby's, the distinguished auction house, took over the auctions from Russ Cochran, with longtime fan-addict and former *Squa Tront* editor Jerry Weist serving as house consultant.

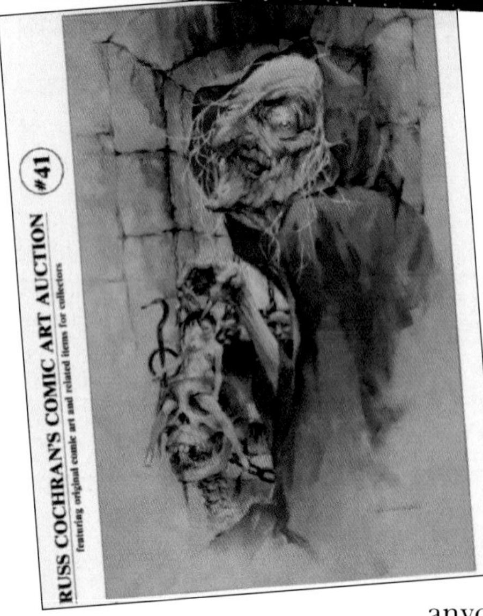

As Gaines released the original art for sale, Russ Cochran prepared catalogs and sent them to interested collectors.

The Stage Is Set

All in all it was a remarkable transformation. From 1956 to 1983, *Tales from the Crypt* had mutated from a drug on the market to a cult favorite to a hot collectible property. The stage was set for the next step, the return of *Tales from the Crypt* and the reintroduction of the Crypt Keeper to television audiences.

Necro-Ghouldwyn-Mayhem, here I come! I'm ready for my gross-up, Mr. Silver. Heh, heh, heh.

Like its comic book predecessor, the HBO series *Tales from the Crypt* is a labor of love. Since its inception, many top actors and directors have worked for scale just to be involved in the grisly glee. Before it could become a labor of love, however, it was a labor of persistence and determination. In an industry where getting anything made is difficult, it took the influence and backing of five of the most powerful figures in Hollywood to bring *Tales from the Crypt* to television.

A Star Is... Exhumed

Tales Resurrected on TV

The reason people love *Tales from the Crypt* is that they're funny and they're gruesome. They're like a guilty pleasure that appeals to the dark side, the murderous rage that every human has in them. They give you a healthy outlet to take pleasure in that fantasy, a pleasure we all enjoy, even though we don't want to admit it.

That's what Gaines and Feldstein did in the comic books, and that's what we wanted translated very specifically to the screen. The episodes had to be stylish, full of irony and satire and black humor, and a lot of that humor comes from the fact that there were characters who had absolutely no redeeming value—the more despicable the characters, the better. At the very first screening when we unveiled the first three episodes, Joel Silver stood up and said, "Ladies and gentlemen, this is *Tales from the Crypt*. This is **not** *Tales from Sesame Street*."

—Robert Zemeckis

First There Were Two

Director and *Tales* executive producer Walter Hill grew up reading the originals. "I was a great fan of EC comics when I was a kid—much to the despair of my mother," he reminisces fondly. "I used to collect them; I was about twelve when they got into trouble with Senator Kefauver and the committee, but I still loved them. One of my ambitions was to get into the comic book world. It was everything I wanted to do. I thought it would be a great life to make up these wild stories, write them, and draw them."

Intent on becoming a cartoonist, Hill briefly embarked on a course of study at the University of the Americas in Mexico City, but returned to the States and settled for a degree in English instead. For several years he drifted in and out of documentary film work before becoming the second assistant director on *Bullitt* (1968), where he found himself responsible for civilian safety during the landmark breakneck chase sequence through the streets of San Francisco. After writing McQueen's hit film *The Getaway* (1972), he landed his first directing assignment, an action movie called *Hard Times* (1975), starring Charles Bronson and James Coburn. Since that time Hill has directed action films in a wide variety of settings, most notably the Nick Nolte/Eddie Murphy buddy pics *48HRS* and *Another 48HRS*, and *The Long Riders*. His film *The Warriors* (1979), which he calls "a comic book version of Xenophon's story" set amidst the gang turf wars of New York, was falsely blamed for a a wave of violent episodes in theaters that accompanied the screenings (an accusation that in many ways paralleled the bum rap the original EC comics got for causing juvenile delinquency). Hill also produced the three box office horror/science fiction successes *Alien*, *Aliens*, and *Alien³*, and is working on bringing a fourth *Alien* to the screen. His most recent film is *Last Man Standing*, starring Bruce Willis and Bruce Dern.

David Giler produced the 1974 thriller *The Parallax View*, directed by Alan J. Pakula and starring Warren Beatty.

Walter Hill's *48HRS*, starring Nick Nolte and Eddie Murphy, put a new twist on the "buddy" picture.

It was hideously cleaver of the five execute-ive prod-oozers to bring me back to life, don't you think?

Hill was directing features at Universal in the early 1980s when he became aware of Russ Cochran's hardcover reprints of the old EC comics, and sent off for a complete set.

When they arrived, he found that they were as enjoyable as they'd been in his childhood. From his adult perspective as a director, however, he now realized that the stories also contained a wealth of material that would translate well to the screen. He showed them to his partner, writer/director/producer David Giler (*The Black Bird*, *Fun with Dick & Jane*, *Parallax View,* and, with Hill, the *Alien* series). Like Hill, Giler had consumed them avidly as a kid, and now reread them with an eye toward their cinematic potential. He liked what he saw. "Walter came to me and said, 'I think we should buy these.' I said, 'I think so too,'" he recalls.

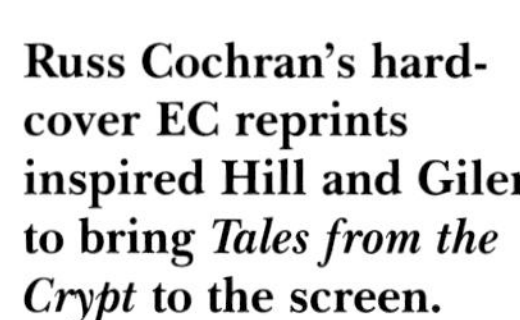

Russ Cochran's hardcover EC reprints inspired Hill and Giler to bring *Tales from the Crypt* to the screen.

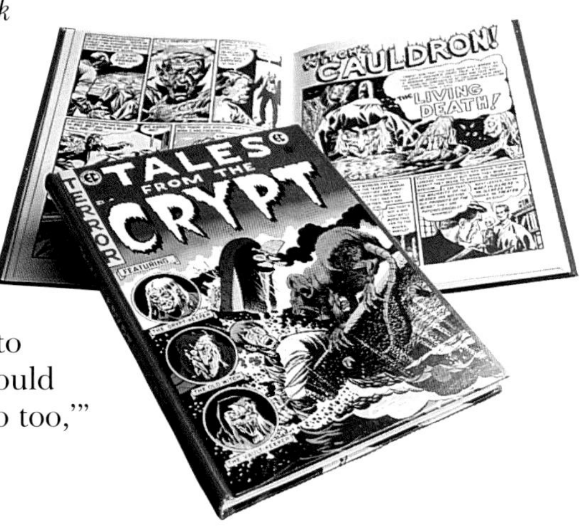

Hill had picked out "The Man Who Was Death" as his premiere segment long before *Tales from the Crypt* debuted on HBO.

Then There Were Three

In 1983, Hill and Giler were working with Joel Silver on *Streets of Fire* when Silver spied Hill's *Tales* reprints. Something clicked. "I told Walter that we should do an anthology feature film based on *Tales from the Crypt*," Silver recalls.

He was preaching to the choir—Hill already had his favorite all picked out. "I know exactly what segment I want to direct," he told Silver enthusiastically. "There's this one great story that I love called 'The Man Who Was Death' (*Crypt of Terror* #17). It's about a guy who's an executioner who thinks that people are real wimpy when they scream, 'I don't want to die!' Then he goes off on his own—sort of a do-it-yourself death squad—and starts killing people who've been 'getting away with murder.' When he gets caught he starts screaming, 'I don't want to die!'"

"I thought it sounded great," recalls Silver. "I called my attorney to see if we could acquire the rights. The three of us bought an option from Bill Gaines. It cost us very little." Gaines was willing to let the option go relatively inexpensively because he knew he was dealing with some of Hollywood's major players. "When we made our contact with Gaines," recalls Walter Hill, "it all went very smoothly because I think he associated us with high-class movie-making. Before this he'd always been dealing with people who just wanted to make horror movies."

"I sometimes say that one of my first ambitions was to do comic books. Now I've achieved it."
—Walter Hill

One More Makes Four

"Nothing happened for more than a year," continues Hill. "Finally Joel called back and told me that Richard Donner was interested. He wanted to know if it was okay to bring him into the project, which was fine by me."

Donner began his career as an actor, but switched to directing with segments of the Steve McQueen television series *Wanted: Dead or Alive*. After directing a number of movies for television, he moved into the horror genre with the highly successful feature *The Omen* (1976).

Donner was a teenager—smack in the heart of Gaines' target audience—during the heyday of the original comic books. They went through a lot of Evereadies in his family—he was a charter member of the flashlight-under-the-blanket brigade. The ECs stuck in his mind into adulthood, and formed part of a deep respect for comic books that he carried into his work.

One of his most successful films was *Superman* (1978), a project he took on out of a sense of obligation to do right by an American icon, and a devotion to Truth, Justice, and the American Way—not to mention "white bread, apple pie, and ham sandwiches," he adds with a grin. "In all seriousness, though, I directed *Superman*

Richard Donner directed all three blockbuster Mel Gibson/Danny Glover *Lethal Weapon* films, which he coproduced with Joel Silver.

because I felt that an American tradition was about to be destroyed. Russian producers who lived in Costa Rica were going to make the film in Italy—with an English director. They had no idea who *Superman* was—he was just a red cape to them. I stepped up and volunteered. After they offered me the opportunity, I rewrote the script—I changed everything. Sure it was exciting to do a big picture with Marlon Brando and Gene Hackman, but I really wanted to take it away from them because they had no idea what they were doing. It would have been a travesty. I was raised on *Superman*, and I really felt like I was salvaging a piece of American heritage."

Richard Donner agreed to direct *Superman* in order to see that Superman's on-screen persona matched his comic book heritage.

Donner made the trio of Silver, Giler, and Hill a quartet in 1986, when he was directing the first *Lethal Weapon*. (Since that time there have been two hit sequels.) "Joel and I were sitting the trailer, this little GMC motor home, during a break in late-night shooting and he said, 'I got this project I want to do—*Tales from the Crypt*.'

"Of course I still remembered it and I offered to help Joel pick up the option. I had no idea what our concept was going to be or how it would evolve, and there were times when everyone near and dear to my life said, 'Don't put any more of your money in this project,' but I stuck with it."

The Quintet Is Complete

The last person Joel Silver brought into the Crypt was Robert Zemeckis, who like Silver was too young to have been caught up in EC comics in childhood. "I came into Bill Gaines' world through *MAD* magazine in the 1960s," recalls Zemeckis. "I became a real fan while I was in film school at USC. That was where I met Bob Gale, my long-time writing partner. He was a comic book aficionado and a major EC buff, and he was the one who reintroduced me to them."

Donner was a charter member of the flashlight-under-the-blanket brigade. EC gave him a deep respect for comic books that he carried into his work.

A Chicago native, Zemeckis grabbed the attention of Steven Spielberg with his student film *Field of Honor*. In 1978 he directed his first feature film, *I Wanna Hold Your Hand*, the story of a group of teenagers who embark on an odyssey to go see the Beatles on *The Ed Sullivan Show*. After writing *1941* (with Gale) for Spielberg and directing *Used Cars* (1980), he had his first megahit with *Romancing the Stone* in 1984, a success he immediately followed with *Back to the Future* the following year.

Zemeckis connected with Silver in 1988 when he convinced him to do a self-parody cameo—as a stereotypical screaming director—in *Who Framed Roger Rabbit?* "While we were filming, Joel mentioned that he was working on getting EC comics on cable, and I thought that was a smart way to do it. I knew *Tales from the Crypt* would never succeed on network television. They'd ruin it. If it was going on cable, I told him I was interested."

Robert Zemeckis' *Who Framed Roger Rabbit*, a seamless mix of live action and animation sequences, was an homage both to cartoons and to film noir.

With the addition of Zemeckis, the quintet was complete and Silver finally had enough firepower to pitch the idea to HBO. Things moved quickly from there. "I hadn't heard much for about a year, then suddenly there was a phone call from Joel," recalls Walter Hill with a smile, picking up the story. It was a classic staccato micro-conversation with Silver. "Joel got on the phone and said 'Bob-Zemeckis-wants-to-do-one-and-Dick-Donner-will-do-one-and-HBO-is-interested-and-could-you-shoot-your-segment-in-five-days?'" When Hill said yes, Silver hung up, and a project which had been on the back burner since Ronald Reagan hit the ground running in his first term in office was suddenly red hot.

Joel Silver: The Spark Plug

A film devotee since childhood, Joel Silver attended NYU film school and broke into Hollywood as an assistant to producer Lawrence Gordon. Gordon already had a relationship with Silver's future **Tales** partner, director Walter Hill, having worked with him on **Hard Times** (1975; Hill's directorial debut). Silver's first project with Gordon was Hill's feature **The Driver** (1978). He was also associate producer on Hill's next film, **The Warriors** (1979). After working on the Burt Reynolds hits **The End** and **Hooper** (both 1978), he and Gordon produced the next three Hill features—**48HRS**, **Streets of Fire**, and **Brewster's Millions**.

In 1985, Silver established his own production company, Silver Pictures, and was responsible for some of the most commercially successful films of the 1980s and 1990s, including **Commando** (1985) and **Predator** (1987), starring Arnold Schwarzenegger, **Jumpin' Jack Flash**, with Whoopi Goldberg (1986), three **Lethal Weapons** featuring Mel Gibson and Danny Glover (1987, 1989, 1992), two **Die Hards** (1988, 1990), starring Bruce Willis, and **Executive Decision** (1996). The **Lethal Weapon** trilogy began his association with another fellow **Tales** executive producer, director Richard Donner.

Joel Silver was a toddler when Bill Gaines was standing up for his comics before Estes Kefauver and the Senate Subcommittee to Investigate Juvenile Delinquency. "The comics were already out of print when I was in my formative years, but sometimes you got lucky when you went to camp or slept over at somebody's house," recalls Silver. "Often the kid's older brother had some. You went through the collection and if you found one you'd pull it out and say, 'I gotta read this —' they were like some kind of forbidden fruit. Everyone knew they weren't ordinary comic books."

Once he got to Hollywood, he kept bumping into them, and one of the biggest bumps was Walter Hill's **Alien**. "I saw a rough cut of the film and was totally blown away by one particular scene," says Silver. "Something had planted eggs in the host; the eggs grew and an alien came bursting out of this guy's chest. It was so startling to me, and I remember talking about how much I liked it with Walter, who told me that the original idea came from an old comic book called **Tales from the Crypt**."

In 1982, horror virtuoso George Romero **(Night of the Living Dead)** filmed **Creepshow**, an homage to the old EC comics that was based on Stephen King's stories, not on the comics themselves. Between his boyhood recollections and later Hollywood contacts, Silver became aware that the EC stories were "out there." Then he saw Hill's reprints, and began putting the deal together that brought **Tales from the Crypt** to life.

Joel Silver made his directorial debut on **Tales from the Crypt**. His episode was entitled "Split Personality," and starred Joe Pesci as a con man who romances a brace of wealthy twins but deludes them into believing that he has a twin brother. Fred Dekker wrote the script, as he had for the premiere episode, "And All Through the House." Often described as the "consummate producer," Silver knew to surround himself with experienced personnel on his maiden voyage as a director. "I wanted the best people I could get, and I had the 'A' team with me," he says with a smile. "In addition to Dekker, David Lowery was my storyboard artist—he later did **Jurassic Park**. Jan De Bont was my cameraman, who went on to direct **Speed** and **Twister**." Silver's initial outing was well received, but he decided that he much preferred producing, and "Split Personality" remains his sole directing credit.

Joel Silver's "A Team" for his directorial debut on Tales from the Crypt included cinematographer Jan De Bont (above), who had served as director of photography for Silver on Die Hard, and Academy Award-winning actor Joe Pesci (right), who had appeared in Silver's Lethal Weapon II and III.

"Joel is a very entrepreneurial fellow," says Hill. "The fact that there is a show is really more because of his entrepreneurial efforts than any other factor."

"Joel Silver would have been one helluva running back in the NFL," laughs Richard Donner in concurrence. "Once Joel gets the ball, forget it. He just took this thing and ran with it."

Getting Gaines' Blessing

First, however, the partners had to convince Bill Gaines. "We had to go back and restructure the agreement," says Hill. "The original contract with Gaines was a feature deal, and he had to be persuaded that HBO was a good way to go."

The idea of an anthology feature film was a dead end on any number of grounds, almost all of which were financial. There had been a flurry of interest in making the movie at one studio, but they wanted to take it out of the hands of the originators and make it as a low-budget film, which was a deal-breaker. Worse yet, recent anthology films with a horror theme, including Stephen King's *Creepshow* and the ill-fated *Twilight Zone**, had not performed well at the box office. Whether or not there was any real similarity between *Creepshow* and *Twilight Zone* and *Tales from the Crypt*, studios were now gun-shy of making a horror anthology for theatrical release.

Gaines agreed that the *Tales* material was too strong for network TV. If a feature was not feasible, cable was his only real opportunity. Besides, cable offered one advantage that a feature film could never match—a chance that all the stories might eventually be filmed. He gave his okay.

The production company ordered multiple copies of Russ Cochran's EC reprints. Some segments follow the comics more closely than others, but the Gaines agreement stipulates that all episodes of *Tales* must originate from the stories that appeared in EC horror comics.

The *Tales* production company also bought the reprints of the EC's science fiction comics, and in the wake of the success of *Tales from the Crypt*, a new cable TV series based on *Weird Science* and *Weird Fantasy* is in the works for 1997. Because *Weird Science* has already been used as the title of a feature film (oddly enough, it was one that Joel Silver produced), the new series will be called *Perversions of Science*.

* Vic Morrow and two child actors were killed in a freak accident during filming.

Four of the five *Tales from the Crypt* executive producers (from left, Richard Donner, Joel Silver, Robert Zemeckis, and Walter Hill) pose with their newly exhumed host the Crypt Keeper. David Giler, the fifth member of the quintet, is shown above.

Into Production

With Donner, Hill, and Zemeckis attached and committed to direct the first three episodes—the "trilogy" as it's known within the *Tales* production company—Silver found that selling the idea to HBO was pretty much a slam dunk. When the green light finally came, however, the timing, of course, was terrible. "Zemeckis had just released *Roger Rabbit*," remembers Silver. "He was about to start shooting *Back to the Future II* and *III* at the same time. He was going to be unavailable for about a year. He told me, 'If you want me to do this, I've got to do it right now.' This was roughly December of 1988. Donner and I didn't have any time either—we were in the midst of shooting *Lethal Weapon II*.

I was reincarnated in all my gruesome glory on slay-ble TV. My show introduced me to a new de-generation of fans, but many still dismembered me from my comic book days.

Setting the Tone—The First Episodes

Despite the time crunch, all of the partners realized immediately that the first few episodes would be crucial because they would set the mood for the entire series, and they all participated in its creation. "The early seasons established a level of quality that set the benchmark for what was to follow," says Bob Zemeckis. For the series premiere, Zemeckis had selected "And All Through the House" (*Vault of Horror* #35) and wanted to do it with his wife, actress Mary Ellen Trainor, in the lead.

Throughout the preparation and the filming, he worked closely with Fred Dekker, who wrote the script, polishing it to make sure it was faithful to the original story. "I wanted to start fresh—I didn't want it to look like we were trying to remake the prior film (which had featured Joan Collins as the murderess). I went back to the comic book—there were lots of images that I wanted to evoke or replicate, including the final image with Santa Claus." (The homicidal St. Nick was played by Larry Drake, best known to TV audiences as *LA Law*'s simple soul Benny, the office boy.)

Richard Donner frames a shot from his first episode, "Dig That Cat...He's Real Gone." Donner is the only *Tales* producer who had prior experience directing for television.

The producers sent it off to Bill Gaines for his assessment. "Gaines gave me just one comment when he read the screenplay," laughs Zemeckis. "He said, 'My only note is that she's got to be screaming her head off at the end.' We took that to heart and in the last scene Mary Ellen gave us one of the greatest onscreen screams ever."

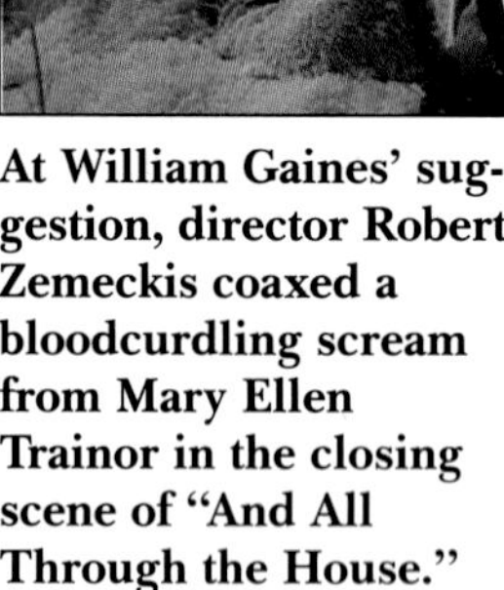

At William Gaines' suggestion, director Robert Zemeckis coaxed a bloodcurdling scream from Mary Ellen Trainor in the closing scene of "And All Through the House."

Walter Hill finally got his chance to film "The Man Who Was Death" early in 1989. "In addition to doing a movie about someone he calls "a twisted human being," he was anxious to try a technique he'd never been able to do in film. "I wanted the character to talk to the camera," he declares. "It's an old technique that I'd seen many times when I was a kid."

Casting a performer who could address the audience directly gave him some problems. "I kept reading actors and I didn't feel anybody really caught the flavor of it. I was in despair. Then Bill Sadler came in. He was great. I said, 'If you can do this exactly the way you did it just now, I'll give you the lead.'"

Sadler, a real *Tales from the Crypt* "friend of the house," starred in the first *Tales* feature *Demon Knight*, had a part in *Die Hard II* (produced by Joel Silver), and also played the lead in Hill's 1989 feature, *Trespass*, which was written by Bob Zemeckis and his writing partner Bob Gale.

Richard Donner, the only *Tales* producer with a TV background, wrapped the last scene in *Lethal Weapon II* late on a Wednesday night in March of 1989. He began shooting his initial *Tales* segment, "Dig That Cat...He's Real Gone," first thing Thursday morning. He intentionally shot the segment "like panels of a comic book. We did the entire show with extreme wide-angle lenses, deliberately distorting people."

Walter Hill offered Bill Sadler the lead in "The Man Who Was Death" only if he vowed to perform it exactly as he had for the audition.

The funhouse mirror unorthodoxy of it was hard to deal with, at least at first. "I was working with a young editor, and after his first cut, I really thought I was going to have to replace him. Instead I said to him, 'I want you to go back into the editing room and do everything you were trained *not* to do. Think of all the bizarre things you thought but never said to all those old farts when you were learning—that nobody has any sense of style, initiative, inventiveness in cutting a film—and do that.' He came back two days later and showed me another cut. It was sensational and totally nonconformist, with a lot of jump cuts. It had a marvelous comic book sensibility and it was exactly what I wanted."

With their three inaugural segments, directors Hill, Zemeckis, and Donner set the mood and the standard for the rest of the episodes.

They also established the wide range of possibility for others to follow. "Bob was interested in things that go bump in the night," says *Tales* associate producer Alex Collett. "Walter has always had a little bit of a darker, psychological edge, and Dick wanted to do something that had a wild, lighter tone. Taken together, they showed the directors who followed them that the work could be gritty and dark, a classic thriller, or wild and way-out-there, with comic overtones."

Once the boundaries had been established, keeping the rest of the series on track was a task that fell primarily to Joel Silver. "Joel is very hands-on," says Walter Hill. "The overall tone of the show has a lot to do with Joel's taste. He selected what shows got made. He decided who got which scripts." In that regard Silver functioned the way Gaines and Feldstein had in the days of the early comics—he matched the material to the creative talent.

"All producing is casting," says Silver firmly, "whether it's casting in front of the camera or behind it. You have to put the players together and make it work. We're always a bit frantic. Sometimes it's a miracle that these episodes come together as well as they do, but the reason they turn out so well is the genius of Bill Gaines and Al Feldstein. The stories are so perfect that they manage to live through whatever occurs, and they survive and succeed."

VIRGIL MIRANO/COURTESY OF BOSS FILM STUDIOS

The *Tales* lead-in, with its camp, creepy Danny Elfman theme song and helter-skelter jaunt through a haunted house, has become almost as much of a trademark of the series as the Crypt Keeper himself. Silver and the other executive producers pushed for a top-notch opening sequence because they knew they'd have to live with it "forever."

Inviting the Audience into the Crypt

The partners understood that the opening sequence had to establish a "Cryptian" tone immediately. Like the splash pages of a comic book story, the lead-in to the series was designed to have a signature feel, one that would physically bring the viewer into the Crypt. This was accomplished through a point of view that approximates walking into a haunted house with a hand-held camera or VCR.

Actually, however, the haunted house is about the size of the 18th hole on a miniature golf course. The lilliputian Victorian mansion was created by Richard Edlund's effects studio, Boss Film. An alumnus of George Lucas' Industrial Light and Magic who began as

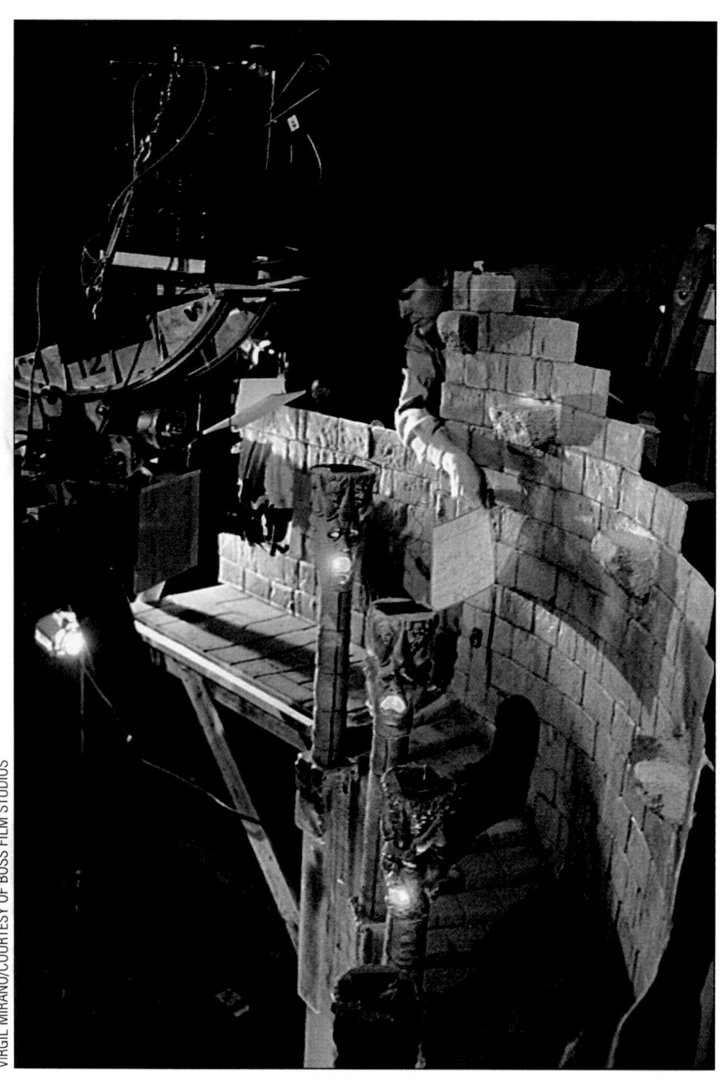

VIRGIL MIRANO/COURTESY OF BOSS FILM STUDIOS

a cameraman on *Star Wars*, Edlund was nominated for a special effects Oscar on *Die Hard* (produced by Joel Silver) and later worked on *Alien*[3] (produced by Hill and Giler). The interior set of the mansion, replete with weird faces and creepy statuary built into the walls of the main hall, the entrance to the Crypt via the secret door in the library, and the webby sepulchral Crypt, was initially sketched by comic book artist Mike Vosburg. Vosburg also drew all of the comic book covers that preface each segment. "I saw EC comics at a very early age and then had them snatched out of my hands," he told Sam Kingston in an interview for the *Tales* fanzine *Horror from the Crypt of Fear*. Dominated by the distinctive *Tales from the Crypt* masthead, Vosburg's covers pay homage to the '50s originals while tying the image to visuals of the current episode.

Bob Zemeckis and Dick Donner supervised the camera movement through the "first floor" of the model—which entailed use of a 65mm snorkel camera with motion control. The descent into the Crypt is actually computer generated; only the Crypt itself is a actual full-size set. Danny Elfman (who also scored *Batman*, *Beetlejuice*, and *The Simpsons*) added the engaging devil-may-care macabre theme—like circus or carousel music run amok—that enhances the giddy anticipation of things to come. Once in the Crypt, the audience is primed for the appearance of the "star," the Crypt Keeper, host of *Tales from the Crypt*.

As part of the technique for physically bringing the audience to the Crypt Keeper, the camera lured viewers down the winding staircase into the Crypt.

***Tales* cover artist Mike Vosberg met Joel Silver through a colleague and was first asked to develop set designs for the interior of the haunted house. Much of his *Tales from the Crypt* cover design work is done on computer.**

Americans have always felt more comfy with a host or guru to guide them through the chills of horror stories, a tradition that dates back to the days of crystal sets and Arch Oboler's *Lights Out*. At about the same time that Wertham's crusade was bearing down on Gaines, Feldstein, and the three GhouLunatics, a new late-night TV show premiered in Los Angeles.

The Horror Host

The program was nothing more than a collection of old horror movies—*The Million Dollar Movie* with a very limited library—but it was hosted by a curvaceous woman sporting three-inch black nails and a slinky black dress. In a good girl age of Peter Pan collars and poodle skirts, it fit her like an Ace bandage and emphasized her astonishing cleavage.

She called herself Vampira. According to David Skal in *The Monster Show*, Maila Nurmi, the woman who portrayed her, claimed the Dragon Lady in *Terry and the Pirates*, the evil queen in Disney's *Snow White*, and silent film vamp Theda Bara as her inspirations. However, Vampira's closest "living" relative is almost undoubtedly Drusilla, the alluring female sidekick that Johnny Craig created for the Vault Keeper. Since that time, female vampire couture has not evolved significantly—both Lily Munster and Morticia Addams apparently used Drusilla's dressmaker. More camp than vamp, contemporary horror hostess Elvira (Cassandra Peterson) is also a direct descendant.

Vampira was followed by other TV movie horror emcees. The most successful was perhaps Roland in Philadelphia, the "Cool Ghoul" who presided over *Shock Theater.* Eventually he moved up to a bigger market, New York, and worked under his own name, Zacherley.

When original horror and thriller programming appeared on television with *Alfred Hitchcock Presents* and *The Twilight Zone*, Hitchcock and writer Rod Serling were present to introduce each segment. Hitchcock in particular had a droll flair for presenting himself with a prop or costume that matched the theme of the episode. When *Tales from the Crypt* was coming on line at HBO, there was no question that the Crypt Keeper would host the program. The only question was what form he would take.

Because of movie commitments, Bob Zemeckis' first episode, "And All Through the House," was already in the can before the Crypt Keeper was developed. HBO liked what they saw, but "they were very concerned about a host," remembers Joel Silver. "In those days even Michael Eisner was hosting the Sunday night Disney series, the way Walt used to do it."

Silver reassured them that a Crypt Keeper was in development. With a commitment for six shows (up from the original three), the production company could afford to amortize the cost of the Keeper and come up with something really inventive.

Look at me in the slimelight—I'm the new Dead Sullivan, bigger than Malice-ter Croak!

"You know… you don't necessarily have to have a nose."
—Robert Zemeckis

"Bob, Walter, Dick, and I, plus others involved in production, began having meetings about what he should look like," continues Silver. "We felt the Keeper was very important. To us the idea of a dead host was even more interesting than having a live one—most of them are dead anyway."

Animatronics expert/puppetmaster Kevin Yagher brought the Crypt Keeper to, er… life. Quite by chance, Yagher, who had created Chucky, the evil doll in *Child's Play*, ran into Joel Silver while retrieving items from his storage facility in Glendale. Silver, who also had materials stashed there, was intrigued when he glimpsed Yagher's monster stuff in the open locker and eventually asked him to work on the Crypt Keeper.

Bob Zemeckis worked closely with Yagher to hone his persona even before work began on his physique. "We talked a lot about the Crypt Keeper's personality traits before I started shaping him," says Yagher. "We built a whole back story for him, about why he's got that snide look and those piercing pale blue eyes. We talked about his breath smelling and the rotting pieces falling off him, which inspired me more than any visual you could ever have. I learned a lot about building a character in the process. The Crypt Keeper is likable, but he's also sly and treacherous—if you turned your back on him, he'd just plunge a knife into you."

"He'll make you laugh, but he may also kill you. He's this little asshole,"

says Zemeckis with a grin. "But he's dead, so he doesn't care what anyone thinks of him—he can say anything he wants to. His attitude is, 'What are you gonna do—kill me?' It's as if he's flipping everyone off from the grave." Which makes the Crypt Keeper, in a way, the Ultimate Slacker.

After meeting with Zemeckis, Yagher did some prototype sketches, then moved into clay mockups. What followed were a series of colorful discussions between Yagher and the executive producers about the physiognomy of the Crypt Keeper—discussions akin to demented sessions of Mr. Potatohead, with Yagher trying out various facial features on the basic design and producers trying to determine which were essential and which were superfluous. It was definitely a case of Less Is More—as the Crypt Keeper shed hair, lips, and teeth, his identity was crystallized and distilled. In his first incarnation, he sported a prominent hook nose. Like a plastic surgeon with a rhinoplasty patient, Yagher tried about half a dozen noses on the Keeper. When Zemeckis suggested that perhaps a nose was extraneous, Yagher carved an indentation into the smooth surface of the clay model and found consensus — almost.

After spending his first couple of seasons in a conservative cloak, the Crypt Keeper became more audacious in his choice of apparel, playing dress-up as Forrest Gump (left), Uncle Sam (center), and Elvis (right).

Walter Hill and David Giler, who had won a brace of special effects Oscars for *Alien* and *Aliens*, had envisioned a host who was a bit more humanesque. Hill in particular thought he might be like British actor James Mason (harking back, perhaps, to Ralph Richardson's portrayal in the films of the '70s). Neither one was quite prepared for the final visage Yagher created. "We looked at it and said, 'Oh my God!'" laughs Giler. "But we were wrong. It made the show."

"Without the Crypt Keeper," says Richard Donner, "I don't think we would have had a series. We would have had a comic book anthology and no thread. The audience needed a personality to hook on to. He became the connection that made it work. People tune in to see the Crypt Keeper as much as the stories. He became a trademark, a legend that everyone could relate to."

In addition to molding him physically, Yagher was also responsible for finding the voice of the Crypt Keeper, actor/stand-up comedian and *Star Search* winner John Kassir. Kassir was the voice of Meeko, the mischievous raccoon in Disney's *Pocahontas*, and is the voice of *everybody* on USA Network's new series *Johnny Time*, which Kassir developed and produced. Kassir drew upon a motley jumble of sources of inspiration—a handful of Alfred Hitchcock, a bit of Rod Serling, a little Henny Youngman here and a pinch of Margaret Hamilton there. (Margaret Hamilton portrayed the Wicked Witch of the West in the *The Wizard of Oz*.) In the end, however, he came up with something all his own to portray what he calls his "cackling bag of bones."

Yagher auditioned several actors, then brought Kassir's tape to Joel Silver with his endorsement. "What got my attention was John's high-pitched, wicked laugh," recalls Yagher. "He also had the raspy 'dead' voice that we were looking for." The gravelly aspect soon became a problem for Kassir—achieving that sandpaper effect was not sustainable for very long. "John could only go so many minutes," says Yagher, "before he had to stop for lots of lemon and honey."

"I have so much fun doing him, but at first my vocal cords were like raw meat by the time we were done with a session," admits Kassir. "I had to lighten him up a little just to keep going." Kassir voices the Keeper not just for the TV series, but for all appearances connected with the *Tales from the Crypt* theatrical films, and for the kids' game show that takes place in the Crypt.

For the first two years, the Crypt Keeper appeared in his standard hooded garb—it was not until the third season that he became more adventuresome in his attire. At the same time, his humor became cheekier and his personality blossomed. "He plays dress-up now," laughs Yagher. "We can put him in sunglasses, or a *Superman* outfit. He's been John Wayne, Bogart, and Brando—and even Howard Stern."

"The Crypt Keeper is a real character, not just a voice or a puppet," says Kassir fondly. "He's evolved, just as a character would in a sitcom. He has grown to enjoy death so much more each year."

The emergence of the Crypt Keeper as a star parallels a period of growth for Yagher himself. With the support and guidance of the *Tales* executive producers, Yagher began directing the "bumper" segments that open and close the show.

He also directed the playful *Tales* episode that chronicled the birth of the Crypt Keeper. Called "Lower Berth," it featured Yagher's brother Jeff, the only actor he knew who'd cheerfully sit still for five hours in Makeup every morning, which is how long it took to outfit him with a second face.

"This has been such a wonderful experience," says Yagher enthusiastically. "They say that when you have dreams of flying you're really enjoying what you're doing during the day—I'd go home from the *Tales from the Crypt* set and dream of flying every night. It's the most fulfilling thing I've ever done."

I'm surrounded by wooden performers... stiffs! My show needs some real hack-tors, genuine scars of the silver scream!

John Kassir, the voice of the Crypt Keeper, has helped his character expand his sense of humor and develop his true personality.

Bringing the Crypt Keeper to Life

A crew of eight people from Yagher's studio built the Crypt Keeper. Yagher sculpted the head himself, and worked closely with *Tales* producers to define his ghoulish features.

It takes six puppeteers to bring the Crypt Keeper's outrageous impudence and his "up yours" demeanor to life. Kevin Yagher has assembled an experienced ensemble troupe, each of whom must operate in concert with their cohorts. They have to think alike and respond in unison.

Many of his puppeteers have been with the Crypt Keeper for a long time — since the days when he still had a nose. Seated behind and underneath the puppet, Van Snowden works the head and body, with his hand inside the cranium. Charles Lutkus, who originally worked in Yagher's shop and was part of the team that built the Keeper's head, sits behind Snowden and manipulates the hands and arms. The Crypt Keeper has half arms that come off the Keeper's shoulder and attach to straps around Lutkus' hands, a technique that Jim Henson pioneered with the Muppets. If the legs are visible, another puppeteer works the lower body. The Crypt Keeper can move his ankles and curl his toes.

Four puppeteers work the Crypt Keeper's facial expressions. His head is actually very large and very heavy, because it is crammed with twenty-seven servo motors. Servos are small motors well known to hobbyists — little different from the Radio Shack specials that power model cars and airplanes.

Erik Schaper is responsible for the sneer. Using four joysticks, he controls the cheek and nostril area in the middle of the face. Mecki Heussen operates the eyes and eyelids. There's one puppeteer (David Stinnett) responsible just for the smile. He works the e's, b's, and t's — all the letters that cause the corners of your mouth to pull back, and of course for the Crypt Keeper's trademark laugh. Servo motors were not powerful enough to work the smile, which instead is operated manually off ten feet of cable.

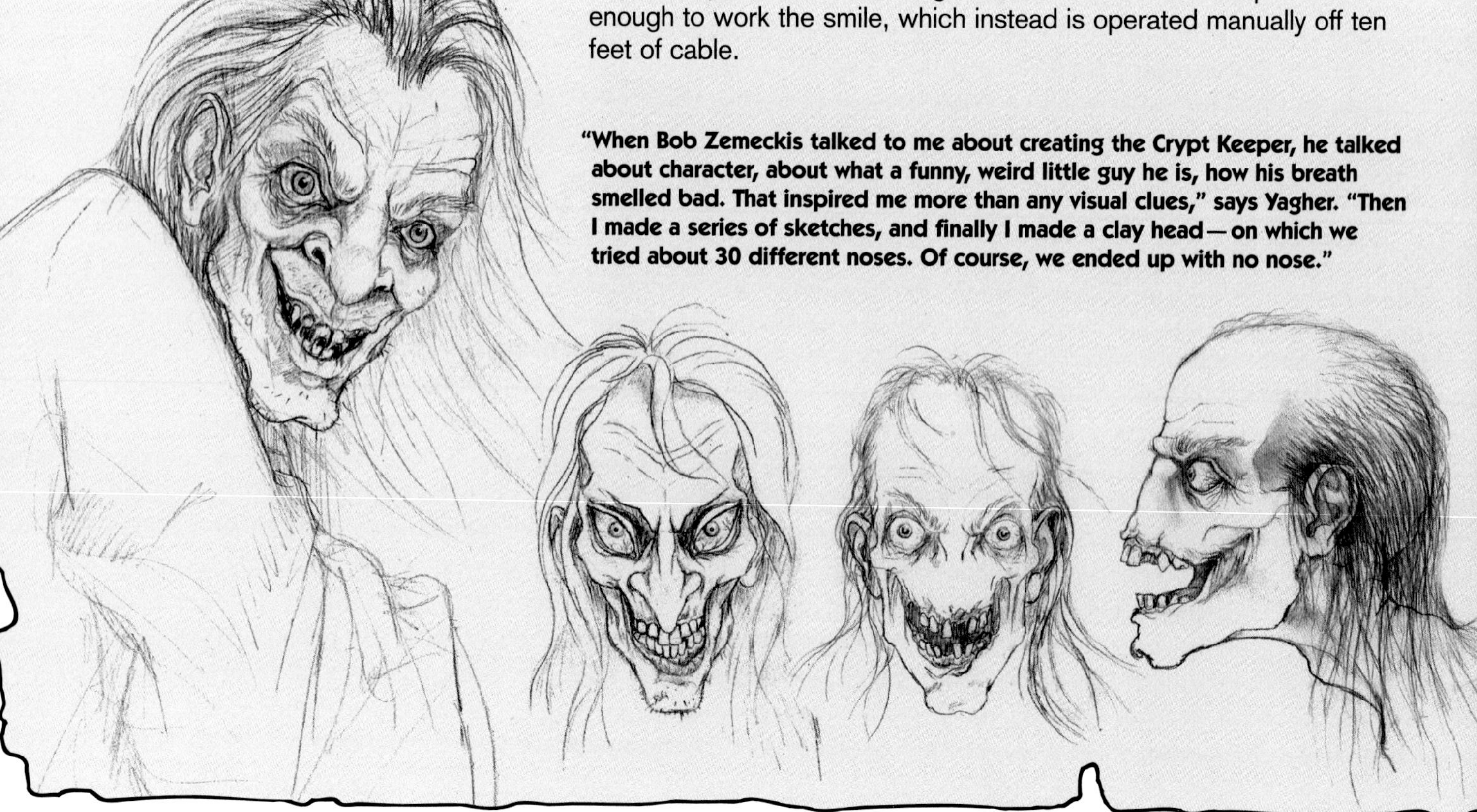

"When Bob Zemeckis talked to me about creating the Crypt Keeper, he talked about character, about what a funny, weird little guy he is, how his breath smelled bad. That inspired me more than any visual clues," says Yagher. "Then I made a series of sketches, and finally I made a clay head — on which we tried about 30 different noses. Of course, we ended up with no nose."

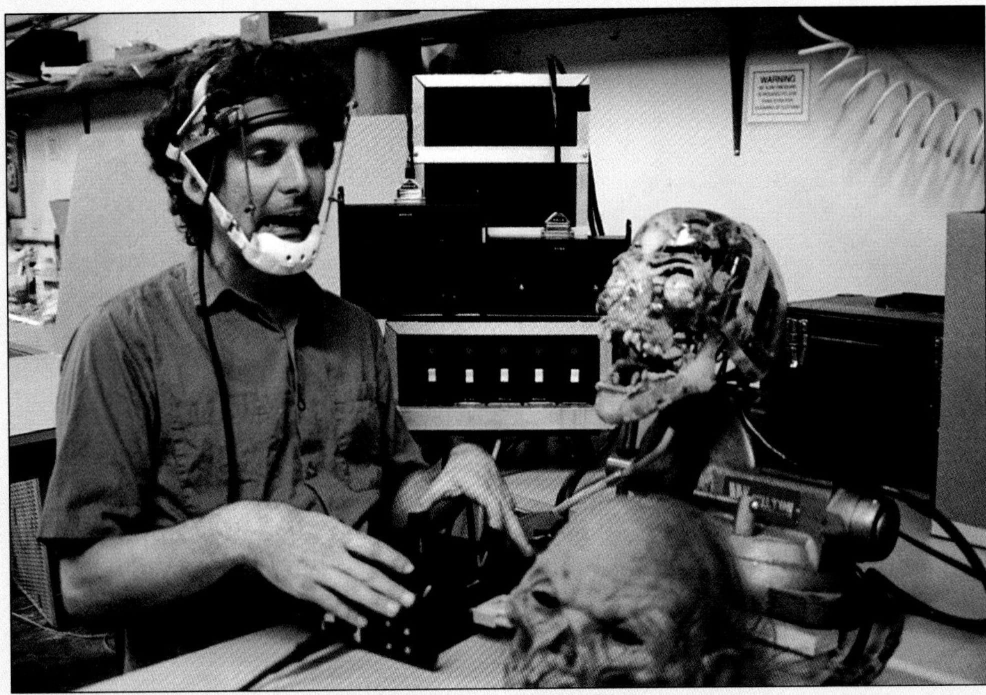

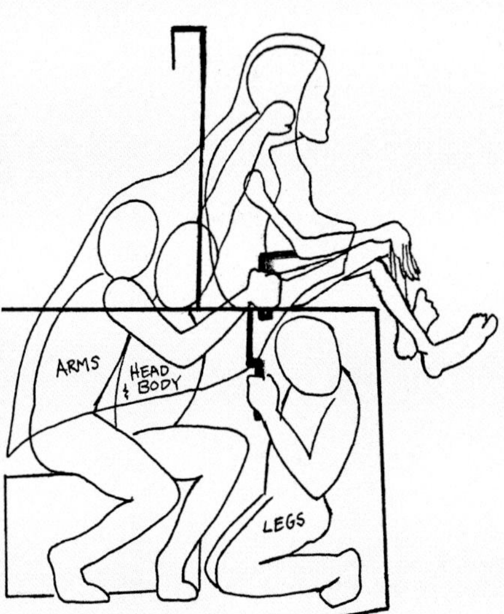

Brock Winkless is the virtuoso responsible for the jaw and mouth, working from a console connected to his own mandible. As Winkless opens his mouth, the Keeper mimics his action. Winkless also manipulates four joysticks on the console to move the lips in sync with the dialogue. He controls four points of movement over each canine tooth, two upper and two lower. Brock is the best lip guy in town," boasts Yagher.

"We have a great time doing the Crypt Keeper live," says John Kassir. For TV, however, he lays down the audio track first. Puppeteers watch Kassir at the microphone and take some of their motion cues from him as he does his voiceover.

Because his foam latex skin rots (how appropriate) the Crypt Keeper gets an annual beauty makeover when the show is on hiatus.

The "In" Thing to Do

At one time or another, the executive producers had worked with most of the biggest names in both film and television, and their commitment to the series gave *Tales from the Crypt* a cachet in the industry that few other television opportunities could match. Although they had planned to call in some old markers and ask some well-known "friends" to appear, they quickly discovered that coaxing and cajoling were unnecessary—stars and directors were calling *them* and asking for a chance to do a segment. The result was a conga line of outstanding talent, both in front of the camera and behind it.

It became a mark of prestige to do a *Tales from the Crypt*. Among the television and movie luminaries who have appeared on the series are Harry Anderson, Francesca Annis, Bruce Boxleitner, Sonia Braga, Beau Bridges, Tim Curry, Timothy Dalton, Blythe Danner, Yvonne DeCarlo, Hector Elizondo, Mariel Hemingway, Margot Kidder, John Lithgow, Elizabeth McGovern, Esai Morales, Cathy Moriarty, Lou Diamond Phillips, Michael J. Pollard, Priscilla Presley, Christopher Reeve, Natasha Richardson, Emma Samms, Martin Sheen, Brooke Shields, John Stamos, Richard Thomas, George Wendt, Adam West, Treat Williams, and Burt Young.

On *Tales from the Crypt*, stars such as Demi Moore, Beau Bridges, Timothy Dalton, Sherilynn Fenn, Isabella Rossellini, John Lithgow, Kelly Preston, William Hickey, and Sonia Braga got a chance to stretch themselves as actors and take on unexpected roles — without a lengthy commitment to a project.

The casting reflects a consciousness of the comic/horror heritage of the series. Adam West played TV's Batman; DeCarlo portrayed Lily Munster on *The Munsters*. Curry was one of the anchors of *The Rocky Horror Picture Show*; and Reeve and Kidder (who appeared in separate episodes) played Clark Kent and Lois Lane in Donner's *Superman*. Much of the cast of the offbeat gothic mystery TV series *Twin Peaks*, including Kyle MacLachlan, Kimmy Robertson, Sherilyn Fenn, Joan Chen, and Grace Zabriskie, have also appeared.

William Teitler guided *Tales from the Crypt* during its first two seasons before going on to produce the features *Jumanji* and *Mr. Holland's Opus*. (Gil Adler has been the series producer since that time.) "There was a huge interest in the creative community in working on the show," recalls Teitler. "We were casting 'Dead Right,' with Howard Deutch (*Pretty in Pink*) directing. We were looking for the perfect person, and it occurred to us that the role was tailor-made for Demi Moore. Joel knows Bruce and Demi quite well. He called her and she agreed to do it. I was stunned that she was going to do a television show, but I was even more stunned by how good it was. On the set there was a real sense that there was something very unusual and wonderful that was happening. Demi just nailed her character, and she was great to work with." Moore played a waitress who married a fat, unsightly man because a fortune teller predicted that he would inherit a fortune and then kick the bucket.

Among the most distinguished actors to work on *Tales from the Crypt* is dimpled legend Kirk Douglas. When the possibility first presented itself, there were those who suggested that appearing on a cable TV show was

The *Tales from the Crypt* executive producers may have the biggest Rolodex in Hollywood. Stars appearing in various episodes include actors who have worked with one or more of the producers previously, those who have worked with the director of a particular episode, and those who are breaking a mold —indulging a desire to do something they've always wanted to do. From the top, among those who have joined in the fun are Christopher Reeve, Meat Loaf, Katey Sagal, Lee Arenberg, Emma Samms, Eileen Brennan, Teri Garr, Andrew McCarthy, Mariel Hemingway, Travis Tritt, Colleen Camp, Harry Anderson, Audra Lindley, M. Emmet Walsh, Yvonne DeCarlo, Carol Kane, Natasha Richardson, and Lainie Kazan.

Because of the great variety of plots and story lines in *Tales from the Crypt*, stars and personalities could find almost any kind of bizarre or despicable character to play. *Tales* episodes have featured Roger Daltrey, Lea Thompson, Catherine O'Hara, Ed Begley, Jr., Traci Lords, Morton Downey, Jr., George Wendt, Sugar Ray Leonard, Burt Young & Joe Pesci, Dan Aykroyd & Kirk Douglas, Judd Nelson & Meat Loaf, Iggy Pop, Jon Lovitz & Sandra Bernhard, Rita Rudner & Richard Lewis, Hector Elizondo, John Astin, Treat Williams, Brooke Shields, and Don Rickles and Bobcat Goldthwait, both of whom are shown with "Morty."

"beneath him." Douglas disagreed and jumped into the Crypt with enthusiasm. "It gets back to the old saying, 'There are no small parts, only small actors,'" states Douglas simply. "Early on, when all the studio heads were saying, 'No one is to go on television,' I was one of the first 'movie stars' who worked in TV. I did a live scene from *Champion* with my costar, Marilyn Maxwell. My *Tales* segment, called 'Yellow,' was directed by Robert Zemeckis. Dan Aykroyd was in it, who I admire very much. It had another actor in it named Eric Douglas, who is my son. I thought it was very well done."

"Kirk was amazing," says Zemeckis. "He was very serious about it. We had some intense story meetings before we started shooting. He broke down every word and every sentence, trying to make the script stronger. He wanted to know the reason for each line. He told me, 'This is where I'm really tough, but on the day I walk on that set, it's your show.'

"Sure enough, when we started shooting if I said, 'Kirk, try it this way,' he'd say, 'Fine. Yes sir. I'll do whatever you want me to do.' For a director it was wonderful to see the incredible discipline that an actor of his caliber has, compared to actors today. He showed tremendous professionalism toward the entire crew." (Zemeckis now has the singular distinction of having worked with all three acting Douglases; he directed Michael in *Romancing the Stone*.)

"Yellow," together with "Showdown," (directed by Richard Donner), and "King of the Road," starring an as-yet-unknown Brad Pitt, was originally supposed to part of 90-minute pilot for an action/adventure anthology series for Fox. Pitt's episode was directed by Tom Holland (*Child's Play*, Stephen King's *Thinner*) and was the tale of a young James Dean-esque street racer who resorted to kidnapping in order to coerce his arch-rival to face him one last time. The series would have been christened *Two-Fisted Tales*, after Harvey Kurtzman's original comic book title, and would have featured Bill Sadler, dressed in black and in a wheelchair, as the slightly off-kilter host. However, Zemeckis and the other partners balked at the censorship demands of the network and spun the three segments back into *Tales from the Crypt*.

Free to Take Chances

Kirk Douglas can now safely play almost any role without endangering his reputation, a luxury many younger actors don't feel they can afford—at least not on the big screen. "If you're an established star," says Zemeckis, "you can't play a despicable character, but actors love that.

On *Tales from the Crypt*, you get a chance to be awful when nothing is at stake.

It is a safe place to have some fun, to be a murderer or whatever. You're not changing your public image; you don't have to sign your life away on a series. It's a one-shot deal."

When Whoopi Goldberg, an early fan of the show, was invited to do an episode, she had just recently won an Academy Award for her role as a medium with a message in *Ghost*. She was delighted, says Alex Collett, who recalls that Whoopi had only one proviso. "The only thing I ask is that you let me be repulsive—really horrible," she told Collett, "because I've been playing a lot of squeaky clean nice people and it's getting to be a drag!" Whoopi got her wish. In 1991 she did a segment called "Dead Wait" directed by Tobe Hooper (*Texas Chainsaw Massacre*, *Poltergeist*), in which she played a voodoo priestess named Peligre who decapitates a man and shrinks his head because she covets his red hair.

"We always assume that we have much greater freedom in Hollywood now than we did 50 or 75 years—or even 30 years ago," says Walter Hill, "and in some ways that's true, especially in the areas of sexual behavior or actual renditions of action sequences, but I think there are much greater restrictions in terms of subject matter in many ways. A movie centered on a villain as the protagonist has literally vanished. The lead can be a flawed personality, but he or she always has to be a good guy."

Don Rickles portrayed an aging ventriloquist with a horrible secret in "The Ventriloquist's Dummy." Directed by Dick Donner and written by Scripter Award winner Frank Darabont (*The Shawshank Redemption*), the episode premiered in the 1990 season, and remains one of the most over-the-top segments in the series. Bobcat Goldthwait plays another ventriloquist who learns that Rickles is a fake and that his dummy, Morty, is actually Don's mutant Siamese twin brother. (As a *Tales from the Crypt* in-joke, Rickles' character was named Ingels, after EC artist "Ghastly" Graham Ingels, who had drawn the original in *Tales from the Crypt* #28.)

In the grand finale, a gory battle ensues between the two (or among the three, depending on how you look at it), in which Rickles gets beaten over the head with a baseball bat and then has to cut off his own hand—which really belongs to Morty. At this point Morty becomes ambulatory and starts scuttling around the room attacking people. Bobcat tries to get rid of it by pushing it into a meat grinder.

"Rickles was a revelation," says producer Teitler. "We all knew his public persona, but in this show he revealed what a great actor he is. He had to do some crazy stuff—blood was spurting everywhere, and little Morty—we had Morty on a fishing pole, chasing him around the room."

"No episodes are alike," says Richard Donner. "Everyone brought their own style and we never said, 'It's wrong.'" Tobe Hooper shot Whoopi Goldberg in "Dead Wait" (right); Russell Mulcahy directed Edward Tudor Pole in "Horror in the Night" (above right). Randa Haines directed "Judy, You're Not Yourself Today," starring Brian Kerwin (above left); William Friedkin did "On A Dead Man's Chest," with Gregg Allman and Yul Vazquez.

I Want to Direct

Name directors, like name actors, clamor for a chance to shoot a *Tales*, and for about the same reason—it's a chance to do something different in a relatively comfortable environment. Some, like Walter Hill, wanted to try a new technique, such as having a character directly address the camera. Others were film directors who had worked very little—if at all—in television. For all of them it was a refresher course in how to propel a narrative. "With *Tales from the Crypt*, what we're doing is making short films, which is what we all did in film school when we first started out," says Bob Zemeckis. "It's a very difficult form to work in, but it's fun because it has to be very cinematic. You don't have a lot of time to set things up. You really have to move the story along in an economic, visual way. It's one of the few opportunities for directors to work in the short film form that isn't completely hamstrung and censor-ridden, the way broadcast television is. You don't have to worry about commercial breaks or censorship of any kind. You just have to do it with complete abandon and go for it."

Zemeckis took his own advice in "You, Murderer," which first aired in 1995. Zemeckis utilized the same CG (computer graphics) techniques that he used in his Oscar-winning *Forrest Gump* to make Humphrey Bogart a character in the segment. "We took old clips and wrote dialogue that bracketed things Humphrey Bogart said in his films, and built shots around it. It was a lot of fun."

Randa Haines (*Children of a Lesser God,*) took on "Judy, You're Not Yourself Today" in 1990. William Friedkin (*The French Connection, The Exorcist*) directed "On a Dead Man's Chest" in 1992. John Frankenheimer (*Birdman of Alcatraz*) directed Blythe Danner in "Maniac at Large" that same year.

Director Russell Mulcahy was working with Denzel Washington and John Lithgow on a theatrical release called *Ricochet* for Joel Silver and asked Silver for a chance to direct a *Tales* episode. "One of the philosophies behind the show was to really make the cinematography, the storytelling, and the acting have the same level of quality as a feature film. I was surprised, however, that there was no 'Bible' for the show—no overall guidelines to follow. Each episode is meant to have an individual look, so that every director has a chance to add his own stamp to the project."

As Bill Gaines and Al Feldstein knew all too well, some of the best outcomes happen as a result of breaking all the rules. Mulcahy, among others, found the opportunity exhilarating. "I asked the producers, 'How far can I go with these?' and they said, 'How far do you want to go?' That was all I got from the production side. I was given the freedom to go all out and have fun."

Isabella Rossellini evoked an image of her mother, Ingrid Bergman, in "You, Murderer," for Robert Zemeckis. In "Showdown," Richard Donner directed David Morse.

Stars Behind the Camera

There have been endless variations of the time-worn joke in Hollywood that everyone wants to direct—on *Tales from the Crypt*, they can make it happen, and they can make it happen in an environment where it is safe to make mistakes, without endangering an eight-figure budget or a "bankable" reputation.

Arnold Schwarzenegger made his directorial debut in the second season with "The Switch," the story of a beautiful young woman (Kelly Preston) hotly pursued by an old millionaire (William *Prizzi's Honor* Hickey) who would spare no expense to win her favor. "Arnold was gracious and undemanding," recalls Bill Teitler. "He always had a great sense of self-deprecating humor about him. He arrived without fanfare in the morning, but we always knew he was here—we could smell the rich aroma of his cigar smoke wafting up from the parking lot!"

In 1992, Tom Hanks, who won Best Actor Oscars for *Philadelphia* and *Forrest Gump*, directed "None But the Lonely Heart," the story of a greedy Lothario (Treat Williams) who specializes in courting and marrying lovelorn older women, none of whom live to celebrate their first anniversary. Michael J. Fox directed "The Trap" in a 1991 segment that starred Teri Garr as an adulterous wife helping her husband to fake his own death in an insurance scam. *Twin Peaks'* Kyle MacLachlan directed "As Ye Sow," the story of a man who hires a killer to bump off his wife's lover, in 1993. Bob Hoskins (Eddie Valiant in Zemeckis' *Roger Rabbit*) directed "Fatal Caper" from the 1996 season.

The only thing *Tales* asked of its star-directors was that they act in at least one scene in the segment, so that HBO could use their likenesses to promote the series. "We gave them an opportunity to do something they'd always wanted to do," says Joel Silver. "All they had to do was lend us their face."

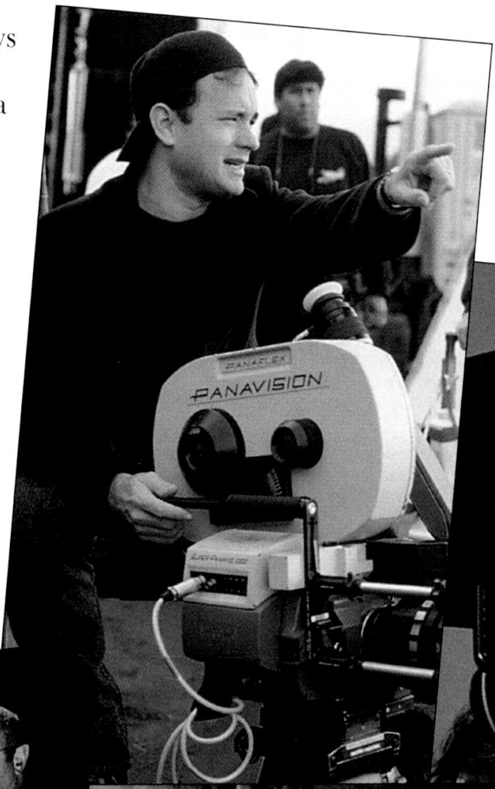

Star directors brought their professionalism to the set, but found it was also a great chance to have some fun on the "wrong" side of the camera. Tom Hanks directed "None But the Lonely Heart" (left); Ah-nold Schwarzenegger took on "The Switch" (below right). Bottom row: Bob Hoskins ("A Fatal Caper"), Michael J. Fox ("The Trap"), and Kyle MacLachlan ("As Ye Sow").

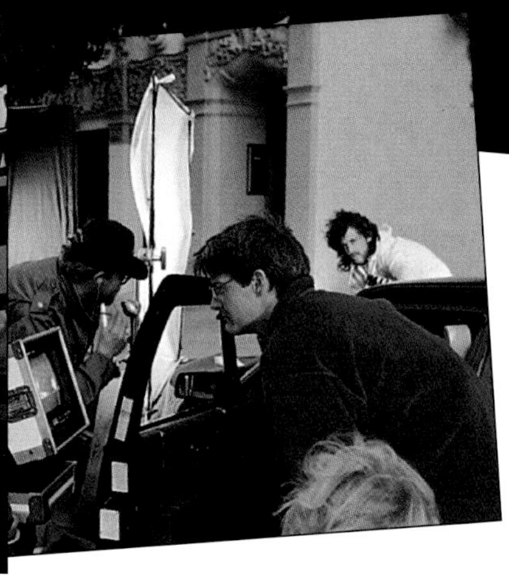

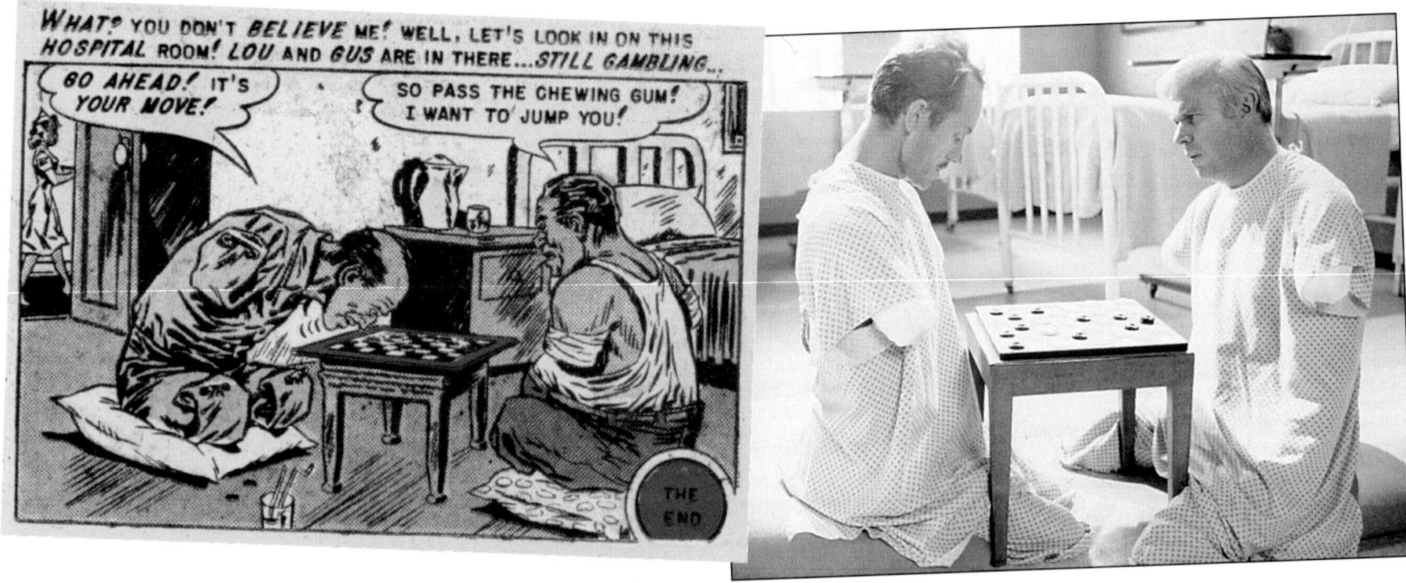

Both Walter Hill, who directed "Cutting Cards" (above), and Joel Silver, who directed "Split Personality" (below), studied the comic book originals, and used them to plan out their shots.

The Link Between Comics and Movies

Any number of live action film and TV features based on comic books or cartoons have crashed and burned because they were unable to capture the feel of the pen-and-ink originals. The executive producers of *Tales from the Crypt* share a commitment to and a fondness for the EC comics that goes beyond their contractual obligation, and it's no coincidence that they have all been credited with having a comic book or cartoon sensibility in their films.

In the eyes of some critics, that's become more of an accusation than a compliment, but none of the five filmmakers sees a comic book outlook as a weakness. "I still look at comics and graphic novels a lot," admits Walter Hill unapologetically. "There is obviously a great carryover from these forms into what we do in motion pictures in terms of storytelling—the economy of visual means and verbal means—how you get it done in an efficient way and still bring mood and character into it."

Zemeckis, of course, happily pleaded guilty to having a cartoon sensibility and made the universally acclaimed *Who Framed Roger Rabbit?* "The thing that's interesting about comic books, and especially about ECs, is that they were ahead of their time in the '50s in terms of style," he says. "They were always extremely visual, with wonderful lighting and low angles. Naturally they were inspirational for a filmmaker. You could take an EC comic and it would trigger images in your mind. The way the panels and images were drawn were very much like movie storyboards."

With *Tales from the Crypt*, the original intentions that Gaines and Feldstein had in mind were always clear," says Joel Silver. "The panels storyboarded each episode for us, and we tried to stay pure to those intentions."

This point of view gets a ringing endorsement from a highly reliable source—author/screenwriter and comic book aficionado Ray Bradbury, whose own works were adapted by Al Feldstein and Bill Gaines for EC horror and science fiction comics. "If you study comics for a lifetime," Bradbury declares, "those are storyboards for films. I knew it when I was ten years old. When it came time for me to write a screenplay, it was just like the comics." In 1956, he shared a screenwriting Oscar with cowriter/director John Huston for *Moby Dick*, which starred Gregory Peck.

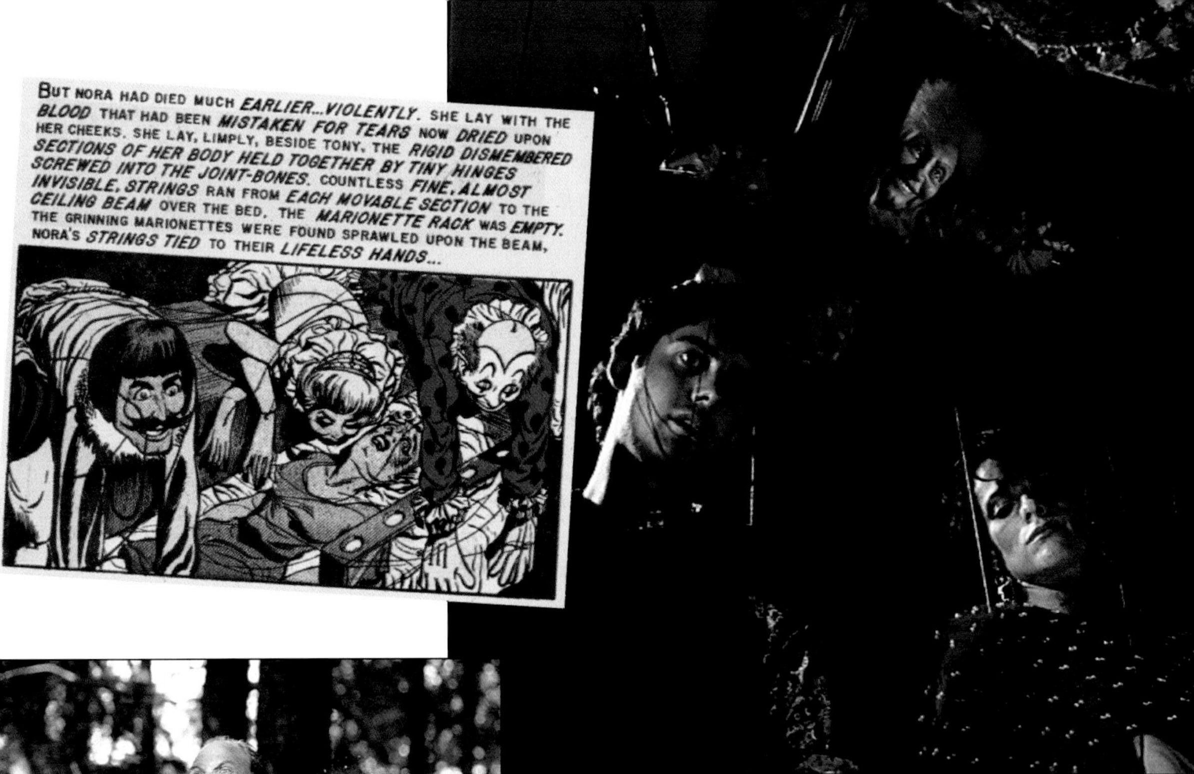

In "Strung Along," director Kevin Yagher chose a different camera angle to convey the scene first depicted by "Ghastly" Graham Ingels. This kind of artistic license was encouraged by the *Tales* executive producers, as it had been by Gaines and Feldstein.

Director Russell Mulcahy modernized the finale of "Split Second," substituting a chain saw for Jack Kamen's axe, and making the scene a one-on-one confrontation between Ted and his boss.

In both "The Reluctant Vampire" (left), and "Carrion Death" (below), the comic book ancestry of the story is clear.

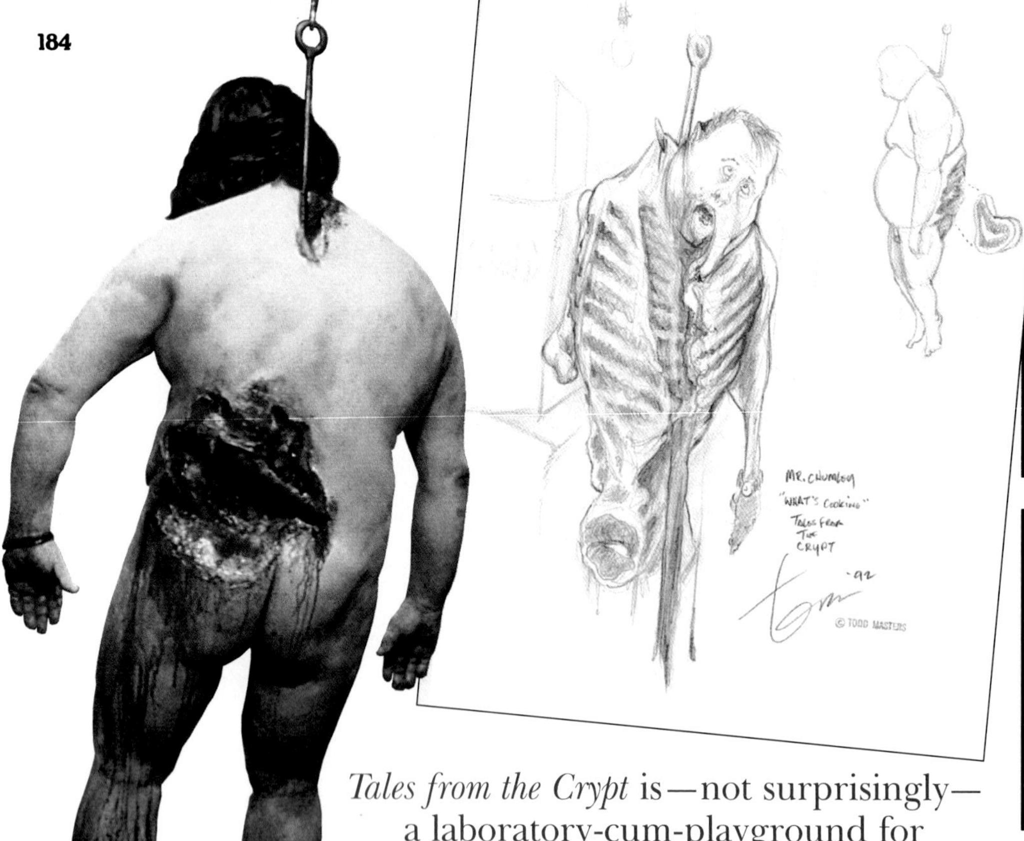

As shown in his original sketch for "What's Cooking" (above), Todd Masters harnessed the resources of the special effects craft to realistically remove a loin steak from actor Meat Loaf.

Tales from the Crypt is—not surprisingly—a laboratory-cum-playground for make-up artists, costumers, and creators of special effects.

Gore Happens

In "Cutting Cards" (1990), directed by Walter Hill, a game of "chop poker" makes dismemberment central to the plot. "Somehow it's always 7 o'clock at the end of a long day when you're trying to get these shots. We're tired—and no one is sure if what we've got is good enough. Next day at the dailies, of course, far from being not good enough, everybody just dies when they see it."

Effects specialist Todd Masters has been associated with the series ever since his company was hired to create Vosburg's sculpted tomb and all the faces lurking in the background. (He also created the demons for the first *Tales* feature, *Demon Knight*.) One of Masters' most challenging episodes was "Forever Ambergris," which first aired in October of 1993. "When Scott Rosenberg's script came in, it was very gooey," remembers Masters. "People were melting and their limbs were falling off, and at the end, Roger Daltrey (*Tommy*'s pinball wizard and lead singer of The Who) has his nose flop into the sink. Steve Buscemi's character had this terrible Ebola-like disease called Jungle Rot. The script called for his face to start bloating and for ooze to be flowing and for his eyeball to swell up and slide down his cheek like a slug. Rather than do it with a fake head, which would have been customary, we

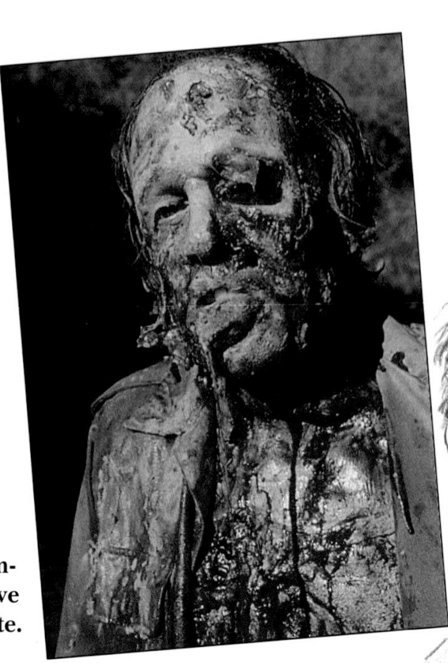

The consensus within the *Tales* production company is that "Forever Ambergris" starring Steve Buscemi (right) is the grisliest episode to date.

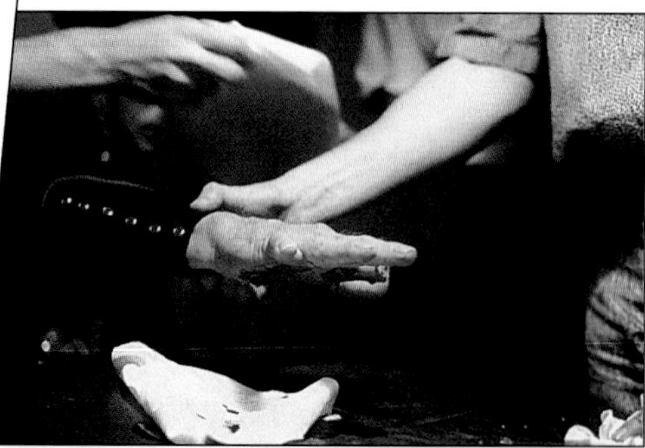

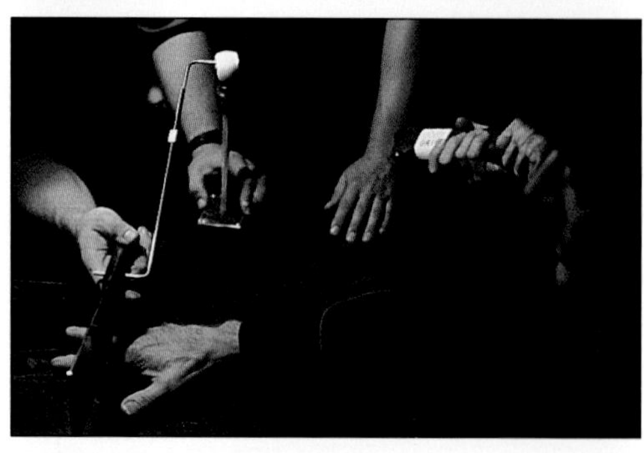

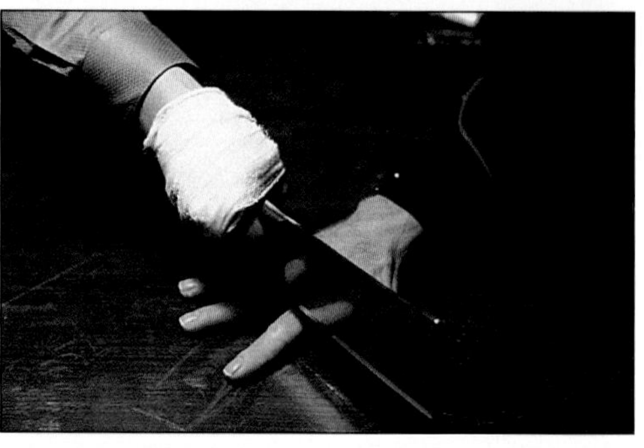

"There's an absolutely horrifying shot in 'Cutting Cards' that I still hear about," says director Walter Hill, "in which a cleaver is used to cut off a guy's finger." The sequence above shows how Hill shot this amputation scene.

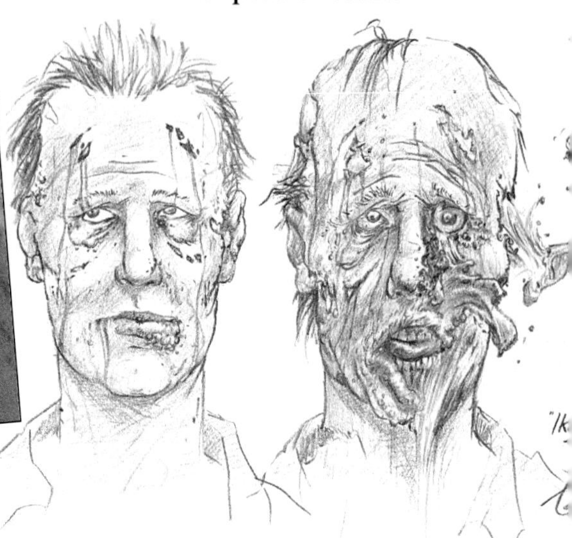

Advancement in special effects techniques makes it possible to realize some effects that were not imaginable in the days of the EC comic books. Below, the cast from "Death of Some Salesman." From left: Tim Curry, Tim Curry, Ed Begley, Jr., and Tim Curry. The inset photo shows Curry in makeup for his role as the most unlovely daughter, Winona.

Todd Masters (center, with cap) mugs with his grue crew and some of their human spare parts.

did it right on Buscemi's face, with a prosthetic. As we did the effect, the entire crew just stood there with their jaws agape, and there was this weird pause as they watched." The next day producer Gil Adler called Masters into his office. With a cocky, rather triumphant grin on his face, he proclaimed, "I just got a call from Dick Donner. He says that we've crossed the line."

"That was the first time I realized that there actually *was* a line on *Tales from the Crypt*," declares Masters. "Other than that one instance, we've never really had anybody telling us what we could or could not do."

Masters is not alone in his appreciation for the artistic elbowroom afforded by *Tales*

As any Hollywood veteran can testify, if you can gross out the crew, you've really got something.

With few limitations from management, *Tales* special effects teams have pushed the envelope to create riveting images such as these protruding shears from "Easel Kill Ya" (left), a bald ghoul and rising cadaver from "Mourning Mess" (lower left, center), and Travis Tritt's blood-drenched, agonized carcass in "Doctor of Horror."

Costumer Warden Neil has Cheech Marin dressed to kill in "Half Way Horrible."

from the Crypt. "My stuff is over the edge when I design for *Tales from the Crypt*, more so than anything else I do," says costumer Warden Neil, who has worked on more than half the episodes. "The producers and directors give me total freedom. They feed me the scenes and I just go from there."

Neil has to juggle a number of factors to maintain a properly "Cryptian" sense of sexy horror, problems that costumers on tamer shows don't have to grapple with—like toplessness. "We also have a lot of costumes that have to be rigged so that blood can fit into them and spurt out in a lifelike manner," says Neil. "It's got to look like real blood and the directors like it dripping in the right way. You can't have blood dripping out sideways."

Blood is director Russell Mulcahy's specialty. He's done a total of four episodes to date, and enjoys the Cryptian sense of gory fun. "Usually there is someone running around with a spritzer of fake blood," he chortles, "and I say, 'No! No! Bring the bucket!!' I run around with the bucket, throwing blood on the walls. The crew now wears protective clothing—those paper suits—when they work with me. I'm known as Russell 'Buckets of Blood' Mulcahy."

Tales from the Crypt was an instant critical and box office success.

The Ultimate Just Dessert

Since its debut, it has garnered a variety of industry honors in a wide range of categories—score, lighting, photography, editing, acting, and directing. Among the trophies are ten CableACE awards, including one for Best Dramatic Series (1990).

For Bill Gaines, the success of the HBO *Tales from the Crypt* series was his final victory over Fredric Wertham and Estes Kefauver, and the ultimate proof of the EC "just desserts" theory that what goes around, comes around, and often in the way you'd least expect it.

"I always knew how near and dear to his heart *Tales* was," says Joel Silver. "I knew it was really very special to him, and I wanted to use his faith in me to honor the material, so I never let it get cheesy. We really tried to preserve the artistry of the material and to remain consistent with the original tone."

"Joel brought Bill Gaines to our studio in Culver City," recalls Bill Teitler, "and it seemed to me that he was quite thunderstruck and very touched by what we were doing. He saw the care we were taking, and how much we respected the original material and the intention behind them. He saw that we hadn't taken the comics and made something else out of them. We really appreciated the comics for what they were, and we loved the same thing about them that he had loved—and still loved.

JEFF KRAVITZ

With Bill Gaines' visit to the *Tales from the Crypt* set, the torch was passed to a new generation.

"He looked around, and I think on some level he saw all of us as another version of what he and Feldstein and the artists had been doing—putting this thing together and having a great time doing crazy stuff. I think he saw our passion and enthusiasm and it really brought it all back for him. There was this great sense of passing the torch—that we got it, we understood it, we loved it—and he got it that we got it. He died fairly soon thereafter."

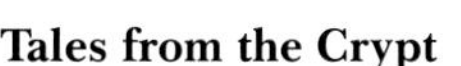

THE CRYPT COMPENDIUM

Since its premiere on Home Box Office in 1989, the reach of *Tales from the Crypt* has become truly global. The series is now broadcast on every continent except Antarctica. The Crypt Keeper hosts his fright nights from Bulgaria to Brazil, from Malaysia to Morocco, from Nicaragua to New Zealand.

Tales from the Crypt has now survived for more years as a television series than it lasted as a comic book. With the conclusion of the seventh season, there are now a total of 93 episodes of *Tales from the Crypt*, all based on stories that originally appeared in the EC horror and suspense comic books of the early 1950s. EC patriarch Bill Gaines passed away before the fourth season aired, but lived long enough to appreciate that his work was in good hands. "I watch *Tales from the Crypt* every time they come on," he told Steve Ringgenberg in a 1992 *Gauntlet* interview, shortly before his death. "I love it, I love it. They've done a splendid job."

Like the *Complete EC Checklist* compiled by Fred Von Bernewitz for EC comics, this *Tales from the Crypt* filmography documents each episode of TV series, and links it to its comic book ancestor.

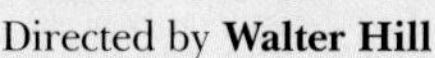

Episode #2

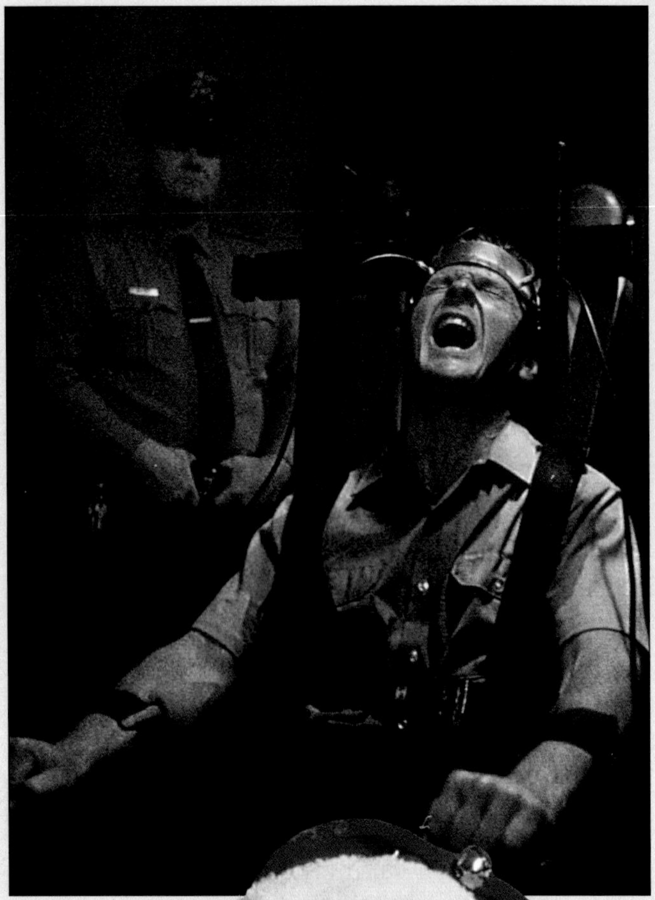

The Man Who Was Death

Directed by **Walter Hill**
Written by **Robert Reneau** and **Walter Hill**
Originally published in *Tales from the Crypt*, No. 17-2
Music composed by **Ry Cooder**
Starring **Bill Sadler**, **David Wohl**, **J.W. Smith**, **Dani Minnick**, **Gerrit Graham**, and **Roy Brocksmith**

Sadler stars as Niles Talbot, a country boy who came to the big city as an electrician and ended up as state executioner. However, the death penalty is repealed and he is suddenly unemployed. His desire to see murderers come to justice turns into a full-time hobby when he begins to stalk criminals who escape through cracks in the system and offs them in various "shocking" ways. He finds himself on the other end of the law and in the hot seat, though, when the cops follow his trail and the death penalty is reinstated just in time to give him the hottest seat in the house at his own electrocution.

Episode #1

Dig That Cat...He's Real Gone

Directed by **Richard Donner**
Written by **Terry Black**
Originally published in *Haunt of Fear*, No. 21-2
Music composed by **Nicholas Pike**
Starring **Joe Pantoliano**, **Robert Wuhl**, **Kathleen York**, and **Gustav Vintas**

Ulric (Pantoliano) is given the chance of a lifetime when a scientist offers to implant a cat's gland inside of him, which will allow him to die and come back to life nine times. The duo turn Ulric's talent into cash, with the help of a carnival barker (Wuhl). They subject him to all manner of horrific deaths — shooting, hanging, drowning — and eight times he astonishes audiences by coming back to life. In a last, desperate attempt to walk away rich, Ulric forces the barker to bury him alive. When he is resurrected in his ninth life, he will take all the profits. Unfortunately, it is only after he is six feet under that Ulric realizes he has flunked math — the cat who died to give him his powers was death numero uno.

Episode #3

And All Through the House...

Directed by **Robert Zemeckis**
Written by **Fred Dekker**
Originally published in *Vault of Horror*, No. 35-1
Music composed by **Alan Silvestri**
Starring **Mary Ellen Trainor**, **Larry Drake**, **Marshall Bell**, and **Lindsey Whitney Barry**

On Christmas Eve, a woman (Trainor) brutally murders her husband (Bell) in order to collect on an insurance policy. What she doesn't realize is that there is an escaped mental patient (Drake) roaming the town dressed as Santa Claus. When he turns up to torment her with an axe, she becomes a victim of her own skulduggery because she cannot call the police or she will be caught. That is, until she figures out a plan to tell the cops that it was the psycho-Santa who offed her hubby. It is a plan that works perfectly... until her little daughter decides to let in jolly old St. Nick, who has an axe to grind with Mom.

Episode #4

Only Sin Deep

Directed by **Howard Deutch**
Written by **Fred Dekker**
Originally published in *Tales from the Crypt*, No. 38-2
Music composed by **Jay Ferguson**
Starring **Lea Thompson**, **Britt Leach**, and **Brett Cullen**

Call girl Sylvia Vane (Thompson) needs money, so she decides to roll a pimp and pawn his jewelry. Instead, the pawnbroker offers to buy her beauty for $10,000, and she willingly accepts. Sylvia then uses her charms to land handsome bachelor Ronnie Price, but soon finds herself aging quickly. Although doctors have no explanation, Sylvia is obviously paying the price for having hocked her good looks. She returns to the pawnbroker, who offers Sylvia her features back for $100,000. Sylvia rushes home for the money, but Ronnie shows up and tries to stop her. She shoots him, and realizes that she is now a fugitive as Ronnie's young, attractive widow. The only way to elude the police is to keep her horrible, wrinkled face.

Episode #6

Collection Completed

Directed by **Mary Lambert**
Written by **A. Whitney Brown, Jr.**, and **Battle Davis** & **Randolph Davis**
Originally published in *Vault of Horror*, No. 25-4
Music composed by **Nicholas Pike**
Starring **M. Emmet Walsh**, **Audra Lindley**, and **Martin Garner**

Pet Sematary director Lambert returns to the call of the wild. After 47 years of work, a grumpy tool salesman, Jonas (Walsh), has a difficult time settling into retirement. His slightly looney wife (Lindley) has an unnatural attachment to her pets. And it is driving him up a wall. She dotes over them, talks to them constantly, even treats her husband as if he were one of them. Jonas decides to curb the local beast population by taking up taxidermy as a hobby. After he has petrified all her pets but her prized feline, she decides to return the favor by killing and stuffing him.

Episode #5

Lover, Come Hack to Me

Directed by **Tom Holland**
Written by **Michael McDowell**
Originally published in *Haunt of Fear*, No. 19-2
Music composed by **Joe Renzetti**
Starring **Amanda Plummer**, **Stephen Shellen**, **Lisa Figus**, and **Richard Eden**

Newlyweds Charles and Peggy find themselves holed up in a decrepit old mansion on their dark and stormy wedding night. After making passionate love for the first time, Charles awakens at the stroke of midnight to discover Peggy doing the same downstairs with another man. His jealous rage quickly turns to horror as he watches Peggy dice up the man with an axe. He realizes that he is witnessing a vision of his bride's mother murdering her husband on their wedding night. When he tries to stop her, he finds himself passing right through her like a ghost. Is he already dead? He awakens with a start, only to find out that history has a nasty way of repeating itself.

2nd SEASON

Episode #10

'Til Death

Directed by **Chris Walas**
Written by **Jeri Barchilon**
Originally published in *Vault of Horror*, No. 28-1
Music composed by **Nicholas Pike**
Starring **D.W. Moffett, Pamela Gien**, and **Aubrey Morris**

A wealthy young plantation owner (Moffett) learns that the land he is about to build his future on is nothing but a quicksand swamp and it is going to cost him a fortune to cover his losses. He devises a plan to woo a wealthy Englishwoman for her fortune. But she won't have anything to do with him, so he seeks out the help of a voodoo priestess. She gives him a potion that will win her over with one drop, and with two, make her his for life. At first the potion appears to have no effect on her, but then it kicks in — with a vengeance. It seems the attraction is stronger than he planned, for when she dies after some meddling by the priestess, she returns, rotting, from the land of the dead to drive him to suicide. But even that's not enough, as the priestess resurrects him, too, for a reunion of sorts.

Episode #11

Three's a Crowd

Directed by **David Burton Morris**
Written by **Kim Ketelsen** and **Annie Willette** & **David Burton Morris**
Originally published in *Shock SuspenStories,* No. 11-4
Music composed by **Jan Hammer**
Starring **Gavan O'Herlihy, Ruth deSosa**, and **Paul Lieber**

For their 10th anniversary, Richard (O'Herlihy) and Della (deSosa) decide to spend time working out their rocky marriage at the island estate of longtime friend Alan (Lieber). It seems Richard has not only lost his job but cannot conceive a child with Della, which makes his stress level rise and sends him into drunken oblivion. Richard begins to believe his wife and friend are having an affair. He sees fit to end it one night in a drunken rage by taking out Alan with a crossbow. When Della shows up, he terrorizes her, finally strangling her to death with a pair of panty hose. While taking her corpse out to the cabin in back for disposal, he discovers he's committed a terrible *faux pas*. A surprise party is waiting for him, a party to celebrate the fact that Della had just found out she was pregnant with his child.

Episode #8

The Switch

Directed by **Arnold Schwarzenegger**
Written by **Richard Tuggle** and **Michael Taav**
Originally published in *Tales from the Crypt*, No. 45-4
Music composed by **Jay Ferguson**
Starring **William Hickey, Rick Rossovich, Kelly Preston, Roy Brocksmith**, and **Ian Abercrombie**

An old millionaire (Hickey) wants badly to win over the heart of a radiant young beauty (Preston) and so he takes the drastic measure of plastic surgery to turn himself young again — for a price. He changes faces with a handsome young stud named Hans (Rossovich). But that's not enough for his love and he eventually spends his entire fortune to exchange bodies with the young man, only to learn that all his true love ever wanted was money and security — which Hans, though old in appearance, now has. And, consequently, he lands the girl.

Episode #12

The Thing from the Grave

Written and directed by **Fred Dekker**
Originally published in *Tales from the Crypt*, No. 22-1
Music composed by **David Newman**
Starring **Miguel Ferrer, Teri Hatcher**, and **Kyle Secor**

Abusive Mitch (Ferrer) turns green with envy when a slick young photographer (Secor) falls for his model girlfriend Stacey (Hatcher) and she doesn't resist. To prove his love, the photographer gives Stacey a necklace that an old woman once told him would hold any promise forever and ever. Mitch kills the photographer, and ties Stacey up in bed, planning to kill her. But Stacey's man rises from the grave just in time to prove that true love never dies — it just becomes zombified.

Episode #9

Cutting Cards

Directed by **Walter Hill**
Written by **Mae Woods** and **Walter Hill**
Originally published in *Tales from the Crypt*, No. 32-3
Music composed by **James Horner**
Starring **Lance Henriksen**, **Kevin Tighe**, and **Roy Brocksmith**

Longtime rival card sharks face off in a small-town casino. They decide to make the stakes high — the loser hightails it out of town…for good. The game? Russian Roulette. Unfortunately, they go through all 6 chambers, only to discover that the gun was loaded with dummy bullets. So they decide to up the stakes to something a cut above — a game of "chop poker." No ante, no pot, just limb-for-limb, based on who wins each hand. The game ultimately lands the two of them in the hospital, limbless, but still vying for best of the best.

Episode #13

The Sacrifice

Directed by **Richard Greenberg**
Written by **Ross Thomas**
Originally published in *Shock SuspenStories*, No. 10-1
Music composed by **Jonathan Elias**
Starring **Kim Delaney**, **Kevin Kilner**, **Don Hood**, and **Michael Ironside**

Hotshot insurance agent Reed (Kilner) decides to murder a bullheaded tycoon and marry his drop-dead wife Gloria (Delaney). The duo scheme up a plan to bump off her husband — quite literally — by knocking him over his balcony. All seems to be going well, until Reed's boss (Ironside) shows up with pictures he has taken of the murder from his apartment across the way. It seems he and the new widow were once married; now he wants her back. He makes a deal with Reed to share Gloria, but it becomes torture for her because her ex-hubby constantly humiliates her. To free Gloria from this degradation, Reed decides to commit suicide and take all the blame for the murder. However, the last laugh is on Reed, because it turns out that his boss and Gloria had been in cahoots all along.

Episode #7

Dead Right

Directed by **Howard Deutch**
Written by **Andy Wolk**
Originally published in *Shock SuspenStories*, No. 6-1
Music composed by **Jay Ferguson**
Starring **Demi Moore**, **Jeffrey Tambor**, **Natalia Nogulich**, and **Troy Evans**

A money-hungry waitress (Moore) goes to see a fortune teller, who predicts that by the end of the day she will be fired and then land a new job. When the prophecy turns out to be reality, the waitress comes back for more. The fortune teller foresees that she will meet a man who will inherit a fortune, then die. Sure enough, she meets a man — albeit a grossly obese one — but for the sake of a promising future, she marries him. The prediction didn't explain that she would be the one to get the money first, by being the millionth customer in an automat, and that she would die by her jealous husband's hand after she tells him to kiss off. Having inherited the cool million, he dies in the electric chair for having stabbed her to death.

Episode #14

For Cryin' Out Loud

Directed by **Jeffrey Price**
Written by **Jeffrey Price** and **Peter S. Seaman**
Originally published in *Shock SuspenStories*, No. 15-3
Music composed by **Michael Rubini**
Starring **Lee Arenberg**, **Katey Sagal**, **Iggy Pop**, **Al White**, and the voice of **Sam Kinison**

A sleazy rock promoter (Arenberg) hears voices in his head, which his doctor attributes to years spent in the music biz. But when he tries to steal the million dollars from an Iggy Pop benefit concert, the voice turns out to be that of his conscience (Kinison), who then tries to talk him out of it. Complicating matters, his banker (Sagal) shows up disguised as a groupie and tries to blackmail him for half of the take. He winds up killing her and stuffing her inside Donnie Osmond's drum case. Now all he has to do is escape, but his conscience leads him to blurt out the truth about the murder. He happily goes to the electric chair to shut up his annoying conscience for good.

Episode #15

Four-Sided Triangle

Directed by **Tom Holland**
Written by **James Tugend** and **Tom Holland**
Originally published in *Shock SuspenStories*, No. 17-1
Music composed by **Scott Johnson**
Starring **Patricia Arquette**, **Chelcie Ross**, and **Susan J. Blommaert**

A runaway young girl named Mary Jo (Arquette) becomes a tortured slave to a nebbish farmer and his cranky old wife. She escapes into the fields, where she has a delusion that the scarecrow reaches out to save her. She begins to use the scarecrow as a source of mental escape, envisioning it as her lover. When the farmer discovers the straw-and-stuffing identity of her "new man," he decides to disguise himself as the scarecrow. His plan backfires, however, when his jealous wife appears in the fields and runs the scarecrow through with a pitchfork to prove to Mary Jo that it's not real. Thinking her straw lover dead, Mary Jo in turn stabs the wife with the pitchfork, thus setting herself free.

Episode #16

The Ventriloquist's Dummy

Directed by **Richard Donner**
Written by **Frank Darabont**
Originally published in *Tales from the Crypt*, No. 28-4
Music composed by **Miles Goodman**
Starring **Don Rickles** and **Bobcat Goldthwait**

A hackneyed ventriloquist named Billy (Goldthwait) seeks out his childhood idol Ingels (Rickles), the best in the business, for some tricks of the trade. Billy is horrified to learn that not only is Ingels a fake, but that he harbors a dark secret: his dummy, Morty, is actually his mutated brother on his "magic" left hand. And Morty has a very murderous streak. When Ingels decides to split up the act by severing Morty from his wrist, Morty winds up killing him, then comes at Billy. But Billy gains the upper hand in more ways than you can imagine.

Episode #17

Judy, You're Not Yourself Today

Directed by **Randa Haines**
Written by **Scott Nimerfro**
Originally published in *Tales from the Crypt*, No. 25-2
Music composed by **Michael Convertino**
Starring **Frances Bay**, **Carol Kane**, and **Brian Kerwin**

Gun nut Donald (Kerwin) and his weirdo reclusive wife Judy (Kane) find themselves up to their necks in witchcraft when an old woman peddler shows up at the house and convinces Judy to try on a necklace. The old woman switches bodies with Judy. Once Donald realizes the switch has taken place, he tricks the old woman into thinking Judy has cancer, and when the two ladies switch back, he blows the hag away and buries her in the cellar. Months later, the witch rises from the dead and switches with Judy yet again. This time, she has a surprise for Donald that he'll never forget.

Episode #19

Korman's Kalamity

Directed by **Rowdy Herrington**
Written by **Terry Black**
Originally published in *Tales from the Crypt*, No. 31-3
Music composed by **David Kitay**
Starring **Harry Anderson**, **Cynthia Gibb**, and **Colleen Camp**

Nebbish *Tales from the Crypt* cartoonist Jim Korman (Anderson) suddenly finds that the grotesque, ghoulish creations that spring from his mind have a way of springing off the page, too — and committing deadly acts of murder. His biggest source of inspiration comes from his bossy, nagging wife (Camp). When a cop (Gibb) on the trail of the grisly crimes traces the murders to the cartoonist and then falls for him, he decides to whip up a suitably nasty creature on his sketch pad to permanently take his wife out of the picture.

Episode #18

Fitting Punishment

Directed by **Jack Sholder**
Written by **Jonathan David Kahn** & **Michael Alan Kahn** and **Don Mancini**
Originally published in *Vault of Horror*, No. 16-2
Music composed by **Stanley Clarke**
Starring **Moses Gunn**, **Jon Clair**, and **Teddy Wilson**

When teenager Bobby's parents die, he goes to live with his Scrooge-like Uncle Ezra (Gunn), a corner-cutting funeral home director. Ezra's cheapskate ways reach new lows when he winds up with an extra coffin and — waste not, want not — decides to fill it with his nephew, murdering him with a crowbar. When the lanky boy proves too tall to fit, he trims off his feet. The boy then returns as a crutch-walking zombie, eager to return the favor.

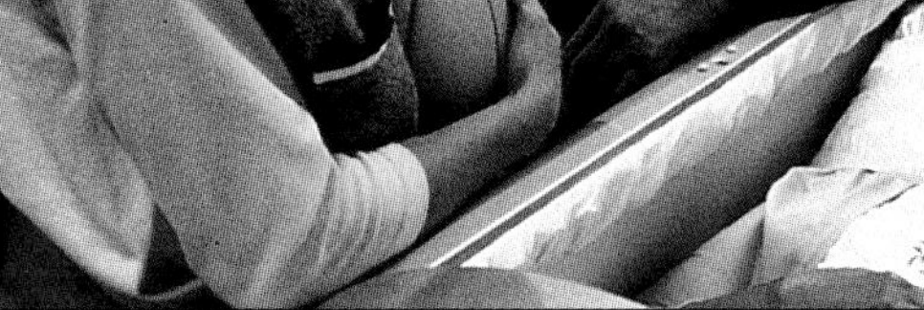

Episode #20

Lower Berth

Directed by **Kevin Yagher**
Written by **Fred Dekker**
Originally published in *Tales from the Crypt*, No. 33-1
Music composed by **Michel Colombier**
Starring **Lewis Arquette**, **Stefan Gierasch**, **Mark Rolston**, and **Jeff Yagher**

The corroded tapestry that is the Crypt Keeper's family history unfolds in this tale of Enoch, the Two-Faced Man (Yagher), a carnival freakshow attraction who has eyes for the 4,000-year-old mummy his keeper has just received in a bargain from a mysterious stranger. When the carny barker discovers the mummy is not only stolen but cursed, he wants to be rid of it — that is, until he notices the sparkling jewels around the mummy's neck. However, the curse states that anyone who tries to lift the ancient family jewels will lose his own, so to speak. The greedy barker decides to swipe them anyway and discovers the sheer magnitude of the curse. This leaves Enoch free to run away with the ghoul of his dreams and sire a bastard creation — the host with the most, the Crypt Keeper.

Episode #21

Mute Witness to Murder

Directed by **Jim Simpson**
Written by **Nancy Doyne**
Originally published in *Crypt of Terror*, No. 18-4
Music composed by **Jan Hammer**
Starring **Richard Thomas, Patricia Clarkson, Reed Birney, Kristine Nielsen**, and **Rose Weaver**

On the eve of her anniversary, a woman (Clarkson) accidentally witnesses a neighbor (Thomas) murder his wife. The shock of the incident leaves her literally speechless and she winds up committed to a hospital. To her horror, she discovers that her doctor is the same man she witnessed commit the crime. The doctor keeps her sedated and tortures her, mentally, all the while keeping her husband in the dark about everything. When the woman finally starts to get through to her husband, the doctor is forced to eliminate him. She finally regains her voice, as well as the will to retaliate, ultimately leaving the evil doctor to die slowly after he accidentally pops something fatal instead of one of his stress pills.

Episode #24

The Secret

Directed by **Michael Riva**
Written by **Doug Ronning**
Originally published in *Haunt of Fear*, No. 24-3
Music composed by **David Kitay**
Starring **Larry Drake, Grace Zabriskie, Mike Simmrin, Georgann Johnson, Stella Hall**, and **William Frankfather**

Twelve-year-old orphan Theodore is adopted by a strange couple, the Colberts, who lock him away in an attic wonderland. It is admittedly every boy's dream, but there's something weird going on. He never gets to go out and the Colberts are always out all day, doing "work." To pass the time, Theodore strikes up a friendship with Tobias (Drake), the house servant. It turns out that the Colberts are actually bloodsuckers who plan on turning little Theodore into one of their own. But little do they realize that Theodore harbors a secret of his own...he's a werewolf with an appetite for vampires.

Episode #22

Television Terror

Directed by **Charles Picerni**
Written by **J. Randal Johnson** and **G. J. Pruss**
Originally published in *Haunt of Fear*, No. 17-2
Music composed by **J. Peter Robinson**
Starring **Morton Downey, Jr., Dorothy Parke**, and **Peter Van Norden**

Sensationalistic, sleazy TV tabloid host Horton Rivers (Downey, Jr.) tries for big ratings by airing live from within a supposedly haunted house, where an old woman hacked up a number of unsuspecting men. Some unusual poltergeist activity begins to scare the wits out of both Horton and his cameraman, but viewers are eating it up, so he has no choice but to plunge farther into the bowels of the abode. When he suddenly discovers his cameraman has been murdered, Horton finds himself alone and at the mercy of a horde of very unruly spectres. Of course, the ratings are through the roof, but Horton winds up being tossed out a window and falls to his death.

Episode #23

My Brother's Keeper

Directed by **Peter S. Seaman**
Written by **Jeffrey Price** and **Peter S. Seaman**
Originally published in *Shock SuspenStories*, No. 16-1
Music composed by **Michael Rubini**
Starring **Timothy Stack, Jonathan Stark, Jessica Harper, Ron Orbach**, and **Valerie Bickford**

Kind Frank (Stack) and obnoxious Eddie (Stark) are Siamese twins. Frank won't agree to an operation that would sever them because he fears being lonely, so Eddie decides to trick him by getting him to fall for a sweet girl named Marie (Harper). He hopes Frank will sign for the operation after she suddenly dumps him. When Marie realizes she actually does love Frank, Eddie murders her in a fit of rage. Frank can't call the cops because if they arrest and sentence Eddie to death, Frank goes too. After they are split up, however, Frank has the final laugh as the cops drag Eddie away.

3rd SEASON

Episode #27

The Trap

Directed by **Michael J. Fox**
Written by **Scott Alexander**
Originally published in *Shock SuspenStories*, No. 18-2
Music composed by **Peter Allen**
Starring **Teri Garr**, **Bruno Kirby**, **Bruce McGill**, **James Tolkan**, **Carroll Baker**, and **Michael J. Fox**

Debt-ridden loser Lou (McGill) sees a way out of the hole by devising a plan to fake his own death and collect on the insurance. He drags both his put-upon wife Irene (Garr) and his coroner brother Billy (Kirby) into the scheme. When Irene realizes that Billy is the kinder, gentler man, she and Billy decide to betray Lou. When everyone thinks Lou's dead, Billy and Irene convince him to fly down to Rio, leaving his money behind to make sure the story sticks. Months later, Lou returns and finds himself in trouble. Billy and Irene won't acknowledge Lou is who he claims to be and he is put to death for his own murder, because his prints were on the murder weapon.

Episode #28

Abra-Cadaver

Directed by **Stephen Hopkins**
Written by **Jim Birge**
Originally published in *Tales from the Crypt*, No. 3-26
Music composed by **Alan Silvestri**
Starring **Beau Bridges**, **Tony Goldwyn**, and **Tom Wright**

Brothers Carl (Goldwyn) and Marty (Bridges) have been feuding for years, ever since Carl played a practical joke that shocked Marty so much it gave him a heart attack. Years later, Marty is on the verge of perfecting a serum that allows the brain to stay receptive even after bodily death. Marty decides to get revenge by turning Carl into his first human test subject. After subjecting Carl to the rigors of witnessing his own death and autopsy, Marty shows Carl that it was all just a trick — or was it?

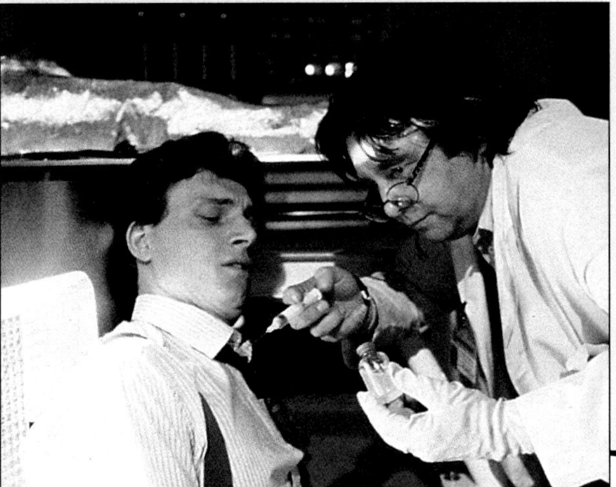

Episode #25

Loved to Death

Directed by **Tom Mankiewicz**
Written by **Joe Minion** and **Tom Mankiewicz**
Originally published in *Tales from the Crypt*, No. 25-3
Music composed by **Jimmy Webb**
Starring **Andrew McCarthy**, **Mariel Hemingway**, **David Hemmings**, and **Kathleen Freeman**

Edward (McCarthy) is a frustrated screenwriter prone to fantasies about his dream girl (Hemingway), even though she won't so much as give him the time of day. He gets an opportunity to win her heart when his mysterious landlord gives him a potion that's sure to make her fall for him. She does indeed become lovestruck for Edward, but a little love goes a long way, and her relentless adoration drives Edward to accept another potion from his landlord to try and kill her. He drinks the poison by accident and winds up in heaven, but at least he's alone and in peace — or so he thinks. However, his true love makes a surprise visit. She has thrown herself out of her apartment window to spend an eternity with Edward.

Episode #29

Top Billing

Directed by **Todd Holland**
Written by **Myles Berkowitz**
Originally published in *Vault of Horror*, No. 39-2
Music composed by **Jay Ferguson**
Starring **Jon Lovitz**, **Bruce Boxleitner**, **John Astin**, **Louise Fletcher**, **Kimmy Robertson**, **Paul Benedict**, **Gregory Cooke**, and **Sandra Bernhard**

Lovitz stars as a struggling actor who would kill to get a part. His girl has just left him, he's been thrown out of his apartment, and his landlord has taken most of his belongings as collateral for back rent. When a longtime rival (Boxleitner) with "the look" lands the lead in a repertory company's production of *Hamlet*, he decides to strangle him to death to take the part. He's horrified to learn, however, that the theater troupe is actually a mental hospital full of dead staff members and escaped nuts.

Episode #26

Carrion Death

Written and directed by **Steven E. DeSouza**
Originally published in *Shock SuspenStories*, No. 9-4
Music composed by **Bruce Boughton**
Starring **Kyle MacLachlan** and **George Deloy**

Diggs (MacLachlan) is a thief on the lam who ends up being caught by a patrol cop (Deloy) after a chase through the desert. When Diggs thinks he gains the upper hand by shooting the cop, he finds he's got a problem — the dead cop has handcuffed himself to Diggs and swallowed the keys as his last act. He tries to make it to the Mexico border, dragging the cop behind him. All the while, a hungry vulture stalks him like the spectre of death. The weight ultimately becomes too much for Diggs to bear and, high atop a cliff, he hacks off his own hand to be free, only to slip and plummet onto the rocks below.

Episode #34

Mournin' Mess

Written and directed by **Manny Coto**

Originally published in *Tales from the Crypt*, No. 38-4

Music composed by **Nicholas Pike**

Starring **Steve Weber**, **Rita Wilson**, **Ally Walker**, **Vincent Schiavelli**, **Nick Angotti**, and **Frank Kopyc**

Weber stars as a lackadaisical reporter investigating a string of murders of street people who gets fired when he fails to deliver the story. He gets a hot scoop, however, when the man everyone thinks is the killer (Schiavelli) comes after the reporter and threatens his life if the newshound doesn't help clear his name. When the man dies and everyone thinks the killings are over, the reporter goes to his gravesite in a cemetery for the homeless, which is sponsored by a group called G.H.O.U.L.S. He discovers what the society is really about — lunch. Beneath the graves lies a series of catacombs, where they dice up and serve the deceased homeless...and guess who's next on the menu?

Episode #32

Easel Kill Ya

Directed by **John Harrison**

Written by **Larry Wilson**

Originally published in *Vault of Horror*, No. 31-1

Music composed by **J. Peter Robinson**

Starring **Tim Roth**, **Roya Megnot**, **Nancy Fish**, **Debra Mooney**, and **William Atherton**

Roth portrays Jack, an artist who finds his niche after he kills a neighbor and paints his version of the bloody aftermath. An eccentric art collector (Atherton) commissions him to paint more of the same, but Jack gives up art for the sake of a new love. When she is the victim of a hit-and-run accident, he decides to murder a man in the hospital parking lot and whip up one more twisted work to pay for the operation that can save her life. Alas, the only one who could perform it was the very man he murdered.

Episode #36

Deadline

Directed by **Walter Hill**

Written by **Mae Woods** and **Walter Hill**

Originally published in *Shock SuspenStories*, No. 12-1

Music composed by **Steve Bartek**

Starring **Richard Jordan**, **Jon Polito**, **Richard Herd**, **John Capodice**, **Rutanya Alda**, and **Marg Helgenberger**

After boozing freelance newshound Charlie (Jordan) finds himself out of work and on the skids, he meets a knockout girl (Helgenberger) who puts the spring back in his step. He vows to go on the wagon and get back on track by finding a hot scoop. Charlie suddenly finds himself smack in the middle of a hot story at a Greek diner when he overhears the owner (Polito) murder his girlfriend. When he gets the frightened man to relate all the dirt and goes to call it in, the woman awakens. She's not dead! More amazing, Charlie is bowled over to discover it's the same girl he met in the bar! Job security comes first, and Charlie strangles her to death to make sure he's got something for the papers. However, the guilt of the incident eventually drives him nuts and lands him in a padded cell.

Episode #30

Dead Wait

Directed by **Tobe Hooper**

Written by **A L Katz** and **Gil Adler**

Originally published in *Vault of Horror*, No. 23-3

Music composed by **David Mansfield**

Starring **Whoopi Goldberg**, **John Rhys-Davies**, **Vanity**, and **James Remar**

A low-life criminal named Red (Remar), looking for a priceless black pearl, locates it at the island estate of ailing millionaire Duval (Rhys-Davies). Red schemes with Duval's mistress Katrine (Vanity) to swipe the pearl, but Duval ends up botching Red's plan when he swallows the pearl so it won't get lost in the scuffle. Red shoots him and digs through his worm-eaten stomach to retrieve it, only to have Katrine turn on him and demand the pearl. Just in time, Duval's spiritual advisor Peligre (Goldberg) shows up to take care of Katrine, but Red finds out the voodoo priestess has far greater plans for him and his priceless red locks.

Episode #31

The Reluctant Vampire

Directed by **Elliot Silverstein**
Written by **Terry Black**
Originally published in *Vault of Horror*, No. 20-2
Music composed by **Cliff Eidelman**
Starring **Malcolm McDowell**, **Sandra Searles Dickinson**, **George Wendt**, and **Michael Berryman**

A blood-sucking night watchman at a blood bank (McDowell) finds he has to do little else to satisfy his appetite than sample from the bank's ample supply. He becomes smitten with pretty secretary Sally (Dickinson), who is being preyed upon by the bank's sleazy owner (Wendt). When the owner declares that he's going to start firing employees, the vampire realizes he has to start replenishing the supplies and satiating his appetite the old-fashioned way. The bank owner discovers the vampire's secret and tries to blackmail him into making a lot of money for his own personal gains, but his scheme backfires when the vampire knocks him out and places him in a coffin.

Episode #33

Undertaking Palor

Directed by **Michael Thau**
Written by **Ron Finley**
Originally published in *Tales from the Crypt*, No. 39-1
Music composed by **Nicholas Pike**
Starring **John Glover**, **Graham Jarvis**, **Aron Eisenberg**, **Scott Fults**, **Jason Marsden**, and **Jonathan Quan**

A group of boys goes undercover to investigate a scam by an underhanded undertaker (Glover) and the town pharmacist, who deliver poison prescriptions and charge a bundle for the funeral after the unlucky victim kicks off. After one of the boys' dads dies at the hands of the dastardly duo, the gang decides to get even. They pull a switcheroo that leads the undertaker to murder his partner in crime; he is then horrified to learn that the boys have been videotaping his evil deeds. They give him a taste of his own medicine by plugging him into a machine that sucks out all his innards, turning him into one of his own high-priced corpses.

Episode #35

Split Second

Directed by **Russell Mulcahy**
Written by **Richard Christian Matheson**
Originally published in *Shock SuspenStories*, No. 4-1
Music composed by **Brian May** and **Nicholas Pike**
Starring **Brion James**, **Michelle Johnson**, and **Billy Wirth**

When lumberjack foreman Dixon (James) weds sexy, bored barmaid Liz (Johnson), he becomes a jealous husband, even though she's constantly teasing the boys. When Dixon discovers her in the sack with young logger Ted (Wirth), he flies into a rage and blinds Ted by whacking him with an ax. Loggers help Ted get revenge by knocking out Dixon, placing him inside a hollow log, and letting the still-chainsaw-handy Ted hone his skills on him...and his wife, too.

Episode #38

Yellow

Directed by **Robert Zemeckis**
Written by **Jim Thomas** & **John Thomas** and **A L Katz** & **Gil Adler**
Originally published in *Shock SuspenStories*, No. 1-2
Music composed by **Alan Silvestri**
Starring **Kirk Douglas**, **Eric Douglas**, **Lance Henriksen**, and **Dan Aykroyd**

During WWI, a general's son realizes he no longer can perform on active duty. Deemed cowardly, his father offers him a way out—if he takes charge of one last mission, he will grant his son a transfer. After fear causes him to leave his fellow soldiers open for a massacre, he flees back to base camp. Nobody believes that he did all he could, and his father has no choice but to sentence him to execution by firing squad. But the firing squad's rifles are loaded with blanks—or are they?

Episode #37

Spoiled

Directed by **Andy Wolk**
Written by **Connie Johnson** and **Doug Ronning**
Originally published in *Haunt of Fear*, No. 26-3
Music composed by **Craig Safan**
Starring **Faye Grant**, **Alan Rachins**, **Anita Morris**, **Tristan Rogers**, **Annabelle Gurwitch**, and **Anthony LaPaglia**

Janet (Grant) is the romance-starved wife of a doctor (Rachins) obsessed with his work. He avoids her every advance and she retreats into soap operas. One day she misses a crucial moment because the TV is on the fritz. She signs up for cable and immediately falls for Abel (LaPaglia), the handsome installer. When the doc realizes they're having an affair, he makes them part of his experiment.

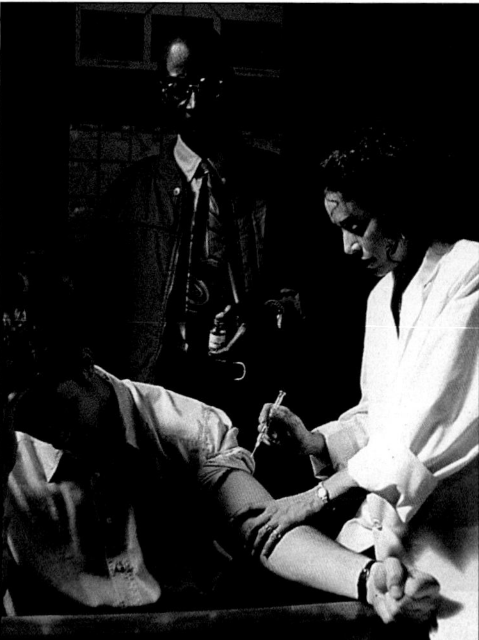

Episode #39

None But the Lonely Heart

Directed by **Tom Hanks**
Written by **Donald Longtooth**
Originally published in *Tales from the Crypt*, No. 33-4
Music composed by **Jay Ferguson**
Starring **Treat Williams**, **Frances Sternhagen**, **Henry Gibson**, **Tom Hanks**, and **Sugar Ray Leonard**

A sleazy man (Williams) makes a killing by marrying wealthy old ladies and bumping them off. His "business partner" fears he'll get caught if he doesn't quit while he's ahead, but the heartless heart-throb wants to try for one more rich widow (Sternhagen). After receiving a series of threatening notes, he knocks off those he suspects, including his partner (Hanks), who manages the dating service he uses to select his victims, and the house butler (Gibson). At last, he poisons the widow. Before he can flee, he is summoned to the cemetery, where he meets a gravedigger (Leonard) who says he's acting on behalf of the vengeful spirits of all the women he's done in over the years — and the greedy young man finds out just how vengeful they are, up close and personal.

Episode #43

What's Cookin?

Directed by **Gil Adler**
Written by **Gil Adler** and **A L Katz**
Originally published in *Haunt of Fear*, No. 12-4
Music composed by **Nicholas Pike**
Starring **Christopher Reeve**, **Bess Armstrong**, **Art LaFleur**, **Meat Loaf**, and **Judd Nelson**

Down on their luck Fred (Reeve) and Erma (Armstrong) need business to pick up fast in their squid café, or their ruthless landlord (Meat Loaf) will evict them. The solution to their troubles comes when employee Gaston (Nelson) shows Fred a really delicious steak recipe — with their landlord as the prime cut. To Fred's surprise, customers start flocking from all over to sample of the tender, juicy beef and he has no choice but to make Gaston a partner. The cops claim they're getting closer to discovering the landlord's murderer, but the knife Gaston used to kill him was Fred's. When Gaston decides it's finally time to pull the rug out from Fred and Erma and make away with the profits, the last laugh is on him and he finds himself the daily blue-plate special.

Episode #40

This'll Kill Ya

Directed by **Robert Longo**
Written by **A L Katz** and **Gil Adler**
Originally published in *Crime SuspenStories*, No. 23-1
Music composed by **Ira Newborn**
Starring **Sonia Braga**, **Dylan McDermott**, and **Cleavon Little**

When scientists Sophie (Braga) and Pack (Little) discover their latest serum contains toxins that will poison the bloodstream and kill anyone they administer it to, their boss (McDermott) tells them to figure out the problem and deal with it. He's an insufferable bastard with no time for details, who's also been seeing Sophie between the sheets for years. He meets his comeuppance, however, after the two scientists accidentally inject him with the poison serum instead of his insulin and he finds himself with only a couple hours left to live. By and by he learns that the two were setting him up and shows up at the lab to return the favor by injecting Pack with the serum, killing him instantly. When he drags the body to the cops and tries to tell his story, Sophie bursts in to tell him it was all just a trick to get him to lighten up — and that the two had just discovered the cure after all.

Episode #44

The New Arrival

Directed by **Peter Medak**
Written by **Ron Finley**
Originally published in *Haunt of Fear*, No. 25-1
Music composed by **Michael Kamen**
Starring **David Warner**, **Joan Severance**, **Zelda Rubenstein**, **Twiggy Lawson**, and **Robert Patrick**

Self-important radio child psychologist Alan Getz (Warner) wants to prove to his boss (Severance) and the world that he really is the best. He accepts the challenge of paying a house call upon an oddball mother (Rubenstein) and her particularly problematic daughter Felicity (Lawson). One by one, the members of his team and, finally, his boss are offed in horrifying ways. But he continues, undaunted, until he discovers he's met his match, as little Felicity turns out to be a little zombie with a penchant for murder!

Episode #41

On a Dead Man's Chest

Directed by **William Friedkin**
Written by **Larry Wilson**
Originally published in *Haunt of Fear*, No. 12-2
Music composed by **Merl Saunders**
Starring **Yul Vazquez**, **Paul Hipp**, **Tia Carrere**, **Sherrie Rose**, **Heavy D**, and **Gregg Allman**

A rocker's ego conflicts with the band's bassist and his woman, a beauty named Scarlett (Carrere). His groupie girlfriend (Rose) tells him to get a tattoo from a very special artist (Heavy D) who doesn't do requests but only translates what the skin tells him to design. To the rocker's horror, he finds his chest emblazoned with Scarlett's face. He does all he can to remove it, but it just keeps reappearing and it finally drives him to murder. In a feverish fit of rage, he strangles Scarlett in a bathtub, but the tattoo continues to terrorize him. He ultimately goes mad, cutting it right out of his skin so that he might finally get the guilt of her murder off his chest.

Episode #42

Seance

Directed by **Gary Fleder**
Written by **Harry Anderson**
Originally published in *Vault of Horror*, No. 25-1
Music composed by **Jimmy Webb**
Starring **Cathy Moriarty**, **Ben Cross**, **Ellen Crawford**, and **John Vernon**

A couple of bumbling schemers (Moriarty, Cross) decide to pull one last fast one on an unsuspecting man named Chalmers (Vernon). The plan is for Cross's character to take pictures while she and Chalmers get cosy, then show them to his wife. But their plot backfires when they find they can't convince Chalmers his wife will be destroyed when she sees the photos. As luck would have it, Chalmers accidentally falls to his death down an elevator shaft. The devilish duo soon discovers the reason Mrs. Chalmers never would have seen the photos — she's blind. When the widow decides she's going to consult with her spiritual advisor, the couple devises a plot. She will pretend to be the medium and he will show up as the dead spirit of Chalmers and tell the woman to give them all her money. However, Chalmers himself really does return and gives the two what they deserve.

Episode #45

Beauty Rest

Directed by **Stephen Hopkins**
Written by **Donald Longtooth**
Originally published in *Vault of Horror*, No. 35-3
Music composed by **Alan Silvestri**
Starring **Mimi Rogers**, **Jennifer Rubin**, **Kathy Ireland**, and **Buck Henry**

Rogers portrays a jealous model who goes berserk when her roommate (Ireland) lands a part she'd thought she had for sure. She's not willing to sleep around to get parts — but she is willing to murder for them. She forces the young lass to o.d. on medication and quickly steps in to take her place as a contestant in a beauty pageant. She comes in second due to the meddling of a jealous competitor (Rubin), and murders her, too. With nobody left to stand in her way, she is crowned the winner. It proves a dubious honor. The title turns out to be Miss Autopsy 1992 — and the spokesmodel has to be among the deceased to accept.

Episode #48

Maniac at Large

Directed by **John Frankenheimer**
Written by **Mae Woods**
Originally published in *Crime SuspenStories*, No. 27-1
Music composed by **Bill Conti**
Starring **Blythe Danner**, **Salome Jens**, **Clarence Williams III**, **Obba Babatunde**, and **Adam Ant**

A mousy new library clerk (Danner) finds herself going nuts over a serial killer on the prowl. The many possible suspects include the library's alcoholic security guard (Williams III), the snotty head librarian (Jens), and a spooky patron (Ant) who is very preoccupied with criminology. When her boss makes her stay late, she's convinced that the serial killer is going to turn her into his next victim. It turns out, however, that she herself is really the killer and, true to the young man's word, makes her boss the next corpse.

Episode #51

Werewolf Concerto

Directed by **Steve Perry**
Written by **Rita Mae Brown** and **Scott Nimerfro**
Originally published in *Vault of Horror*, No. 16-1
Music composed by **Rick Marotta**
Starring **Timothy Dalton**, **Dennis Farina**, **Walter Gotell**, **Charles Fleischer**, **Reginald VelJohnson**, **Lela Rochon**, and **Beverly D'Angelo**

A brutal murder at a backwoods resort hotel is suspected to be the work of a werewolf. The hotel manager (Farina) assures everyone that among them walks a werewolf expert who will get to the bottom of the case and deal with the beast. Meanwhile, suave Lokai (Dalton) is on the trail of both the mystery guest as well as a gorgeous, elusive woman (D'Angelo). Everyone is suspicious of one another, but the general consensus is that Lokai is the werewolf hunter. However, when the moon grows full, he shows his true fur and goes out on the prowl for romance — only to discover the woman of his fancy is not only the werewolf hunter, but a vampire to boot.

Episode #50

Strung Along

Directed by **Kevin Yagher**
Written by **Yale Udoff** and **Kevin Yagher**
Originally published in *Vault of Horror*, No. 33-4
Music composed by **Jay Ferguson**
Starring **Donald O'Connor**, **Patricia Charbonneau**, and **Zach Galligan**

O'Connor plays an aging puppeteer who obsesses over his young wife (Charbonneau). His only solace is his favorite marionette, Koko, who seems to know his every cynical, nasty thought. When his wife and her lover (Galligan) make him think he has caused Koko to murder her, it induces a heart attack in him that leaves the two to continue their passionate affair. But Koko has a mind of his own and enacts a bloody revenge — with no strings attached.

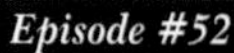

Episode #52

Curiosity Killed

Directed by **Elliot Silverstein**
Written by **Stanley Ralph Ross**
Originally published in *Tales from the Crypt*, No. 36-2
Music composed by **Walter Werzowa**
Starring **Margot Kidder**, **Kevin McCarthy**, **J. A. Preston**, and **Madge Sinclair**

A husband (McCarthy) who can no longer stand the nagging ways of his wife (Kidder) conspires with his best friend (Preston) and his wife (Sinclair) to keep a youth-giving serum away from her. When she thinks the trio is trying to kill her, she poisons them. As they wither, she samples the real formula. So does the family pup, who suddenly has a voracious appetite.

Episode #47

King of the Road

Directed by **Tom Holland**
Written by **J. Randal Johnson**
Originally published in *Two-Fisted Tales*
Music composed by **Warren Zevon**
Starring **Raymond J. Barry**, **Brad Pitt**, **Michelle Bronson**, and **Jack Keeler**

Pitt stars as a cocky drag racer who provokes an aging ex-racer-turned-cop named Iceman (Barry) into one last contest. When Iceman chooses not to return to the reckless days of his youth, the young man woos his teenage daughter (Bronson) and holds her captive until the Iceman changes his mind. Finally, he's willing to come out of retirement to get his daughter back. He proves he's still got the touch, tricking the youngster by changing course at the last second, sending him careening to an explosive death.

Episode #46

Showdown

Directed by **Richard Donner**
Written by **Frank Darabont**
Originally published in *Two-Fisted Tales*, No. 37-4
Music composed by **Michael Kamen**
Starring **David Morse**, **Neil Gray Giuntoli**, **Roderick Cook**, and **Thomas F. Duffy**

A gunman is tracked down by another fast draw (Morse) in a ghost town and the two shoot it out in a wild west showdown. The young man easily bests his rival, but finds himself haunted by his ghost and the spirits of all of his past victims. He has taken a potion from a traveling medicine salesman who was killed by one of the gunman's stray bullets. The spectres haunt the young man and, ultimately, take him down in a bloody shootout in the center of town, where he joins their ranks and becomes a legend himself.

Episode #49

Split Personality

Directed by **Joel Silver**
Written by **Fred Dekker**
Originally published in *Vault of Horror*, No. 30-1
Music composed by **Michael Kamen**
Starring **Joe Pesci**, **Jaqueline Alexandra**, **Kristen Amber**, and **Burt Young**

A gambling man named Stetson (Pesci) who's always had the desire to date twins has his chance after his car breaks down. He winds up in the home of two beautiful, reclusive daughters (Alexandra, Amber) of a deceased and quite wealthy architect. He decides to play both angles, as it were, and "create" his own twin by telling the girls he will be going away while his brother stays with them. Each of the girls marries one of the "brothers." Stetson plans to reap double the wealth when he eventually knocks them both off. What he doesn't realize is that these ladies share and share alike. When he trips up and the two figure out they've actually married the same guy, they carve him up with a chainsaw, just as they'd done to their father years before, so that there will be enough of him to go around.

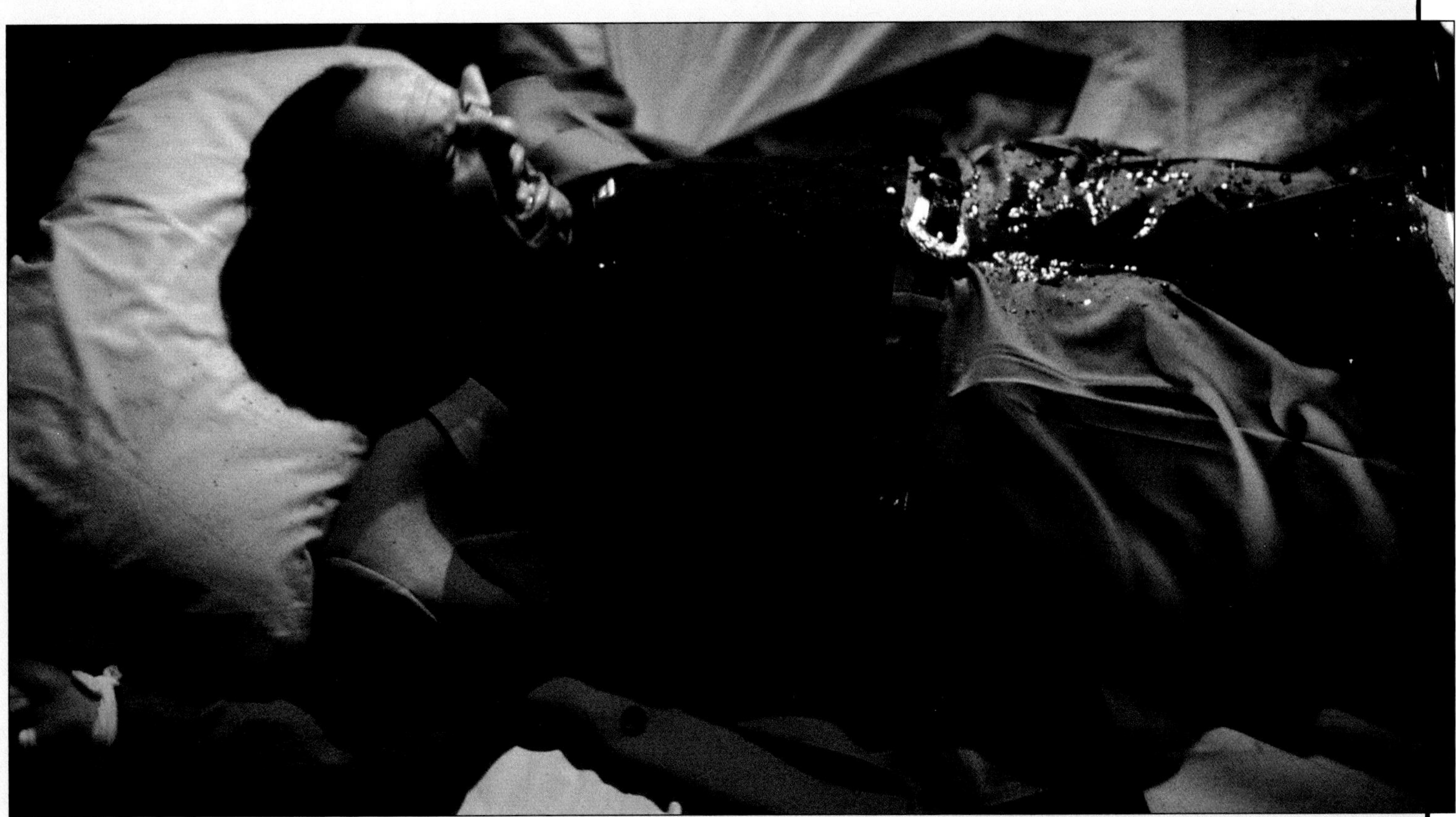

Episode #54

As Ye Sow

Directed by **Kyle MacLachlan**
Written by **Ron Finley**
Originally published in *Shock SuspenStories*, No. 14-4
Music composed by **Branford Marsalis**
Starring **Hector Elizondo**, **Patsy Kensit**, **John Shea**, **Sam Waterston**, **Adam West**, and **Miguel Ferrer**

MacLachlan directs this torrid tale about a husband (Elizondo) who hires a detective (Waterston) to spy on his lovely Irish wife (Kensit). The husband suspects a smooth-talking priest (Shea) of fooling around with her and pays the investigator $100,000 to have him taken care of. After he realizes he's been suckered, he slips into the confession booth to do the job himself. Suddenly his wife comes in. He hears her confess that she wasn't cheating, just afraid to have sexual relations because her mother died in childbirth. Upon hearing the good news, the husband happily reunites with his wife — only to be shot down by the very hitman he hired.

Episode #57

People Who Live in Brass Hearses

Directed by **Russell Mulcahy**
Written by **Scott Nimerfro**
Originally published in *Vault of Horror*, No. 27-2
Music composed by **Brad Fiedel**
Starring **Bill Paxton**, **Lainie Kazan**, **Brad Dourif**, and **Michael Lerner**

Two-bit criminal Billy (Paxton) plots to break into the safe of the ice cream warehouse where he once worked. In revenge he plans to frame the man who put him away, Mr. Byrd (Lerner). Billy uses his half-wit brother, Virgil (Dourif), as the front man, but complications ensue. There's no money in the warehouse safe — Byrd must have taken it home with him. When the two brothers bust in on Byrd, they catch him off guard and Billy blows him away. Little does he realize that Byrd has a brother, too — a Siamese twin attached to his back who serves up vengeance upon Virgil and Billy...à la mode.

Episode #58

Two for the Show

Directed by **Kevin Hooks**
Written by **A L Katz** and **Gil Adler**
Originally published in *Crime SuspenStories*, No. 7-4
Music composed by **Nicholas Pike**
Starring **David Paymer**, **Vincent Spano**, and **Traci Lords**

When a husband (Paymer) believes his wife (Lords) is having an affair, he murders her. A cop (Spano) shows up to investigate, but finds nothing except a very nervous man who won't let him near the bathtub (where her body is floating). He chops her up, tosses her in a steamer trunk, and hops a train out of town to dispose of the body. The cop follows him, so he switches his trunk for a similar one. When he opens the trunk to prove to the cop that he's not a killer, he gets a most unpleasant and inexplicable surprise — the trunk he stole also contains a corpse.

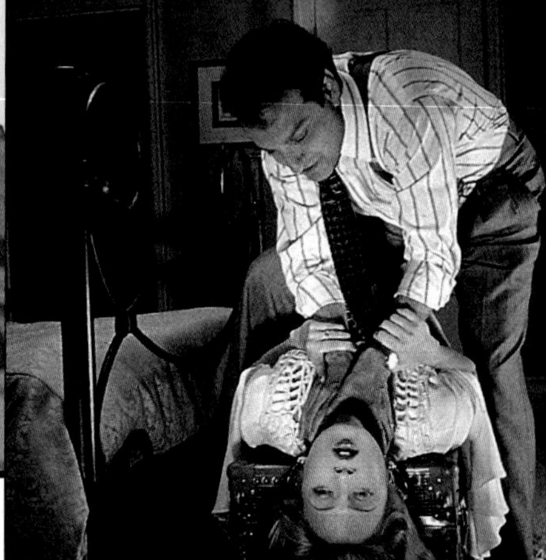

Episode #55

Forever Ambergris

Directed by **Gary Fleder**
Written by **Scott Rosenberg**
Originally published in *Tales from the Crypt*, No. 44-1
Music composed by **Jay Ferguson**
Starring **Roger Daltrey**, **Steve Buscemi**, and **Lysette Anthony**

Seasoned combat photographer Dalton (Daltrey) finds himself second banana to up-and-comer Ike (Buscemi). He's also become smitten with the young man's sexy wife (Anthony). While on assignment in South America, Dalton sends Ike into a germ-warfare-plagued area. When he returns, he becomes stricken overnight with a fatal disease that eats him from the inside out. Dalton then takes Ike's work and returns to the States to claim it as his own. He tries to claim his sexy widow as well, but she's one step ahead of him. Her dying hubby sent her a letter detailing how he was set up by Dalton. She sacrifices herself by smoking some poison weed Ike sent her from the decimated village and then infects Dalton during intercourse.

Episode #53

Death of Some Salesman

Directed by **Gil Adler**
Written by **A L Katz** and **Gil Adler**
Originally published in *Haunt of Fear*, No. 15-4
Music composed by **Michael Kamen**
Starring **Tim Curry**, **Ed Begley, Jr.**, and **Yvonne DeCarlo**

In a downright grotesque triple play, Curry portrays Ma, Pa, and beyond-homely daughter Winona. A sleazy, fast-talking traveling salesman (Begley, Jr.) who makes a killing selling false cemetery plots shows up at their door, without realizing that the family has a thing against salesmen. To save his hide, he agrees to wed the repulsive Winona. When he learns of a fortune buried in the cellar, he escapes to the basement while Winona disposes of Pa and Ma, who disapprove of the marriage. After she shows him where the treasure is buried, the salesman shoots Winona and gets to work digging, only to unearth an unsavory discovery — the family really isn't dead and the hole he just dug is his own burial plot.

Episode #56

Food for Thought

Directed by **Rodman Flender**
Written by **Larry Wilson**
Originally published in *Tales from the Crypt*, No. 40-1
Music composed by **Sylvester Levay**
Starring **Ernie Hudson**, **Joan Chen**, **John Laughlin**, **Phil Fondacaro**, **Kathryn Howell**, and **Margaret Howell**

Circus psychic Zambini (Hudson) dominates his lovely assistant Connie (Chen) by invading her every thought. When he discovers she has eyes for the Big Top fire eater (Laughlin) and that she plans to run off with him, he torches the poor man to a crisp. Connie flees in disgust. Days pass and she doesn't return, so he tries his powers of telepathy to call her home. However, Zambini's mind control instead coaxes the circus's man-eating gorilla out of her cage and she tears the psychic limb from limb.

Episode #63

Oil's Well That Ends Well

Directed by **Paul Abascal**
Written by **Scott Nimerfro**
Originally published in *Vault of Horror*, No. 34-2
Music composed by **Frank Becker**
Starring **Lou Diamond Phillips**, **Priscilla Presley**, **Noble Willingham**, **Alan Ruck**, **John Kassir**, **Steve Kahan**, and **Rory Calhoun**

Two scheming lovers (Phillips and Presley) devise a plot to pull a fast one on some good ol' Southern boys by convincing them that there's oil buried beneath a cemetery. All they have to do is buy the land and it's theirs to drill. When the men figure out they're being taken for a ride, the two lovers already have that base covered. She fakes killing him to make it seem like she's on the level, planning to bury him and dig him up later so they can run away with their earnings. When she unearths her lover, she finds it's one of the men instead — the guys are all in cahoots to pull a fast one on her. They're all shocked, however, when they discover there really is oil under the graveyard — then she drops a cigarette in it and blows them all sky high in a self-sacrificing last attempt at revenge.

Episode #61

Creep Course

Written and directed by **Jeffrey Boam**
Originally published in *Haunt of Fear*, No. 23-1
Music composed by **Jay Ferguson**
Starring **Jeffrey Jones**, **Anthony Michael Hall**, and **Nina Siemaszko**

A bookish young student (Siemaszko) reluctantly agrees to assist the class jock (Hall) so that he won't flunk history, despite the intentions of the strict professor (Jones). She finds that extracurricular activities are getting deadlier after her professor and the jock lock her in a basement tomb to become an offering for a very unruly mummy. But she proves to be smarter in the subject of ancient history than either teacher or student, and charms the bandaged ghoul in the guise of his eternal love, Princess Nefra. Meanwhile, the professor poisons the jock so that the mummy's riches will be all his. But when he goes to check on his handiwork downstairs, the young woman turns the mummy on him by making the ancient one jealous and, thus, incredibly angry.

Episode #65

Till Death Do We Part

Written and directed by **Peter Iliff**
Originally published in *Haunt of Fear*, No. 12-3
Music composed by **Alan Silvestri**
Starring **Kate Vernon**, **John Stamos**, **Robert Picardo**, **Frank Stallone**, **Johnny Williams**, and **Eileen Brennan**

Stamos stars as a gigolo who's been "bought" by an aging old woman (Brennan) with a flock of goons by her side at every moment. After she discovers her man is cheating on her with a pretty young thing (Vernon), she orders him to pull the trigger on the lass out in the woods under her watchful eye. Instead, he blows away her henchmen and then comes after her, his new love by his side, in a bloody shootout inside a seedy bar. The hapless young man is disheartened to find that the young woman has turned on him…or so he perceives. In actuality, he's been fantasizing about what might happen if he lets her go, so he really does go through with the deed and blows her head off.

Episode #60

Well-Cooked Hams

Directed by **Elliot Silverstein**
Written by **Andrew Kevin Walker**
Originally published in *Tales from the Crypt*, No. 27-1
Music composed by **Walter Werzowa**
Starring **Martin Sheen, Billy Zane**, and **Maryam D'Abo**

Demon Knight's Zane is a hack magician who blames others for his mediocrity, even going so far as to fire his pretty assistant (D'Abo). When he comes across a true magical genius (Sheen), he decides to bump off the old man and steal his illusions. In trying to do one of the master's tricks, however, he finds himself a stuck pig after some tampering by his ex-assistant. As the would-be magician gasps his last breath, the old man materializes right in front of him to prove that art and trickery are all in the eyes of the living…or is it the dead?

Episode #59

House of Horror

Written and directed by **Bob Gale**
Originally published in *Haunt of Fear*, No. 15-2
Music composed by **Alan Silvestri**
Starring **Keith Coogan**, **Michael DeLuise**, **Courtney Gains**, **Brian Krause**, **Jason London**, **Meredith Salinger**, **Wil Wheaton**, and **Kevin Dillon**

Pledge night turns into hell night when mean-spirited frat president Wilton (Dillon) decides to scare three young pledges out of their wits by sending them on a journey through a supposedly haunted mansion. Along for the ride is a sexy young coed (Salinger) with eyes on one of the pledges (Wheaton) and the hope that her sorority can form a bond with the frat. When the pitfalls Wilton has set up inside the house prove to be nothing compared to a possible real-life phantom who may be stalking them, everyone turns on Wilton and it's his turn to see who's the toughest by going up into the attic. There, he is met with a ghastly surprise — the sorority sisters turn out to be a horde of vampire vixens, handy with the buzzsaw and hungry for some fresh meat.

Episode #64

Half Way Horrible

Written and directed by **Greg Widen**
Originally published in *Vault of Horror*, No. 26-3
Music composed by **Donald Markowitz**
Starring **Clancy Brown**, **Martin Kove**, **Costas Mandylor**, **Charles Martin Smith**, **Jon Tenney**, **Brian Wimmer**, and **Cheech Marin**

Manufacturer Roger Lassen (Brown) buries a friend alive in the South American jungle to complete the development of a chemical preservative, then is plagued by guilt over the incident. The preservative will make him a fortune, but he can't seem to get it past FDA regulations. Visions of his dead buddy force him to admit having done the deed, only to have his buddy's zombified corpse show up to get revenge. Lassen kills his friend once again, this time beheading him. When a mysterious voodoo priest (Marin) shows up at Lassen's house to offer him the chance to exorcise his murderous "evil side" for good, he readily accepts, but finds the operation leaves him only half the man he used to be.

Episode #62

Came the Dawn

Directed by **Uli Edel**
Written by **Ron Finley**
Originally published in *Shock SuspenStories*, No. 9-2
Music composed by **Christopher Franke**
Starring **Brooke Shields**, **Perry King**, **Michael J. Pollard**, and **Valerie Wildman**

Lonely Roger (King) is driving along a mountain road to his cabin when he spies a young woman (Shields) stranded on the side of the road. After he invites her up to his place, he learns that there's been a murder nearby. The killer, who favors an axe, is on the loose in the area. The young woman schemes to tie Roger up and escape, but his estranged wife shows up and botches everything. While she desperately searches for a way out, she makes a horrifying discovery — the female voice she heard isn't Roger's wife but Roger himself...and it is Roger's rather irate female side who turns out to be the killer.

6th SEASON

Episode #72

The Pit

Written and directed by **John Harrison**
Originally published in *Vault of Horror*, No. 40-3
Music composed by **Kevin Gilbert**
Starring **Mark Dacascos**, **Debbe Dunning**, **Marjean Holden**, **Stoney Jackson**, and **Wayne Newton**

A bloody Ultimate Fighting Championship-style steel cage match is about to get under way between two longtime rivals, the greatest fighters in the universe. The real heat, however, is not between them but between their back-stabbing, controlling, power-and-money-hungry wives, who were once fighters themselves. The two fighters realize that they really don't hate each other at all. With the help of a Las Vegas showman, they set up their wives so that they both think the other is trying to sabotage the match. As the two lethal ladies go head-to-head in their own brutal battle, the cameras are rolling and the greatest pay-per-view event of the century is on!

Episode #69

Operation Friendship

Directed by **Roland Mesa**
Written by **Rob Ross**
Originally published in *Tales from the Crypt*, No. 41-1
Music composed by **Peter Bernstein**
Starring **Tate Donovan**, **Michelle René Thomas**, **John Caponera**, and **Peter Dobson**

Mild-mannered computer genius Nelson (Donovan) is everything his childhood pal and mischievous alter ego Eddie (Dobson) isn't. When Eddie discovers Nelson is letting a coworker (Caponera) stomp all over him and steal his ideas, he tries to get him to stand up for himself, but it's no use. Nelson is a hopeless case. That is, until he meets his lovely new next-door neighbor Jane (Thomas) and fumbles his way into her heart. Suddenly fearful that Nelson no longer needs him, Eddie nags at him to find a way to get rid of Jane because she's only going to ruin their friendship. When Nelson won't agree, Eddie becomes quite physical and tosses Nelson's "good side" out a window and the suave, cutthroat power player he's had buried deep inside takes over.

Episode #74

Staired in Horror

Directed by **Stephen Hopkins**
Written by **Colman deKay** and **Teller**
Originally published in *Vault of Horror*, No. 23-4
Music composed by **Jay Ferguson**
Starring **D. B. Sweeney**, **Rachel Ticotin**, and **R. Lee Ermey**

A criminal on the lam (Sweeney) seeks refuge in the home of a wrinkled old woman (Ticotin). He soon discovers the house has a curse on it after the woman comes downstairs in the night as a gorgeous young beauty — who quickly turns ancient and pruned again. She explains that long ago, her husband found her cheating on him and put a curse on both her and the house. She will never come downstairs a young woman again and any man who tries to ascend to her bedroom will find himself aging before his very eyes. When the police show up, she tells him to go upstairs and EC justice takes over.

Episode #66

Let the Punishment Fit the Crime

Directed by **Russell Mulcahy**
Written by **Ron Finley**
Originally published in *Vault of Horror*, No. 33-2
Music composed by **Vladimir Horunzhy**
Starring **Catherine O'Hara**, **Peter MacNicol**, and **Joseph Maher**

An ambulance-chasing lawyer (O'Hara) gets her comeuppance when she becomes trapped in small-claims court hell. She's hauled in for having too many digits on her license plate and discovers that not only is she dealing with a kangaroo court, but a town with a history of swift, strict, and brutal punishment. She is repeatedly run through the system and finds the true meaning of hard justice when she's finally delivered her sentence — public service. She doesn't realize her lawyer (MacNicol) has just been relieved from being stuck in this lawyer's version of hell and treats himself to the electric chair, while she must stay behind to take his place.

Episode #73

The Assassin

Directed by **Martin von Haselberg**
Written by **Scott Nimerfro**
Originally published in *Shock SuspenStories*, No. 17-3
Music composed by **Frank Becker**
Starring **Shelley Hack**, **Chelsea Field**, **Jonathan Banks**, **Marshall Teague**, and **Corey Feldman**, with **Bill Sadler** as The Grim Reaper

Suburban housewife Janet (Hack) finds her home invaded by a group of operatives, headed by the lethal Gwen (Field), who believes she is in great danger from her ex-CIA assassin husband. Gwen dispatches one of the team members (Feldman) to neutralize the homemaker in the basement, but she seduces and then offs him, proceeding to take out the other guy as well. Gwen thinks she has the drop on Janet, but the housewife has a little surprise for her.

Episode #71

The Bribe

Directed by **Ramon Menendez**
Written by **Scott Nimerfro**
Originally published in *Shock SuspenStories*, No. 7-2
Music composed by **Pray for Rain**
Starring **Terry O'Quinn**, **Kimberly Williams**, **Benicio Del Toro**, **Hal Williams**, **Max Grodenchik**, and **Esai Morales**

Recently appointed fire marshal Zoeller (O'Quinn) plans on closing down The Naked Experience strip club in order to get back at its sleazy owner, Puck (Morales) and his partner (Del Toro) for letting his daughter (Williams) dance there. He coaxes an arsonist to torch the club. Only after burned corpses are being lifted out of the remains does he discover that his daughter had been inside, partying with Puck and his friends.

Episode #75

In the Groove

Directed by **Vincent Spano**
Written by **Jack Temechin** and **Colman deKay**
Originally published in *Crime SuspenStories*, No. 21-2
Music composed by **Greg De Belles**
Starring **Miguel Ferrer**, **Linda Doucett**, and **Wendie Malick**

Frustrated talk radio DJ Gary Grover (Ferrer) is half owner of a failing radio station and his sister (Malick), the station manager, has given him a new partner, a sexy looker named Val (Doucett), who quickly reestablishes him as the hottest dirty-talking DJ around. But when the subject of mothers comes up, he goes bonkers on the air. As a result, his sister fires him. At Val's suggestion, he decides to murder his sister in her home, but she's waiting for him with a gun. Poor Gary's been part of a plot by the two ladies to replace him with Val.

Episode #70

Revenge Is the Nuts

Directed by **Jonas McCord**
Written by **Shel Willens**
Originally published in *The Vault of Horror*, No. 20-4
Music composed by **Ulrich Sinn**
Starring **Anthony Zerbe**, **Teri Polo**, **John Savage**, **Bibi Besch**, and **Isaac Hayes**

Patients at a run-down home for the blind suffer under the cruel torture of its owner (Zerbe). Pretty Sheila (Polo) is a new "inmate" who becomes an unwilling pawn when the owner says he will lighten up on the others, if she agrees to sleep with him. Also a veritable prisoner in the home is Benny (Savage), a kindly simpleton who saves Sheila and helps the rest of the blind victims to lock up the heartless owner.

Episode #68

Whirlpool

Directed by **Mick Garris**
Written by **A L Katz** and **Gil Adler**
Originally published in *Vault of Horror*, No. 32-1
Music composed by **Nicholas Pike**
Starring **Rita Rudner** and **Richard Lewis**

Comedienne Rudner stars as a *Tales from the Crypt* story artist who becomes trapped in a twisted, repetitious hell, reliving the same events over and over again. First she goes to the office, where her no-nonsense boss (Lewis) tears her latest story idea to shreds and fires her. Then, she goes down to a bar and gets drunk, only to return late at night to ask for her job back and end up shooting her boss. This scenario reoccurs over and over in a bad case of déjà vu.

Episode #67

Only Skin Deep

Directed by **William Malone**
Written by **Dick Beebe**
Originally published in *Tales from the Crypt*, No. 38-2
Music composed by **Nicholas Pike**
Starring **Peter Onorati**, **Sherrie Rose**, **Stephen Liska**, and **Diane Dilascio**

A conceited young man (Onorati) meets up with a strange, sexy woman (Rose) at a masquerade party. They go back to her place to make love, promising to remain anonymous. Next morning he breaks his vow and she becomes enraged. She goes back to bed and tells him not to be around when she wakes up. Stumbling around her apartment, he finds a glass case, housing the preserved faces of her previous conquests. In a fit of rage, he tries to remove her mask, only to find that it's not a mask at all but her horrifically disfigured face. She then murders him and adds one more face to her collection.

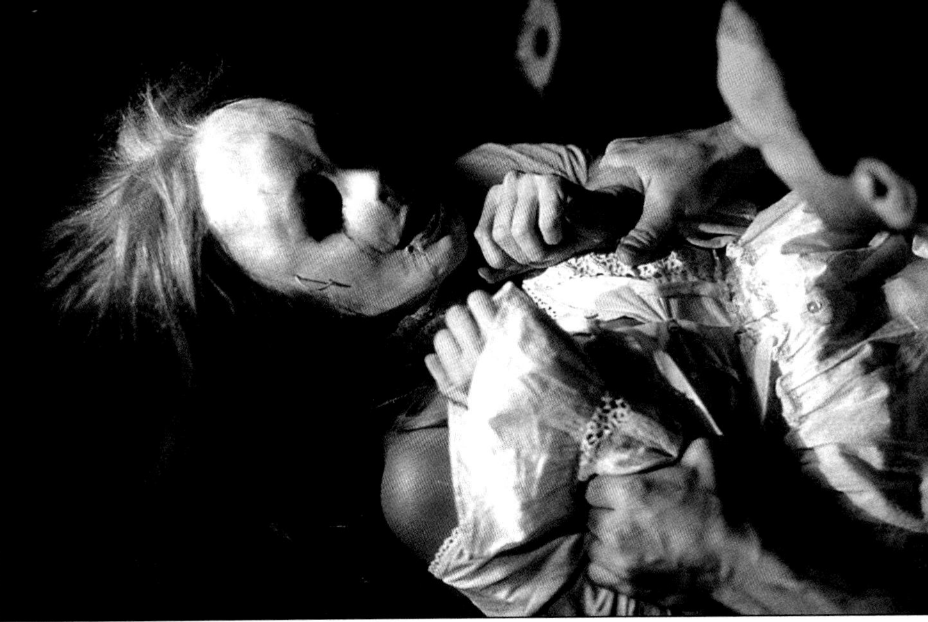

Episode #78

Comes the Dawn

Directed by **John Herzfeld**
Written by **Scott Nimerfro**
Originally published in *Haunt of Fear*, No. 26-4
Music composed by **Frank Becker**
Starring **Bruce Payne**, **Vivian Wu**, **Susan Tyrrell**, and **Michael Ironside**

An ex-Army colonel (Ironside) and his sergeant buddy (Payne) are out poaching bear in the wintry wilds of Alaska. They seek the aid of a woman, the most renowned hunter in the area (Wu). While on the hunt, she tries to persuade the sergeant to stiff the colonel. Instead, the two men decide they don't need the woman anymore, and try to kill her. But she's been leading them on all along—right into a den of dormant and very ravenous vampires. The sergeant shoots and sacrifices the colonel, retreating to his cabin just as the sun is due to come up, but he has forgotten one important detail—Alaska is currently locked in six months of permanent darkness.

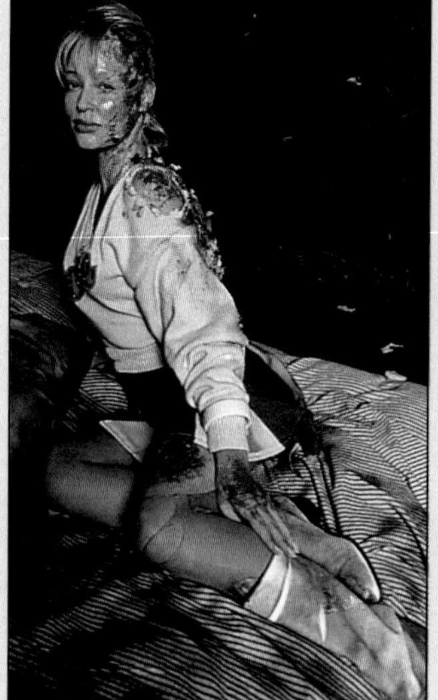

Episode #76

Surprise Party

Directed by **Elliot Silverstein**
Written by **Tom Lyons** and **Colman deKay**
Originally published in *Vault of Horror*, No. 37-1
Music composed by **Walter Werzowa**
Starring **Adam Storke**, **Clare Hoak**, **Jake Busey**, and **Rance Howard**

After murdering his father to inherit a house that burned down years ago, a young man (Storke) arrives to find the house intact and packed with dancing, drunken youngsters. A sexy young siren claims things really heat up at the stroke of midnight. Truer words were never spoken, for when the girl's jealous boyfriend (Busey) shows up, the young man is forced to kill both of them. When he tries to burn them to hide the evidence, he finds that he's repeating the deeds of his father, who burnt the place down the first time.

Episode #77

Doctor of Horror

Written and directed by **Larry Wilson**
Originally published in *Vault of Horror*, No. 13-3
Music composed by **Jay Ferguson**
Starring **Hank Azaria**, **Travis Tritt**, **Ben Stein**, and **Austin Pendleton**

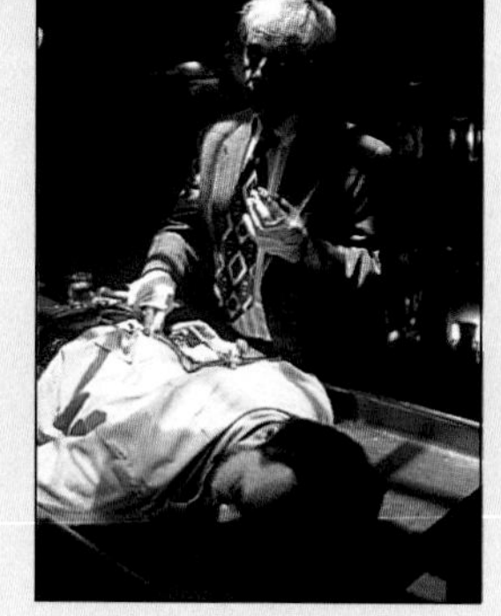

Bumbling morgue security guards Richard (Azaria) and Charlie (Tritt) are offered $500 by a doctor (Pendleton), who needs a body for experimental research. It seems he's trying to locate and excise the soul from the top of the spinal column, just before it disappears. When their boss (Stein) figures out what they've done, Richard is forced to kill him. But Charlie's having second thoughts and so Richard decides to bump him off, too. The doc successfully extracts Charlie's soul; Richard then chops up his simpleton friend. Later, he receives a visit from the soulless Charlie, who's now all evil and looking to get revenge.

Episode #80

You, Murderer

Directed by **Robert Zemeckis**
Written by **A L Katz** and **Gil Adler**
Originally published in *Shock SuspenStories*, No. 14-3
Music composed by **Alan Silvestri**
Starring **Humphrey Bogart**, **John Lithgow**, **Isabella Rossellini**, **Sherilyn Fenn**, and **Robert Sacchi**, with a special appearance by **Alfred Hitchcock**

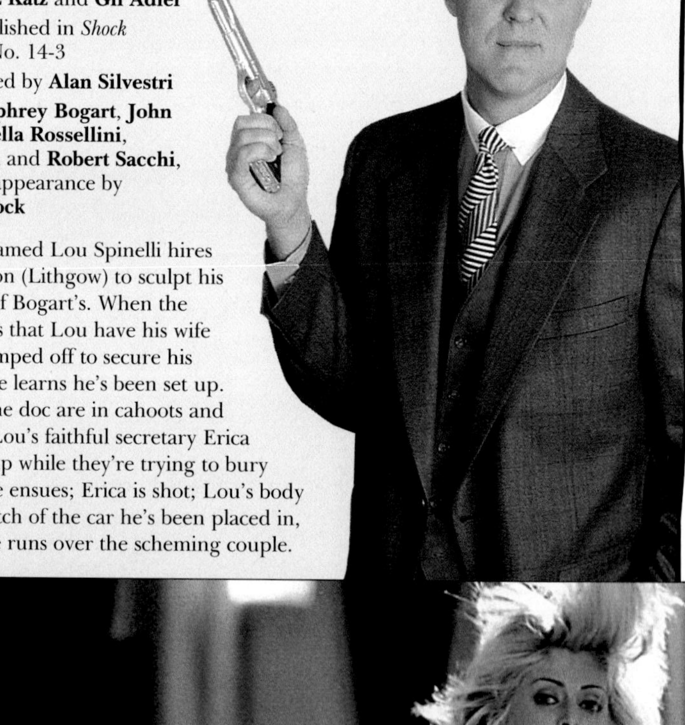

An ex-crook named Lou Spinelli hires a plastic surgeon (Lithgow) to sculpt his face into that of Bogart's. When the doctor suggests that Lou have his wife (Rossellini) bumped off to secure his new identity, he learns he's been set up. His wife and the doc are in cahoots and murder Lou. Lou's faithful secretary Erica (Fenn) shows up while they're trying to bury him. A struggle ensues; Erica is shot; Lou's body falls on the clutch of the car he's been placed in, and the vehicle runs over the scheming couple.

Episode #79

99 and 44/100% Pure Horror

Written and directed by **Rodman Flender**
Originally published in *Vault of Horror*, No. 23-2
Music composed by **Jay Ferguson**
Starring **Bruce Davison**, **Cristi Conaway**, **Darin Heames**, **Kelly Coffield**, and **Ricky Dean Logan**

Self-infatuated artist Willa (Conaway) is enraged her pushover soap magnate husband (Davison) informs her that his company has decided to drop her ad campaign. Willa vows to come up with something new, but nobody's interested. The last straw comes when Willa learns that her husband's company is going with a graffiti artist for their new campaign. Furious, she bashes her hubby's head in with a giant soap-bar statuette and disposes of his body in a vat of his own product. She decides to have a little fun and shower herself by using one of the bars created from his innards, only to find her skin bubbling and melting due to the acids his remnants contain.

7th SEASON

Episode #81

A Fatal Caper

Directed by **Bob Hoskins**

Written by **Colman deKay** and **A L Katz** & **Gil Adler**

Originally published in *Tales from the Crypt*, No. 20-2

Music composed by **Jay Ferguson**

Starring **Leslie Philips**, **Bob Hoskins**, **Natasha Richardson**, **Greg Wise**, and **James Saxon**

Before dying, elderly Mycroft (Philips) decides to disinherit his greedy sons Justin (Wise) and Evelyn (Saxon). His lawyer, Fiona Haversham (Richardson), changes his will, so that unless the two find their missing brother, Frank, Mycroft's millions go to charity. Fiona, however, has her own agenda. Evelyn plots with her to murder Justin by tricking him into thinking he sees Mycroft's ghost, hoping to give him a fatal heart attack. Justin survives, but is also conspiring with Fiona—to kill Evelyn. Justin shoots Evelyn, but when he tries to bury him, he receives a nasty surprise. Mycroft is alive. The last laugh, however, belongs to Fiona—she's really Mycroft's long-lost son, Frank, who's had a sex change operation.

Episode #84

Escape

Directed by **Peter MacDonald**

Written by **A L Katz** and **Gil Adler**

Originally published in *Vault of Horror*, No. 16-4

Music composed by **Nicholas Pike**

Starring **Martin Kemp**, **Nickolas Grace**, **Nick Redding**, and **Roy Dotrice**

An English WWII traitor (Kemp) is confined to a prison camp. One of the men he turned on shows up, badly scarred and burned. When he recovers, he will reveal the Englishman's true nature. He kills the invalid before he has a chance to squawk, then flees with one of the prisoners in tow. However, he's the victim of an elaborate setup: the truck he escapes in takes him to a refuse pit of discarded bodies, where he becomes the next addition.

Episode #82

Last Respects

Directed by **Freddie Francis**

Written by **Scott Nimerfro**

Originally published in *Tales from the Crypt*, No. 23-2

Music composed by **Frank Becker**

Starring **Emma Samms**, **Kerry Fox**, **Julie Cox**, **Michael Denison**, and **Dulcie Gray**

Three sisters think they've found a way out of their financial woes when they discover a monkey's paw. Dolores (Fox) wishes for a million pounds. Moments later, youngest sister Marlys (Cox) learns she's inherited 3 rare fountain pens worth $750,000. Lavonne (Samms) goes with Marlys to make sure she gets her share, but there's been a mistake and there is no money. On the way home, Marlys and Lavonne get into a crash that kills Marlys. Dolores then wishes her back exactly as she was before the accident. The wish comes true, but Marlys is still dead—she was first drowned by Lavonne to collect on her insurance. Dolores gives her third wish to Marlys, whose wish is apparently to return as a zombie and terrorize Lavonne.

Episode #83

A Slight Case of Murder

Written and directed by **Brian Helgeland**

Originally published in *Vault of Horror*, No. 33-3

Music composed by **Chris Boardman**

Starring **Francesca Annis**, **Chris Cazenove**, **Elizabeth Spriggs**, and **Patrick Barlow**

Sharon (Annis) is a testy mystery novelist who can't stand the bothersome queries of Mrs. Trask, her nosy neighbor (Spriggs). When Sharon's jealous ex (Cazenove) shows up, she tries to toss him out, but he draws a gun on her. After a struggle, he knocks her out and buries her in the cellar. While he basks in his deed upstairs, the neighbor sends her Milquetoast son over to dig Sharon out. As the son (Barlow) runs next door to get a gun to take care of her ex, Sharon comes alive and is bent on doing the same. All three burst in on each other with weapons and end up bumping one another off, much to the delight of the nosy neighbor, who had plotted the setup all along as research for her next book.

Episode #86

Cold War

Directed by **Andy Morahan**
Written by **Scott Nimerfro**
Originally published in *Tales from the Crypt*, No. 43-2
Music composed by **J. Peter Robinson**
Starring **John Salthouse**, **Jane Horrocks**, **Ewan McGregor**, **Colin Salmon**, and **Willie Ross**

After she bungles yet another job, Cammy (Horrocks) decides she's had enough of the "foolproof" plans of her lover-in-crime, Ford (McGregor), and walks out on him. At a bar, she meets a handsome black man named Jimmy, whom she lures into bed in order to enrage Ford. He threatens and insults Jimmy for being a mere human. Ford and Cammy, it turns out, are zombies. They try to kill Jimmy, but he's got a little something up his sleeve by way of retort—he's a vampire. After a scuffle, all three fall out a window. Jimmy turns into a bat and flies away, while the lovers plummet to the sidewalk. They live to see another day, albeit with mangled bodies. At least they've still got each other.

Episode #89

Smoke Wrings

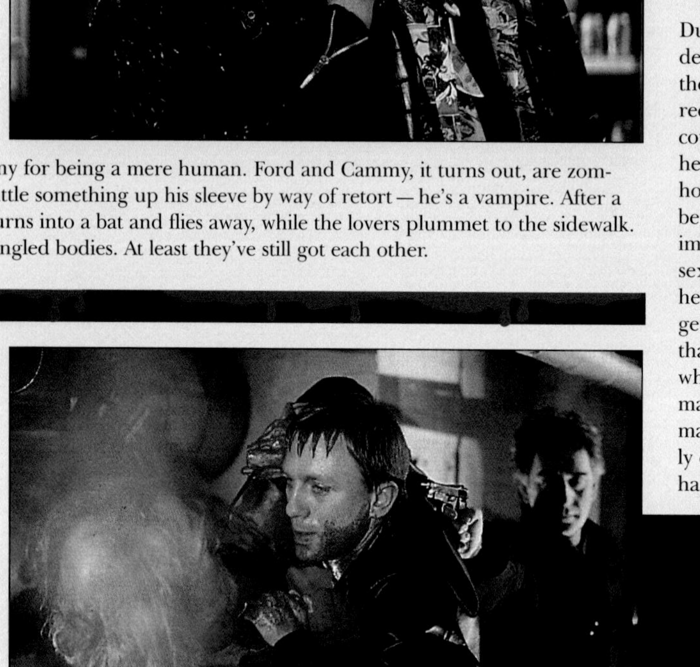

Directed by **Mandie Fletcher**
Written by **Lisa Sandoval**
Originally published in *Vault of Horror*, No. 34-3
Music composed by **Jay Uhler**
Starring **Ute Lemper**, **Chris Stanton**, **Tres Hanley**, **Daniel Craig**, **Gayle Hunnicutt**, **Denis Lawson**, and **Paul Freeman**

When self-important ad exec Jacqueline (Lemper) hires Barry (Craig), she's delighted to find he's got her rival, Frank (Lawson), running scared. But Barry knows nothing about advertising and is really working for Alistair Touchstone (Freeman), the agency's founder, who was ousted years ago. He gives Barry a device to use that gives new meaning to the term "subliminal advertising." When Barry's cigarette ad campaign is a smash, Jacqueline gives him Frank's position, but Alistair has a few nasty surprises for everyone.

Episode #87

The Kidnapper

Directed by **James Spencer**
Written by **John Harrison** and **Scott Nimerfro**
Originally published in *Shock SuspenStories*, No. 12-3
Music composed by **Jay Ferguson**
Starring **Steve Coogan**, **Julia Sawalha**, **Tim Stern**, and **Serena Gordon**

Pawn broker Danny Skeggs (Coogan) takes in pregnant single mother Teresa (Sawalha), so that she will not have to hock a family heirloom to have her child. All seems well until Danny becomes jealous of Teresa spending too much time with the newborn. He makes arrangements to have it stolen, but she's even worse without the little tyke around. He tries to buy the kid back from the crooks he hired to steal the baby in the first place. But a deal's a deal and the black marketeer threatens to sic his henchman on Danny. Desperate, he attempts to steal another woman's baby, only to be caught and beaten to death by the henchman, just after realizing the infant he tried to pilfer was Teresa's.

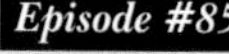

Episode #85

Horror in the Night

Directed by **Russell Mulcahy**
Written by **John Harrison**
Originally published in *Vault of Horror*, No. 12-3
Music composed by **J. Peter Robinson**
Starring **Elizabeth McGovern**, **James Wilby**, **Roman Vibert**, **Edward Tudor Pole**, and **Peter Guinness**

During a jewelry heist, Nick (Wilby) decides to double-cross his partner, then holes up in a hotel, where he requests that he not be disturbed. Of course, his conscience apparently hasn't heard, for he begins to have a series of horrifying visions that may or may not be alcohol-induced figments of his imagination. They center around a sexy, mysterious woman (McGovern) he finds in the hotel lobby, who won't get out of his head. He finally learns that she's an old flame he screwed over who has returned to haunt him and make life generally difficult, until the man who hired Nick and his supposedly dead partner burst in and blow the hapless thief away.

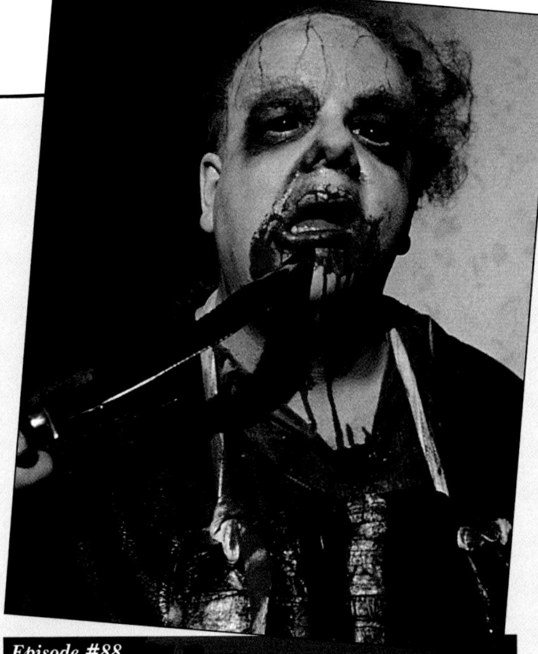

Episode #90

About Face

Directed by **Tom Sanders**
Written by **Larry Wilson**
Originally published in *Haunt of Fear*, No. 27-1
Music composed by **Vladimir Horunzhy**
Starring **Anthony Andrews**, **Imelda Staunton**, **Anna Friel**, **Paddy Navin**, **Finty Williams**, **Emma Bird**, **Pip Torens**, and **Lane Vidal**

When Jonathan (Andrews) discovers that he has two long-lost daughters named Angelica and Leah (Friel), he decides to accept them as his own, much to the chagrin of his current girlfriend, Sarah (Staunton). Angelica, however, won't let Jonathan see Leah, for fear that her ugly sister will cause Jonathan to have a change of heart about taking them in. Sarah, on the other hand, spends some time with Leah and finds her repulsive. When Jonathan plots to leave Sarah and the uglier of the sisters behind, Leah decides to strike back at her father. Jonathan is forced to kill Leah and only afterward does he realize that he's murdered Angelica as well — they were Siamese twins.

Episode #91

Ear Today...Gone Tomorrow

Directed by **Christopher Hart**
Written by **Ed Tapia**
Originally published in *Tales from the Crypt*, No. 24-1
Music composed by **Jay Ferguson**
Starring **Robert Lindsay**, **Phil Davis**, **Richard Johnson**, **Gretchen Palmer**, and **David Gant**

Malcolm (Johnson) discovers that Glynn (Lindsay), the expert safecracker he hired to pull off a heist, doesn't have the same hearing he once had. He prepares to kill him, but Malcolm's beautiful wife Kate (Palmer) suggests that he be given another chance. While Malcolm is away, Kate suggests Glynn see a specialist who can repair his hearing, then the two can break into Malcolm's safe and run away together. When unforeseen complications arise, Glynn gets an earful from Kate and Malcolm.

Episode #88

Report from the Grave

Written and directed by **William Malone**
Originally published in *Vault of Horror*, No. 15-3
Music composed by **Frank Becker**
Starring **James Frain**, **Siobhan Flynn**, **Jonathan Firth**, **Gordon Peters**, **Julian Kerridge**, and **Roger Ashton-Griffiths**

Elliot (Frain) believes he's on the verge of a fantastic discovery — the ability to harness thoughts from the dead through the use of a machine of his own design. He wishes to make an infamous murderer named Tymrak (Ashyon-Griffiths) his test subject, and takes the lovely Arianne along as an assistant. But complications ensue and Arianne (Flynn) is killed, leaving him in a state of morbid guilt. He discovers that he can bring her back through his machine. But Tymrak comes, too! Elliot solves this cruel dilemma in the worst possible way.

Episode #92

Confession

Directed by **Peter Hewitt**
Written by **Scott Nimerfro**
Originally published in *Shock SuspenStories*, No. 4-2
Music composed by **Julian Nott**
Starring **Eddie Izzard**, **Ciaran Hinds**, **Ashley Artus**, **Alun Armstrong**, **John Benfield**, and **Mark Spalding**

A serial killer is decapitating women all over the city, and Jack (Hinds), an interrogation expert, pinpoints a prime suspect — a screenwriter named Warhol Evans (Izzard). Warhol looks like a classic psychopath, but other heads roll before the story ends.

Episode #93

The Third Pig

Directed by **Bill Kopp & Pat Ventura**
Written by **Bill Kopp**
Music composed by **Nathan Wang**
Voices **Bobcat Goldthwait**, **Cam Clarke**, **Brad Garrett**, **Jim Cummings**, **Charlie Adler**, **Jess Harnell**, **and Cory Burton**

In this cartoon reworking of the tale of the Three Little Pigs, the two slobby, ignorant pigs are eaten and the smart third pig, Dudley, is charged with their murders because the courts are populated solely by wolves. But the ghosts of his deceased brethren come to him and tell him to build a zombie Frankenpig to avenge their deaths, and he does. The monster devours the Wolf, but Dudley discovers he has a few other swinish problems.

Now a Major Motion

With the 1995 film *Demon Knight*, the Crypt Keeper made the transition from the little silver box to the big silver screen. Directed by Ernest Dickerson *(Juice)*, and produced by the same fearsome fivesome responsible for the TV series (Richard Donner, David Giler, Walter Hill, Joel Silver, and Robert Zemeckis), the film is a morality play of unabashedly Biblical proportions, bracketed by an Intro and an Epilogue from horror's Alistair Cooke, the Crypt Keeper.

PICTURE

As the host, the Crypt Keeper materializes à la vintage Cecil B. DeMille, sporting a riding crop, a beret, and a megaphone. As he directs a scene from his own horror flick, he is mightily displeased with the scenery-chewing of the actor who plays Carl—or what's left of him. With a bone-shattering "Cut!" he tells off "Carl" (John Larroquette in an unbilled cameo), saying he's no Gorey Cooper or Robert Deadford, then settles his audience in for the beginning of *Demon Knight.*

HBO's *Tales from the Crypt* wasn't even on the air when the *Demon Knight* screenplay was first developed. The story began as a late-night skull session among three pals, all former NYU Film School students. Ethan Reiff, Cyrus Voris, and Mark Bishop collaborated on a first draft 1987—and hung in there through a raft of changes and near-misses until the film was finally shot in 1994.

They rolled out the dead carpet for the Crypt Keeper at the *Demon Knight* Hollywood premiere.

Director Tom Holland thought it might make a suitable follow-up to *Child's Play* (whose evil doll, Chucky, was created by Keepermeister Kevin Yagher). In an interview with Anthony C. Ferrante in *Fangoria* magazine, screenwriter Cyrus Voris indicated that Holland was convinced the movie would succeed or fail on the strength of its villain, who at that time was called the Salesman. Holland was hoping to make the film with Chris Sarandon as the Salesman/Collector and Tommy Lee Jones as Brayker, but went on to make *Fatal Beauty*, a bomb starring Whoopi Goldberg as a narcotics cop. The next director to show an interest was Mary Lambert (*Pet Sematary*, Madonna's music videos *Material Girl, Like a Virgin, Like a Prayer*), but she ultimately chose to make *Pet Sematary II* instead. When that movie failed at the box office, financial backing for her realization of *Demon Knight* evaporated.

"This is when we thought this script was cursed," screenwriter Ethan Reiff told Ferrante. "The joke was, the curse wasn't on us, but whoever optioned the script usually had serious career problems afterwards if they didn't make the movie. When the project ended up with the *Tales from the Crypt* production company, it got the attention of Ernest Dickerson, who like other younger Crypt fans had been a *Famous Monsters* devotee in his youth. Dickerson worked with Reiff, Voris and Bishop to buff up the script. Before settling on Zane and Sadler, Dickerson's short list of candidates for the leading roles included Willem Dafoe as the Collector and Val Kilmer as Brayker.

John Larroquette has an unbilled cameo as a vengeful corpse in the Crypt Keeper's movie-within-a-movie.

Frights! Camera! Hack-tion!

The Big Scream!

There is a serious tradition to the horror movie genre, as Ernest Dickerson, director of *Demon Knight,* understands. "The way the demons are born definitely suggests [Ray] Harryhausen. There is an image that sticks in your head forever and becomes a part of your psyche when the skeletons are formed from the Hydra's teeth in *Jason and the Argonauts,"* he observed to Anthony C. Ferrante in a special *Tales* magazine produced by the editors of *Fangoria*. Prior to rising in the ranks of Hollywood directors with the gritty contemporary drama *Juice,* Dickerson worked as a cinematographer on many notable films, including *Malcolm X*, *Jungle Fever*, and *Do the Right Thing*.

Director Ernest Dickerson, right, grew up as a *Famous Monsters* and H. P. Lovecraft fan, and over the years developed a *Jeopardy*-class encyclopedic knowledge of horror, gore, monster, and vintage gothic fright films.

To capture the true EC flavor, Dickerson would not settle for any Alfred Hitchcock subtleties, but as his reference to Ray Harryhausen, one of the pioneers of Hollywood special effects, suggests, Dickerson was looking for more than just shock. "We thought that if the eyes are the window to the soul, why not also let the soul escape [when you kill the demons]? So I didn't want to make it as easy as just shooting out the eyes. It's sort of like in *Alien*—when you kill the aliens, you have to make sure you don't get hit by any of that blood."

It was difficult to avoid being splashed with blood on the set of *Demon Knight*. Todd Masters supplied gallons of the stuff, and there would have been more, if Dickerson, Adler, and Katz hadn't modified the original script. The demon attacks got fairly repetitive," Dickerson told Ferrante. "It was a lot like *Alien* in that it was a constant raging war and gun battle, and one of the things I wanted to do was play up the attacks and have them become more psychological. And I think we beefed up the characters and made them stronger, and also worked with the mythology.

"There are a lot of classic, mythic themes at play in this movie," observes Dickerson. "The mythology is really something that everybody had access to, and it's a twist on the ideas we've been presented with all along. The film basically takes the tack that the stories in the Bible are essentially information that has been passed down through word of mouth for hundreds of years before anybody wrote it down. So basically, you start to question how much of the information is real—and the movie speculates that the Bible has part of the story, and there's another part that isn't told to us. We find out later, through our characters, what's really going on."

With *Demon Knight*, the personality of the Crypt Keeper as a ghoul-about-town flowered. Theatre audiences also glimpsed a rare sight—the Crypt Keeper walks! As in the comic books and in the TV show, his bad puns and humorous asides reminded the audience that it was "just a movie."

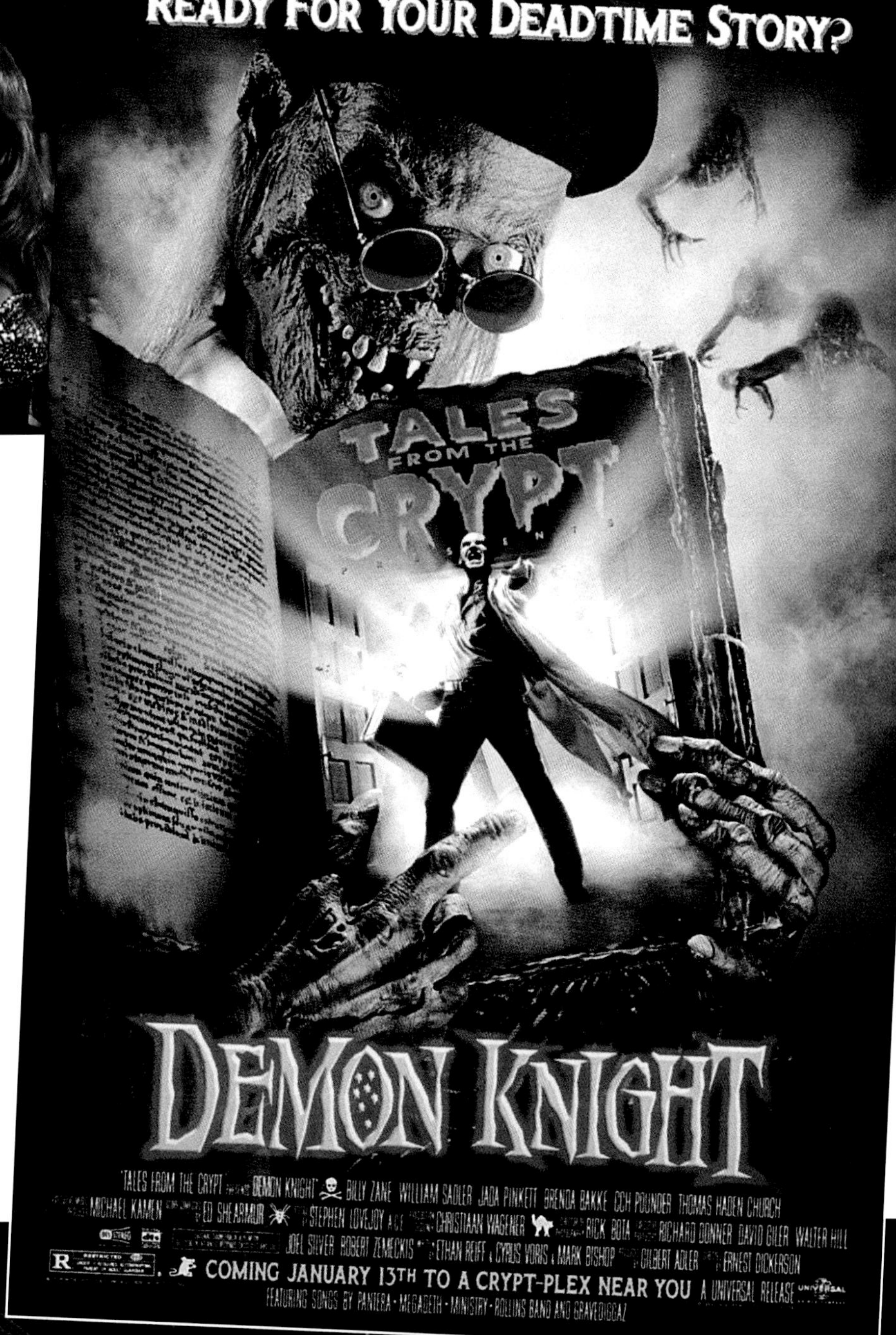

Producer Gil Adler notes that the Crypt Keeper is a sort of safety valve for all of the unremitting horror of *Demon Knight*. "After people are through getting the pants scared off them, they like a good laugh," he says. "Since the Crypt Keeper's already dead, he's free to laugh at it all. What he does is let the audience know that it's okay to go home and turn off the lights. There's nothing under the bed—at least, nothing you need to worry about right away." As Adler points out, the Crypt Keeper's comic presence is also part of a horror tradition: "Sick humor actually has a long and honorable lineage. In Shakespeare's plays—*Hamlet* and *Macbeth* come to mind—you have clowns cracking wise even as the bodies are falling all around them."

Tales from the Script

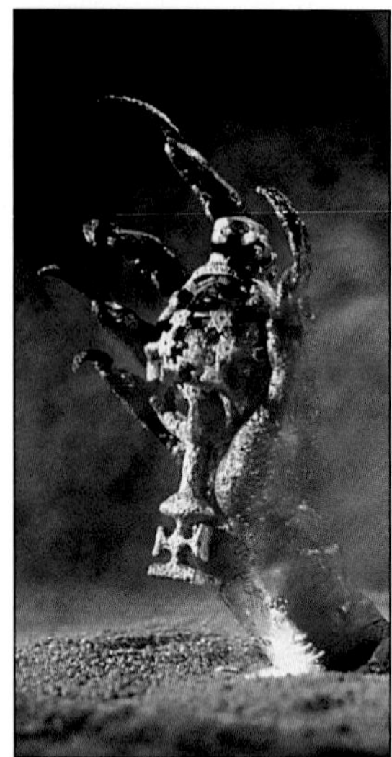

The story turns on one of the classic plot conventions of the horror genre—a motley bunch of misfits, thrown together by chance and confined to a single location, who must make it through the night, even though they are besieged by the Forces of Evil.

Those Forces are led by a suave character known as The Collector, played by Billy Zane *(Dead Calm, The Phantom)*. The Collector is a gatherer both of souls and of antiques. His archrival, a mysterious careworn paladin named Brayker (William Sadler of *Die Hard II* and Walter Hill's first HBO episode, "The Man Who Was Death"), has something he very desperately wants to complete his collection—an ancient mystical amulet. The talisman is a key filled with a dark liquid, the only one of seven originals remaining in safe hands on the terrestrial side of the River Styx. His Satanic Majesty's forces hold the others, and Brayker's key is all that stands between the human race and an Armageddon in which all the smart money would be on the really baaad dudes in black from across the river.

A Mystical Omen

It's a dark and stormy night as the two adversaries clash on the outskirts of Wormwood, New Mexico. Outskirts are all Wormwood really has—it's a town quite literally in the middle of nowhere. Their arrival comes with a bang (as it were)—a pedal-to-the-metal car chase ending in a fiery crash that destroys both vehicles. Now on foot with the Collector still in pursuit, Brayker removes a black leather driving glove to reveal a strange symbol tattooed on his right palm. It is a circle with seven stars—four are part of the circle; the other three glow within. As he tries to steal a car at the local greasy spoon to continue his journey, Brayker is surprised in the act by a small boy and must abort the theft. Instead he takes refuge in a no-stars residence hotel, the only one in town. The Mission Inn is a desanctified old church that was converted into a rooming house in the '50s and has seen very little maintenance since. Arriving at the inn, Brayker takes another look at his hand. The glowing stars within the circle in his palm have realigned themselves on the outer ring. This is the omen he's been waiting for, and Brayker realizes he must now rally a septet of reluctant denizens of a ramshackle rooming house to defend their species.

Ship of Fools

The Mission Inn is truly a ship of fools run aground, since the only people left in Wormwood were too poor or too stupid to leave when the silver mines ran out and the interstate highway bypassed the town. The grande dame of the establishment is Irene Galvin, a no-nonsense battle-axe of a matron with a toothpick permanently grafted between her front teeth. The lodgers include Cordelia, Wormwood's only professional woman—her profession is the world's oldest. There is

also Wally Enfield, a recently defrocked mailman; Uncle Willy, the town drunk; and Roach, Cordelia's boorish client and the fry cook at the local cafe. Lastly there is Jeryline, a beautiful young parolee who earns her keep as sort of a neo-Cinderella, cooking meals, sweeping up, and changing the sheets—which, given Cordelia's line of work, is no small task.

Resisting Arrest

Tipped off that Brayker was the would-be car thief at the cafe, two members of the local constabulary, Sheriff Tupper and his rather dim-witted deputy, Bob, arrive at the rooming house to arrest him. With them is the Collector. Displaying an unctuous charm and impeccable manners, he has convinced the cops that Brayker's key is rightfully his. As proof, he produces an ancient wooden reliquary with a niche carved inside it that exactly fits the talisman. As Sheriff Tupper seizes the key and begins to arrest Brayker, he receives information from headquarters that *both* vehicles involved in the inferno were stolen, and moves to take the Collector into custody.

Up to this point, viewers are not really certain whether Brayker or the Collector is the supernatural bad guy. The first clue the audience gets is when the Collector resists arrest and punches out Sheriff Tupper—at which time his fist flies through the sheriff's face and out the back side of his head.

The Battle Is Joined

After Brayker brands the key into the Collector's cheek, the stage is set for a pitched battle over possession of the talisman. While Brayker tries to assert some sort of discipline and unity over the not-so-brave and not-so-noble little band of ordinary folk under siege in their own private Alamo, the Collector marshals his support troops, inscribing a cut in his palm and summoning up demons from a handful of greenish blood that he spatters to the ground. The *Homo sapiens* are badly outnumbered.

The demons waste no time assaulting the inn; Brayker's first task is to seal off all the entrances, a job for which the dark liquid in the key's vial is essential. He moves through the rooming house anointing each point of entry with a drop from the key. The liquid is blood, and a drop or two in a door-jamb or on a window ledge creates a neon red seal, like a big "Do Not Enter" sign to the demons. Those who try are vaporized.

An Ancient Burden

The only other way to do in a demon is to go for the eyes. Grisly eyeball removal has a long history in works of horror—it was

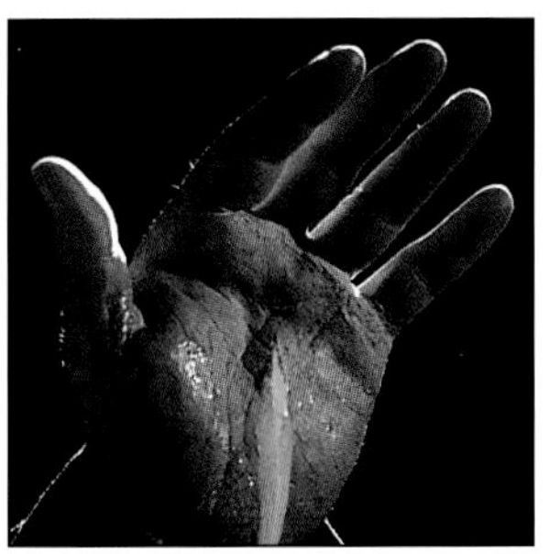

one of Max Gaines' original no-nos and a particular bugaboo to Fredric Wertham. In *Demon Knight*, however, it's a major weapon in the hands of the beleaguered humans.

Brayker's burden is indeed an ancient one. The original blood in the key came from Golgotha itself, but over the centuries it has been mixed with that of all who have carried the terrible burden. Each guardian of the amulet has refilled it with his own blood and passed it to his successor upon his death. Brayker has been the custodian since World War I, when he received it in the fields of France from a dying comrade (named Dickerson, after the film's director). With the key, he also inherited the 7-star tattoo on his palm. Tonight he will pass it to one of the other occupants of the Mission Inn.

Six, Five, Four, Three, Two…

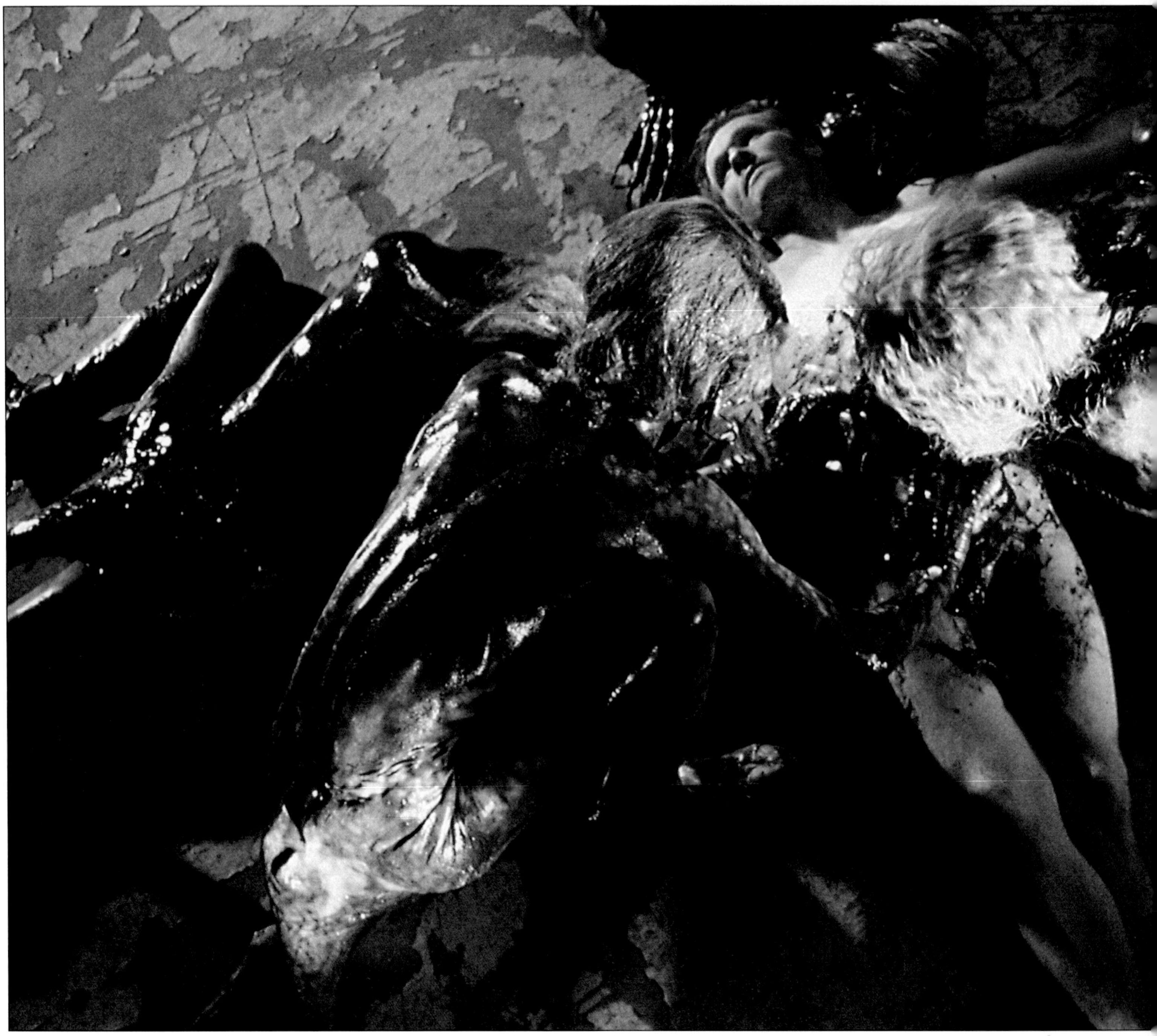

The Collector and the demons begin a game of seven little Indians, whittling down the members of the party one by one. Irene the landlady loses an arm; tough old broad

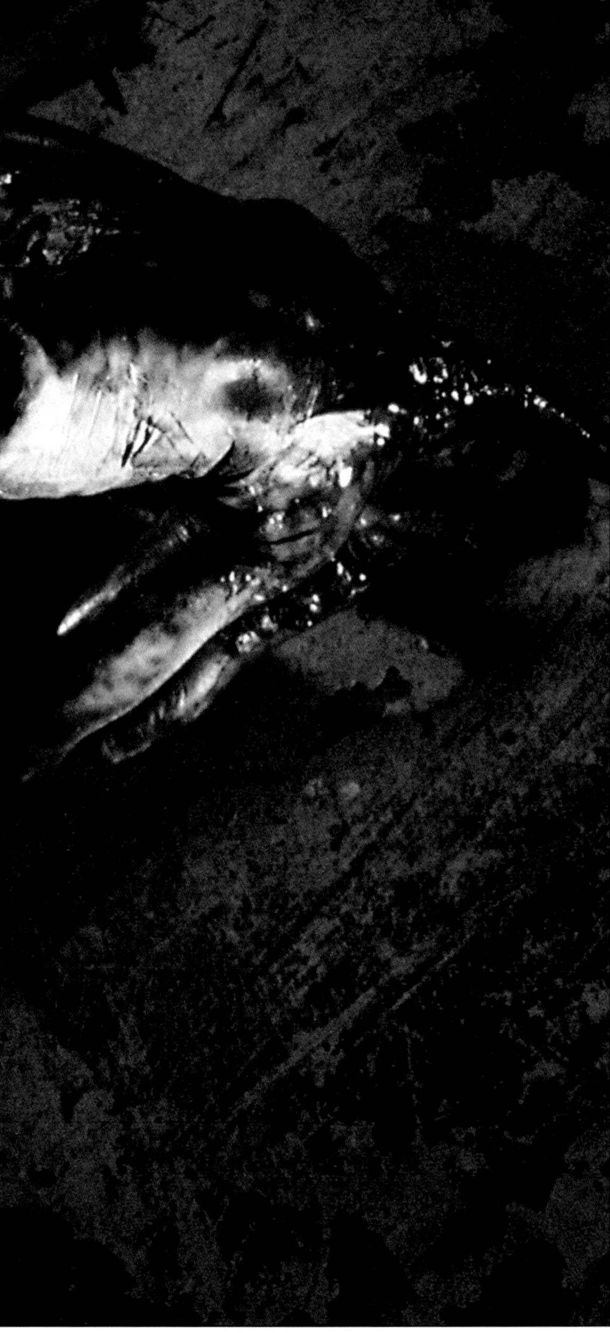

that she is, it barely slows her down. What the demons cannot attain by full frontal assault, the Collector accomplishes by guile and cunning. He knows the all-too-human foibles of each member of the group, and preys on their weaknesses. He seduces Cordelia with her need to be loved, and wins Uncle Willy with booze. He tries to lure Jeryline with promises of the good life in Paris—and fails. When Brayker learns that she has rebuffed the Collector, he knows that she is destined to be the next guardian. In a scene that parallels his own receipt of the key in 1917, he passes it—and the tattoo—to Jeryline. Before dying, he gives her the same advice he had received—"Watch your back." When dawn breaks, she flees what's left of the seedy rooming house, with all the furies of hell in pursuit.

DEMON KNIGHT
Credits

Starring
Billy Zane
William Sadler
Jada Pinkett
Brenda Bakke
CCH Pounder
Thomas Haden Church
and
John Kassir
as the voice of the Crypt Keeper

Executive Producers
Richard Donner
David Giler
Walter Hill
Joel Silver
Robert Zemeckis

Written by
Ethan Reiff
Cyrus Voris
Mark Bishop

Produced by
Gilbert Adler

Directed by
Ernest Dickerson

Director of Photography
Rick Bota

Production Designer
Christiaan Wagener

Film Editor
Stephen Lovejoy, ACE

Executive Music Producer
Michael Kamen

Score Composed by
Ed Shearmur

Coproducers
Alan Katz
Scott Nimerfro
Wendy Wanderman

Special Effects Makeup Designed and Created by
Todd Masters

Costume Designer
Warden Neil

Some of the images used by director Dickerson evoke the Biblical legacy of the key (left), but the demons get to everyone eventually, including a young boy named Danny (above right), and even Brayker himself (top). Only Jeryline survives.

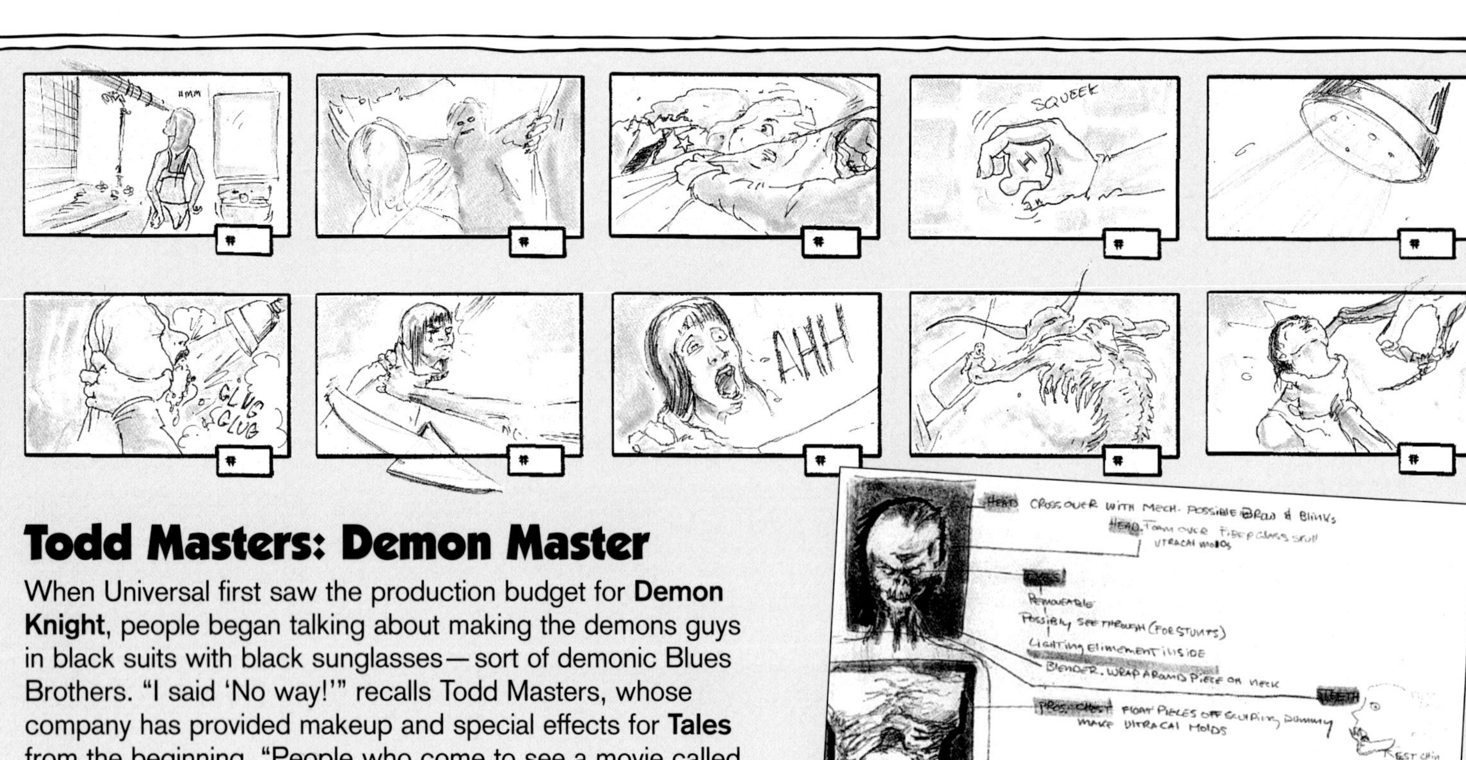

Todd Masters: Demon Master

When Universal first saw the production budget for **Demon Knight**, people began talking about making the demons guys in black suits with black sunglasses—sort of demonic Blues Brothers. "I said 'No way!'" recalls Todd Masters, whose company has provided makeup and special effects for **Tales** from the beginning. "People who come to see a movie called **Demon Knight** want to see real demons."

Masters came up with a fresh, less expensive design concept. "We envisioned very thin, waiflike people with hideous faces and exaggerated body parts. I used prosthetics and make-up to give them a frightening, feline look." The design was a solution to an economic problem, but it gave the producers a new creative direction. EC fans have noticed that the demons look like figures in some of the Graham Ingels drawings, but Masters did not refer to them in his work.

"Basically, we have these gaunt people running around in full body makeup. They're practically naked, with horrible masks, a crotch piece that holds a battery belt for the tails, extended fingers, and extended legs and hooves. And they do look like demons."

Masters drew a series of sketches with notes and sculpted a maquette to express his vision of the demons.

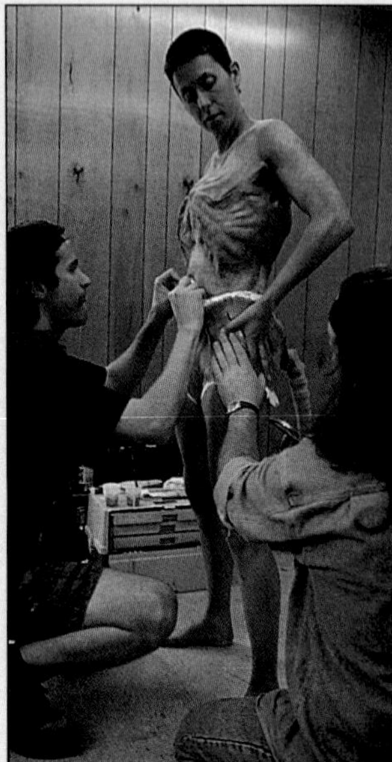

Each day the demon actors—Walter Phelan, Josh Patton, Kay Kimler, and Jimmy Roberts—arrived early to go through the long body makeup process before the day's shooting.

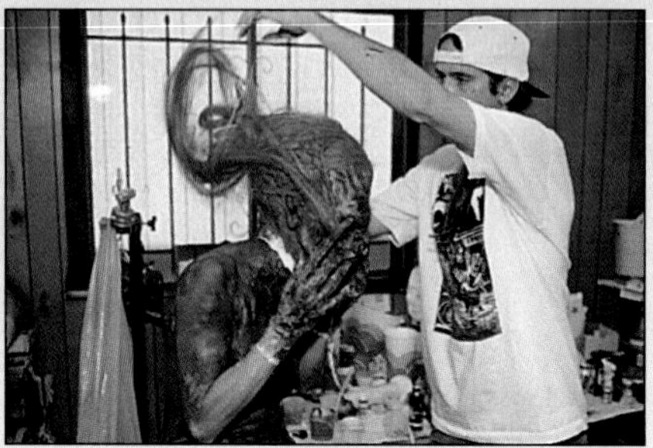

Everything was glued to the actor's bodies: the torso piece, ribcage piece, crotch piece (with radio-controlled tail), and stiltlike leg extensions. Then they stood out in the hot sun to be spray-painted with demonic latex before working 16-hour days, often involving strenuous gymnastic stunts. For the film, however, it was worth it. The sinister wraiths (right) are a big improvement over the sunglass-clad "killer yuppie" demons that were originally proposed.

Bordello of Blood

The Crypt Keeper's macabre sense of humor introduces audiences to *Bordello of Blood*, the second *Tales from the Crypt* movie, released in August of 1996. *Bordello* is the tale of the resurrection of Lilith, the Mother of All Vampires and the most bloodthirsty seductress in history. This hooker with a heart of fire (and brimstone) is played by redhead Angie Everhart (*Jade*, *Bullet*, and a fixture of the *Sports Illustrated* swimsuit calendar). Lilith springs back to life with a vengeance at the hands of Vincent, a malevolent dwarf. It's taken him a decade to procure the four pieces of her shriveled heart, and now he reunites the pieces and places them on her chest. When she revives, she's hungry, *very* hungry—and quickly indulges her craving for organ meats—served blood rare. Lilith feasts on Vincent's travelling companions, and it is only his possession of an ancient talisman—the blood-filled key from *Demon Knight*—that prevents her from devouring him as well.

The key is the only holdover from *Demon Knight*; everything else about *Bordello* is new. Although *Demon* had its fair share of double entendres, *Bordello of Blood* pokes its tongue much farther into its cheek than its predecessor—and into other body cavities as well.

Bordello producer/director/cowriter Gil Adler (right), a _Tales_ veteran, also produces the television series and produced the first feature film, _Demon Knight_.

The Madam from Hell

With a bevy of lovely young vampires to titillate patrons, Lilith—truly the Madam from Hell—sets up shop in the heart of the Bible Belt, turning on her red light in a hideaway conveniently located beneath the McCutcheon Mortuary. A coded password (ask for "the Cunningham Wake") and an E-ticket coffin ride through the funeral home's crematorium bring clients into her parlor, where girls in various stages of deshabille entertain the clientele. For the johns, however, it's a one-way trip to a one-night stand—there are no repeat customers. Lilith's ladies set up the guys, then she comes in to finish them off in a manner that gives "deep kissing" a whole new dimension.

Beneath a funeral home, Lilith's vampire harlots show their johns a real good time (below left), but clientele turnover is very rapid. Some end up in the mortuary's embalming room (below right).

Lilith, played by super-model Angie Everhart (left), finds that Rafe Guttman (Dennis Miller) is just her (blood) type.

A Missing Brother/ A Rock 'n' Roll Preacher

One of Lilith's patrons is a young punk named Caleb (Corey *Stand by Me* Feldman). Into heavy metal, black leather, and body piercing, Caleb visits Lilith's brothel in the company of his friends and fellow sociopaths,

"Hunting vampires is probably easier than making a movie about it."
—*Bordello* cowriter A L Katz

going AWOL from the "normal" suburban home he shares with his sister, Katherine. Blond, comely, and virginal, Katherine Verdoux (Erika Eleniak—late of *Baywatch* and the second generation Elly Mae in the movie version of *The Beverly Hillbillies*) is as straight-arrow as her brother is twisted. She is a devout follower of rock 'n' roll tele-vangelist Reverend Jimmy Current (Chris Sarandon, *Fright Night*, *Child's Play*). Current broadcasts from a high-tech Crystal Cathedral, outfitted with laser beams, a

Movie-making is a collaborative medium. The morphing of Lilith at the film's finale involves a small army of camera and sound operators, plus special effects personnel who manipulate various parts of her increasingly repulsive anatomy.

Puppeteers (far left) operate the Lilith "doll" by remote control. For some scenes, Angie Everhart was in Makeup for up to six hours as technicians layered on Lilith's latex appliances (near left and below). Some sequences utilized Everhart's "better half" (lower left), but make-up and prosthetics effects coordinator Chris Nelson designed a gaping 20-inch axe wound as a customized accessory for her purple gown. (He also made twenty-five sets of fangs.)

BORDELLO OF BLOOD
Credits

Starring
Dennis Miller
Erika Eleniak
Angie Everhart
Chris Sarandon
Corey Feldman
and
John Kassir
as the voice of the Crypt Keeper

Executive Producers
Richard Donner
David Giler
Walter Hill
Joel Silver
Robert Zemeckis

Story by
Bob Gale & Robert Zemeckis

Screenplay by
A L Katz & Gilbert Adler

Produced and Directed by
Gilbert Adler

Director of Photography
Tom Priestley

Production Designer
Greg Melton

Film Editor
Stephen Lovejoy, ACE

Executive Music Producer
Michael Kamen

Score Composed by
Chris Boardman

Coproducers
Alan Katz
Alexander Collett

Visual Effects by
Available Light Ltd.

Additional Prosthetic Effects Designed & Created by
Todd Masters Company

Filmed on location in Vancouver, the *Tales* production team created a deliberately over-the-top set at the BC Pavilion, located downtown at the site of EXPO '86. On the altar of Reverend Jimmy Current's Crystal Cathedral–type sanctuary, they constructed a 28-foot motorized cross, which split down the middle to accommodate a rising 12-foot animatronic devil.

sound system worthy of the Mormon Tabernacle, and an animatronic devil that he summons (and vanquishes) on cue. Katherine works for the minister as an all-purpose administrative assistant-cum-adoring sycophant. Turns out, however, that the Reverend Current—or JC, as he's known to his disciples—has another employee—a swarthy midget named Vincent.

An Insolvent Gumshoe

Frustrated because the police won't look for her brother, Katherine hires down-and-out detective Rafe Guttman (Dennis Miller, *Disclosure*, *The Net*, and of course, *Dennis Miller Live*). Rafe gets a hot tip on where to find some hot action, learns that Caleb was last seen headed for a whorehouse, and pays a call on the McCutcheon Mortuary.

A Pact with the Devil

Knowing her brother went to the whorehouse but not his ultimate fate, Katherine's close brush with Sodom and Gomorrah prompts her to ask Current for permission to make a fundamentalist documentary about the evils of lust. "Onward Christian soldier," he says, blessing her crusade—for Current and his flock, the fight with Satan is a daily struggle. His next appointment is with another true believer—"Brother" Vincent the dwarf.

The Reverend Current, it seems, sponsored Vincent's quest for Lilith's heart and her resurrection—all in the name of the Lord. Jimmy believed that Lilith and her harlots would rid the world of adulterers, one fornicator at a time, but now her whorehouse has taken on a life of its own. Vincent,

"These guys want to scare the pants off you and then make you laugh."
—Dennis Miller

During ministry broadcasts, the devil rises so that Rev. Current can vanquish him, but with the preacher out of the picture and Lilith on the loose, the fate of the world rests in the hands of Katherine Verdoux (Erika Eleniak, above right) and detective Rafe Guttman (Miller).

Denied entry to the Cunningham Wake, Rafe commits a little breaking and entering and finds a piece of Caleb's nose jewelry in the embalming room.

Just Her Type

When Rafe finally takes his own coffin ride into the brothel, he meets up with Tamara, Lilith's newest recruit. Tamara is into B&D, or as he calls it, "medieval foreplay." Only by turning the tables, as it were, on Tamara does Rafe manage to escape from the torture devices in the brothel's dungeon room. In making his getaway, however, he leaves his wallet behind. Tamara still has a bit of Rafe's blood on her fingers, and Lilith decides he's just her type—blood type, that is. In her own way, she considers Rafe a delicacy. "I haven't tasted this since Ivan the Terrible," she says with gusto as she sucks on Tamara's digits, "and that was eight centuries ago. We gotta keep this guy alive!"

for his part, is convinced that he should be getting more personal financial reward from the bordello and is bent on making his own deal with Lilith to hijack the operation.

In disguise, Current trails Vincent to his rendezvous with Lilith at a sleazy strip joint, only to be interrupted by Katherine's documentary film crew. Current, Vincent, and Lilith hightail it out the back door, but not before Katherine has filmed an Interview with the Vampire for her documentary. In the showdown in the back alley, Vincent abandons Current and throws in with Lilith. In the ensuing fracas, the ancient key is shattered.

The Truth Is Transparent

Katherine rushes her videotape back to the studio. She recognizes Reverend Current, despite his disguise, but is even more amazed to find that her footage shows her pointing her microphone at an empty chair. There is no image of Lilith on film. While she is showing her footage to Rafe, she gets a panicky phone call from Caleb, asking to meet them in an abandoned power plant.

When they find him, Caleb is alive—or rather, undead. Rafe is knocked unconscious as he and Katherine attempt to get away. When he comes to, Katherine is nowhere to be found, and he's strapped to a hospital bed, trying to explain how vampire prostitutes are taking over the city to an incredulous cop. A nurse enters, asks the officer's help with the patient in the other bed, then sinks her fangs into his neck—it's Rafe's old nemesis, Tamara. Defending himself with garlic salad dressing, Guttman and Tamara scuffle, disturbing the patient in the other bed—none other than Whoopi Goldberg. Tamara is done in, not by Rafe, but by a shaft of sunlight. Although she is wearing sunblock to protect herself, the light hits her skin through a tear in her uniform and she vaporizes.

Joel Silver's other commitments precluded his involvement in *Bordello of Blood* on a daily basis, but he still worked closely with Gil Adler's production team. "I put in my two cents," he says.

"I'm very proud of the fact that we were able to take this *Tales from the Crypt* idea and build it into something that is really like a cottage industry."

—Joel Silver

The Water of Life and Death

Rafe flees the hospital and heads for the funeral home. Using his car as a battering ram, he crashes through the mortuary wall, armed with his pistol and—a neon Super Soaker. There he finds the Reverend Current. Outfitted with spikes, a hammer, and a knife, the preacher has come to try to undo the havoc he has wrought. Realizing that Current is still on the side of the angels, Rafe tosses him a water pistol.

Both the pistol and the Super Soaker are filled with holy water, deadly for the vampire trollops, but useless against Lilith herself. "The only way to kill her," says Current, "is to draw and quarter her heart." Current and Guttman drench the whores in a soggy shootout. Hookers melt, sizzle, ooze, and explode as the brothel is destroyed. The two rescue Katherine, then take on Lilith. Rafe takes a Lizzie Borden whack at her with an axe. Down but not out, she retreats to regroup, but not before she mortally wounds Jimmy. With his dying breath, Current tells Katherine to broadcast the word from the cathedral.

The Vampire Gospels

With Rafe manning the camera, Katherine stands on the altar/stage, preparing to comply with JC's last wish. As she does so, however, the Devil figure rises from beneath the platform, splitting the cross. Lilith, it seems, has taken over the control room, generating special effects all her own. She handcuffs Rafe to a railing, then goes for Katherine. In the ensuing catfight, Katherine is definitely getting the worst of it until Rafe gets to the laser control panel with his foot. Stretching himself to the limit, he painstakingly manipulates the laser with his toe until he finally succeeds in using its beam to separate Lilith's auricles and ventricles into their four component parts. Morphing rapidly into a hideous monster, Lilith comes after him, but disintegrates before she can wreak her revenge.

Sex and Sunblock

With the aid of a rabbi, Rafe and Katherine incinerate the last of Lilith in the McCutcheon Mortuary crematorium. As they leave the mortuary with Lilith's ashes in a little wooden reliquary, all of Katherine's sanctimonious demeanor has vanished. Now playful and more than a little flirty, it looks as though the smoldering attraction between Rafe and Katherine might finally burst into flame. However, when Rafe comments on her perfume, she tell him it's sunblock—just before she sinks her fangs into his neck.

That's a wrap!

A Kinder, Gentler Keeper

For two years, *Tales from the Cryptkeeper*, the kiddie version of *Tales from the Crypt* from Nelvana Productions, haunted ABC's Saturday morning cartoon lineup. Executive producer Toper Taylor saw the Crypt Keeper as an ideal candidate to replace the *Beetlejuice* series. As he told *Fangoria*'s Anthony Ferrante, "We saw there was a need for another horror-type property. Those have always worked, as far back as *Scooby Doo*, but ABC was clearly not ready for EC horror on Saturday morning. We're a lot more cautious with regard to bloodshed and the acts of violence underneath it all."

Nelvana retained child psychologist Brian Newmark to review the scripts and make sure they were suitable for the target audience. They had originally considered using Kevin Yagher's Keeper as the host, but they eventually decided that the puppet was a bit too "boo" for very small children, and went with a cartoon likeness instead. To further take the edge off him, they gave him some long-dormant but nevertheless familiar sidekicks—the Vault Keeper and the Old Witch—who traded wisecracks with him and bantered with one another over who was going to take control of the show.

John Kassir is the voice for the animated Crypt Keeper, as he is for the nighttime edition, but he found that adapting to a G-rated version of the character took some adjustment. "Nelvana created a kinder, gentler personality for the children's Crypt Keeper, and it feels a little uncharacteristic at times," he admits. Although the cartoon series only ran for two seasons, it spawned an astonishingly diverse collection of Crypt merchandise and memorabilia.

With the Crypt Keeper as "jeer-leader," *Secrets of the Crypt Keeper's Haunted House* is a new TV game show in which young contestants face challenges such as The Incredible Shrinking Room and The Swamp from Hell—environments enhanced by computer-generated virtual reality and Hollywood FX technology.

The *Tales from the Cryptkeeper* cartoon series had its share of spooky images, but each episode was a morality play for children portraying the consequences of unprincipled behavior.

Buying Up the Past

A "collectible" is anything that people collect, whether or not that item had any intrinsic market value when it was first produced. Captain Midnight decoder rings are a great example. So are baseball cards and political campaign buttons. …So are *Funnies on Parade*, Max Gaines' original 1933 giveaway comic books that were offered as inducements for purchasing Wheatena and Canada Dry.

Everything about the 1939 New York World's Fair is collectible—as is anything about *The Wizard of Oz*. "If they'd made a *Wizard of Oz* condom in '39 when the Judy Garland movie came out, it would qualify," says Jerry Weist, comics collectibles consultant for Sotheby's, only half in jest.

Generally speaking, the hottest collectibles, like those from the World's Fair and *The Wizard of Oz*, are associated with cultural phenomena—events that

- became shared experiences that bonded us together;
- caused us to see the world differently; or
- caused controversy.

YESTERDAY'S MEMORIES… TOMORROW'S TREASURES

Tales from the Crypt bonded kids together.

It set a new standard for comic art and storyline and changed the way readers thought about horror comics. And it was awash in controversy. As a bona fide cultural phenomenon on all three grounds, virtually anything associated with *Tales from the Crypt*, in either its early or later years, is collectible.

All EC comics from the 1950s are collectible, but first issues and special editions such as these are particularly valuable. Copies that don't look their age are the most prized by connoisseurs.

EC comic books cost just a dime when they were first published; now they can fetch hundreds of dollars. Generally they are worth considerably more than other comic books of their time, even those that originally outsold them on the newsstand.

Much of this financial premium is in effect a "banned books" bonus. Dr. Fredric Wertham is just one of a long line of unsuccessful guardians of morality throughout history, a skein of shortsighted individuals that extends from the Renaissance popes who tried to exterminate the "heretical" works of Galileo, to the prudes of the 1960s who risked deafness (not to mention brain damage) in a bootless effort to decipher the sub rosa "dirty" lyrics in "Louie Louie,"* to those who would now put fig leaves over the works of Robert Mapplethorpe. Although generation after generation of censors have been surprised at the outcome, over the centuries these efforts to bowdlerize works of art, music, and literature have almost uniformly produced the same result. Unwittingly the censors' efforts made the objects of their wrath more precious, the polar opposite of what they'd intended.

Nearly broke and unable to market *Shock* #3, Bill Gaines ordered almost the entire print run of 250,000 destroyed. Less than 200 copies were hand-bound, making this issue the "Hope Diamond" of EC comics.

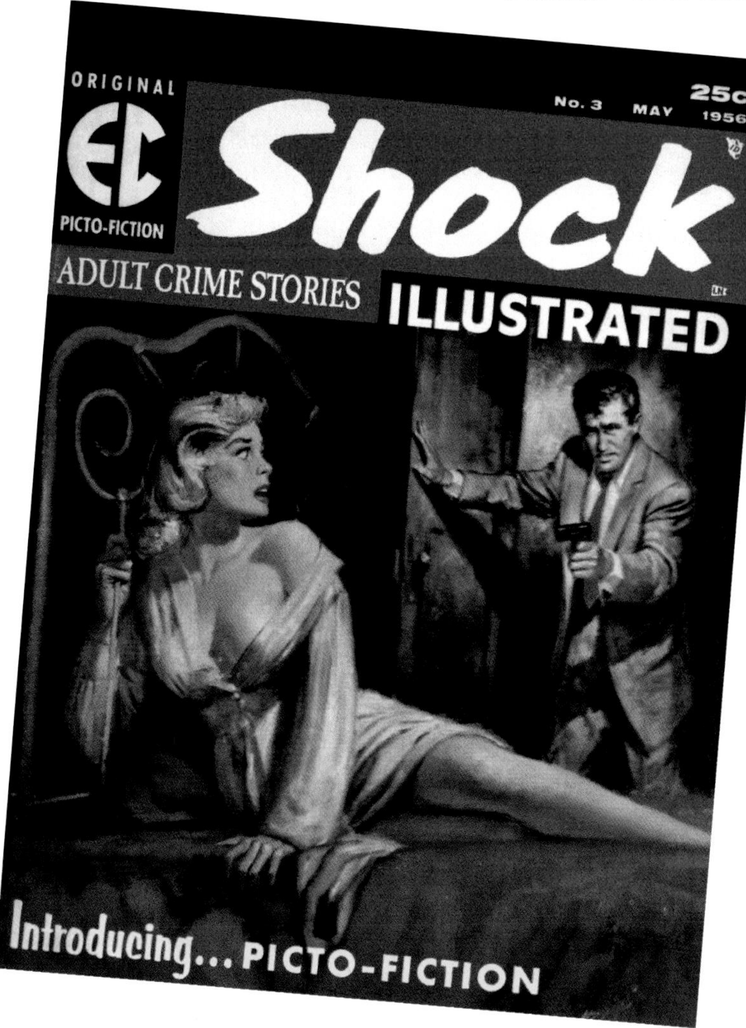

Early fan-addicts who squirreled away copies of *Tales from the Crypt*, whether they did so with a clairvoyant eye toward eventual financial gain or merely out of a packrat mentality, find that their comic book dimes have realized increases in value that exceeded all but the most bullish stocks on the Dow Jones Industrial Average.

Today a pristine copy of an early *Tales from the Crypt* is worth $1,500, a 15,000% return on a 10¢ investment.

Even those who started collecting in the 1960s or 1970s and paid prices that seemed at the time like sheer gougery—$2 for a 10¢ comic—find that their investment has handsomely outperformed the market.

The *Overstreet Guide*, a price catalogue published by first-generation EC fan-addict Bob Overstreet, monitors the pulse of the comic book market, from the first comics of the 1930s through the most contemporary. Overstreet works with a network of dealers across the country who funnel data to him about prices and trends; his guide is the comic equivalent of the automobile *Blue Book*. Year after year, *Tales from the Crypt* and the other EC *New Trend* comics are among those reported to be the most valuable, provided they are in excellent condition.

LONI SPECTER

Fans almost always begin by amassing comic books, but serious collectors often move on to purchase the original pen-and-ink artwork. Original comic art, such as this Johnny Craig cover owned by jazz guitarist Grant Geissman, is the hottest segment of the collectibles market.

*Grownups could not find the "dirty" lyrics because they did not exist. According to Dave Marsh, author of *Louie Louie* (Hyperion), they were a fiction invented to twit disapproving adults.

The Ravages of Time

Comic books don't age well, and keeping them in nice condition is a problem that only increases with time. Like picture postcards, and movie posters, comic books are "ephemera"—a fancy name for stuff that was never meant to last. From the flimsy rust-prone staple that holds them together to the cheap, highly acidic newsprint, comic books were designed to be read a few times and tossed away. Because these mementos of the past are so vulnerable, the highest prices are garnered by comics that are in "mint" or "near mint" condition—meaning they've never or almost never been read.

When *Tales* comics were new in the fifties, the main enemies of preservation were all too visible. They were familial—compulsively tidy moms rooting out "junk" and little brothers armed with crayons and peanut butter. Today, the enemy is far more insidious because it is invisible. It is the air itself—exposure to heat, humidity, sunlight, and smog cause irreversible damage. To keep the paper from yellowing and turning either moldy or brittle, collectors store their comics in archival envelopes. Serious collectors handle their comics as if they were radioactive, using the same gloves worn by film editors. Nevertheless, repeated contact inevitably diminishes the value.

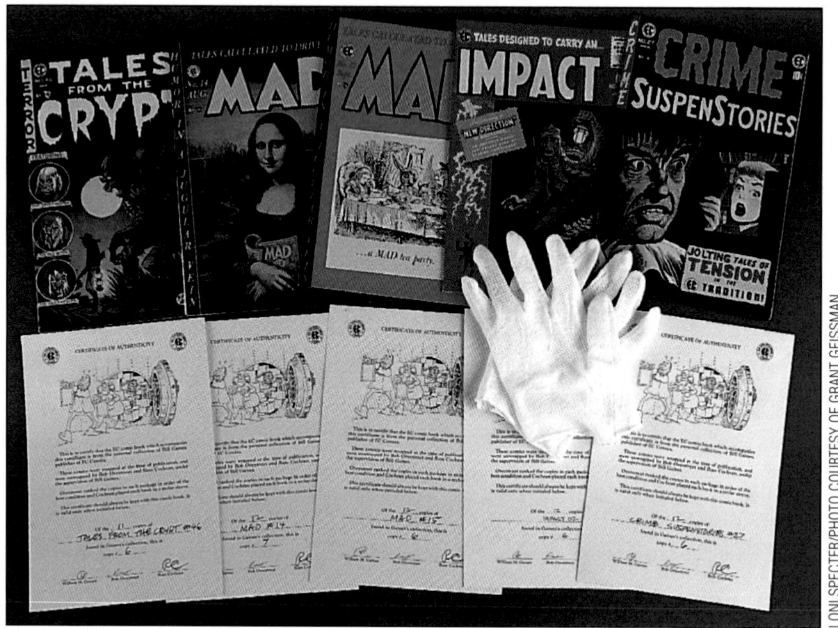

Gaines began selling mint-condition EC file copies in 1990. Each one came with a pair of film editor's gloves, and a Certificate of Authenticity.

LONI SPECTER/PHOTO COURTESY OF GRANT GEISSMAN

LARRY STARK/FRED VON BERNEWITZ COLLECTION

Gaines, Fred von Bernewitz (center), and Ted E. White (right) are shown in December 1955 poring over bound volumes of EC comics. Von Bernewitz is the compiler of the *Complete EC Checklist*, which indexed all EC *New Trend* comics, and is a valuable resource for collectors.

Tales from the File

Bill Gaines was a saver—he was sentimental about his comic creations and felt a personal attachment both to the works and to the people who produced them. He also knew or at least suspected that his *New Trend* comics had the potential to appreciate in value. Among the items he saved for posterity were a dozen file copies of each EC comic book. Four were kept for family members—his children Cathy, Wendy, and Mike, and his wife Annie. Beginning in 1990 the remaining copies were sold, some individually, some in complete sets, together with initialed certificates of authenticity—and a pair of film editor's gloves. Because they had been carefully stored, they had not significantly yellowed. It was as if they were brand-new—those who saw them said they still smelled of fresh ink. Not surprisingly they brought three to four times the value indicated in the *Overstreet Price Guide*.

There are other high-grade collections of EC comics, most notably what has become known as the "White Mountain Collection," amassed by a man from the granite hills of New Hampshire whose car dealer father had been a connoisseur of vintage automobiles. Inspired by the concours standard of his father's collection, he bought one of almost every EC and stockpiled them meticulously in metal file cabinets, where they were insulated from fluctuations in heat and humidity. Pristine comics such as the EC file copies and the White Mountain Collection redefined the meaning of "mint" in the collectibles world. New sources do surface from time to time. It's possible that the mother lode of mint EC comics remains entombed with the 40-year-old Velveeta in some decommissioned fallout shelter in Winnemucca, Nevada—or anywhere in the high desert where the air is dry and cold.

Grant Geissman: The Ultimate Collector

Grant Geissman is an accomplished jazz musician who leads a double life as one of the foremost collectors of EC and **MAD** materials in the world.

"I'm considered what's called a second-generation fan, and I got into it when I discovered **MAD** when I was about eight years old. It was this whole window on the adult world—I was astounded that such a publication could exist and you could ride your bike down to the drugstore and pick it up. When the Ian Ballantine EC reprints showed up at the bookstore in 1964, I bought them and recognized Wally Wood and Joe Orlando and all the **MAD** guys. From then on, I was hooked. I hung on to my Ballantine EC books, and I read 'em to death. When I found out that you could actually go back and buy the original comics, I started doing that as well. I began getting in touch with collectors and dealers. "When I began collecting, I could still buy all the original comics for a few dollars. In 1967 I was going to send $3 to a dealer to buy **MAD** #20, but my dad urged me to save my money for a few weeks so that I could buy **MAD** #1. I'm glad he did. It was a thrill to own it—as well as a bargain."

"I've actually had several collections over the years, but I've sold pieces when I wanted to buy other things. Recently, I sold a number of comics to purchase original paintings from Al Feldstein and Johnny Craig. I'm one of the few people who has tried to collect all the comic books, all the related paraphernalia, and some of the good paintings, too. For example, I have a pair of the EC cufflinks that Gaines had made for his staff, and a charm from the EC charm bracelet that Bill gave to the ladies. Stuff like that is what pushes my buttons. It's just more personal than the comic books."

Geissman toured with Chuck Mangione and played guitar on the album **Feels So Good**. His tenth and most recent solo album is **Business As Usual**. In addition, he is the author of **Collectibly MAD**.

"I was a guitar player early in life. I practiced diligently but my comic book collection was always a little closet hobby that I had. My mother always said, 'Why are you wasting your time with this crap? It'll never amount to anything!' My real life was playing in bands, but I never threw the stuff away. It was always there. Now I have my own house and this, well, shrine."

LONI SPECTER

Guitarist Grant Geissman, author of Collectibly MAD (Kitchen Sink Press), poses in his home museum with his collection of EC memorabilia.

Collectors of original art frame it for display (below); many also pursue specialty artwork. A 1972 limited edition print of the cover art from *Weird Science-Fantasy* #29 was hand-colored and signed by artist Frank Frazetta, and marketed by Russ Cochran.

The Cult of Personality

The Crypt Keeper is a bona fide star, and at least as many people tune in to revel in his grisly cornpone humor as to see the episodes themselves. The persona of the Crypt Keeper is the medium by which *Tales from the Crypt* fans identify with the TV show and the films. "The whole zeitgeist of the horror phenomenon hangs on the Crypt Keeper, this wisecracking Groucho Marx-y kind of character," says collector/musician Grant Geissman, "and for some reason that grabs people. We've always been fascinated with scary stuff—it's a way to measure reality against fiction. I think it's connected to the urban myths described by Jan Harold Brunvand. These are widely held beliefs, stories that everyone thinks are true, like the choking Doberman who has fingers in his throat, the couple necking on lovers' lane who hear radio bulletins warning of a one-armed murderer and later find a prosthetic hook dangling from the handle of their car door.... Some of what goes on in the TV series is a little over the top—deliberately so. What they've done is take the EC stuff to the next level. They're titillating and outrageous for today, just like EC was titillating and outrageous for the '50s. It's just been turned up ten notches because it's the '90s—and the Crypt Keeper ties it all together."

Some collectors seek out new works with the first generation keeper, such as Al Feldstein's "The Original EC Crypt Keeper & Friends" (above). Others prefer the "lifesize" 1990s Crypt Keeper replica (below) from Spencer Gifts. (Naked lady not included).

Future Antiques

Jack Wohl, president of *Tales from the Crypt Productions*, is the marketing mastermind behind the growing array of contemporary Crypt Keeper collectibles, and is personally involved in their creative development. He also coproduced *Secrets of the Crypt Keeper's Haunted House*, a new action/adventure game show which debuted this fall on CBS. There are Crypt T-shirts, a "museum-quality" scale-model Crypt Keeper kit from Screamin' Products, and "Have Yourself a Scary Little Christmas," a Crypt-Keeper-as-Bing-Crosby album of Ghoultide favorites. Backed by the Salivating Army Band and the Santa Clarita All Ghoul Choir, the Keeper croons such old favorites as "Deck the Halls with Parts of Charlie." The CD also includes a reprint of "...And All Through the House," the classic Johnny Craig *Vault of Horror* story (and HBO series premiere) about the murderess whose young daughter admits a homicidal maniac into the house because he's dressed as St. Nick. There's a trio of GhouLunatic cold-cast porcelain statues by William Stout. There are *Tales from the Crypt* trading cards with scenes from the TV series, and a *Tales from the Crypt* phone card for making toll calls away from home. There's even a *Tales from the Crypt* pinball machine.

The softer *Tales from the Cryptkeeper* cartoon series, targeted at younger viewers, has also generated a host of spinoff products. Marketing of these items peaks in the fall to coincide with Halloween, a holiday that has been growing rapidly in commercial importance. Novelty items include *Cryptkeeper* Halloween masks and costumes, cylinders of Halloween candy topped with *Cryptkeeper* finger puppets, and a Barbie-size *Cryptkeeper* doll that cackles just like John Kassir. Some of the goods are conventional costume and magic store fare, such as hyperthalmic Googley Eyes (reminiscent of Marty Feldman's—or the Cookie Monster's—except they glow in the dark), Ghoul Guts, and Cadaver Putty that very much resembles its generic cousin, Silly Putty. What makes them collectible is that they have been packaged with the kinder, gentler Cryptkeeper of the Nelvana cartoon series on the label.

Are Ghoul Guts and Cadaver Putty the anchors of tomorrow's collection of *Tales from the Crypt* treasures? It's possible, says Jerry Weist of Sotheby's. Survivorship is important—the rarer an item is, the more value it has—even if it was made in the millions and only a few remain. "As long as you have a mother or fiancée who throws it out—or a Religious Right that buries it—there's going to be a market for it twenty-five years later," he adds with a chuckle.

Collectibles from the Crypt

on the cover

Crypt Keeper Bust

Hollywood artist/designer Greg Aronowitz has sculpted a nine-inch cold-cast porcelain bust of the Crypt Keeper as part of his "Legends in Three Dimensions" series.

Crypt Keeper Mask and Hands

Collegeville/Imagineering manufactures a Crypt Keeper mask and hands as the basic components of a Halloween dress-up costume.

The GhouLunatics in Porcelain

Graphitti Designs has produced a limited edition set of cold-cast porcelain statues of the EC comic version of the Crypt Keeper, the Vault Keeper, and the Old Witch, sculpted by William Stout.

EC Charm, Cufflinks

Bill Gaines had about two dozen sets of gold-plated EC cufflinks (left) made for the men on his staff in the early 1950s. Women received larger EC charms (right). These very rare items are highly prized by collectors.

Crypt Keeper Collectibles

The Crypt Keeper "franchise" has generated a host of collectible items for fans of the television series and of the two feature films. Shown below are Crypt Keeper trading cards, audio-CDs, novelizations of the movies, and a 13-video series, each containing three episodes of the TV show.

Tales from the Crypt T-Shirts

Tales T-shirts, with or without the image of the Crypt Keeper, are popular with younger collectors. Some were given away as prizes in a **Tales from the Crypt** phone-in horror trivia contest.

Juvenile Cryptkeeper Merchandise

Nelvana's **Tales from the Cryptkeeper** cartoon series generated a multitude of collectible novelty items of special interest to kids.

Cryptkeeper goodies for kids include **Tales from the Crypt** candy, Googley Eyes, Cadaver Putty, wrist watch, and horror action figures. Not all novelty items use the cartoon Cryptkeeper image. Some, such as the do-it-yourself Cryptkeeper model kit (far left) and Cryptkeeper dolls (below) are based on the contemporary "adult" Crypt Keeper.

Ballantine EC reprints, GhouLunatic bookends

The black-and-white Ballantine EC reprints of the mid-1960s rekindled interest in EC comics, and have themselves become collectible. So are the GhouLunatic bookends.

This Bud's for You

In 1995, the Crypt Keeper was a spokesman for Anheuser-Busch breweries, a role that spawned a collection of commercial novelties.

Pinball Machine

The colorfully animated, elaborately designed pinball machine from Data East of Chicago was never sold to individuals. Marketed to commercial establishments as an arcade game for $3,000 apiece, the pinball machine sold out quickly and has not been available for several years. This is one of the rarest and most costly of the EC collectibles.

A Worldwide Boom in Tales Memorabilia

"There are thousands upon thousands of people seriously collecting comic books," says Weist. "It's a global phenomenon. Sotheby's last auction had over 750 people on the floor, but the real auction was the 1800 to 2000 other absentee buyers who were bidding long distance from places like Scotland, Hong Kong, New Zealand, Tokyo, Seoul, Sydney, and Toronto.

"Back issues of *Tales from the Crypt* are the highest in demand," continues Weist, "higher than *Weird Science*, higher even than *MAD*. People love the title above all others. *Tales from the Crypt* has more of a dramatic ring to it than *Vault of Horror* or *Haunt of Fear*, and of course the Crypt Keeper has always been a more popular figure—he's the #1 comic book character of that whole era, the Superman of his time."

The Crypt Keeper even has his own place in cyberspace. At the *Tales from the Crypt* website, http://www.cryptnet.com, net surfers can pull down video and audio clips, and look at original screenplays. The website will also be selling Crypt merchandise.

By far the hottest segment of the collectibles market, however, is original comic art. When Bill Gaines began releasing the EC original illustration boards for sale at auction, numerous collectors of comic books segued into collecting art. The auctions, first through Russ Cochran and later through Sotheby's, brought record prices and spirited bidding. Many of those who have collected comics for any length of time know one another, at least by name or reputation. Familiar rivals vie amicably (but intensely) with one another for the choicest lots, some of which have realized astonishing increases in value in a very short time. "A *Tales from the Crypt* Feldstein cover, like #24, which ten years ago sold in Russ's auction for $1,400 and five years ago would have been worth $2,700, was valued at $4,000 two years ago. You couldn't get it now for $15,000," declares Jerry Weist. "Overstreet's comic book price guide has been coming out now for a quarter of a century, but now there's an Overstreet's for collecting original comic artwork." The blossoming of the market for originals occurred for any number of reasons, the foremost of which is the mystique and magic behind the fact that there's only one of what you've got.

Like Barbies in their original boxes, every hair in place, or Steiff teddy bears that still have their FAO Schwarz price tags, there is something sterile and more than a little sad about a perfect comic book that's never given a kid a thrill. The passion for immaculate copies of old comics—and the prices people are willing to pay for them—baffles some of those most intimately involved in creating them. "Collectors of old comic books are paying $200 to $250 for a lousy ten-cent magazine!" marvels *Tales* cocreator Al Feldstein. "Bill Gaines went to the comic book conventions, but now I go because it's really an ego trip. I see these dealer displays and they've got a *Tales from the Crypt* Number 22 or 25 with my artwork on it and there's a price of $475 on it. I didn't get $475 to do the original artwork and the eight-page lead story together!! It's funny...I say to a dealer, 'Would you like me to sign that?' After he realizes who I am he pauses, like a ten-second pause, because he's turning it over and over in his head, wondering whether my signature would make his copy more valuable because it's me or less valuable because his copy would no longer be mint."

It's an agonizing question that sparks controversy among condition-conscious collectors, a notoriously persnickety lot. A first edition of *Dracula* signed by Bram Stoker is worth more than an unsigned copy, but *Dracula* is not a comic book. Although some would say that Feldstein's John Hancock adds value to a vintage comic, Jerry Weist of Sotheby's maintains that, "Generally, any autograph to the cover of a comic book sends the value down because basically comic book people are anal fanatics. If an *Action Comics* Number 1 (Superman's debut) were signed by (Superman creators) Joe Shuster and Jerry Siegel, it would be worth less." In other words, mint is mint—as if it had just come off the presses, even before it had been placed on the newsstand where it might have been...handled. (Many of the finest surviving EC comics originally belonged to subscribers, whose issues arrived by mail and were never subjected to the pawings and maulings of the newsrack.)

They don't call me a keeper for nuthin. Heh, heh, heh.

Bill Gaines
An Appreciation

When Bill Gaines passed away in 1992, his place in the history of American popular culture was already secure. Most people knew him primarily as the godfather of **MAD** magazine, but with the ongoing success of **Tales from the Crypt** on TV, many more fans have come to appreciate how broad his vision really was. Not only did he work intensely with Al Feldstein to develop EC's horror and science fiction story lines, he also served as the creator and sustainer of EC's atmosphere of hothouse looniness — a benevolent bedlam that fostered some of the finest comic artwork ever produced in the United States.

"EC was an amazingly happy group of very creative people. There was genuine caring and affection," remembers Nancy Gaines fondly.

"I used to sit in the office opening mail while Bill and Al plotted out the stories. It was such fun to be there."

Nancy, who came to work in EC's subscription department at the age of seventeen, married Bill in November of 1955, just as the EC empire was crumbling. "On the plane returning from our honeymoon he said, 'I didn't want to tell you this before we left, but we're bankrupt.' It didn't bother me, because I knew Bill could do anything."

Bill and Nancy were married for fifteen years and had three children, Cathy, Wendy, and Mike, all of whom were born after the heady days of the horror comics. Even after EC's demise, however, Gaines' offbeat creativity and macabre sense of fun didn't leave him when he went home from the office. "We went to zeppelin shows (Bill was an avid collector...He took us on picnics in graveyards. He was a wonderful father!" says Cathy Gaines Mifsud enthusiastically. "He always had fun things for us to do — not normal things. He and I spent one summer going to every French restaurant in New York City.

No matter where we went, he taught you something. He put a clever twist on it, something cute or funny, to make you want to learn and remember. I hear myself doing the same thing with my own children."

Mike Gaines runs his own business and keeps watch over the memorabilia in the family vault. By Bill's arrangement, Wendy Gaines Bucci became the guardian of the EC legacy after her father's death. With the help of Gaines' longstanding advisors, Jack Albert and Dorothy Crouch, she makes sure that contemporary uses of EC images and materials are in keeping with the intent of the originals. Her responsibility has given Wendy an enhanced appreciation for her father and his work.

"It all makes sense now. When I was younger, EC didn't really mean anything to me, but I've come to have an enormous respect for the material."

Wendy Bucci also admires the artwork. "I understand about Feldstein, Davis, Craig, Kamen and the others, and the impact they had on the world."

Bill himself was also aware of their impact, both on the world at large and on his own world, and acknowledged it throughout his lifetime. Although he owned the EC artwork outright, when Russ Cochran's reprints began generating money and when the sales of the original illustration boards began, Gaines sent royalty payments to his former artists. Bill even tracked down the reclusive Graham Ingels, who had repudiated his association with horror, and convinced him to take the money, if only to donate it to charity. Payments to surviving artists have continued since his death.

"The public may remember Bill best for **MAD**, but **Tales from the Crypt** and the other horror comics always had a very special place in his heart — as did the people who made them," says Annie Gaines, who first met Bill in 1972. They were married in 1987.

"He loved the material, and he loved the fact that there were all these loyal fans who wouldn't let it be forgotten.

He was so pleased when it became a successful TV series. It was a great vindication."

After seeing his horror comics reviled as instigators of juvenile delinquency, Bill Gaines lived long enough to see them become sought-after collectibles. He also made the deal that brought them to life on television, reaching a new level of popularity with a whole new generation of fans. "After my father died," recalls Wendy Bucci, "someone had drawn a cartoon of Dad standing in heaven with his new wings on, facing his Maker. He was saying, "God, put me in Fredric Wertham's section." It would be the final justice, EC style.

A Final Gift from the Crypt

In the waning days of December 1995, Sotheby's consultant Jerry Weist and his lifelong friend and fellow fan-addict, Roger Hill, made their annual pilgrimage to West Plains to visit with Russ Cochran. Weist was there on a busman's holiday to select some artwork for a forthcoming Sotheby's auction.

On New Year's Day, 1996, Weist opened a drawer in one of the tall antique wooden filing cabinets in Cochran's recycled bank vault, unfolded the butcher-paper wrappings on one of packages, and was bewildered. "It wasn't anything I recognized," says Weist, "but the light was very bad. I carried the package out to show Russ and Roger, but they didn't recognize it either. Then I looked at the markings on the bottom. It said *Shock Illustrated* #4."

Shock Illustrated #3 was the last issue of *Picto-Fiction* that was ever printed, but it never made it to the newsstands. Weist had found the artwork for an entire unpublished issue of *Picto-Fiction*. The file drawer contained four packages with art for nineteen complete stories, which were prepared for *Confessions Illustrated* #3, *Terror Illustrated* #3, *Crime Illustrated* #3, and *Shock Illustrated* #4.

Weist, Hill, and Cochran were elated, but fast on the heels of their jubilation at the discovery came the realization that artwork was all there was. There was no story on the illustration board, just white space above each panel. Fortunately, Mike Gaines, Bill's son, still maintains the family vault in Manhattan. Armed with a description of the art, he was able to sift through the family mementos and find the text.

This story, "The Mother," is Bill Gaines' last gift from the Crypt. Although the authorship of the story is still uncertain (further research may yet confirm it), the artwork is by Jack Davis. Entombed for forty years, it is published here for the first time.

THE MOTHER

It had begun to rain, and under the lowering night sky, the ramshackle house squatted like a giant misshapen frog, ugly and cold. Part of the roof had long since fallen in, and the ruins of a brick chimney lay scattered amid the tangled weeds and bushes where there had once been a garden.

The mother shuddered and clutched all the tighter two small hands placed so trustingly in her own. The children . . . a boy of nine and a girl of eight, with pale pinched face . . . were frightened. She could feel their fright.

"Mama, I don't like it here," the boy whined, shivering.

"It's a place to stay, baby," the mother soothed him. "We . . . we don't have any other . . . "

In the darkness, the mother's eyes turned to her husband. Not angrily. Not even accusingly. There was no feeling of any kind left in her for this great hulking unshaven man with the reek of cheap whiskey perpetually hovering about him.

"Well?" The alcohol-thickened voice snarled a challenge. The bleary eyes focused. "Wha' did you want t' do? Sleep in the street? We got thrown out of that crummy furnished flat we paid good money for every month! Remember?"

"We wouldn't have been put out if we'd *paid* every month, Frank!" The mother was patient. Eternally, irrevocably, forever patient.
The father, however, was not. He swung at her suddenly, savagely . . .
Dirty fingers left a harsh imprint on her cheek.
"Meaning I'm a bum, eh?" A red, thick-featured face was shoved close to her own. "Meaning I used our dough for booze 'stead of payin' the rent, eh? Okay! So what! I found this place, didn't I? I'm takin' care of my family, ain't I? So don't you give me any of your lip, y'hear? Nobody gives Frank Krebs any lip! Nobody. . .
The snarl trailed off. "C'mon. There's beds inside. Nobody's been near this dump for years."
The mother followed, holding tightly to the cold trembling little hands.
There was no door. Just a black, yawning cavity. Krebs struck a match. And instantly there was a running, a skittering, a scratching.
"Rats!"
They were everywhere. Tiny red eyes gleamed in dark corners. Musty grey bodies beneath glimmering cobwebs. Rattling claws on rotted wood.

Upstairs, there were two dark rooms. In one, was a bed. Broken, sagging, covered with a mildewed rancid blanket . . . but still, a bed. Krebs fell on it, and he was asleep almost at once.

The mother took the children into the other room. For them, there was a musty pile of moldy rags. She stayed with them until they had fallen asleep.

Then she kissed them and left the house. It was past midnight and she had eight hours of work ahead of her . . . downtown, in the office building where she was a charwoman.

Krebs did not see the huge beady-eyed rat which leaped up onto the foot of his bed, later, and sat there, staring at him.

But he saw it in the morning. Saw it and hurled a broken chair after it as it dove through a hole in the wall.

The chair smashed against the already-cracked plaster, gouging a great chunk of the rotten stuff loose, and sending a hollow reverberation echoing through the abandoned old house.

Krebs was feeling mean, the way he always did after a drunk. When the children, awakened by the noise, ran in, frightened and crying, he heaved himself up from the filthy bed and started after them, mumbling:

"Shut up! Whining brats! Hanging onto me like . . . "

But the mother was home by then. She appeared suddenly, got in Krebs's way, stood between him and her children.

"Get out of my way!" he snarled.

"No, Frank!" The mother was rock.

"I'll take care of them," she said as she turned away. "Now come downstairs. There's an old stove. I bought some groceries and got a fire going. You'd better have something to eat."

But Krebs did not eat. Sometimes, when he was sober, he was almost afraid of his wife. She was so . . . so . . . Blast her! And those brats of hers too!

Her cheap pocketbook was on the bed. He rifled through it, found a dollar and some silver in it.

"Just wait till your mother is gone, " he told them softly. But it was the mother who came understanding.

"I told you," she said. "You're not going to touch them. You'll have to kill me first . . . "

It happened so suddenly. The rage came like fire. Krebs's fist swung in a short jolting arc, and the mother was flung backward.

Her head slammed against the foot of the bed, and she sunk to the floor. Blood seeped slowly into the splintered boards.

And behind Krebs there was a scratching. The rat had come out of its hole and now sat on its haunches, watching him.

Suddenly, Krebs was sober. Suddenly he was on his knees beside his wife, shaking her, screaming at her.

"Get up, get up, get up . . . "

Only she would never get up. Because the mother was dead. He'd killed her.

He sat there stupidly beside her in an alcoholic daze. And the rat watched.

Until Krebs stumbled to his feet, and kicked at it viciously, and it dove twittering back into its hole.

Krebs stayed in his room all that day. It was not until night, until the children had cried themselves to sleep upon their bed of rags, that he left the old house. There was a lumberyard he knew . . .

When he staggered back, he was carrying a stolen hundred-pound sack of builders' plaster.

Breaking down the wall in the room where he slept was easy. All it meant was enlarging the opening he had already put in it. But there was the rat . . .

It appeared suddenly. And it watched. It watched, twittering and restless, as he tore down the moldy plaster and the rotting lath underneath. It watched when he stooped and lifted the corpse and carried it awkwardly to the wall. And then, suddenly, it leaped . . .

For a wild, horrible moment, its teeth were tearing at Krebs's throat, its claws ripping for a foothold on his liquor-stained filthy clothing.

The corpse fell, thrashing stiffly. Krebs sprawled. And the fetid breath of the thing was in his nostrils; its slavering yellow fangs were slashing at his jugular vein.

His fist smashed down on the rat's spine like a hammer.

The rat shuddered from the blow and lay still.

Krebs struggled to his feet, his breath coming in great rasping sobs, his intestines writhing.

It took hours to hide the corpse behind a wall of fresh plaster, cunningly smeared and splattered with dirt so that it looked as old and scabrous as the other walls.

Then Krebs turned back to the rat. But it was gone. It had been stunned, not killed.

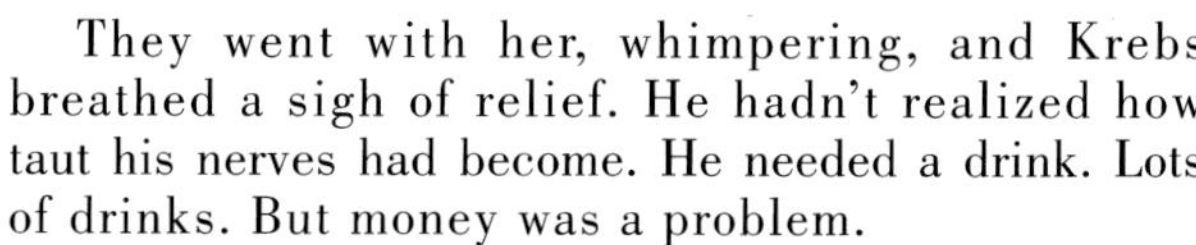

In the morning, Krebs went to the children.

"Your mother's gone," he told them brutally. And between their tortured, unbelieving sobs: "She ran out on you! Like I always knew she would!"

The policeman he found later believed his story. And why not? One look at him . . .

That same afternoon a woman from the Welfare Board came and took the children away.

They went with her, whimpering, and Krebs breathed a sigh of relief. He hadn't realized how taut his nerves had become. He needed a drink. Lots of drinks. But money was a problem.

He solved that problem, though. There was a woman he followed into the park. A woman who screamed when he snatched her purse and ran . . .

In the purse, there was more than eighty dollars. And so, that night, Krebs brought two dozen bottles of fiery whiskey to the bedroom. Within an hour, he was sodden. Within two, he was in a drunken stupor, asleep on the grimy bed.

But he awoke. Suddenly. To the smell of fetid breath. To see two tiny red eyes, burning in the darkness. Eyes!

The rat perched on the ragged pillow beside his head, black lips drawn back in a snarl of hate. Another moment and those yellow teeth would have sunk into Krebs's throat . . .

Krebs screamed. Out of sudden horror.

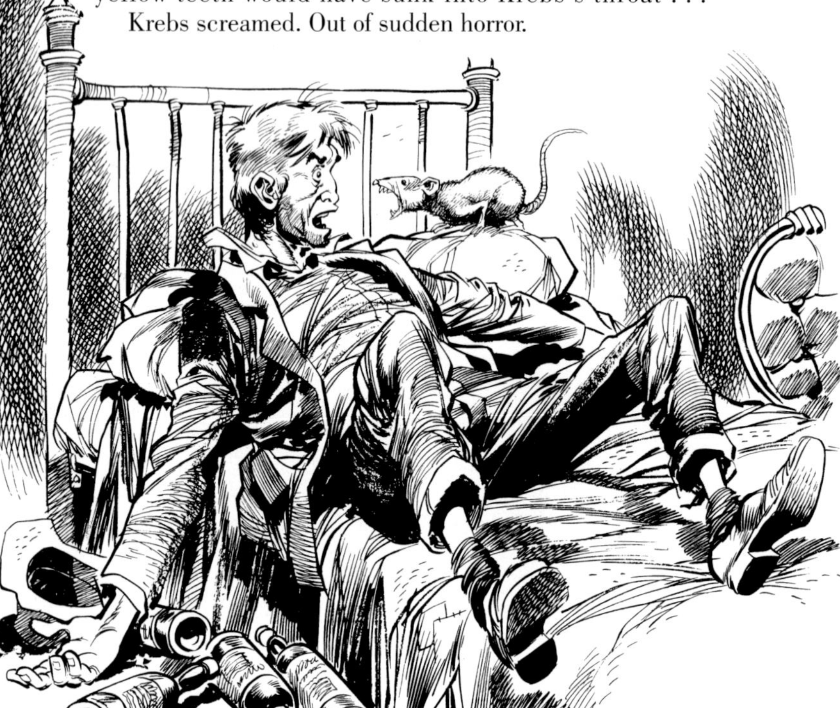

The rat vanished. But it did not go far. Near its hole, it stopped, sat up to stare at him. With a baleful look that was calculating, cunning, and patient . . .

Patient!

That was when Krebs first began to suspect.

"You!" he breathed. "You!"

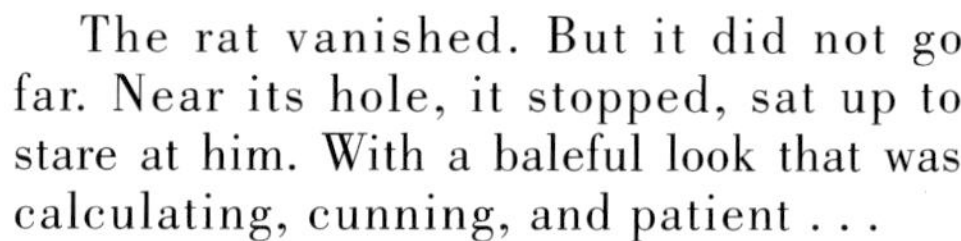

But that was insane! A corpse is a corpse! The life, the hate of a dead woman does not enter the body of a rat!

And yet, afterward, the rat was always there. The two dozen bottles dwindled to ten, eight. But drunkenness was not enough to blot out that nagging persistent thought . . .

Once, Krebs had a wild idea. He went to the wall where he'd hidden his handiwork, and put his ear to it. He listened, hearing only the sound of his own heartbeat.

Until he heard the other sound. The soft restless stirring . . .

No! The dead are dead! The rat! It must be the rat! Moving inside the wall!

But the rat sat at the other end of the room, snarling.

And each time that Krebs went to the wall, the rat snarled. As if it knew!

"You said . . . you'd take care of the kids!" Krebs yelled at it finally. "All right! The kids are gone! Why don't you go find them? Leave me alone!"

The rat drew back a little, but otherwise, it did not move. It watched. Perpetually. A hundred times during the long black nights, it crawled up onto the filthy bed; a hundred times, Krebs waiting until it was close to his throat . . . and then struck savagely. But always, the rat avoided the blow. Always, it returned to stare, and wait, patiently.

There was no doubt, after a while, that the rat was stalking Krebs. It chilled him. But he could not leave. Not so long as there was that patient look in the rat's eyes. Not so long as the rat lived. It was a contest . . . a duel. In Krebs's clouded brain, the rat became his wife, and his wife became the rat. He set traps for it, contrived killing snares. But the rat avoided them. Twice, he plugged its hole in the wall with shards of broken glass so that the rat could not dive to safety in time of danger. But those yellow fangs created new holes.

Some nights, Krebs lay on his bed, bottle in hand, and spoke to the rat. Placatingly. Almost pleadingly. "Please," he would slobber. "Leave me alone. I . . . I never hurt the kids!" And when the rat would remain immobile, the bottle would suddenly be hurled, to splinter against the floor or wall. And Krebs would scream: "All right! So you were a good mother! Well you weren't good enough to keep me from sending your brats to a home, were you? You think you'll get revenge, don't you? But you won't! I'll kill you first! I'll kill . . . you . . . "

Only . . . only . . . hadn't he already *done* that? Sometimes he remembered. Other times he didn't. His head spun in alcoholic confusion. He would have to kill the rat. That much he knew. So he planned its death cunningly, shrewd with whiskey. But his plans never worked.

Finally, there was a night when Krebs drank too much, even for him. He pounded on the wall, daring his wife to come out, daring the rat to come out.

And it did. It darted between his legs, and when Krebs went after it, he stumbled and fell.

He lay on the musty rotten, floor, unable to move, paralyzed with drink.

And it was only the pain that woke him from his lethargy. He put a hand to his throat, stupidly. And his fingers brushed furry softness, came away wet.

Blood. His blood. The rat . . .

He screamed.

And the rat scurried away . . .

It was not a deep slash. He had luckily stirred too soon. But the next time.

There could be no next time! Next time, the rat would win! If he remained as he was . . .

Krebs drank no more that night. Dulled as his senses were, he knew enough for that. Despite the burning, yearning ache deep in his gut, he did not touch the last of the full bottles. Not that night nor the next day. By then, he was stone sober.

In the cellar, he found the tarnished remains of an old brass lamp.

The lamp stand, ripped from its base, made a heavy, four foot long club of solid metal.

There was a grim resolve in Krebs's every move when he climbed the rotting staircase with its rickety balustrade to the bedroom.

Claws skittered all about him as he walked. But those rats did not matter. Only *the* rat mattered!

By the flickering light of the candle stub, Krebs sat in the dismal bedroom later . . . waiting.

And in time, the rat's lumpy body crawled out of its hole in the wall . . .

Krebs struck. The brass pole splintered the rotten flooring. Again! Again! And still again! Wild, seemingly aimless blows that the rat dodged easily. But there was a method to Krebs's attack. Each blow drove the rat closer to the open bedroom door. And at last, there was no place else for it to go.

It dodged through the opening, avoiding a savage final assault.

Then . . . it paused. It reared back, bristling spine against the peeling balustrade. And Krebs grinned in triumph.

"I was right," he hissed. "You won't leave this room, will you? You won't leave your body, will you? You *are* her, aren't you? *You are*!"

It was so simple. Always, the rat had appeared in that bedroom! *No where else*!

"Now, we'll see!" Krebs stood in the doorway. "C'mon! Let's see you get back inside!"

The brass club was raised, ready. Krebs was almost crooning now.

"C'mon! C'mon, c'mon, come on . . ."

He could even smile. "Come on, little . . . *Mother*! You want your revenge don't you? You want to pay me back for what I did to your brats, don't you?"

The rat did not move. Only its beady eyes flickered. As if it were planning. Calculating . . .

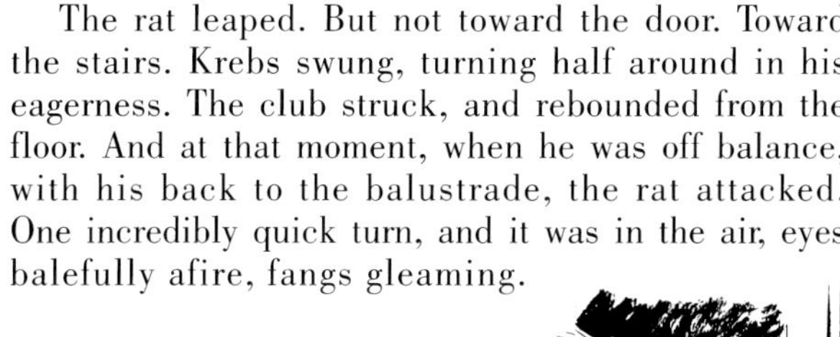

The rat leaped. But not toward the door. Toward the stairs. Krebs swung, turning half around in his eagerness. The club struck, and rebounded from the floor. And at that moment, when he was off balance, with his back to the balustrade, the rat attacked. One incredibly quick turn, and it was in the air, eyes balefully afire, fangs gleaming.

Krebs dropped the club, threw up his arms, and the impact of the rat's body drove him back so that he had to grasp at the balustrade for support.
The balustrade . . . which broke beneath his weight with a rotten, dry, tearing gasp.
Krebs dropped into nothingness, screaming. The brass pole fell after him.
Krebs struck first.
Flat on his back, so that his spine was shattered in a dozen places.
Just before the jagged end of the brass pole pinned him to the floor.
From above, the rat looked down. But Krebs did not move. Slowly, the baleful fire vanished from the rat's eyes.
Content, the rat turned, went back into the bedroom, to its hole in the wall. It moved slowly. There was no need to hurry. Not any more. The intruder was no longer cause for concern.
Through the tunnel gnawed in the moldy lath. Past the corpse rotting slowly in the darkness . . .
The rat quickened its pace.
To the nest, where four miniature replicas of itself waited.
The rat's babies were hungry. And now that the danger to them had been removed, there was no other thought in the tiny brain of . . . the mother.
THE END

For Further Reading

Boyll, Randall. *Tales from the Crypt Demon Knight* (novelization). Pocket Books, 1995.

Case, Sigurd, ed. *Postcrypt* (fanzine), published quarterly, 214 Wheeler Road, Frewsburg, New York, 14738.

Daniels, Les. *Comix: A History of Comic Books in America*. Bonanza Books, 1971.

Decker, Dwight, and Groth, Gary. "An Interview with William M. Gaines." *Comics Journal,* May 1983: 53-84.

Ferrante, Anthony C. "Tales from the Script," *Fangoria* #140 (March 1995), pp. 20-24+.

Gaines, William. "Madman Gaines Pleads for Plots," *Writers Digest*, February 1954.

Geissman, Grant. *Collectibly MAD: The MAD and EC Collectibles Guide*. Kitchen Sink Press, 1995.

Goulart, Ron. *The Great Comic Book Artists, Volume 2*. St. Martin's Press, 1989.

Halberstam, David. *The Fifties*. Fawcett Columbine, 1993.

Hardy, Phil, ed. *The Overlook Film Encyclopedia: Horror*. The Overlook Press, 1995.

Hegenberger, John. *Collector's Guide to Comic Books*. Wallace-Homestead, 1990.

Jacobs, Frank. *The MAD World of William M. Gaines*. Bantam, 1973.

Kingston, Sam. *Horror from the Crypt of Fear* (fanzine).
2648 Manor Drive
Salt Lake City, UT 84121

Kurtzman, Harvey. *From ARRGH to ZAP!: A Visual History of Comics*. Prentice Hall Press, 1991.

Lupoff, Richard, and Thompon, Don. *All in Color for a Dime*. Arlington House, 1970.

Malloy, Alex G., ed. *Comic Book Artists: Profiles of 150 Major Illustrators with Listings and Values for Their Comics*. Attic Books/Wallace Homestead Book Company, 1993.

Michlig, John. "EC Comics: A Strange Undertaking," *Boomer*, March 1994.

Nyberg, Amy Kiste. "William Gaines and the Battle Over EC Comics," *Inks: Cartoon and Comic Art Studies*, February 1996, Volume 3, No. 1, pp. 2-15.

Overstreet, Robert M. *The Official Overstreet Comic Book Price Guide*. Avon Books, published annually.

Reidelbach, Maria. *Completely MAD: A History of the Comic Book and Magazine*. Little Brown, 1991.

Ringgenberg, S.C., "Jolting Words with Al Feldstein in the EC Tradition," *Comics Journal*, May 1995.
—— "Spaced Out with Al Williamson," *Comics Journal*, May 1984: 63-91.

Sassienie, Paul. *The Comic Book*. Chartwell Books, 1994.

Skal, David J. *The Monster Show: A Cultural History of Horror*. Penguin, 1994.

Sotheby's *Comic Books and Comic Art* sales catalogues. Sotheby's, 1991, 1994, 1995.

Tales from the Crypt, *Haunt of Fear*, *Vault of Horror*, and other EC Comics reprints
(By direct order only)
Russ Cochran, Publisher
PO Box 469, West Plains, Missouri 65775
(417) 256-2224

Teitelbaum, Sheldon. "Filming Comic Book Horror: Tales from the Crypt," *Cinefantastique*, January 1990, pp. 16-29+.

Thompson, Don, and Lupoff, Richard. *The Comic-Book Book*. Arlington House, 1973.

Voger, Mark. "The EC Story," *Comics Scene Spectacular*, September 1992, pp. 52-61.

Wertham, Fredric. *The Seduction of the Innocent*. Rinehart, 1954.

Index